SHAKESPEARE'S UNIVERSE: RENAISSANCE IDEAS AND CONVENTIONS

Shakespeare's Universe: Renaissance Ideas and Conventions

Essays in honour of W.R. Elton

Edited by

John M. Mucciolo
with the assistance of Steven J. Doloff
and Edward A. Rauchut

SCOLAR PRESS

Published by
SCOLAR PRESS
Gower House
Croft Road
Aldershot
Hants GU11 3HR
England

Ashgate Publishing Company
Old Post Road
Brookfield
Vermont 05036-9704
USA

British Library Cataloguing-in-Publication data.

Shakespeare's Universe: Renaissance Ideas
and Conventions – Essays in honour of W.R. Elton
  I. Mucciolo, John M.
  822.33

Library of Congress Cataloging-in-Publication data.

Shakespeare's universe: Renaissance ideas and conventions : essays in honour
  of W.R. Elton / edited by John M. Mucciolo, with the assistance of
  Stephen Doloff and Edward A. Rauchut.
    p. cm.
  ISBN 1-85928-193-1
    1. Shakespeare, William, 1564–1616—Criticism and interpretation.
  2. Renaissance—England. I. Elton, William R.
  II. Mucciolo, John M. III. Doloff, Steven J. IV. Rauchut, Edward A.
PR2894.S44   1995
822.3′ 3—dc20   95-8834
                                                                  CIP

ISBN 1 85928 193 1

Typeset in Sabon by J.L. & G.A. Wheatley Design, Aldershot and
printed in Great Britain by Biddles Ltd, Guildford.

Contents

Part Five   Shakespeare, Art and Music

Part Six   Shakespeare and Criticism

Preface

To the gift of critical imagination – the twin of poetry itself – it is rare to find superadded the scholar's knack of subtle and laborious knowledge, yet precisely this combination has marked William Elton for one of the great scholar-critics of Shakespeare. His magisterial study, *King Lear and the Gods*, changed the way this tragedy is to be understood, and not just in details, here or there. *King Lear and the Gods* provides a model for the serious critique of 'values', in that it overturned a facile, ungrounded, fantasizing picture of a great work of art. The modern reader had been typically invited, by R.W. Chambers and Bradley before him, to believe that Shakespeare's *Lear* was designed to redeem the suffering King, as it were in a Christian purgatory, finally crowned (according to one critic) in 'a victory of true love'. This Christian reading of the play seemed to enjoy inherent plausibility – not only was the play saturated with doctrinal allusion, it was also structured so as to whet an enormous appetite for redemption, an audience-wish equal to the massive scope of the play itself. Lear, like Gloucester, had suffered so horribly, and had in some sense so deserved his suffering, that it was felt (so to speak) only right and proper that a deep religious poetic justice should at the last transfigure the dying Titan. This Christian wish-fulfilment had for decades the force of critical authority. Hence, Elton needed something beyond intuition, beyond sceptical finesse, if he was to dislodge such a fixed piece of misguided false consciousness. The resulting volume, *King Lear and the Gods*, showed how such intuition and finesse could be supported by magisterial learning. The critique of *Lear* is only one side of Elton's work; the book was equally, and inevitably, an education in Elizabethan and Jacobean values, as these were reflected in a wide religious, philosophical and ethical reading.

Elton's discursive texture is like no other: the most detailed allusions to historical materials are wedded to a minutely exacting exegesis. The learning is textured, then, in conformity with the Shakespearean mind; it surprises. And yet, critical imagination is finally the gift most movingly evident, as Elton gradually extracts certain truths about the play, of which he says: 'The complexity of the drama and the varying viewpoints involved allow for a free and ironical interplay of seemingly contradictory positions.' At the very moment when, as Bacon's essay 'Of Atheism' would have it, one would expect Lear to incline to piety, he 'seems to bow the other way'. At every point,

Elton investigates the sceptical tragedy Sheakespeare *in fact* had given his audience, in this way defending the splendour of Shakespeare's mind against a sentimental reduction borne of Victorian optimism. *King Lear and the Gods* refuses to belittle human suffering by lumping it all together as a pain to be cured by a careless Christian redemption. Elton's reading of a sceptical *Lear* was necessarily many-sided, so that, for example, he could show how the double plot reveals contrast as well as parallel between Lear and Gloucester. This last might not seem novel; where Elton differs, say, from the intelligent director finding Gloucester and Lear so different on the stage, is that the chapter on 'Double Plot' is no less richly tied to Elizabethan thought than any of the more doctrinal discussions.

Critics familiar with the Elton texture, with its forested learning, will recall that, quite wondrously, he exits from the history of ideas whenever it suits him. He comments always on the action of the play, on character and personae within the play, as these notably develop. He discovers a general principle of Shakespearean dramaturgy, as based upon structural irony, in a final chapter which dramatistically supports his radical thesis that the play was, in sum, 'a syncretically pagan tragedy'. Such a reading was bound to shock the school of Christian Humanists. But its truth was overwhelmingly demonstrated in Elton's treatise, and no compelling reason has more recently been advanced to undermine the central insight – that *King Lear* refuses any optimistic Christian redemptive pieties. The tragedy Elton perceived was coloured, and has remained coloured, by a questioning light, diffracted through serious, many-sided, syncretic ironies. If it is true that an exemplary subtlety of learning marks the critique provided by *King Lear and the Gods*, it is no less appropriate to gather a wide variety of essays to honour William Elton's lifework, which has continued the sceptical quest of his *Lear*.

Tracing the varied essays comprising this *Festschrift*, the reader will discover a principle of Shakespearean criticism which, while it underlies William Elton's scholarly texture – critique through genuine historical research – finds its centre in the central document of Shakespeare criticism: Johnson's *Preface* (1768). There are two sides to this Johnsonian inheritance. Shakespearean drama, the *Preface* states, is 'the mirror of life', a depiction of our lives, our natures and our characters so vivid and yet so universally 'general', that it will therapeutically clear us of our fantasies, our 'delirious ecstasies'. So strong is the Shakespearean appeal to 'general nature', that, to quote Dr Johnson again, the poet creates 'scenes from which a hermit may estimate the transactions of the world, and a confessor predict the progress of the passions!' Johnson, arguing for a universalizing stability in the Shakespearean drama, is arguing for 'the stability of truth', which he distinguishes from the glittering 'pleasures of sudden wonder'. Shakespeare has lasted now a good four centuries, only because, as the other Johnson memorably put it, 'he was not of an age, but for all time'.

Universalizing a general nature is but one half of the picture, however. There is always a microstructure, for the individual, for the culture. If research into the past leads archaeologically to a level of infinitely fine texture, it might be thought Dr Johnson opposes such research. Yet to think so is to neglect his vast effort in the *Dictionary of the English Language*, whose historical novelty was its use of quoted sentences, where a word could be observed in use. Similarly with the Shakespeare *Preface* and the edition, with its notes, the Johnsonian inheritance is rich with historical nuance, and in the same fashion our scholars honouring Professor Elton range, at times, down to the most precise microstructural level of textual commentary. This width of scope, of course, betokens Shakespeare's canonical status, and his commentators' response to canonicity. The broader implication can only be that universal appeal cannot result from *mere* generality; it must equally feed off the natural which, in turn, must exist primarily at the level of textual specificity.

This twin inheritance, shared by Elton, and honoured in the essays that follow, inevitably expresses itself in the most varied terms. Yoshiko Kawachi contrasts Shakespearean and Kabuki transvestism. Richard Levin, S.F. Johnson, and Raymond Waddington analyse the boundary conditions of gender difference. John Steadman recalls the Renaissance imperatives of the woman's dowry, with all the pragmatic, as well as dramatic, implications possessed by gendered inheritance patterns. While these papers on gender issues are, to our eyes, of immediate present concern, they are nonetheless closely linked to the topics broached in a highly focused set of politically motivated essays: the late Professor Harry Levin – in his last essay, written for this *Festschrift* – develops a virtually complete picture of political myth-making in *Richard II*, while David Norbrook analyses 1601 responses to the play's rebellion. Politics and religion are never separate for Renaissance drama, and G.K. Hunter focuses this bond in a reading of *Henry VIII*. While George Williams goes to the central political question of obedience in *Hamlet*, Jones-Davies and Jonas Barish analyse the devices and desires, and the dramatic mechanisms, by which Shakespeare and other dramatists sought to manipulate their audiences' political self-awareness.

If, like all drama, the Shakespearean canon requires analyses of class structures, social and political groupings, their interactions and conflicts, it is also true that the aesthetic imperative is finally even stronger than the sociopolitical significance of the plays. Hence it is fortunate that a goodly number of the *Festschrift* papers directly discuss dramatic art. John Demaray, Jay Halio and Andrew Sabol deal with stage illusions, staging in general, and with the important influence of theatrical music and masking, as these project a world of imaginative freedom. Such criticism shows how Renaissance plays, as well as their protagonists, may seek expressive power. A similar concern for drama as the stage *realizes* it, for dramatic embodiments, will be seen to animate essays by Thomas McAlindon on the representation of staged villainy, François Laroque, who shows how *Troilus and Cressida* is both in and about perspective, and Sidney Thomas, who discusses the stylistics of mannerism in *Love's Labours Lost*. All these essays broach Shakespeare the dramatist – the dazzling craftsman.

A final set of essays, on language and on criticism, rounds out the larger picture. T.H. Howard-Hill explores derivations of speech from class differences in *Othello*; Marvin Spevack examines the Shakespearean use of etymological wordplay; Werner Habicht finds in the *Sonnets* a topos of ineffability. These essays point to central questions of recent philosophy, with its 'linguistic turn'. Meanwhile Kenneth Muir explains why it took 350 years to make *Troilus and Cressida* and *King Lear* into acceptable theatrical fare. Philip Edwards reconsiders G. Wilson Knight on the late plays while, to conclude, Klaus Uhlig surveys recent trends in Shakespeare studies, as these relate to *King Lear*.

So ends a broad conspectus of Shakespearean thinking at the present time. The reader will have seen and experienced the natural canonical response – Shakespeare generates an unequalled variety of interests, as the present collection attests, and an unparalleled mobilization of the mind in concert with the heart.

Here we return to the occasion of this volume of essays, Professor Elton. His colleagues in the field of Shakespearean scholarship have long appreciated his overriding concern with *Lear* and *Troilus*, two works that test our sense of early modern history. *Troilus and Cressida*, particularly, as Kenneth Muir's essay shows, could not yield to general understanding until, as Muir puts it, 'History has made us catch up with Shakespeare'. History, with all its modern horrors, dwarfs the ancient horrors of the drama. And yet the very existence of the Shakespearean texts, with all their conventions and their originalities, modifies this triumph of history.

Elton and those who, with him, want criticism to ally itself with probing textual research, can show that history can force us to catch up with Shakespeare, only because our research (be it on the printed page or on the modern stage) instructs us in a readiness toward general nature. This generality has life, because it is manifest speech by speech, word by word. Elton's lifelong concern with a questioning of conventions is only one of his contributions, but a central one. For it liberates difficult truth, and gives us ways of experiencing the extreme situations in *Troilus and Cressida*, *Lear*, or other tragedies and histories. There can be no higher commendation of scholarship than to note the scholar's willingness to follow the text, no matter how disturbing the pursuit may be. Paradoxically, it might seem, Professor Elton has insisted on subtlety in the discovery of grand narratives. Hence his reading of staged religious experience is always secularized, always tested and purged by currents of disbelief, so that we – students of the plays – may the more fully, one might say more truthfully, experience the full weight of the drama, as poem. The careful analysis of tracts and their contextualizing relevance paradoxically allows the play to become less of a tract. By learning an intellectual and religious and emotional context for older works, we are enabled to put aside anachronistic rationalizing; we can now liberate what we can only call 'the poetry'.

There is a strange, exploratory novel by Herman Melville, *Pierre: or, The*

Ambiguities. Elton always gives us, on the grandest scale, *Shakespeare: or, The Ambiguities*. In an age like ours, when so many would like to return to fascistic or fundamentalist templates, Elton's work stands out, learned, lively, unexpectedly and tenaciously humane. He teaches us to respect the art of poetry.

PART ONE

Shakespeare, Politics and Religion

CHAPTER ONE

Sitting upon the Ground
(*Richard II*, IV, i)

Harry Levin

Kingship (or queenship) has established a highly traditional framework –
or, at all events, a frame of reference – for the perspectives of English life.
Shakespeare confronted that institution directly and dealt with it upon a duly
majestic scale. A succession of eight kings parades through his double set
of historical tetralogies (the later kings appearing in the earlier set): two
Richards and four Henries, plus two Edwards (the younger one assassinated
before he could be formally crowned), with still another Henry to preside
over an updating afterpiece. Those last two Henries belonged to the more
recent house of Tudor, having staked their claim through a marital alliance
with the Lancasters and reinforced it by a subsequent intermarriage with the
Yorks, so that their own accession could be looked upon as a happy ending
to the wars so bitterly fought in the name of the Roses. That preceding
Richard could be looked back upon as a terminal figure in England's formative
dynasties, a childless son whose father, the legendary Black Prince, had died
before succeeding to the throne, and who himself would bequeath it to the
contentions of his York and Lancaster cousins through the greater part of
the fifteenth century. Thus Shakespeare had ample occasion to ring the
changes on the monarchic theme; and the unhappy reigns of those two
dissimilar Richards – the Second all too passive, as contrasted with the
hyperactive Third – gave him a deepening opportunity to tilt his histories
in the direction of tragedy.

Neither Richard could justly be regarded as a hero in the honorific purport
of the term, which may be more readily accommodated to the epic than to
the drama. Richard III looms large, both physically and morally, as the
very archetype of the arch-villain, his inner nature scarcely masked by his
avowed hypocrisy; a man of action whose external acts constitute a series
of unalleviated misdeeds, more melodramatic than tragic in their utter disregard for the ethical implications. Richard II, in contrast, is rather a weak

The editors wish to thank Mrs. Elena Levin for her kind assistance in providing this, Professor
Levin's final essay, which was written for this *Festschrift*. Thanks are due also to Professor
G.B. Evans for reviewing the manuscript, and to Bette Anne Farmer for transmitting a
typed version.

than a wicked human being, prone to irresponsibility rather than malevolence. Over-indulged and self-indulgent, coddled into that seat of grandeur which Richard III would struggle toward so ferociously, he neglects its duties and obligations while enjoying its privileges and exploiting its prerogatives. Yet, quite unlike his misshapen namesake, he cuts a self-consciously personable figure, and responds with increasing sensitivity to the circumstances that turn against him. Experience is enlarged, not by his vainglorious round of public appearances, but by the cramping retreat that overtakes and confines him, while his evolving private voice engages our belated sympathies. Words come to him easily, while deeds do not; he is at ease when surrounded by the court, but less so when afield – least of all on the battlefield. Unlike that other Richard, who strives so brashly for it, worldly greatness has been thrust upon him, and he hesitates in facing its emergent demands.

A man of passion rather than action – passion in its primary sense of suffering – Richard feels those sufferings all the more keenly because he has been spoiled by his privileged status. Hence he bears and bespeaks his feelings with greater eloquence than any Shakespearean characters have previously done. None of them will more fully express or personify what Walter Pater would call 'that irony of kingship': the histrionic routines, the long-winded protocols, the childish punctilio, the authorized egocentricity, the merely human limitations under the awe-inspiring mantle of majesty – viewed from the inside, an all but impossible job. The earliest history-plays must come to terms with the wickedness of Richard III, with the weakness of Henry VI, with both of those faults in King John. Shakespeare would sound the depths with Richard II, before addressing himself to the upward mobility of the fourth and fifth Henries. 'Up, cousin, up', is Richard's descending counsel to his successor, Bullingbrook (III, iii, 194). But except for the latter, who will wear his crown with some uneasiness, and more distinctively his son, Prince Hal/Henry V (despite a notably wayward apprenticeship), none of Shakespeare's English rulers could serve as models for their exalted roles. Shortcomings too obvious to be overlooked would have to be rationalized by the medieval doctrine of the king's two bodies, the ideal of divinely hedged supremacy cohabiting with the realization of mortal frailty.

Yet royalty, so often at war with itself, held self-evident dangers as a corpus of subject-matter, even more through the exposure of its weaknesses than through the abuse of its powers. *Richard II*, by dwelling on both of those recurrent issues, would bring Shakespeare as precariously near as he ever came to the political complications and troubles of his own day. Viewed from a more classical, an Aristotelian standpoint, his elevated protagonist could hardly have seemed more nonchalant in his *hubris*, more self-centred in his *hamartía*, or more abject in his *peripéteia*. Crowned heads are ideally supposed to betoken a glorified incarnation of humanity at large, which cannot altogether look up to them when they themselves do not really live up to their own exceptional standards. Their inherent pride will sometimes risk, and always exacerbate, an ominous fall. We are invited to sympathize, and to a certain extent we do, with such failures in the highest places. But, while we are witnessing the downfall of those who have lorded it over such ordinary mortals as ourselves, our reactions may be shaded with a slight tinge of *Schadenfreude*. In sharing that shock of reversal on the kingly plane, we may also feel some democratic release in rehearing the humiliations of *lèse-majesté*. That makes for an ambivalent catharsis, though it subserves the ends of poetic justice, allowing us to commiserate with the fallen even while we are welcoming the forces that have been destined to supplant them.

Tragedies, as composed in the Middle Ages, were not plays but narratives illustrating the scriptural dictum, 'How are the mighty fallen!' Boccaccio had transcribed and collected a good many salient examples, from the primal Adam to the Renaissance despots, with his *De Casibus Virorum et Feminarum Illustrium*, which would be emulated in Middle English verse by John Lydgate's *Fall of Princes*. Chaucer's Monk defined the genre in outline as the story of a falling-off from the height of prosperity to the most wretched misery, each successive case exemplifying the mutability of worldly fortunes. Claiming to have gathered together a hundred such case-histories, and prompted to recite a number of the earliest ones, he had been cut off by his bored fellow pilgrims after the seventeenth. The influential compilation, *A Mirror for Magistrates*, would be published, several times reprinted, and augmented by various poetic hands throughout the Elizabethan period. Its title evoked a conventional symbol for the didactic function of literature, as a cautionary reflection of life which edified its viewers by showing up the exemplary mistakes of their official predecessors. Its *Induction* by Thomas Sackville, Earl of Dorset, framed the whole sequence within the nightmare-vision of a journey to the underworld, while the ghosts of worthies mainly from the British past would deliver their respective plaints. More than thirty histories would be dramatized from these versified lives of illustrious but ill-starred men and women.

Richard II was brusquely and adversely reflected in the *Mirror for Magistrates*. Shakespeare's treatment had more in common with the balanced metrical narration of Samuel Daniel's *Civil Wars*. He would also draw upon conflicting accounts in the prose chronicles of Raphael Holinshed, Edward Hall and Jean Froissart; and certain French witnesses may have inclined him toward a rather more sympathetic view of his subject. His Richard is supremely conscious of his personal visibility in the magistral looking-glass. Hastening back from his inauspicious war in Ireland to face the crisis of Bullingbrook's return from banishment, the execution of his own sycophantic henchmen, and the defection of supporting forces from Wales and the North, he eloquently oscillates from one extreme to the other, from reassertions of regal authority to admissions of helpless defeat. But the trend runs downward: from the divine right of his anointed sovereignty to his 'talk of graves, of worms, and epitaphs' (III, ii, 145). Weeping for joy when he lands at its Welsh shore, he immediately salutes what he takes to be the compliant soil of his loyal kingdom. Within a few minutes his body sinks down upon what has

suddenly become that 'barren earth', like another Job bemoaning his fate.
Whereupon this prodigal prince aligns himself with the figures in Sackville's
ghostly procession:

> For God's sake let us sit upon the ground
> And tell sad stories of the death of kings:
> How some have been depos'd, some slain in war,
> Some haunted by the ghosts they have deposed,
> Some poisoned by their wives, some sleeping kill'd,
> All murthered ...
>
> (155–60)

Later on, while playing his own part in that hapless spectacle, taking leave
of his queen, and gravitating toward his own obituary, he will enjoin her:
'Tell thou the lamentable tale of me' (V, i, 44). Only then, when her listeners'
tears will have put out its fire (V, i, 40–49), will the blackness of its ashes
attest 'the deposing of a rightful king' (50). Now, to depose means literally
to put down, a customary paradigm in tragedy. That thematic stricture,
ringing through the play, has by then reached its dénouement and been
acted out in what has come to be known as the Deposition Scene. The
basic verb falls from Richard's lips repeatedly; and it will prove ironic that
he himself first used it (in another sense) with reference to the armed rival
claimant, Bullingbrook, when asked for a deposition (a sworn statement
of his intentions): 'Depose him in the justice of his cause' (I, iii, 30). A
mock-heroic echo – 'Depose me?' – will be voiced in the playacting scene
of 1 Henry IV, when Falstaff is called upon by the Prince to step down from
his impersonation of the King.

But there remains a generic difference between Richard and his storied
precursors. We listen to their sad stories; we witness his, from step to
step, as it is being enacted; and, while their storytelling points a collective
moral for us to reconsider from our own vantage-point, his dramatic
characterization offers a psychological bond that enables us to participate
in his actions and to suffer through his emotions vicariously. For this we
find a closer prototype in Marlowe's Edward II, which is equally if not
more intensely concerned – in Charles Lamb's phrase – with 'the reluctant
pangs of abdicating royalty', and which would be set above Richard II
by Swinburne and Rupert Brooke. Shakespeare's pioneering contemporary
had made the most spectacular impression through his overreaching protagonists, and through such 'sky-aspiring and ambitious thoughts' as Richard
would vainly attempt to suppress in others (I, iii, 130). By centring upon
a royal weakling, influenced at that stage perhaps by the Henry VI plays,
Marlowe for once could work out a more Shakespearean pattern of interaction with the other characters. The weakness that makes Edward seem
most vulnerable, as rendered in Marlowe's tenderest lyrical strains, is the
King's homoerotic infatuation with his French courtier, Piers Gaveston. Their
vengeful challenger, the Earl of Mortimer, is due to break down in his
Machiavellian turn, whereas Richard's triumphant antagonist, Henry

Bullingbrook, now Duke of Lancaster, will dethrone him and assume his crown as Henry IV.

If *Richard II* formed a sorrowful prologue to the cycle of a more auspicious regime, it had been preceded – possibly suggested – by the sorrows of another drama, the anonymous *Thomas of Woodstock*. Here the titular character, officially Duke of Gloucester, is victimized for his principled opposition to the caprices that have been leading his nephew, the youthful monarch, astray. By farming out gainful franchises to his self-serving favourites, and thus empowering them to collect the revenues from taxes and from leases on public lands, Richard has been negligently squandering the resources of his country, and will be forced to pay the price himself in Shakespeare's sequel. There the death of Woodstock will be recalled by his mourning Duchess, and his patriotic admonitions will be carried on by the two surviving brother-uncles, the Dukes of Lancaster (John of Gaunt) and of York. Since so much of Richard's 22-year reign had been crowded into *Thomas of Woodstock*, *Richard II* would be free to concentrate upon its two last years – the last two years of what Barbara Tuchman would designate as 'the calamitous Fourteenth Century'. Its most fearful calamity almost seemed to have been ordained from on high; countless lives were lost by the intermittent visitations of the bubonic plague, the Black Death. Military strife throughout this epoch, the Hundred Years' War on the Continent, was aggravated at home by movements of social protest that culminated in the Peasants' Revolt.

We can revert more happily to those years while we are reading Chaucer; but, if we open Wycliffe's contemporaneous Bible, we are reminded of the heretical Lollards, of the dissidence and persecution that ushered in the Reformation. What was broadly and gradually happening would become an embattled transition from feudal oligarchy to centralized monarchy. But that would not take place until the baronial claimants had eliminated one another's claims, and a more popular rule had taken command through the dynamic personality of Henry V. It will be he who confides, on the eve of Agincourt, speaking incognito to three common soldiers, 'I think the King is but a man, as I am. ... His ceremonies laid by, in his nakedness he appears but a man'. And Shakespeare's Henry, going on to invoke 'thou idol Ceremony', will soliloquize over those undemocratic distinctions which it has so arbitrarily raised between man and man. Richard II, seen in that retrospective light, has ruled by taking advantage of such distinctions, and has maintained his princely rank by proceeding from one ceremony to the next. His First Act is prearranged accordingly, with formal pomp, theatrical display and heraldic flourishes. He inaugurates it by mounting a scaffold and standing high before Windsor Castle, while two contending peers appeal to his less than decisive judgment. Ominously Herford (Bullingbrook) and Mowbray (Duke of Norfolk) accuse each other of treason, recapitulating past conflicts and portending eventual disasters.

That ceremonious opening soon deteriorates into an unheroic anticlimax.

Richard keeps trying to reaffirm, with all his wavering dignity, that he was 'not born to sue, but to command' (I, i, 196). Yet his mediation is powerless to resolve the quarrel or to appease the irreconcilable rivals, who press their mutual accusations by flinging down their gauntlets (as 'gages' of their determination), and thereby exchanging knightly challenges to a trial by single combat. This opens the way for an even grander – and consequently more anticlimactic – ceremonial, set in the chivalric lists at Coventry. Trumpets sound, banners wave and armour flashes, as the heralds marshal in the hostile champions. Their militant steeds are conventionally declared to be awaiting them backstage, and will not be needed as it turns out (conveniently for the staging), though the prospective riders will figure on horseback when Mowbray's son recalls and narrates the episode in *2 Henry IV*. Here, at the most expectant moment, Richard throws down his own gage, the ruling baton, and with that commanding gesture calls the tournament off. Both of the would-be combatants will instead be banished. 'The note of banishment', as the self-exiled James Joyce would comment, 'sounds uninterruptedly' throughout Shakespeare's works; and it is sounded here with a special poignance through Mowbray's lament, because it will exclude him forever after from hearing or speaking the English language:

> What is thy sentence then but speechless death,
> Which robs my tongue from breathing native breath?
> (I, iii, 172f.)

On the other side, the rare word 'regreet', dropped negatively by Richard and picked up twice by Bullingbrook, will become a positive augury (I, iii, 67, 142, 186). Bullingbrook's expatriation will be temporary, somewhat commuted in deference to his grieving father, John of Gaunt, and actually to be cut short by Gaunt's imminent death. Richard's sudden and arbitrary decision has marked an end of the usages of chivalry, as well as the beginning of his own reverses, the first in a sequence of guidelines pointing downward. 'Oh, when the King did throw his warder down ...', the younger Mowbray will pronounce in his later reminiscence, 'Then threw he down himself (*2 Henry IV*, IV, i, 123, 125)'. Gaunt's deathbed speech – enunciated at the play's moral centre, like the dream of Clarence in *Richard III* – is both a warning and a prophecy for the condition of England. 'This blessed plot, this earth, this realm' is patriotically eulogized up to a point – a critical point where the apprehension and insights of the dying man downgrade that fertile terrestrial metaphor into a paltry piece of real estate, a heavily mortgaged farm (II, i, 50). When Richard pays his frivolous visit, he is admonished that, in his extravagance and exploitation as 'landlord of England', he has been acting to depose himself (113). Callously he meets the announcement of his uncle's death by appropriating the ducal estates, in order to finance his ill-advised Irish expedition; and this is what motivates Bullingbrook to return and reclaim his Lancastrian inheritance.

Meanwhile the reported voices of both nobles and commons have been rising to a virtual chorus of resentment and disaffection. It is York, the very last survivor among the seven sons of Edward III, appointed as governor during the sovereign's absence from England, who likewise inherits from his older brother the conscience of a *raisonneur*. Under that twofold commitment, his articulate but ineffectual position must be 'neuter'; he must disregard the family connection ('uncle me no uncles'); he can neither abet nor oppose the *coup d'état* dethroning Richard and enthroning Henry (II, iii, 87, 159). More and more widely recognized and accepted, as both of the rivals turn homeward from opposite directions, and as the followers of the straying leader desert him for the ranks of his more purposeful adversary, the overturn becomes inevitable. Each encounter is a comedown for Richard, after the bad news greets him in Wales and pursues him to Flint Castle. His initial response is to stiffen his haughty posture as God's deputy. But, as the pressures mount, he lapses into self-pitying monologues: 'Cry woe, destruction, ruin, and decay ...' (III, ii, 102). I have already quoted part of the passage in which he relates himself to the bygone spirits of deposed and murdered kings. Sitting there on the ground (this blessed plot? this barren earth?), and waiting now to be royally unseated, he continues by tragically dramatizing his less than stately role:

> ... for within the hollow crown
> Keeps Death his court, and there the antic sits,
> Scoffing his state and grinning at his pomp,
> Allowing him a breath, a little scene,
> To monarchize, be fear'd, ... and humor'd thus
> Comes at the last and with a little pin
> Bores through his castle wall, and farewell king!
> (160–70)

The funereal jester will have the ultimate word, even as a mirror for magistrates foreshadows a dance of death. Ready now to surrender without resisting, Richard discharges his dwindling retinue: '... hence away, / From Richard's night to Bullingbrook's fair day' (217f). That daylight is the habitual ambience of royalty, radiating from the sun itself, from the King himself. The earlier farewell of Bullingbrook – 'This must my comfort be, / That sun that warms you here shall shine on me' – will in the long run be less polite than portentous (I, iii, 144f.). Under the immediate stress upon Richard, his imagery is shifting to sunsets and clouded skies. In the next play, reviewing the train of events, Henry IV will candidly recount to his wayward prince how he braved comparison with 'the skipping king' and managed to appropriate Richard's aureole of 'sunlike majesty'.

Their confrontation eventually comes to pass at Flint Castle, which 'royally is mann'd', now that Richard has taken refuge there (III, iii, 21). So Bullingbrook is informed by young Harry Percy, who will be better known afterwards as Hotspur, and much less friendly to the Lancastrian party. Richard again makes his formal appearance aloft ('*on the walls*'), looking down from the battlements. The elevation is still kinglike, but the illumination is darkling – a modulation likened by Bullingbrook to that of 'the blushing discontented sun' when 'the envious clouds are bent / To dim his glory' (63, 65–6). A preliminary interview pits Richard's stern reproof against the more conciliatory approach of Northumberland (Percy's father, Bullingbrook's spokesman). But Richard has come a long way from his angry rhetorical question, 'am I not king?', when he beseeches his captors, 'What must the King do now?', and counterbalances the changing alternatives: 'My gorgeous palace for a hermitage, ... And my large kingdom for a little grave' (III, ii, 83; iii, 143, 148, 153). He cannot refuse the bidding to come down into the lower courtyard, where Bullingbrook, whose 'heart is up', awaits him; yet he is acutely sensitive to the symbolism implicit in this descent, and Shakespeare's stage was well suited to the blocking of these bodily ups and downs (194). Richard goes through the motions ceremonially and histrionically, reproving his foes and critics in rhymed couplets that formalize his predicament on a literary plane:

> Down, down I come, like glist'ring Phaëton,
> Wanting the manage of unruly jades.
> In the base court? Base court, where kings grow base,
> To come at traitors' calls and do them grace.
> In the base court, come down? Down court! down king!
> For night-owls shriek where mounting larks should sing.
> (178–83)

The classical allusion is an admission; for the scion of the mythical sun-god, Icarus, was disastrously unable to drive Apollo's blazing chariot across the sky; and Richard, while blaming the horsemanship (*manège*) for the mismanagement, ignores what Shakespeare elsewhere mentions: that the earth was badly scorched by Phaëton's disaster. A double pun is unfolded in the following couplet: if that lowest courtyard (not the *cour d'honneur* but the workaday *basse cour*) befits the abasement of the degraded king, then the adjective *base* can also be accorded to his teacherous courtiers. In the concluding trope the visual antitheses of *night/day* and *sunlight/clouds* are vocalized into bird-calls.

Whenever a climax looms ahead, we may hopefully speak of rising to it; and this can be said of Richard's behaviour, which becomes more outstandingly eloquent as the difficulties arise before him; yet each consecutive encounter sustains and accentuates a falling movement, which abases him more deeply than the last one. The scene that intervenes between his surrender and his condemnation functions as a choric interlude in much the same vein as Gaunt's dying prediction, which was placed between the two scenes presenting court assemblies. Here we get our clearest glimpse of Richard's touching queen, whose mutually affectionate relations with her husband diverge very strikingly from the estrangement of Marlowe's indifferent Edward and his faithless Queen Isabel. Shakespeare has embroidered upon the historical facts, since Richard's first wife (Anne of Bohemia) was dead, and the spouse of his diplomatic second marriage (Isabelle of France) was barely adolescent at this time. The Queen, as Shakespeare conceives her, is seeking but not finding a few moments of relief from her conjugal worries. The setting that attracts and fails to distract her is a garden (the Duke of York's), which colours the ensuing diction with the cluster of images that Caroline Spurgeon has traced – as a characteristic point of departure and return – through all of Shakespeare's writing. The Wars of the Roses were launched in the Temple Garden; the Battle of Agincourt is resolved by a peace that should recultivate France into 'this best garden of the world'.

Iago will humanize the metaphor: 'Our bodies are our gardens'. Ophelia's madness will seek expression by handing out flowers, King Lear's in distributing weeds. 'Richard, that sweet lovely rose' is invidiously compared with 'this thorn, this canker Bullingbrook' amid the Percies' afterthoughts in *1 Henry IV*. With *Richard II* it is the play itself that elicited Pater's comment, 'What a garden of words!', and Shakespeare has gone beyond his sources to introduce this scene. It is a gardener in person who recites the *topos* and elucidates the allegory, likening the cultivation of the land to the proper tending of a commonwealth. That suggests a query from his assistant which will bring out his overheard disclosure: why should this little patch of ground be tended so conscientiously, when 'our sea-walled garden, the whole land,' has been so neglected, and indeed is now so overgrown and 'swarming with caterpillars?' (III, iv, 43, 47). Those pernicious worms denote Bushy, Bagot, and Greene, 'The caterpillars of the commonwealth', the self-serving courtiers who have so grievously misled their king and so shamefully profited from their flattery (II, iii, 166). The Gardener's answer is to report their deaths, along with Bullingbrook's capture of Richard himself, who is 'depress'd' (put down) if not yet 'depos'd' (III, iv, 68). The idiom of gardening extends to the round of seasons, with autumn – in its vividly Anglo-Saxon synonym – as the visible embodiment of tragic decline:

> He that hath suffered this disordered spring
> Hath now himself met with the fall of leaf.
> (III, iv, 48–9)

The oracular significance of this dialogue is rounded out when the Queen envisages the Gardener as old Adam, re-enacting 'a second fall of cursed man'; and, after her departing curse upon this other Eden, he plants 'a bank of rue' for ruth – for pity – in commemoration of her plight (76, 105). Their anxious colloquy brings down to earth the restless visions expounded so much more schematically by Ulysses in *Troilus and Cressida*, the cosmic oscillation from order to disorder.

Everything in the first three acts builds up to the single continuous scene that comprises the fourth. This might well be termed a *scène à faire*, in the language of Francisque Sarcey – or, as phrased by William Archer, an 'obligatory scene'. For both of those very practical critics, the most clear-cut test of a playwright's talent was his ability to pick out and treat that segment

of his narrative material which would best lend itself to effective drama-
tization. In the present instance the material happened to be associated
with problems that extended far beyond the stage. During the final period
of the Virgin Queen's long sovereignty, the unsettling issue of what would
come next – of who would become her successor – was much in the air.
Analogies would be discerned, most sharply by Elizabeth herself, between
the Earl of Essex's conspiracy and that of the future Henry IV against
Richard. A suspiciously opportune revival of *Richard II* in 1601, a private
performance half a dozen years after its première, was officially countered
by the arraignment and interrogation of Shakespeare's company. Perforce
the Deposition Scene was omitted from the text of the first three quartos,
and not published until the fourth, after King James had more or less
comfortably settled down on the throne. Shakespeare in the mean time was
advancing from the histories toward his tragical period, and the play is
entitled a tragedy in all the quartos. In the Folio its title reads: *The Life and
Death of King Richard the Second*.

There does not seem to be much valid historical basis for this grand scene,
which interlinks Richard's abdication with Henry's coronation. Two disparate
and mutually antagonistic episodes seem to have been fused together, through
a propagandistic twist of the chronicles in smoothing the way for the
Lancastrian dynasty. Contemporaneous testimony, most expressly from a
French fellow prisoner in the Tower of London, Jean Créton, handed on
the report that Richard raged and wept when he received the parliamentary
judgment against himself, and that he accused Henry of committing treason.
Shakespeare has transferred the background to Westminster Hall – just in
time, since that edifice had been erected at the King's command only a few
years before. There, even while divesting himself of the office he has abused,
Richard comes to dominate the proceedings of parliament. The act has started
out with the wrangling nobles ready to throw down their gages once more,
and will end with the clerics expressing their expectations of further turmoil.
It pivots around a speech of prophetic protestation from the loyal Bishop
of Carlisle, who defends the legitimate line of kingship, and foresees the
consequent disasters 'if you raise this house against this house' (IV, i, 145).
He is arrested at once, and what should ensue is the requisite climax: lines
154–318, which came under the Elizabethan censor's ban, and would be
printed as 'new additions' in the Fourth Quarto (and from a more authoritative
Jacobean text in the Folio).

Enter Richard then, heralded by York as 'plume-pluck'd', stripped of his
majestic feathers, and followed by attendants bearing the contested regalia,
the crown and the sceptre (161). Summoned as a prisoner to acknowledge
his capitulation and act out his humiliation 'in common view' before the
national assembly, he is just beginning to shake off his own 'regal thoughts'
(155, 163). His successful competitor, having taken full charge, is ready to
publicize their new relationship, which Richard proclaims his discomfiture
in accepting, or bending a courtier's knee to this usurper. Recalling how very

recently he himself has been the object of such flattering salutes, he cannot but reproach the surrounding courtiers for their disloyalty. If their hypocritical 'All hail!' is to be paralleled with that of Judas, it follows that he is casting himself in the role of Jesus – an identification that he confirms at a later stage by recasting them as 'Pilates', unable to wash away their sin of delivering him to a kind of martyrdom (169, 240). Richard's own career could hardly qualify as an *imitatio Christi*; yet some of his chroniclers, notably Créton, were willing to draw that sacrosanct analogy; and Richard has now involved himself in the enactment of a passion-play. The ambiguity of the situation is heightened when the abdicating monarch cries 'God save the king!', and no one cries 'amen' because no one definitely knows for which potential incumbent that blessing has been invoked (172).

Submissively Richard inquires: 'To do what service am I sent for hither?' (176). York answers by reminding him that his 'tired majesty' has freely offered to resign in Henry Bullingbrook's favour, and that his resignation must here and now be made public (178–80). If this is an enforced renunciation of authority, for Richard it is also an open invitation to stage a culminating ceremonial. 'Give me the crown' is his very last command – not that he would wrest it back from his conqueror, but that a meaningful act of abdication should be fully realized and nobly enacted (181). Grasping one side of that golden diadem and enjoining Henry to hold up the other side, he visualizes their opposing fortunes as a pair of buckets within it, moving downwards and upwards respectively through a figurative well: Henry's bucket 'ever dancing in the air', continually ascending even while Richard's, heavily laden with all his griefs, completes its lachrymose descent – and the doleful noun 'grief' is more frequently heard in this play than anywhere else in Shakespeare:

> You may my glories and my state depose,
> But not my griefs; still am I king of those.
> (192f.)

The tongues of both men, like Scroop's in a previous scene, have become 'care-tun'd' (III, ii, 92). When Henry matter-of-factly speaks of 'cares' that are being passed on, this inspires four lines of Richard's wordplay in which the keyword reverberates nine times (IV, i, 195–8). For the former it signifies the assumption of responsibilities; for the latter it can only mean the continuation and intensification of anxieties. Responding to the former's straight question, 'Are you contented to resign the crown?', again Richard plays upon words, upon the most elementary monosyllables: 'Ay, no, no ay'. *Yes* and *no* are meaningless, 'for I must nothing be' (200–1). There can be no identity under such conditions: no 'I', and 'Therefore no no', neither assent nor denial (202).

Yet he is never more personally himself than when he proceeds, slowly and proudly, to renounce the ancestral rights of royalty and give up its vested trappings, to

> ... give the heavy weight from off my head,
> And this unwilling sceptre from my hand,
> The pride of kingly sway from out my heart.
>   (204–6)

A ritual is being uniquely improvised, a coronation in reverse, wherein every intimate gesture reinforces an attitude of widening detachment from his consecrated grandeur:

> With mine own tears I wash away the balm,
> With mine own hands I give away my crown,
> With mine own tongue deny my sacred state.
>   (207–9)

And, as it moves through the legal and political to the religious consequences of his decision, Richard's blank verse is formalized into rhyme, grimly sealing off his own retirement, graciously congratulating his opponent, and envisaging the next regime in its brightest aura:

> God save King Henry, unking'd Richard says,
> And send him many years of sunshine days!
>   (220–1)

This is where the speaker might well have preferred to conclude his demonstration. But he has still to reckon with Northumberland, who steps forward to demand a confession, so that the detailed articles of indictment will show the commons that their erstwhile king has been 'worthily depos'd' (227). Weeping, Richard demurs and condemns himself for having complied with these encircling enemies by lending himself to their treacherous accusations. It has left him, after living through the chill of so many winters, in a seasonal change with 'no name, no title' – since name and title depended upon the rank that has just been 'usurp'd' from under him (255, 257). He envisions his repudiated self in the serio-comic image of a snowman, deliquescing under the solar radiance of his ascendant rival for the kingship:

> O that I were a mockery king of snow,
> Standing before the sun of Bullingbrook,
> To melt myself away in water-drops!
>   (260–2)

When Northumberland produces a legalistic script and urges him to sign it, Richard's hesitation finds its voice in a self-conscious expression of undiminished vanity. Not that he is reluctant to confess; after all, that is the best opportunity he has left to talk about himself. But a piece of paper is not the source of inspiration he needs; he can best peruse his sins in the book of his own face. It is a looking-glass, therefore, that he requests, and with Bullingbrook's permission receives, to crystallize the occasion: 'Give me that glass, and therein will I read' (276). To hold it up to himself should induce a mood of introspection, and yet his first reaction is to be gratified that his features have not been wrinkled more deeply by his griefs. But that cannot be the truest reflection of the saddening part that he has been walking through. The mirror-image may unduly flatter him, as – he now understands – his opportunistic followers have so guilefully done. Scrutinized more thoughtfully, his glass becomes another mirror for magistrates, and he becomes another passer-by in that weary procession of failed authorities. Nearing a rhetorical climax, Shakespeare conjures up the most romantic precedent, 'the face that launch'd a thousand ships' in the unforgettable salutation of Marlowe's Doctor Faustus to Helen of Troy:

> Was this the face
> That, like the sun, did make beholders wink?
> Is this the face which fac'd so many follies,
> That was at last out-fac'd by Bullingbrook?
> (283–6)

Richard will no longer shine in the light of, nor abide comparison with, the tutelary orb of kings, whose very brilliance caused men's eyes to blink. This valediction is coupled with two further wordplays on 'face': the realization that he has countenanced too many follies, and the concession that he has now been put out of countenance by Bullingbrook.

It is Richard's climactic stroke, at this juncture, to signalize the 'brittle glory' of his face and of his office by dashing down the glass against the ground into 'an hundred shivers' (287, 289). To Bullingbrook, the 'silent king', he divulges a moral: 'How soon my sorrow hath destroy'd my face' (290–1). To this his more businesslike and literal-minded listener interposes a word of correction: 'The shadow of your sorrow hath destroy'd / The shadow of your face' (292–3). The darkness of his troubles has momentarily cast its shade upon his perception of himself. Richard, in his melancholy, is willing to embrace that umbrageous revision: 'Say that again, / The shadow of my sorrow!' (293–4). Shadow, as the antithesis to sunlight, befits his current unkingly stance; and, even more profoundly, as the insubstantial counterpart of substance, it redirects him from the world of outer appearances to a sphere of innate realities. For this shared insight he thanks King Henry, and asks for but one more courtesy. And it is Henry's condescension that elicits Richard's final irony: since a king is politely flattering him, he must now be 'greater than a king' (305). The granted boon is simply 'leave to go'; and, since no destination has been named, Henry issues the order to his attendants: 'Go some of you, convey him to the Tower' (313, 316). His choice of verbs prompts Richard to a parting shot of linguistic one-upmanship, inasmuch as – to the Elizabethans – 'conveyer' was a euphemism for 'thief':

> O, good! convey! Conveyors are you all,
> That rise thus nimbly by a true king's fall.
> (317f.)

This concludes what the Abbot of Westminster describes as 'a woeful pageant' (321). Like the other spectators and incidental speakers, he has consciously fallen in with the overt theatricality of Richard's stage-managed departure. Predictably, if not anticlimactically, the Fifth Act will do all it can to tie up the looser ends of unfinished business. The Queen has but two appearances of any importance, the one before and another just after the Deposition Scene, and the latter is the only scene that brings her onstage with her husband. Together only to separate forever, she is retiring to her native France, while he – in a shifted sentence – will be imprisoned not at the nearby Tower of London but far north at Pomfret Castle. Their leavetaking could not be more formally observed, dwelling upon his posthumous reputation, evoking such allusions as ancient Troy, and trading verses in stichomythy. Richard's prophetic rebuke to Northumberland, when the Earl interrupts this elegiac duet to send them on their penitential ways, will be recollected ironically by the King in 2 Henry IV, after the former allies have turned against one another as predicted. 'As in a theatre', but at a second remove, we overhear the Duke of York telling his Duchess about the triumphal procession in which King Henry is hailed and ex-King Richard is humbled (V, ii, 23). Horses prance verbally, if not literally, through Elizabethan drama. To ride in triumph, for Marlowe's Tamburlaine, was to achieve his imperial ambitions.

If horseback could be seen as a mode of enthronement, then to be unhorsed could stand for dethronement, as was so conclusively demonstrated by Richard III. The equestrian deposal of Richard II will be tearfully brought home to him when his last visitor, a groom from the royal stable, tells of Henry riding to his coronation on Richard's favourite steed, Roan Barbary. This will round out the reversals of Act V. Conspiracy will have raised its head again; and the Yorkist plot of Aumerle will be thwarted, exposed by York himself and pardoned by Henry: yet its impact will continue to be felt as a threat undermining Lancastrian prospects. So long as Richard is alive, however, he dominates his prison cell as he did his courtly surroundings, now revelling in the moods and changes of his adversity. Having cried woe and destruction, having arrived at ruin and decay, he is well aware that 'The worst is death' and prepared to accept the fact that 'death must have its day' (III, ii, 102–3). His receding thoughts move up and down through 66 lines of soliloquy, recapitulating his course from the worldly pride of kingship to the suicidal dejection of beggardom, grasping ineffectually at the consolations of proverbial wisdom, and belatedly evincing an empathy for other roles than his own:

> Thus play I in one person many people,
> And none contented
>
>   (V, v, 31)

Then the unexpected sound of music in the distance – broken music – shifts his meditation to the rhythms of time, with the recognition that his time is up. 'I wasted time, and now doth time waste me' (49). His murder is unavoidable but ambiguous, since Henry is not to be held responsible for the regicide, but must repudiate the assassin who is doing him such a service,

Pierce Exton, and then must rather guiltily promise to do penance with a crusade – a promise that will soon be intercepted by battles to retain his English conquest. Richard is aroused at long last to redeem his stature with a valiant fight against his murderers, and to reverse the emphasis on his descension with an expiring gasp:

> Mount, mount, my soul! thy seat is up on high,
> Whilst my gross flesh sinks downward, here to die.
> (111f.)

It is a pious sentiment; but from the lowest depths, the absolute bottom of his imaginary well, the sole remaining outlook for him cannot be other than upwards; and Richard has shown less resistance as he has been sinking from one station of his pilgrimage to the next. At his last agony he is still clinging to hope and pretension, though he might more definitely be declaiming the tag-lines of Jonson's *Sejanus*:

> For whom the morning saw so great and high,
> Thus low and little fore the 'even doth lie.

Jonson would be translating loosely from the *Thyestes* of Seneca; but this *sententia* was also quoted from the original Latin by Marlowe in *Edward II*; and, as a concise formulation of tragedy, it was often quoted during the English Renaissance. The composition of *Richard II* has been singled out, by some of Shakespeare's interpreters, as a dress rehearsal for *Hamlet*. Composed in the mid-1590s, it might be considered to mark his literary coming-of-age, using what he had learned from the widespread experimentation of his apprentice years and prefiguring mature developments. Richard may indeed anticipate Hamlet in the full disclosure of his mind, but his is a shallower mind. Hamlet not only lamented the cursèd spite that kept opposing him; he deliberately sought it out and, however unsuccessfully, tried hard to strike back. An undramatic lack of bilateral conflict led Yeats to criticize *Richard II* as 'a play without a hero'. Coleridge had said that it was 'for the closet', and George Pierce Baker would argue that it provided 'no good acting part'. Those cavils could be somewhat neutralized by E.K. Chambers' description of Richard as 'a born actor', even though he fails so crucially in living up to his inherited role. Moreover, his role-consciousness can be partly attributed to Shakespeare's medium-consciousness at the verge of his fullest technical mastery. If Richard seems continually aware that he is acting a part, Shakespeare leaves us similarly aware that he has been writing a play.

Happily, the matter suits the manner – and even the mannerisms, which might not have fitted so neatly into a less elaborate or symmetrical context. The earlier plays are more open and more uneven; the later ones range more freely through their individualized effects; this one seems to have been moulded into its ornate artistic form. The formalities of its construction are matched by the regularities of its style. It never stoops from verse to prose,

as do nearly all of the others. The absence of comic characters has helped
to eliminate that relaxing convention; even the earthy Gardener has his
moralistic vein of iambic pentameter. To walk with Richard from scene to
scene is like turning the illuminated pages in a medieval Book of Hours.
Shakespeare, writing at the apogee of what we regard as his Lyrical Period,
was moving from history and light comedy toward tragedy with *Romeo and
Juliet*. But he would still be celebrating the brightest span of history itself
by moving on with the Henries, and incidentally cutting through the Ricardian
grandiloquence to a more colloquial vein. Prince Hal is conspicuous by his
absence from *Richard II*, notoriously 'at London, 'mongst the taverns' (V,
iii, 5). As the diction moves from hollow court to mellow tavern, so does
the ethos. Bullingbrook will be denounced as a 'vile politician' by the chivalric
Hotspur, 'policy' being commonly understood as Machiavellian realism. To
the cynical Bastard in *King John*, the watchword for the interplay of motives
had been 'commodity' (self-interest).

The backward glance does not seem altogether fair, when we reconsider
the sixteenth-century Shakespeare in the forward-looking light of his Jacobean
achievements. Doubtless with maturity and practice he came to understand
more comprehensively and to render more convincingly the psychology of
his dramatic personages. But latterday critiques may not have made due
allowance for the formalism and the conventions of his still-developing
medium, when G.I. Duthie could denominate Richard 'an artist miscast as
a king', or when Mark Van Doren could recast him as 'a minor poet, not
a king'. Reversing that formula, a modern poet, Louis Aragon in 1940,
could ease the strains of German occupation and French resistance with a
recollection of Richard accepting the loss of his state and glories, but not
of his griefs: 'Still am I king of those'. That became the consolatory refrain
of '*Richard Deux Quarante*': '*Je reste roi de mes douleurs*'. (Aragon would
go on to commemorate a more heartening exemplar, the crusader buried in
France, with '*Richard Coeur-de-Lion*'. But, although England's second King
Richard might have seemed outdated in his own or in Shakespeare's lifetime,
his reappearance may strike us today as quite timely. It is *Richard III* that
no longer holds the favourite place it occupied in the repertory of the
eighteenth and nineteenth centuries. That became the first – and for many
years the most popular – Shakespearean production in the United States,
possibly because it transmitted so adverse a picture of royalty.

Such a chronological reversion from Richard III to Richard II may
symbolize a significant permutation in the cultural climate, while the strong-
minded century of Balzac was being displaced by Kafka's age of anxiety. It
would be hard to imagine the same actor as both kings, as Richard the ranting
tragedian and Richard the lyrical self-questioner; but styles of acting change
too, along with the times. It is easy to think of John Gielgud as Richard II:
slight in stature, sensitive in mien, mellifluous in enunciation. The part is
his by nature, and he has played it well. As for the play itself, it somehow
became the most familiar vehicle for Maurice Evans, who patterned his

interpretation on Gielgud's and who managed to set records with it on both sides of the Atlantic. Gielgud, in his turn, appeared successfully in the title role of a new play on the same subject, *Richard of Bordeaux*, written for him under the pseudonym of Gordon Daviot. At any rate, our century has refuted those prior criticisms regarding the actability of this Shakespearean history. And, though its stage history is fairly sparse in the early record, there were some unusual occasions, such as the problematic revival that got itself implicated with the Earl of Essex against Queen Elizabeth. And just a few years after that unique episode – to be exact, the recorded date is 30 September 1607 – *Richard II* was performed by the crew of the good ship *Dragon*, off the coast of Sierra Leone on its voyage to East India.

Those sailors were allowed to engage in dramatics, as we learn from the journal of their captain, William Keeling, in hopes that such recreation might divert them from indulging in games more unlawful, or from the sleep or silence into which they might otherwise have bogged down. But why they should have chosen this particular offering, in addition to two shipboard performances of *Hamlet*, rather than two easier choices for so amateur a group of players, fosters speculation if not explanation. Both offerings were deeply rooted in the Europe from which they were being carried away, but neither could have imbued its nautical cast with much nostalgia. Though the *Dragon* was heading for an older world, it was animated by the adventurous spirit that had currently begun to settle a new one. In the developing culture of that new world even the unkinged Richard would find some recognition, as we have noticed (and Hamlet, the disinherited prince, would find a good deal more). Walt Whitman, the self-proclaimed bard of democracy, would take his hand-bound copy of *Richard II* along when he rode on a Broadway bus, and would counteract the street noises by loudly spouting from it to his fellow New Yorkers. Even more surprisingly, Abraham Lincoln, who was fond of reading Shakespeare aloud or reciting from memory to his friends, seems to have weathered some of his discouragements by quoting from an unlikely speech and speakers: 'For God's sake let us sit upon the ground / And tell sad stories. ...'

To have drawn together such polar opposites is to touch upon the canon of universality, in spite of some readers who may have been put off along the way by the palpable artifice and the residual preciosity of a talent so consciously realizing itself. In its resulting fusion of poetry into drama, in what E.M.W. Tillyard has reckoned as the 'most formal and ceremonial' of Shakespeare's plays, music has been more than a recurrent metaphor; it has become an operatic *lietmotif*. That note is sounded first on Mowbray's expulsion, and linked with language – but negatively, since he must put English behind him. Henceforth his tongue can mean no more to him

> Than an unstringed viol or a harp,
> Or like a cunning instrument cas'd up,
> Or being open, put into his hands
> That knows no touch to tune the harmony.
> (I, iii, 162–5)

If departure means silence for Mowbray, the last words of Gaunt are accorded
a special attention, 'like deep harmony' (II, i, 6). And he introduces his
predications by linking the image of a dynastic sunset with the dying fall of
a musical composition, together with a couplet that echoes Shakespeare's
thirtieth sonnet ('remembrance of things past'), which will be re-echoed in
the latterday context of Proustian memories:

> The setting sun, and music at the close,
> As the last taste of sweets, is sweetest last,
> Writ in remembrance more than things long past.
> (12–14)

But for the moribund Richard, as the timing broke down, the sweetness turned
sour. Alas, that, after all those elegant intonations, it should come to this!
'So is it in the music of men's lives' (V, v, 45). And, since history can be
perceived as the music of time, it is fitting that the close of Richard's life
should have its musical accompaniment, but also that its tones should
orchestrate the discordant pitch as well as the faltering rhythms of his career
in office: the neglected 'concord of my state and time' (47). Projecting that
same metaphor, the chronicler Hall had given it a more affirmative twist by
looking ahead toward the victorious Lancasters: 'Things decay through
discord, ... through concord they are revived'. But this is not quite yet their
hour; it is the end of Richard's; and his erstwhile glories are overwhelmed
by his present griefs. That, of course, is the fundamental outline of all
tragedies, and his is an archetypal example because its comedown is so
steep and spectacular. The sweet fruition for Richard III, as for Marlowe's
most heroic protagonist, was an earthly crown. For Richard II it is a crown
of sorrows.

CHAPTER TWO

Shakespeare and the Church
G.K. Hunter

At the end of Shakespeare's *Henry VIII*, when the infant Elizabeth is baptized into a proto-Anglican communion by Archbishop Cranmer, we are given a characteristically Anglican mixed message, both secular and sacred:

> Truth shall nurse her,
> Holy and heavenly thoughts still counsel her;
> She shall be loved and feared: her own shall bless her;
> ... In her days every man shall eat in safety
> Under his own vine what he plants, and sing
> The merry songs of peace to all his neighbours.
> God shall be truly known, and those about her
> From her shall read the perfect ways of honour
> And by those claim their greatness, not by blood.
>
> (V, iv, 28–38)

Looked at closely this is an extraordinary mish-mash. The language draws on a number of biblical sources, especially Micah, Chapter 4, verses 1–6 (quoted here in the Geneva version):

> But in the last days it shall come to pass that the mountain of the house of the Lord shall be prepared in the top of the mountains ... Yea, many nations shall come and say, let us go up to the mountain of the Lord ... and he shall judge among many people, and rebuke mighty nations afar off; and they shall beat their swords into mattocks and their spears into scythes: nation shall not lift up a sword against nation, neither shall they learn to fight any more. But they shall sit every man under his vine, and under his fig tree; and none shall make them afraid ... For all people will walk every one in the name of his god, and we will walk in the name of the Lord our God for ever and ever ... And I will make her that halted a remnant and her that was cast far off a mighty nation; and the Lord shall reign over them in Mount Zion for ever and ever ... Now also many nations are gathered against thee, saying Zion shall be condemned ... But they know not the thoughts of the Lord. Arise and thresh, O daughter of Zion: for I will make thine horn iron, and I will make thy hoofs brass: and thou shalt beat in pieces many people: and I will consecrate their gain unto the Lord.[1]

It is needless to labour the applicability of such a vision of the apocalypse to the militant Protestant sense of Elizabeth's reign. Shakespeare allows its full resonance; but his transformations mirror the political pressures that had moved the established Anglican Church away from theocratic fervour of a coming apocalypse towards the political stability that alone would allow it to survive. In Micah the elect nation is only an aspect of the power of the Lord. Shakespeare points our attention instead towards the political facts of his own age. The success of Queen Elizabeth is to be the success of a nation-state that can survive being 'cast off' and the 'rebuke [of] mighty nations afar off' because it had achieved a national consensus in which the knowledge of God and the establishment of a service aristocracy are two sides to one coin. 'Truth ... Holy and heavenly thoughts' must be seen in this mixture less as ends in themselves than as guarantees of a political order from which all the other social and personal (and even religious) goods will flow.

Modern critics and modern directors obviously find it difficult to know what to do with the scene of Elizabeth's baptism. The Cambridge production of 1931 turned it into what might in religious terms be called a charismatic experience but in the secular terms of the modern theatre can only be expressed as a rave-up, lobbing the baby doll Elizabeth from one person to another and finally, while the stage revolved faster and faster 'with a shout the company tossed the baby into the audience'.[2] As a rave-up the scene had a great theatrical impact and the excitement no doubt translated into modern parlance something of the effect intended; for few modern theatregoers are prepared for a serious charismatic experience. But even fewer are prepared for a historical understanding of or sympathy with the political roots of the English church here exposed. Anglicanism as 'the Tory Party at prayer', as is sometimes said, is a communion which by one means or another has managed to equate an 'established religion' (the very words are like a knell) with an established secular hierarchy in which the squire and the parson are brothers in function, as they often were, through the nineteenth century, in literal fact (and rejoiced at for their consanguinity).[3] We should notice that much, even among the more revolutionary aspects of the reformed religion, pointed inevitably (and paradoxically) in this political direction. The demand for a learned clergy that could refer the problems of individual conscience to a wealth of biblical and patristic reading was a demand for an élite clergy, university educated and so separated by status and interests from the lives of its parishioners.[4] The parson's élite education absorbed his life into the conformist social élite of the squirearchy, and the ecclesiastical injunction to peace remained what it is in *Henry VIII* – an injunction to the peace of obedience to the political establishment.

The modern world – at least the intellectual part of it – tends to equate 'truth' with subversion; thus truth is usually seen as an uncovering of what the social authorities prefer to conceal. And among theatregoers Shakespeare has enjoyed continuous popularity as a truth-teller whose humane revelations and capacity for laughter undermines the stuffiness of stability and tradition. But in the case of 'Shakespeare and the Church' we seem at first glance to be facing a connection that places him against rather than with that modern conception of truth. The question whether this was an impediment to his genius or an enabling circumstance is the question this paper is mainly designed to raise.

As we all know, Elizabethans were forbidden by proclamation to write plays 'wherein either matters of religion or of the governance of the realm shall be handled or treated, being no meet matters to be written or treated upon, but by men of authority, learning and wisdom, nor to be handled before any audience but of grave and discreet persons' (Proclamation of 16 May 1559 (cited in E.K. Chambers, *The Elizabethan Stage*, IV, 263)). The general issue is well known, as I say; what is less often noticed is the strangeness to modern (especially American) ears of the combination, even the equation, of 'religion' and 'the governance of the realm'. But it is a standard feature of the period. A parallel injunction of 13 June 1559 establishes control of the printing of 'books of matters of religion or policy or governance', the objectionable books being defined as 'heretical, seditious and unseemly for Christian ears'. The same control is to be exercised over 'songs or ditties that be vile or unclean, especially in derision of any godly order now set forth and established' (Chambers, IV, 264–5). 'Heretical... unseemly... vile... seditious' – these adjectives reflect a view of social opposition to 'godly order' as a beast with several heads but only one purpose: to attack or undermine the vulnerable political system of the country and so render defenceless its spiritual being.

The aim of the foundation documents of Elizabeth's reign was to bind together in one definition the fissiparous elements of reformed doctrine with the true and tried cement of patriotism. This is not surprising (compare the fortunes of theoretical Marxism in Russia's 'Great Patriotic War'). The Reformation had dissolved one cement of social order, the universal church with its claim to an unalienable possession of the keys to the kingdom – a claim which 'naturally' bound every soul to its directives. Into the space left vacant by the Protestant revolt against this doctrine flooded all the socially dangerous ideas of *sola fides*, of the priesthood of all believers, of the supremacy of individual conscience, of an omnipresent Devil that only the individual could keep at bay, and of the requirement to find the answer to every particular difficulty in an individual reading of an open Bible. Only if England could be defined in terms of Micah's 'remnant' turned into a 'mighty nation', as a besieged minority, a flickering light in a darkened world, whose political status was essential to God's plan, could the demand for social conformity have equal charismatic force with the new demands of the individual conscience. And looking across the Channel it could well seem as if the minority status of a 'saving remnant' was indeed God's gift to the nation.

The rhetoric of a sacramental state, an elect nation chosen by God to establish the new Jerusalem was, of course, almost as dangerous to the Elizabethan polity as the basic anarchism of reformed doctrine. To control the one by espousing the theocratic notions of the other was no victory at all for secular state organization; and the early history of the English Church 'as by law established' is a history of attempts to retain the advantages of God's supposed English sympathies without having to set up a social and ecclesiastical system that corresponded too closely to that fact. The use that could be made of Old Testament analogies to suggest a necessary connection between the clergy and the secular authorities certainly could be pushed in an Erastian direction. John Jewel in his *An Apology of the Church of England* cites 'Moses, a civil magistrate' giving 'Aaron the priest ... a vehement and sore rebuke' (ed. J.E. Booty (1963), pp. 115–17). He offers Joshua, David, Solomon, Hezekiah, Jehoshaphat, Joash and Jehu, together with the Roman Emperors of the first five centuries of the church, as proto-Elizabethan examples of sovereigns who took control of the ecclesiastical hierarchy. Collinson's magisterial treatment of 'Magistracy and Ministry' (*op. cit.*, chapter 4) stresses the capacity for settled coexistence that emerged in England. Yet the two halves of this diarchy were never in fact pulling in the same direction (see especially Collinson's pp. 178–82 on this); and eventually the lessening of the external political pressures allowed the internal stresses to pull the union apart and create conditions within which a civil war became conceivable.

Elizabethan longing for peace and stability after the violent alternations of the preceding reigns and especially after the martyrdoms and foreign interference of the immediately preceding one, was no doubt a powerful factor in favour of Elizabeth's tightrope act. If we read the *engagées*, the articulate, the theoretical (as historians tend to do), we hear mainly of dispute, anger and instability. From Jewel, from Foxe, from Cartwright and Perkins and a hundred others we hear passionate discussion of the Eucharist, of Purgatory, of ecclesiastical celibacy, of vestments, of the intermediacy of the Virgin and the saints. But that these passions descended far into the lives of the theatre-going laity I take liberty to doubt. From the enthusiastic point of view, and in accordance with *Revelations*, 3.16, lack of enthusiasm for doctrinal positions was a sign of incipient atheism; but this is to give a negative value to what must most often have appeared as a conscious and positive choice. If heresy and treason are pushed together, then social conformity can easily come to be seen as a version of religion, specifically of an Anglican version of religion where, as George Bernard Shaw remarked, 'churchgoing is an alternative to religion'. What undoubtedly did sink into the national consciousness was the rejection of Papal supremacy. And this surely happened because Papal supremacy affected an issue that lay people did care about passionately – nationalism. Innocent III appears in Bale's *King Johan* under the Morality title of 'Usurped Power'. The Pope was a foreigner, an interloper, an exporter of English coinage, an impediment in the way of direct communication between the English people and the English sovereign. As the Act of Supremacy of the first Elizabethan Parliament put it in its Preamble, the purpose of the Act was 'the utter extinguishment and putting away of all usurped and foreign power and authorities out of this your realm'. The oath to be administered to every 'ecclesiastical person' required him to assert that 'no foreign prince, person, prelate, state or potentate hath or ought to have any jurisdiction, power, superiority, preeminence or authority, ecclesiastical or spiritual, within this realm'. Something of the same instinctive nationalist response can be seen in the attachment to an *English* Bible. Elizabeth's capacity to call on these symbols, sympathies and prejudices allowed her to command loyalty to the religious establishment without defining doctrine in any precise way, allowed her to make the *via media* look like a crusade rather than a political finagle. And of course throughout the whole period the looming Spanish threat kept up a useful pressure on English self-definition.

I am making here what seems to be a necessary distinction between an intellectual élite and the mass of the population, between those for whom religion raised passionately held issues of doctrine – matters of truth not dependent on nationalism – as against those whose religion was carried by ethical and social practice and so intimately tied to the conformities of the nation. And these were the conformities that the Crown was anxious to bring into primary focus. It would be a mistake, of course, to suppose that such engaged intellectuals were always churchmen. There can be little doubt that the voices of the Catholic apologists were clearly heard and listened to intently by university men of many persuasions. For the intelligentsia of the age the appeal of Rome remained powerful, having the advantage of doctrinal rigour and the social convenience of a system of private devotion that was little different from that of the English church.[5] But the Catholic appeal for intellectuals seems to have had non-religious components as well. There was widespread admiration, for example, for Campion and Southwell as intellectuals, scholars and writers, avant-garde figures in the highly coloured emotional style of the Mannerists,[6] and this seems to have been able to coexist with revulsion against them as secular subversives who would bring back the fires of Smithfield and Spanish intervention.

Thus we find a figure like Ben Jonson moving uneasily from one side to another and back again. Less well known than Jonson's case, but more revealing, is that of William Alabaster.

> In his early years he was a Calvinist [but] the validity of the Elizabethan Church settlement ... began to appear questionable ... he began to feel a greater tenderness of heart towards Christ's cross and passion than ... the Protestants were wont to feel ... [and suddenly saw] that nothing could be false that the Catholic Roman Church did propose ... I leapt up from the place where I sat and said to myself 'now I am a Catholic'.[7]

Alabaster saw that only the Church of Rome could provide the infallible authority in matters of doctrine that he needed. And so he chose to join the Society of Jesus, because it demanded the most unquestioning obedience. After a spell in Rome he returned to England determined to die a martyr, but when he arrived he confessed his knowledge and abhorrence of Catholic *political* intrigue. In 1606, after the Gunpowder Plot, he wrote to Robert Cecil offering his services as a spy against politically active Catholics. But after this he went back to Rome and wrote in defence of Catholic faith. However his book was found heretical and he abandoned the Jesuits and denounced Father

Parsons and the Holy Office. Then he repented his revolt from Rome. By 1613/14 he was again a Protestant. King James commanded Cambridge to make him a Doctor of Divinity and by 1617 he was a chaplain to James.

Hearing such a story it is tempting to dismiss Alabaster as simply an opportunist turncoat; and of course there may have been elements of that. But his case points us to a real situation in these years. The doctrinal relation of the two churches was such that any man committed to the search for a truth that stood above political exigency was bound to waver. Such is the fate of intellectuals.

We ought to allow, I believe, that Shakespeare gives no sign of being an intellectual in these terms, that is of being a man tormented by the possibility that he might attain to a sufficiency of Truth. As represented by the attitudes that appear in his plays, he appears rather to be a person, not of course with an ordinary mind, but one whose created worlds are full of people with ordinary minds, people with short-term rather than long-term anxieties and ambitions, who regard long-term ends with a degree of vagueness (accompanied by trepidation). It is clear that he could enter with sympathy and understanding into such minds; that he could enter with sympathy and understanding into a mind like Alabaster's is by no means as clear.[8] Of course Shakespeare's plays show churchmen in plenty, but they are churchmen in their social roles; the nearest he comes to his own time and place is with Cranmer and Wolsey, both judged, as good and bad, by their socio-political activities, one a humble conformist to the royal will, the other a counter-politician, an exponent of church *against* state. Wolsey judges himself at the end of his life – and clearly we are intended to confirm the judgment – as someone who has allowed his conformist spiritual role to be swallowed up by a wholly inappropriate appetite for political power and whose only hope of goodness now lies in renewed conformity to the interrelated wills of God and king.

There are also friars in plenty in Shakespeare. Does this mean that their creator longed for a reinstatement of the religious orders? To say so is to confuse art and life. Friars are an essential part of the social life depicted in the *novella* tradition that Shakespeare drew on so heavily for his plot material, for their social situation, outside the rigid class hierarchies of the secular world, gives them a freedom of movement (especially a freedom of access to women) that enables intrigue to be handled with a degree of social realism. There are also plentiful references in Shakespeare to grace, repentance, mercy, forgiveness, despair and providence, and these words as they appear in the plays regularly require a religious gloss, such as '*despair* here does not refer only to a psychological state but also to the theological condition of the *desperate* man, alienated from God's grace'. And in this characteristic Shakespeare is not to be differentiated from other Elizabethan writers. The vocabulary of the Elizabethans is shot through with ecclesiastical and doctrinal references, and many of these have connotations firmly anchored in the practices of the Roman church. The issue is, however, entirely explicable as a linguistic phenomenon and does not impose any doctrinal consequences. Words always carry traces of the meanings they had when we first heard them; and we should remember that Shakespeare's father and mother (those from whom he learned to speak) had lived their lives inside the Catholic fold. Official regulations can change official behaviour, but at the deeper level of speech meanings do not disappear. Shakespeare's Catholic vocabulary and his sensitivity to its historical resonance is part of his freedom as a writer and does not allow us to decide that he was either a Protestant or a Catholic in doctrine or sympathy. One might also make the point that the state's prohibitions as well as its calculated vagueness about doctrine allowed the skilful writer to enter into a greater range of psychologies and experiences, applying doctrinal words, with their powerful traditional charge, to humanly various situations. In this respect at least the government's requirement that the writer avoid doctrinal matters (in a vocabulary still loaded with doctrinal echoes) looks like an extraordinary boon, and may be one part of the means by which Shakespeare was able to move into a 'modern' world of psychological creativity. Borges has remarked, I believe, that censorship has the great advantage of providing a writer with metaphors. The secularization of statements about religion in Elizabethan plays may well have operated to much the same advantage.

Take the case of *Measure for Measure*, the play which probably more than any other draws on a specific church organization and which uses a vocabulary in which secular conflict is continually referred to spiritual values. Vienna's ruler appears also as a father confessor and his self-justification is represented as both downright (as a ruler) and devious (as a friar). The heroine is likewise both a heroic adventurer and a frigid nun, active in deed and reclusive in desires. Temperaments which in an un-Elizabethan society might find embodiment in social roles that allow a religious fulfilment are here contained inside situations that reflect the straight political require-ments of justice and obedience. This does not mean that the resonance of alternative possibilities is suppressed. Shakespeare's imagination is obviously very engaged here with details of theological minutiae. I have discussed elsewhere[9] his surprising acquaintance with the status of the Poor Clares and with the theory of manducation. One might also point to his interest in this play in setting fatherhood-in-God and brotherhood-in-God against the corresponding blood relationships. But these interests are part of the orchestration not of the melodic development. The complications of the story as told depend on the negotiations of ambivalent individuals with the demands of secular life and issue in secular solutions, which require, of course, ambiguities and compromises rather than absolutes, and are all the more real for that. It seems that immersion in the world of the English Church provided for Shakespeare and his fellows an excellent training in the complex negotiations that dramatists have to conduct between absolutes and existencies, values and realities, inner aspirations and outer behaviour.

NOTES

1. Compare 1 Kings, 4:25 and Isaiah, 36:16.
2. See Norman Marshall, *The Other Theatre* (1947), pp. 66–7.
3. See the beginning of Book VI of Wordsworth's *The Excursion*:

> Hail to the State of England! And conjoin
> With this a salutation as devout
> Made to the spiritual fabric of her Church;
> Founded in Truth; by blood of Martyrdom
> Cemented; by the hands of Wisdom reared
> In beauty of holiness, with ordered pomp
> Decent and unreproved. The voice that greets
> The Majesty of both shall pray for both
> That mutually protected and sustained
> They may endure long as the sea surrounds
> This favoured land, or sunshine warms her soil.

Patrick Collinson (The Religion of Protestants (1982), p. 3) is right enough to say that Anglicanism of this nineteenth-century kind is 'drained of the dynamism of the Elizabethan church politics'; but my point about the continuity of the church and state mixture still stands, I believe.

4. See Collinson, *op. cit.*, Chapter 3.
5. Thus Father Parsons's *Christian Directory* could be taken over by Anglican pietists and with only a few modifications could then enjoy a continuously successful career as an Anglican devotional manual.
6. Campion's History of Ireland appears in Holinshed's Chronicles as the work of a 'rare clerk'. Ben Jonson remarked to Drummond of Hawthornden that he would have been content to destroy many of his own poems 'so he had written that piece of his [Southwell's], the Burning Babe'.
7. See *The Sonnets of William Alabaster*, ed. G.M. Story and Helen Gardner (1959), pp. xiiff.
8. The obvious problem-figure here is Hamlet, who must be allowed to be an intellectual in the full sense, not simply a person who is made to use intellectual discourse to represent ordinary human hopes and fears. But even Hamlet, insofar as he thinks in Christian terms (in terms of Providence, Grace, the after-life) does not go beyond the ideas that link Christians rather than separating them. Purgatory is both affirmed and denied, allowed as a poetic possibility and rejected equally in the terms of 'what a man might say'. There is no evidence in the play that the uncertainty of these matters contributes to Hamlet's mental turmoil.
9. 'Six Notes on *Measure for Measure*', *Shakespeare Quarterly* XV (1964), 167–72.

CHAPTER THREE

Hats, Clocks and Doublets: Some Shakespearean Anachronisms

Jonas Barish

Shakespearean drama, as we all know, is riddled with anachronisms. Repeatedly the plays jolt us out of the historical moment in which their stories are supposed to be unfolding, by reference to some event or custom or historical person that could not, so far as we know, have coexisted with the setting. Hector quoting Aristotle – several centuries before Aristotle was born; the future Richard III, while Duke of Gloucester, measuring his own ruthlessness against that of the murderous Machiavel – at a time when Machiavelli was still in his infancy; Hamlet attending an as-yet-unfounded Wittenberg University; Cleopatra playing billiards: these are the kinds of error from which our most universally revered culture hero seems not to have been exempt.

The first thing, however, that needs to be said about these and similar oddities of temporal displacement is that anyone composing a fiction based on a past epoch is virtually doomed to fall into anachronism, even when making strenuous efforts to avoid it. Some degree of chronological incongruity would appear to be inherent in the attempt to recreate a *past*, hence by definition a *lost* and *alien* culture, and therefore to some extent an irrecoverable one. We cannot, after all, know any former epoch with the kind of intimacy with which it was known to its original inhabitants, nor can we divest ourselves of our own immersion in our own epoch, so that when transplanting ourselves imaginatively into the past we are more or less certain to stumble into mistakes: our modernity is sure to betray us in ways we can neither predict nor control. And this would apply even to works written about past eras close to our own – to plays on relatively recent American history, for example, such as Robert E. Sherwood's *Abe Lincoln in Illinois* (1939); or *Sunrise at Campobello* by Dore Schary (1958), which chronicles the emergence of Franklin D. Roosevelt onto the American political scene, not without many compressions, ellipses and rearrangements of recorded fact; or (most recent of all) *A Walk in the Woods* by Lee Blessing (1987), in which an American and a Soviet negotiator on nuclear arms control engage in a private conversation while walking in the Geneva woods, removed from direct surveillance by their respective governments. This last-named play succeeds precisely to the extent that it deals with immediate, virtually contemporary history, the actual walk in the woods on which the play is based having taken place only five years earlier than the play itself. Even then it concerns a series of wholly invented conversations that conform to certain stereotyped notions of how a zealous young American and a more seasoned Soviet negotiator in such circumstances might perhaps have been expected to behave, but which nevertheless did not escape severe comment in the press on the distorted picture it implied of the actual process of international debate over ways of forestalling a nuclear holocaust. As little as five years after the event, the play seemed already, to some, to be caught in a time warp. All plays on historical subjects, then – and they are legion – lend themselves inevitably to anachronism, and the fact should cause no surprise.

But these American instances at least presuppose a certain degree of familiarity on the part of spectators with the basic historical materials – with Lincoln, with Roosevelt, and with the deadlocked negotiations on arms control between America and the Soviet Union. Such would not have been the case with spectators in 1595 or 1605, a fact which the playwrights of that epoch did not fail to exploit, since some of Shakespeare's contemporaries indulged in anachronism much more promiscuously and, it would seem, knowingly, than he, indifferent to coherency of setting or historical veri-similitude. Cleopatra's billiards, it appears, were suggested by an earlier play of George Chapman's, *The Blind Beggar of Alexandria*, first performed in 1598. At least, so thought a late nineteenth-century commentator cited in the Furness Variorum edition of *Antony and Cleopatra*. To which Furness himself, quoting the *NED*, appended the relevant observation that in the same play (i.e. *The Blind Beggar*) 'the hero flourishes a pistol, smokes tobacco, swears by "God's wounds", and talks fair modern Spanish, in the time of the Ptolomies.'[1] In other words, Chapman simply rides roughshod over all considerations of chronological plausibility, and glories in doing so. Chapman of course may have thought that that was part of the fun of what is, after all, an exceedingly casual throwing together of miscellaneous elements designed to produce a comic romance. Dekker's and Marston's *Satiromastix* (1601), similarly, picks up certain characters from ancient Rome, others from the streets of Elizabethan London, and plunks them down in the days of William Rufus, without the slightest attempt to make the eleventh-century setting even minimally believable. The king in the play, seeking to exercise his *droit de seigneur* over the betrothed of one of his vassals, might just as well be named Hadrian the Seventh or Harlequin the Ninth as William Rufus. Here, as in the case of *The Blind Beggar*, we might be said to be dealing with an identifiable subgenre, pseudo-historical romance, peculiar to an epoch in which history in our sense had not yet fully disengaged itself from fiction.

Furness's observation is relevant also because it reminds us that Shakespeare offers very few examples of such wanton flouting of temporal plausibility. Though he cannot be said to have attempted anything like the rigorous adherence to documentary sources aimed at by Ben Jonson in his tragedies *Sejanus his Fall* and *Catiline his Conspiracy* or (to a lesser degree) in his 'comical satire' *Poetaster* – all of which, despite their author's massive scholarship and his labours of archaeological reconstruction, are themselves open to criticism for their lapses from the annals and other records on which they are presumably based – Shakespeare too was plainly aiming at a persuasive recreation of older cultures. In consulting the English or Scottish chroniclers or the Roman or Greek historians, he selects the details that matter to him with a remarkable degree of artistic conscience.

The fact is that most of Shakespeare's anachronisms are discreet, sometimes to such a point that editors today do not always trouble to comment on them. The New Arden editor of *King John*, E.A. Honigmann (Methuen, London, 1954), for example, has nothing to say about the repeated references in that play to *cannon*, a weapon not invented until several centuries *after* John's reign. No more does A.R. Braunmiller, editor of the Oxford Shakespeare edition of the same play (1989), or L.A. Beaurline, editor of the play for the New Cambridge Shakespeare (1990). Nor do editors bother to remark on the engines of war Lady Hotspur has heard her restless husband call out in his sleep – the basilisks and culverins along with the cannons – in equal defiance of chronological possibility. John Dover Wilson, in his Cambridge New Shakespeare (1946), again of *King John*, glosses 'basilisk' and 'culverin' but says nothing about their being anachronisms. The New Arden editor of *King Lear*, lastly, Kenneth Muir, passes in silence over the oddity by which, in a play set in ancient Britain, Edgar is made to disguise himself as a 'Bedlam beggar', a thousand years or so before Bedlam – Bethlehem Hospital – even came into existence, let alone became a byword for a lunatic asylum. And so with most of the other editions of these plays that I have been able to consult.

In short, in none of these instances is the anachronism felt *as* an ana-chronism, even today. The reason, I suspect, is that Shakespeare, in these as in dozens of comparable cases, manages the references so unobtrusively, makes them seem so natural and inevitable a part of his story that it simply would not occur to us to question them unless someone questioned *us* about them. And if we, with our historical noses to the ground, do not scent historical falsity in these cases, surely no Elizabethan theatregoer, far less schooled than we in detecting historical discrepancies, would have noticed anything amiss, or would have cared two pins if he had.

One sort of anachronism, which I do not recall seeing mentioned elsewhere, smote me between the eyes as I was pondering this topic. It crops up in a speech in *Troilus and Cressida*, when Troilus, having just witnessed Cressida's betrayal, is asked by Ulysses whether he is as moved as his agonized outburst seems to indicate. 'Ay, Greek,' replies Troilus, 'and that shall be divulged

well / In characters as red as Mars his heart / Inflam'd with Venus' (V, ii,
162–4).[2] With reference to the memorial token bestowed on Cressida,
Troilus's presumably ornamental sleeve – itself an anachronism – which
Cressida has now conferred on Diomed, Diomed has sworn to display it on
his helmet in the next day's battle. Troilus declares grimly,

> That sleeve is mine that he'll bear on his helm.
> Were it a casque compos'd by Vulcan's skill,
> My sword should bite it. Not the dreadful spout
> Which shipmen do the hurricano call,
> Constring'd in mass by the almighty sun,
> Shall dizzy with more clamor Neptune's ear
> In his descent then shall my prompted sword
> Falling on Diomed ...
>
>   (V, ii, 169– 76)

Here we encounter references to four gods in the Olympic pantheon: Mars,
Venus, Vulcan and Neptune. Why, I found myself asking, should Troilus,
at the height of the Trojan War, many centuries before the founding of Rome,
refer to those gods by their *Roman* names? Why not Ares and Aphrodite?
Hephaestos and Poseidon?

Does Shakespeare, I wondered, *ever* give these deities their proper Greek
names? At this point I resorted to the Harvard Concordance for some
checking, and made an enlightening discovery. In the course of the canon
Shakespeare alludes at least 56 times to Mars, including numerous instances
in *Troilus, Timon of Athens*, and *The Two Noble Kinsmen*, all set in ancient
Greece, but never once to Ares. Less often, but quite often enough, he
mentions Venus, Vulcan and Neptune, also Juno, Hercules and Ceres. Very
often indeed – 137 times – he refers to Jove or Jupiter, but not once in any
of these cases does he use Hellenic nomenclature. Against 14 references to
Mercury I found only a single one to Hermes. I thought these statistics
striking, and I sought then to learn whether any editor had commented on
the situation. I could not find that any had.

Digging further, I unearthed another curious fact: even the (relatively)
erudite Chapman – whose translation of the first eight books of the *Iliad*
(published in 1598) apparently served Shakespeare as a source for *Troilus*
– even Chapman, working (at least largely, we assume) from the Greek,
also gave *his* gods their Roman names – Jupiter, Jove, Juno, Neptune,
Venus and Mars – almost as though by this means to *anglicize* them.
When, in Book I, he departs from this practice (perhaps for metrical reasons)
and calls his Olympian artificer 'Ephaistus' [*Hephaestos*], he carefully
supplies a marginal note to explain that this was 'a name of Vulcan', and
he follows the same note with three others in which he insists on the more
familiar Roman term, including one in which he identifies 'Ephaistus' as
'Vulcan skinker [i.e. tapster, or drawer] to the Gods'.[3]

We know too little about Chapman's early years even to speculate about
his education – he may have been mainly self-taught – but for Shakespeare

the explanation is probably simple enough. Shakespeare, trained in the Stratford grammar school, saturated in the Roman classics – particularly Ovid, but also Virgil, Horace, and Terence, and in Renaissance authors like Erasmus and Palingenius – must from childhood have been completely at home in the ancient pantheon. He knew the characters in those myths under the Latin names by which they had been known in his schoolbooks, and he knew them like the back of his hand. He probably knew their Hellenic equivalents but would not naturally have used them, or put them in the mouths of his characters. Doubtless even his literate auditors would have been in the same position; they would have found the Greek names Greek indeed. The fact that we, with our even less Greek than Shakespeare, find ourselves in essentially the same plight, would seem to be borne out by the ease with which we too accept what in all historical rigour is a striking anachronism, and by the silence of editors on the subject (whom I do not in the least mean to be faulting on this score).

What this all suggests is that audience recognition of anachronism is very much a sometime thing, dependent on the nature of the specific instance and on how adroitly the playwright works it into his discourse. The reason that audiences never think to bristle at Hotspur's being shown as the same age as Prince Hal, when in actual fact he was older than King Henry IV, is that they do not know it. Instead of unconsciously monitoring the play's presentation of history, audiences – including alert and instructed audiences – are in fact usually learning their history *from* the play. The reason that hats, clocks and doublets spring to our attention as they do is that they belong to the world of visible, tangible objects, in two cases familiar items of clothing that the characters on stage must either wear, or which, if they do not wear, must open an awkward and disconcerting gulf between what we hear and what we see.

Hats have given a good deal of trouble in Act II of *Julius Caesar*. Lucius, Brutus's page, tells his master that the conspirators have arrived. 'Their hats are pluck'd about their ears,' he says, 'And half their faces buried in their cloaks' (II, i, 73–4), prompting a memorable reply from Brutus concerning the stealth, and indeed the hypocrisy, to which he and his associates are driven by the nature of their undertaking. A memorable editorial response to the incident came from Alexander Pope in his edition of Shakespeare. Pope, horrified by the thought of ancient Romans wearing hats, simply omitted the word; rather than attempting any emendation, he left a blank in the text, as though deleting a foul expletive. Later, when editing *Coriolanus*, he altered his strategy, this time changing 'hat' to 'cap'.

John Dover Wilson, in his New Cambridge edition of the same play (1949), p. 127, suggested that 'Shakespeare, knowing nothing of Roman headgear, "dressed his Romans in the slouch hats of his own time"', citing the Clarendon Press edition of 1884. But T.S. Dorsch, the play's New Arden editor (1955), points out that, on the contrary, 'the Romans did use headgear of various kinds: the *petasus*, a broad-brimmed travelling hat or cap, the *pilleus*, a close-fitting, brimless felt hat or cap, worn at entertainments and festivals, and the *cucullus*, a cap or hood fastened to a garment.' (p. 38, line 73n.). Dorsch however offers no hint as to which of these varieties of headgear – if any – might most appropriately be worn in the scene in question. In any case the reason for editorial debate over such a detail stems from the fact that here the hats form part of the visible furniture of the scene, part of its material substance, which we are asked to gaze upon and recognize as lending a disquieting furtiveness to their wearers. They play their part, these hats, in establishing the conspiratorial atmosphere and helping to articulate the morality of the episode. They cannot therefore simply be brushed aside, but must either be shown or their absence somehow accounted for.

The same would be true, certainly, of the 'sleeve' already mentioned, which Troilus bestows on Cressida, Cressida gives to Diomed, and Diomed swears to affix to his helmet in sign of his proprietorship over Cressida. Here too we are dealing with a palpable stage prop that carries a high emotional charge, something that must be seen and its psychic and social meanings grasped; but this time we are once again dealing with legendary history, pseudo-history, of an epoch so unfathomably remote from our own time – from ours *or* the Elizabethans' – that our ignorance protects us, as it doubtless protected its author, from *feeling* as such the anachronism in which, no doubt, the entire play must strictly speaking be said to be saturated.

Comparable, but of lesser moment, would be the 'doublet' Caesar is said to wear when offered the crown, which in a theatrical gesture he is reported to have plucked open so as to offer his throat to the people, and the 'sleeve' by which Cassius tells Brutus to tug Casca as he passes by – though of course the Roman toga had no sleeve – or the 'lace' which Cleopatra begs Charmian to 'cut' in a moment of emotional agitation – though ancient Egyptian ladies did not wear lace that required cutting. In such instances as these, the allusion is so transitory, and the action so distanced from us (in the case of Caesar) or so confined to words alone (as in the other cases) that we scarcely notice. Very likely Shakespeare did not notice either.

As for the clock that strikes so insistently in the orchard scene and later in *Julius Caesar* and which serves, according to the New Oxford editor, Arthur Humphreys (1984), to 'stress the inexorable drive of time toward the climax' (II, i, 193n., p. 139 – a strained and portentous reading, to my mind), it has caused less trouble than the hats precisely because it need not be seen. It need only be *heard*, as it is heard also in *Cymbeline*, warning Iachimo that it is time to leave Imogen's chamber, where he has been hiding to collect the data he needs in order to win his wager.

Cymbeline of course, provides a kind of total immersion in anachronism, since it seems to be set simultaneously in Renaissance Italy and in the Rome of classical antiquity, as well as in ancient Britain. Yet this logical absurdity, which outraged Dr Johnson, is in fact negotiated so as not to abuse our credulity. During the Italian scenes we are plainly in a corrupt Italian milieu, inhabited by characters with names like Philario and Iachimo, whereas in

Britain we find ourselves in the ancient world, in an outpost of the Roman empire, with a Roman general named Caius Lucius declaring war on the rebellious Britons in the name of Caesar Augustus, in order to enforce the payment of tribute. All this being the case, such trifling incidental anachronisms as Pisanio's provision of a man's disguise for Imogen, including 'doublet. hat, hose', can hardly be said to be disturbing.

Perhaps generic considerations come into play here, with Shakespeare himself attempting the sort of romance *cum* history or history *cum* romance that popular writers like Chapman, Marston and Dekker had dealt in so freely. Shakespeare, as usual, succeeds in both honouring the hybrid genre and turning it to his own more serious and probing purposes. On the one hand he is plainly continuing his prolonged inspection of Romanitas, of the character of Rome itself as the great ancestral matrix from which Elizabethan England was thought to have sprung, while simultaneously recreating a version of England's more indigenous past, that of the native Britons, along with the folklore and fairytale elements that (in his representation) belonged to that domain. He thus dramatizes the colliding, and with the reconciliation at the end, the ultimate merging, of the two main currents that (in his understanding) fed into and eventuated in his own composite culture.

As for Renaissance Italy, part of the anachronistic 'confusion of the names and manners of different times' that Dr Johnson complained of,[4] it would not of course have been 'different times' or 'history' at all to Shakespeare's audiences, but rather the *contemporary* world, *their* world, at a slight geographical remove, vividly glimpsed and serving to warn impressionable Englishmen to cease aping Italian manners or risk being infected by Italian vices. In the story of the wager they would have seen a once-honest and in most respects exemplary British gentleman, Posthumus Leonatus, converted by residence in Italy into the incarnate devil not long since denounced so scathingly by Roger Ascham.[5] They would then have seen his return to Britain as restoring him to the more wholesome air of his own country, causing him to abandon Italianate jealousy and revenge in favour of forgiveness, repentance, self-castigation and self-amendment. They would have watched the rage and quarrelsomeness picked up in Italy now no longer directed against a malicious rival (from whom he has also learned boastfulness and suspiciousness) but in honourable battle against the invaders of his native soil.

If this conjecture is right, we are less likely than Dr Johnson to regard the mingle of disparate elements as an instance of 'unresisting imbecility'. We are less likely, that is, to be unnerved by the play's hybrid nature, or offended by its temporal irregularities, since we may take a less rigorous view of the playwright's obligation to adhere to the letter of the chronicles, or to the unities of time and place, and care less than Johnson did about fidelity to the separation of genres. The romance ahistoricism, or *anti*historicism of *Cymbeline* is so deliberate, its collapsing of diverse historical elements so unabashed, and yet the imaginative pressure fusing these ingredients reaching such a pitch of incandescence, that it ends by creating a new chemical compound, with its own odour, taste and colour, its own unique and recognizable character. They serve at one and the same time, these disparate elements, to explore England's past, to warn against some of the dangers of its present moment, and to stake out valid and meaningful alternatives for the future.

In short, and to make an end, I would stress three simple points: first, *some* element of anachronism is all but inescapable in any fictional recreation of a past epoch, as it no doubt must be in *any* historical writing, however scrupulously the author may struggle to deal with what Sidney would have called his 'mouse-eaten records' – his archives, his documentary proofs, his archaeological relics. Second, the Elizabethans were doubly vulnerable to anachronism, given the fact that fiction and history had only barely begun to acquire the separate and distinct characters we have until recently assumed them to possess. And third, Shakespeare, by the instinctive tact and poetic intensity with which he worked, somehow managed almost to *dissolve* the element of anachronism into the mainstream of his discourse, so that most of the time it passes us harmlessly by, unnoticed, or when we do notice it, as in *Cymbeline*, it succeeds in conveying wisdom that the playwright is unmistakably eager for us to acquire.

NOTES

1. Horace Howard Furness (ed.), *The Tragedie of Anthonie, and Cleopatra*, A New Variorum Edition of Shakespeare (Philadelphia, Lippincott, 1907), pp. 128–9.
2. Citations from Shakespeare will be to *The Riverside Shakespeare*, ed. G. Blakemore Evans *et al.* (Boston, Houghton-Mifflin, 1974).
3. Allardyce Nicoll (ed.), *Chapman's Homer*, Bollingen Series XLI, (New York, Pantheon, 1956), I (*Iliad*), 40–1.
4. *Selections from Johnson on Shakespeare*, ed. Bertrand H. Bronson with Jean M. O'Meara (New Haven, Yale University Press, 1986), p. 307.
5. *English Works*, ed. William Aldis Wright (Cambridge, The University Press, 1904), p. 229.

CHAPTER FOUR

'A Liberal Tongue': Language and Rebellion in *Richard II*

David Norbrook

A consistent theme of W.R. Elton's teaching, at once daunting and bracing, has been that for all the volume of commentary generated by Shakespeare's plays, there is still a great deal to be done in understanding their initial contexts. *Richard II* is a case in point. It is generally accepted that it is the play of which the Lord Chamberlain's Men staged a special performance on 7 February 1601; the following day, eleven members of that audience took up arms in Essex's rebellion. The interpretation of that evidence, however, is much more problematic. I believe that the play has been widely misinterpreted – or at least very selectively interpreted – by a misunderstanding of its contexts in political and intellectual history. But it will be a long time before those contexts have been fully recovered; we still lack a full study of the politics of Essex and his circle; and the analysis of political discourse in the 1590s is not nearly as well developed as for the mid seventeenth-century period. In the limited space available, I shall try to question the validity of some long-current contexts and offer some alternatives, on the basis of which I shall attempt, in a necessarily very tentative way, to reconstruct some of the ways in which the audience of 1601 might have responded to the play.[1]

* * *

The play's opening line can put us on the right track. But all too often it has done the reverse. 'Old John of Gaunt, time-honoured Lancaster': the ethos is of age and tradition, looking back to a medieval past. From the nineteenth century onward, the medieval era has conjured up an image of an organic community, of a harmonious hierarchy united by a simple religious faith, with deferential peasants and mystically sanctioned rulers. That image of the middle ages became hardened during the reaction against the French Revolution, and it was in that period that conservative readings of the first tetralogy as expressing nostalgia for a lost social unity became current.[2] E.M.W. Tillyard's reading of the histories, while more historically grounded, drew on similar patterns of analysis.

The nostalgic readings gained a new lease of life with the publication in 1957 of Ernst Kantorowicz's *The King's Two Bodies*. Kantorowicz reads *Richard II* as dramatizing the theory that the monarch has two bodies, one natural and mortal, the other artificial, mystical and immortal. The tragedy of the play lies in the emerging split between these two bodies. Stage by stage Richard's sacramental unity becomes violently severed until in the deposition scene his body becomes 'now devoid of any metaphysis whatever'.[3] This pattern of explanation throws the emphasis firmly on Richard, and Kantorowicz acknowledges a debt to Walter Pater's analysis of the poet-king. His political sympathies are clearly with Richard. One of 'Richard's so-called "tyrannies"', his claim that the laws of the realm were in his head, in fact 'merely referred to a well known maxim of Roman and Canon Laws'.[4] His accusers, then, were merely betraying their provincial ignorance. That emphasis is characteristic of Kantorowicz's strategy in his book, which is to uncover a buried vein of metaphysical mysticism in what had traditionally been seen as the hard-headed empiricism of English common law. His reading of Shakespeare is strongly marked by the conservative German tradition, and *The King's Two Bodies* retains traces of his early allegiance to the mystical monarchism of the poet Stefan George.[5]

Kantorowicz's reading has exercised a powerful influence on recent new historicist criticism: it brings together favoured themes of the body, power and display, and comes with a strong recommendation from Michel Foucault.[6] Although in the article that named the 'new historicist' movement Stephen Greenblatt drew attention to the need to set interpretations of *Richard II* in their political contexts,[7] this principle has not been very consistently followed, and it is possible to detect strong residues of older conservative readings in later new historicist work.[8] Greenblatt's own subsequent downplaying of the possible radicalizing effects of Shakespeare's histories on their audiences reflects the growing influence of Foucault's scepticism about agency.[9] But he was, I believe, right in his original insistence that the 1601 performance was a significant pointer to elements in the play's political rhetoric; the emphasis on mystical bodies has distracted attention from very different aspects of the play and of Elizabethan political discourse in general.

For if the Elizabethans did feel nostalgic for the medieval past, it was not necessarily for mystical bodies that they yearned. 'Old' and 'time-honoured' would not have conjured up unequivocally monarchist associations for the rebel party of 1601. And, indeed, for any reader of Holinshed.[10] The reign of Richard II as there described is no timeless idyll of metaphysical unity, but a period of sharp contestation: popular rebellion, attempts at religious reformation under Wyclif, and struggles to maintain or increase the status of Parliament. In those struggles, London plays a key role: Richard tries as far as possible to hold Parliaments out of that city for fear that they will be swayed by growing extra-parliamentary pressure on the MPs. The House of Commons begins calling for annual Parliaments, to which Richard retorts that he would rather submit himself to the King of France than to his own subjects. A group of lords try to keep Richard under strict control to the point of threatening to depose him.[11]

If the late fourteenth century offered an object lesson for readers of the 1590s, it was not because subjects were nostalgic for absolutism but because they feared its recurrence. Those chivalric spectacles that look so quaint and archaic today had a sharp political edge: as Richard McCoy has shown, Essex and his circle vindicated traditional aristocratic ideas of honour against the monarchy's attempt to centralize honour in loyalty to the monarch. Essex tried to revive feudal offices that had served to restrict monarchical power.[12] An increasingly important body of antiquarian thought was beginning to formulate the concept of feudalism and to heighten public awareness of long-lapsed constitutional precedents for challenges to royal power.[13] The remedies of annual Parliaments and aristocratic councils were to be looked to increasingly under the early Stuarts. When the Civil War broke out, Parliamentarian leaders consciously looked back to the Middle Ages; for them, absolutism was an innovative phenomenon to be resisted by an appeal to deep-rooted constitutionalist traditions.[14] Sir John Hayward's *The Life and Raigne of King Henrie IIII*, which opened with Bullingbrook's challenge to Mowbray, was republished in 1641, 1642 and 1643. The Parliamentarian leaders saw themselves as offering a comparable trial by battle, and indeed individuals were still ready to engage in trial by combat.[15]

This aristocratic constitutionalism could blend with classical republicanism: Roman history too could be read as a struggle between independent aristocrats and tyrannical sovereigns. Republican discourse was circulating in England in the 1590s: Hayward's history, the first major synthesis of classical Tacitean discourse with English history, appeared two years before the Essex rebellion, with a dedication to the Earl.[16] The leading republican theorist of the later seventeenth century, Algernon Sidney, was to remember how his ancestors had been betrayed by monarchical deceit:

> Henry the Fourth was made king by the earl of Northumberland, and his brave son Hotspur ... but [he could not] think himself safe, till his benefactor was dead.[17]

Sidney was proud of his connections with the earls of Northumberland, a traditionally independent aristocratic dynasty. The seventh earl had been executed in 1572 for his part in the northern rebellion, and the family were forbidden to venture into their traditional territories north of the Trent. (For members of the family, the scene in *1 Henry IV* where the Percies are awarded that territory would have been very poignant.) The eighth earl was accused of treason and found dead in suspicious circumstances. The ninth earl, brother of the conspirators and husband of Essex's sister, distanced himself from Essex, but his heterodox views made him suspect, and he was to be imprisoned by James for many years under suspicion of involvement in the Gunpowder Plot. Unsurprisingly, the tenth earl, Algernon Sidney's uncle, sided with Parliament in the Civil War. He allegedly opposed the punishment of those responsible for the execution of Charles I in 1649, declaring that 'the example might be more useful and profitable to kings, by deterring them from such exorbitances'.[18]

In this context, it is very interesting to note that two of the three commissioners of the 1601 performance were Charles and Jocelyn Percy, brothers of the ninth Earl of Northumberland. Far from being nostalgic for the loss of sacramental absolutist monarchy, they would have feared its recurrence. And we have fascinating evidence of how one member of their circle responded to the next play in the tetralogy. A notebook has recently come to light containing detailed notes apparently taken at a performance of 1 Henry IV; amongst the lines singled out are Worcester's reminding Henry that he owes his own crown to men like himself and Northumberland (I, iii, 10–13), and Henry's account of the stratagems by which he gained popular favour, 'opinion', even in the presence of the king – but this commentator has pointedly changed the last word to 'Queene'. The notebook also contains heterodox religious opinions, questioning God's existence, and the author may have been Thomas Harriot, a close associate of the ninth earl, or else a member of the Essex circle. Greenblatt's brilliantly intuitive link between Harriot's subversiveness and Shakespeare's plays may turn out to have had concrete grounding.[19] Though written before Hayward's history, the play does, as Richard Tuck suggests, display something of the critical scepticism found in Tacitist discourse.

The young Percies, then, would have had a particular interest in seeing their house at a period when it was a kingmaker; and Richard II presented their rebellious activities in a somewhat more favourable light than its successors. Shakespeare and his company had close links with Essex's circle in the 1590s, Essex himself being a regular playgoer, and the revival of this by now 'old' play would have been a reassuring evocation of a familiar cultural world. We may still wonder why the Essexians did not choose a more directly and overtly rebellious play like Woodstock, which handles resistance to Richard and his favourites in a more starkly critical mode. Richard II is more oblique in its handling of the motives for rebellion. Yet insofar as there is a sense of caution, of evading direct statement on such key issues as Richard's implication in Gloucester's death, that sense of blocked communication could have served to heighten the political tension. The rebels had long been urging Essex to overcome his reservations about rebellion and take a stand to redeem the country's honour; here was a play that demonstrated a slow and painful process of formulating opposition.[20] The issue of blocked communication is at once internal and external to the play: the most sensitive moment, Richard's self-deposition, seems to have been omitted for political reasons from the early quartos.[21] The chronicles were full of stories of monarchs who tried to consolidate their power by stifling Parliaments and other outlets for public discussion. The preservation of a guaranteed space for debate and criticism was a major concern of those worried about the growth of royal absolutism, whether in the fourteenth century or the sixteenth. Shakespeare's play embodies that concern, both in the story it tells and in its medium, opening up in a public theatre areas of debate that absolutists wanted to keep veiled as mysteries of state.

*   *   *

The opening part of the play involves continual anticlimax, a repression of political and military action which serves only to fuel the underlying conflicts. Bullingbrook's combat with Mowbray, whose political conse-quences would have been known by an informed audience to be explosive, is deferred in the first scene and again in the third. Actual conflict is sub-limated into a war of words: Bullingbrook threatens to bite off his tongue and spit it out at Mowbray (I, i, 190). Despite his attack on mere words as womanish (I, i, 48), however, Mowbray, like all the protagonists, is an able rhetorician, and he will lament that exile makes it no longer possible for him to use his language. Shakespeare has given this feudal society an anachronistic inflection of civic humanism, a concern with the dignity and political importance of full and open speech. (Modern critics' model of language in the plays as a 'fall' from plenitude into rhetoric suppresses the centrality of language as a mode of action in pragmatically-oriented humanist rhetoric.)[22] Mowbray pleads for 'free speech', which Richard allows him (I, i, 55, 123). But we are aware of ironies: Richard and Mowbray cannot afford to speak too freely since they are engaged in a cover-up. And the fact that Richard 'allows' free speech is one of the points at issue: how far should such freedom be a grace offered from above, rather than a constitutional right?

For the more Richard tries to stifle dissent, the more he undermines himself. His own position is vulnerable because he increasingly places his own and his favourites' private interests against the common good, his party dwindling to 'some few private friends' (III, iii, 4). Only as he is falling from power does he realize that his mystical conception of kingship needs a material foundation, that his role as head of the body politic depends on 'the blood of twenty thousand men' (III, ii, 76). By contrast, in the opening scenes his opponents rediscover a threatened sense of corporate identity.[23] The first scene had opened with an address to Gaunt, the second opens with his pondering 'the part I had in Woodstock's blood', which acts with his widow's reproaches to stir him to resistance; and the Duchess loses no opportunity to reinforce the appeal to blood and to a sense of common identity: 'Yet art thou slain in him' (I, ii, 25). Gaunt's language registers a struggle to overlay such sentiments with a discourse of patience and submission; to which the Duchess starkly retorts, 'Call it not patience, Gaunt, it is despair' (I, ii, 29); her 'old Gaunt' (54) rings reproachfully against the play's opening words. Gaunt's struggle continues in the ensuing scene. Bullingbrook celebrates the energy he gains from 'the earthly author of my blood' which gives him 'a twofold vigour' (I, iii, 69–71). Gaunt goes along with his banishment, but his language registers the crisis of language and agency into which he has been plunged:

> But you gave leave to my unwilling tongue
> Against my will to do myself this wrong.
> (I, iii, 245–6)

Bullingbrook, however, is by now starting to break loose from such restrictions, and there is exhilaration in his concluding self-description as 'a true-born Englishman' (I, iii, 308). His stance is modulating from an exclusively aristocratic to a generally national one; the play's strong sense of nationalism is another anachronism with a strong contemporary resonance. There was a certain appropriateness in eighteenth-century editors' spelling 'Bullingbrook' as 'Bolingbroke', associating Shakespeare's protagonist with the spokesman for a form of monarchism that was deeply influenced by classical republicanism.[24] In the ensuing scene we see the courtiers contemptuously discussing his courting of the people at large. Richard's description of the commoners as 'slaves' (I, iv, 27) confirms the opposition's claims that the absolutist faction want to enslave them (II, i, 291); contempt for the commons is a consistent characteristic of the court party (cf. II, ii, 128ff, III, iii, 89, V, i, 35).

It is in this context of escalating opposition that the Essexians would have read a speech that has tended to dwindle to a mass of patriotic clichés: Gaunt's 'sceptred isle' speech. The tension between submission and resistance that has so beset him finds a resolution in his determination to make a final appeal to the king through rhetoric rather than arms, and he musters all his rhetorical forces. But York is sceptical: flattery has deafened the king's ear. And though Gaunt feels a prophetic afflatus, there is a certain irony in the fact that it comes before the king has arrived, so that his greatest appeal to a common patriotic spirit serves to vent his own feelings rather than to sway the king. The reference to Eden does conjure up a nostalgic mood, but it should also be noted that greater emphasis is placed on the island's prowess in war, a somewhat un-Edenic activity crucial both to the feudal aristocracy and to the 'war party' around Essex. It is because of their skill in war that Gaunt reveres the kings of the past. As the huge sentence with its suspended verb builds up, we feel the strain of Gaunt's dying powers, as if the very intensity of his rhetoric is serving to destroy him: 'I die pronouncing it' (II, i, 59).

Shakespeare has boldly placed this set-piece speech, which he must have known would quickly enter anthologies, at a potentially anticlimactic point: how will Gaunt be able to follow it up when Richard does arrive? Richard's first words apply the 'aged' label, but with a perfunctory insensitivity that graphically registers how the same words can perform widely different speech-acts: 'What comfort, man? How is't with aged Gaunt?' (II, i, 72). After parodying Richard's brittle symmetries in skirmish of bitter punning, Gaunt launches into a speech that pushes at last beyond the threshold of obedience: he imagines Edward II as deposing Richard, and indulges at least in imagination in rebellion. As 'landlord', Richard has reduced a political realm, one in which law and public accountability predominate, to a mere house-hold economy where the subjects lack political rights.[25] Richard cuts off his speech, overruling the 'ague's privilege' that transgresses normal rules of speech, and gives Gaunt's words a vivid, self-destructive materiality:

> Wert thou not brother to great Edward's son,
> This tongue that runs so roundly in thy head
> Should run thy head from thy unreverent shoulders.
>   (II, i, 121–3)

Again discourse is brought to the brink of violence but holds back: Richard pays grudging tribute to feudal bonds. But this provokes Gaunt into his climactic charge: at last he holds back no longer and directly accuses him of complicity in Woodstock's murder. The audience have been waiting for this moment since the opening scene. In civic humanist spirit, Gaunt's finest rhetorical hour is not the lyrical meditation of the 'sceptred isle' speech but his last moment of strenuous active engagement.[26]

And it is at this point that Northumberland enters the play, bearing the news of Gaunt's death with a characteristically acerbic irony:

> My liege, old Gaunt commends him to your Majesty.
> What says he?
>   Nay nothing, all is said;
> His tongue is now a stringless instrument[.]
>   (II, i, 147–8)

This further 'old Gaunt' reminds the audience of Richard's recent irreverence, the Duchess's rebukes, and the play's opening words. The Percies in the audience would have had a special interest in Northumberland's role: would the open opposition now begin? But there is yet another moment of anti-climax: York now takes on the role Gaunt had earlier occupied, struggling desperately not to topple over the verge into rebellion. But for him it is even harder: his often-protested patience (II, i, 163, 169, 207) is coming to seem more and more like cowardice. York makes one last appeal to common bonds between Richard and his peers, to the common memory of Edward III: 'His face thou hast' (II, i, 176). He engages in a series of sharp antitheses between Edward's patriotism and Richard's absolutism; but the sharpness of those antitheses, undercutting any possible resemblance, itself becomes seditious, and York breaks off:

> O Richard! York is too far gone with grief,
> Or else he never would compare between –
>   (II, i, 184–5)

If you continue as you are, he resumes, 'Be not thyself': Richard's personal identity must depend on being bound up with a larger community. Such paradoxes are not enough to contain York's sense of facing a discursive crisis that he does not know how to resolve. His final sentence begins 'Now

afore God – God forbid I say true!' (II, i, 200): to call on God for him not
to speak truly is a desperate recourse. If you continue, says York,

> You lose a thousand well-disposed hearts,
> And prick my tender patience to those thoughts
> Which honour and allegiance cannot think.
>   (II, i, 206–8)

This speech brings out explicitly what the whole opening part of the play
has implied: that quite apart from external censorship, absolutism depends
for its maintenance on self-censorship, on keeping subversive thoughts away
from the threshold of consciousness. In the following scene we have another
glimpse of that process, as York momentarily confuses the queen with the
Duchess of Gloucester, whose death the servant has forgotten to announce.
The audience are reminded that the Duchess had despairingly abandoned
an invitation to him as she bowed out of the play (I, ii, 62ff). York is
troubled by his inability to formulate a response to her fidelity to Gloucester's
memory. The Duchess's abandoning of her request to 'commend' her to
York has re-echoed in Northumberland's heavily ironic 'old Gaunt commends
him to your majesty'.

But Northumberland is by now emerging as the agent of a different policy,
crossing the threshold to active resistance. The aristocrats who linger after
the king's departure in Act II scene i emphasize the continuity of agency from
one generation to another:

> Well, Lords, the Duke of Lancaster is dead.
> – And living too, for now his son is duke.
>   (II, i, 224–5)

Northumberland's role is to translate seditious thoughts into effective action.
When Ross laments that

> My heart is great, but it must break with silence,
> Ere't be disburdened with a liberal tongue
>   (II, i, 229–30)

it is Northumberland who tells him to 'speak thy mind' (II, i, 230). Ross's
'liberal' does not of course have its modern sense, and carries with it rather
the pejorative charge that would have been the response to Richard's careless
speaking of his 'liberal largess' (I, iv, 44); but the play does have an emotional
and intellectual pressure toward wishing for more open communication. To
encourage his friends, Northumberland remains within a very traditional
discourse of obedience: like York, he claims that 'The king is not himself'
(II, i, 241), that he is merely led by flatterers. We may however suspect
disingenuousness at least on the part of Northumberland, who reveals himself
as a determined political manipulator; certainly the Richard of the play takes
the initiative rather than being manipulated by courtiers, who often find it
hard to get a word in edgeways (cf. III, ii, 213ff). Northumberland's role
is to sharpen the contrast between common feudal bonds and allegiance to

the king, and he does so in an economical antithesis: Richard has exiled 'His noble kinsman – most degenerate king!' (II, i, 262; cf. York at II, ii, 114). Northumberland titillates his fellows by claiming that 'I dare not say' what his hope is; but Ross appeals to the common bonds of aristocratic solidarity:

> We three are but thyself, and, speaking so,
> Thy words are but as thoughts; therefore be bold.
>   (II, i, 276–7)

The transition is about to be made from purely verbal to military opposition.

Northumberland's imagery as he urges decisive action is one of opening out, of bringing the private once more into a public realm:

> If then we shall shake off our slavish yoke,
> Imp out our drooping country's broken wing,
> Redeem from broking pawn the blemish'd crown,
> Wipe off the dust that hides our sceptre's gilt,
> And make high majesty look like itself,
> Away with me in post to Ravenspurgh;
> But if you faint, as fearing to do so,
> Stay, and be secret, and myself will go.
>   (II, i, 291–8)

Northumberland's language negotiates between loyalty to the monarchy and a wider patriotic loyalty, one in which public resistance is preferable to secret compliance. The suppressed pun on 'guilt' at line 294 (to be echoed at V, i, 69) associates the king with the dust that hides the monarchical sceptre. But the imagery of shaking off yokes, of opening out wings, points beyond a narrowly monarchical conception of national interest, while leaving the precise constitutional implications tautologically vague ('make high majesty look like itself').

What ensues as the play moves to its climax is certainly not a straight-forward celebration of rebellion, and Northumberland does not emerge in a light that would have been unequivocally appealing to his descendants. Though Shakespeare plays down the full extent of his role in the rebellion, he emerges as a cool and ruthless operator, ready to flatter Bullingbrook's nascently regal 'discourse' as 'sugar' (II, iii, 6–7), outrageously quick to redefine treason for the new political order (IV, i, 150). Nevertheless, it is important that he does offer the audience a perspective on events distinct from any simple dualism between Richard and Bullingbrook. While modern critics tend to concentrate on his personal moral duplicity, an audience of the 1590s would have been equally alert to his role in trying to maintain a discourse of the aristocratic, and occasionally of the common, good, independently of whichever monarch may be in power. When he laments 'civil and uncivil arms' (III, iii, 102), the play on words seems to be echoing the opening line of Lucan's *Pharsalia* ('Bella ... plus quam civilia'), whose republican sympathies were gaining it interested readers in the 1590s; Marlowe's translation of Book I had been printed the year before the Essexians' performance.[27] Northumberland's discourse thus has a tinge of civic humanism; and in the deposition scene he is more keen than Bullingbrook to keep attention on constitutional issues as opposed to Richard's personal emotions. It is Northumberland who keeps urging Richard to read out the 33 articles – the evidence of what Kantorowicz termed Richard's 'so-called tyranny' – so that the commons 'May deem that you are worthily depos'd' (IV, i, 227, cf. 272). Northumberland's language here directly echoes that of Holinshed: the articles were read 'to the end the commons might be persuaded, that he was an vnprofitable prince to the common-wealth, and worthie to be deposed'.[28] The 'and' in that sentence is pregnant with a whole set of decidedly unmetaphysical political assumptions. The play's closing speech is given to Bullingbrook's desire to wash away his guilt; Northumberland has bowed out of the play on a characteristically less emotive note: 'My guilt be on my head, and there an end' (V, i, 69). We are made to condemn the harshness of the separation of king and queen, and Northumberland's justification with the conventionally suspect, Machiavellian term 'policy' (V, i, 84). That is, appropriately, his last word in the scene. Feudal rebellion has merged with a more modern form of political agency. Even those of the audience who did not approve of Northumberland would have had to acknowledge the dangers of a lack of 'policy'.

*   *   *

When Charles and Jocelyn Percy watched *Richard II*, then, they would have found much to fire them in emulation of a medieval past that was far from cravenly monarchical. And they would not necessarily have been daunted by the pathos of Richard's fall, any more than their nephew the tenth earl was moved by the cult of the royal martyr to unequivocal condemnation of the execution of Charles I. By concentrating on the aristocracy's role in the play, it is possible to see how limited is the perspective that sees it as offering a straightforward choice between Richard and Bullingbrook. That is not to say, however, that the aristocratic viewpoint is finally endorsed. In *Richard II*, the voices of other social groups are by and large excluded, being reserved for the *Henry IV* plays. The effect is to heighten the sense of an archaic, hieratic political order that has so swayed some critics. But there are hints of alternative perspectives.

It is in the garden scene that members of the lower orders make their only extended appearance. Critics have emphasized this scene's formal, archaic quality. It is indeed particularly dense with sacramental rhetoric. But it is important to note how that rhetoric is placed. It is here associated with the Queen; it is consistently the favoured discourse of the Yorkists. And in this scene it is placed in direct contrast with different conceptions of political order. Of course we are made to sympathize with the queen's grief and shock; but this should not blind us to structural problems in the scene's discourse. The queen initiates the contrast as soon as she sees the gardener and his servants: she decides to hide and eavesdrop, convinced that

They'll talk of state, for everyone doth so
Against a change; woe is forerun with woe.
                    (III, iv, 27–8)

For the queen, this talk of 'state' by the lower orders is a subversion of order.
The gardeners, however, have their own conception of order, which looks
back to Gaunt's 'this England' speech, though it lacks his feudal militarism.
They insist on the predominance of public over private interest, and on the
need for active intervention to remedy abuses even at the cost of violence:

Go thou, and like an executioner
Cut off the heads of too fast growing sprays,
That look too lofty in our commonwealth:
All must be even in our government.
                    (III, iv, 32–6)

The word 'commonwealth' here, along with the emphasis on evenness, and
the reference to decapitation of favourites, carries an oblique tinge of
republican discourse. The rhetoric is literally radical: the role of the head
gardener is to 'root away' the weeds, a role which he himself compares to
Bullingbrook's (37, 52). It is one of the under-gardeners who initiates direct
political discussion, converting the literal discussion of the garden into a
political allegory and asking why they should work while their leaders let
the realm go to ruin. The head gardener has enough of a sense of hierarchies
of discourse to ask him to 'Hold thy peace'; but he goes on to develop the
allegory, contrasting the gardeners' skill with the courtiers' incompetence,
and building up to prophesying that the king will be deposed.
    At this point the queen angrily intervenes:

O, I am press'd to death through want of speaking!
Thou, old Adam's likeness set to dress this garden,
How dares thy harsh rude tongue sound this unpleasing news?
What Eve, what serpent, hath suggested thee
To make a second fall of cursed man?
Why dost thou say King Richard is depos'd?
Dar'st thou, thou little better thing than earth,
Divine his downfall? Say, where, when, and how
Cam'st thou by this ill tidings?
                    (72–80)

The queen's opening words return the play yet again to the theme of
suppressed discourse; though in this case the queen has imposed the limitation
on herself. Her grief at the news is displaced by anger at its bearer for breaking
her rigidly hierarchical conceptions of language: it is not for such underlings
to meddle with mysteries of state. She finds his tongue 'harsh' and 'rude':
understandable though her response is under the circumstances, it does recall
Richard's preference for euphemistic harmony over unwelcome truth. The
queen lives in a world of absolute oppositions between rulers and people
as between good and evil, and she recasts the gardener's horticultural
discourse in authoritarian terms. Like all the Yorkists, the Duchess speaks

disparagingly of the lower orders; and she appeals to a theological conception of political order, with any intervention by the commons presented as a fall of man. Her interpretation of the garden thus contrasts sharply with the gardener's less mystical, more interventionist garden/state allegory. And the gardener stands his ground. He describes Richard's fall not in a traditional mode of the Fall of man or *de casibus* tragedy, but in a secular language of balance of power: reinforced by 'all the peers', Bullingbrook is bound to triumph in the end. Richard falls not because God has withdrawn his favour but because he has neglected the proper political means. Let her go to London – the centre of England's public sphere – and she will find the truth. The Queen's response is to curse the gardener's plants. The gardener, however, gracefully deflects this destructive speech-act, planting an emblematic bank of rue. If the scene thus ends on a pathetic and organic register, it has arrived there by a far more complex route.

This scene is entirely of Shakespeare's invention, and it bears scrutiny as an allegory not only of political discourse but of the role of Shakespeare's company in politics, of their disposition of their flowers of rhetoric. Several critics have noted that the gardener's reference to cutting off heads may allude to a story in Livy about Tarquin's sending an execution order through an agricultural code so that the messenger would not understand it. In this case, however, it is the messenger who understands more than the queen. The scene opens on a note of courtly recreation: the queen asks her ladies to divert her, and they offer to engage in whatever activity pleases her. In place of aristocratic festivity, the gardener offers a more didactic form of entertainment, one ultimately too didactic for the queen, who considers that it interferes in mysteries of state and halts the narrative. This scene immediately precedes the deposition scene, which was of course not printed in full in the Elizabethan quartos. *Richard II* contains an oblique prophecy of its own censorship: the play is aware that it is touching on sensitive areas of political discourse, areas that displace a top-down hierarchy. And yet it protests that those above may need that commoners' discourse at least as much as the commoners need them.

In this play, however, the commons remain spectators, not agents. Emphasis is placed on aristocratic agency – the gardener's own analysis of the power structure refers only to the aristocracy, not to the commons. To some degree, that omission reflects changes between Shakespeare's own time and the period he represents, that growth in the public sphere in which the theatre formed a signficant part. It might have been better for the aristocratic rebels of 1601 to have taken this point. Though they enjoyed some passive support from the London populace, their coup sought legitimacy from feudal traditions rather than from wider consultation, and was ultimately short on 'policy'. When, on the morning after the play's performance, Essex rode through the city asking for the Londoners' support, counting on their admiration for his aristocratic dash and charisma, he failed to reckon with the fact that they might find him impulsive and irresponsible. In the play

the citizens are presented as fickle and politically immature, turning easily
from Richard to acclaim Bullingbrook in his passage through London. When
Essex and his followers made their entry to the city, in a display of their
aristocratic authority, the citizens of 1601 stayed in their houses, and watched,
and waited.[29]

NOTES

1. Most studies of the play's audience have been cast in ahistorical terms or
    have assumed the play's designs on the audience to be highly orthodox: Phyllis
    Rackin, 'The Role of the Audience in Shakespeare's *Richard II*', *Shakespeare
    Quarterly*, 36 (1985), 262–81 (267), assumes that the audience will exper-
    ience rebellion as a 'terrible crime'. For more historically specific readings
    see J.H. Hexter, 'Property, Monopoly, and Shakespeare's *Richard II*', in
    P. Zagorin (ed.), *Culture and Politics from Puritanism to the Enlightenment*
    (Berkeley, Los Angeles, and London: University of California Press, 1978),
    pp. 1–24; Ernest W. Talbert, *The Problem of Order: Elizabethan Political
    Commonplaces and an Example of Shakespeare's Art* (Chapel Hill, NC: Uni-
    versity of North Carolina Press, 1962) and Graham Holderness, *Shakespeare's
    History* (Dublin: Gill and Macmillan, New York: St Martin's Press, 1985).
    Leeds Barroll, 'A New History for Shakespeare and his Time', *Shakespeare
    Quarterly*, 39 (1988), 441–64, gives a salutary rejoinder to some exaggerated
    accounts of the play's political subversiveness, but his scepticism on some
    points seems to me exaggerated. Barroll argues that the rebels '*misconstrued*'
    (454, italics his) Shakespeare's play. A misconstruction which came from
    figures at the centre of a powerful international network of political intelli-
    gence and cultural patronage, on the basis of several years of continuing
    familiarity with the work of Shakespeare's company, might have some claims
    to being an alternative, rather than an italicized 'mis', construction. Quotations
    from *Richard II* are from the New Arden edition, ed. Peter Ure (London:
    Methuen, 1961).
2. See especially the writings of the strongly legitimist writer Adam Müller, who
    formulated long before Tillyard a theory of the second tetralogy as registering
    a historical shift from feudalism to the modern state, with a concomitant division
    in the monarchy. Richard II, in his view, represented the warning example of a
    monarch whose excessive rigidity led to revolution (Louis XVI offered the
    obvious parallel). See Roy Pascal, *Shakespeare in Germany 1740–1815*
    (Cambridge: Cambridge University Press, 1937), pp. 31–3, 153ff; and on
    comparable developments in English criticism, Jonathan Bate, *Shakespearean
    Constitutions: Politics, Theatre, Criticism 1730–1830* (Oxford: Clarendon
    Press, 1989).
3. Ernst H. Kantorowicz, *The King's Two Bodies: A Study in Medieval Political
    Theology* (Princeton: Princeton University Press, 1957), p. 40.
4. Kantorowicz, *The King's Two Bodies*, p. 28 n.5
5. For fuller discussion see David Norbrook, 'The Emperor's New Body? Ernst
    H. Kantorowicz, *Richard II*, and the Politics of Shakespeare Criticism', forth-
    coming in *Textual Practice*.
6. See Michel Foucault, *Surveiller et punir: naissance de la prison* (Paris: Gallimard,
    1975), pp. 33–4.
7. Stephen Greenblatt, 'Introduction' to *The Power of Forms in the English
    Renaissance* (Norman, Oklahoma: Pilgrim Books, 1982), pp. 3–6.

8. The first detailed application of Kantorowicz's paradigm, Marie Axton's *The Queen's Two Bodies: Drama and the Elizabethan Succession* (London: Royal Historical Society, 1977), clearly demonstrated that there were rivals to the 'two bodies' theory, a nuance lost in later accounts such as Leonard Tennenhouse, *Power on Display: The Politics of Shakespeare's Genres* (New York and London: Methuen, 1986), pp. 77–8, and Christopher Pye, *The Regal Phantasm: Shakespeare and the Politics of Spectacle* (London and New York: Routledge, 1990), pp. 64, 73, 85ff, 101.

9. For the claim that 'the audience does not leave the theatre in a rebellious mood' see Stephen Greenblatt, 'Invisible Bullets: Renaissance Authority and its Subversion, *Henry IV* and *Henry V*', in Jonathan Dollimore and Alan Sinfield (eds), *Political Shakespeare: New Essays in Cultural Materialism* (Manchester: Manchester University Press, 1985), p. 41; and for a subsequent modification, *Shakespearean Negotiations: The Circulation of Social Energy in Renaissance England* (Oxford: Clarendon Press, 1988), p. 55. Greenblatt was perhaps reacting against the overstated terms in which he had at first presented the play's subversiveness, for correctives to which see Barroll, 'A New History'.

10. See Annabel Patterson, *Reading Holinshed's Chronicles* (Chicago and London: Chicago University Press, 1994).

11. Raphael Holinshed, *Chronicles of England, Scotland, and Ireland*, ed. Henry Ellis, 6 vols (London, 1808), II, 735ff, 717, 721, 734, 775, 791ff.

12. Richard C. McCoy, *The Rites of Knighthood: The Literature and Politics of Elizabethan Chivalry* (Berkeley, Los Angeles and London: University of California Press, 1989), ch. 4. See also Mervyn James, 'At a Crossroads of the Political Culture: The Essex Revolt, 1601', in *Society, Politics and Culture: Studies in Early Modern England* (Cambridge: Cambridge University Press, 1986), pp. 416–65.

13. J.G.A. Pocock, *The Ancient Constitution and the Feudal Law: A Study of English Historical Thought in the Seventeenth Century* (Cambridge: Cambridge University Press, 1957; reissue, 1987).

14. J.S.A. Adamson, 'The Baronial Context of the English Civil War', *Transactions of the Royal Historical Society*, 40 (1990), 93–120 (95 n.13).

15. George Wither's poetic defence of the regicide, *The British Appeals* (London, 1651) saw the Parliamentarians' victory as a divinely-approved trial by combat.

16. Richard Tuck, *Philosophy and Government 1572–1651* (Cambridge: Cambridge University Press, 1993), pp. 106–7.

17. Algernon Sidney, *Discourses Concerning Government*, in J. Robertson (ed.), *Sydney on Government: The Works of Algernon Sydney*, pp. 240–1, cited by Jonathan Scott, *Algernon Sidney and the English Republic 1623–1677* (Cambridge: Cambridge University Press, 1988), p. 46.

18. Ibid., pp. 48, 44.

19. Hilton Kelliher, 'Contemporary Manuscript Extracts from Shakespeare's *Henry IV, Part 1*', *English Manuscript Studies 1100–1800*, 1 (1989), 144–81. Amongst the passages cited are I, iii, 6–14, II, i, 80–82, III, ii, 40ff.

20. James, 'At a Crossroads of the Political Culture', p. 447.

21. Janet Clare, *'Art Made Tongue-Tied by Authority': Elizabethan and Jacobean Dramatic Censorship* (Manchester and New York: Manchester University Press, 1990), pp. 47–51. Barroll, 'A New History', pp. 448–9, points out that there is no firm evidence of censorship and argues that the lines missing in the earlier quartos may have been added later by Shakespeare in an expansion of Richard's 'psychic identity'. But the scene also contains elements which were not purely psychological in interest, such as Northumberland's insistence on satisfying the commons that the king was worthily deposed, an elaboration on Holinshed.

22. See James L. Calderwood, *Metadrama in Shakespeare's Henriad: 'Richard II'*

to 'Henry V' (Berkeley, Los Angeles and London: University of California Press, 1979), and Joseph A. Porter, *The Drama of Speech Acts: Shakespeare's Lancastrian Tetralogy* (Berkeley, Los Angeles and London: University of California Press, 1979), both of which read the plays in terms of a fall from an older, unified linguistic order, an analysis which leads them to concentrate on Richard at the expense of other figures in the play. Calderwood, *Metadrama*, p. 191 n.12, argues that the pre-modern linguistic world resembled the 'primitive' thought of Tasmanian aborigines. Tuck, *Philosophy and Government*, exemplifies a much more sophisticated development of speech-act theory in the analysis of discourse.

23. On the importance of blood and lineage among Essex's followers, see James, 'At the Crossroads of the Political Culture', pp. 435ff.

24. Phyllis Rackin, *Stages of History: Shakespeare's English Chronicles* (London: Routledge, 1990), p 47 n.14.

25. On the way this line has often been glossed in a misleadingly absolutist sense see Donna B. Hamilton, 'The State of Law in *Richard II*', *Shakespeare Quarterly*, 34 (1983), 5–17.

26. For an excellent analysis of this scene see George D. Gopen, 'Private Grief into Public Action: The Rhetoric of John of Gaunt in *Richard II*', *Studies in Philology*, 84 (1987), 338–62.

27. Shakespeare may also have engaged with Lucan via Daniel's *The Civil Wars*, whose opening echoes Lucan's: see George M. Logan, 'Lucan–Daniel–Shakespeare: New Light on the Relation between *The Civil Wars* and *Richard II*', *Shakespeare Studies*, 9 (1976), 121–40. See also McCoy, *The Rites of Knighthood*, pp. 116–18.

28. Holished, *op. cit.*, II, 859. Holinshed goes on to call the articles 'heinous', a word echoed by Richard at IV, i, 233. It is characteristic of the Ricardian emphasis of modern editions that Ure, pp. 138, 191, should cite the 'heinous' parallel but omit the 'worthily'.

29. As Giles Fletcher revealingly put it, the citizens held back from rebellion 'being faithful subjects, and careful of their estates' (James, 'At a Crossroads of the Political Culture', p. 453); on the later shift toward more Parliamentary forms of opposition, see pp. 462ff.

CHAPTER FIVE

Historical Consciousness and Convention in Shakespeare's First Tetralogy

M.T. Jones-Davies

To Henry IV who is meditating on the 'book of fate', Warwick explains how by observing 'the revolutions of the times' (III, i, 45–6), or rotations in history, one may safely conclude on a certain predictability of events:

> There is a history in all men's lives
> Figuring the nature of the times deceas'd;
> The which observ'd, a man may prophesy
> With a near aim, of the main chance of things
> As yet not come to life, who in their seeds
> And beginnings lie intreasured
> (*2 Henry IV*, III, i, 80–5)

hence the many prophesies that echo from play to play and show kings and people as creatures of God's divine providence ('God is my fortress', as Talbot proclaims, *1 Henry VI*, II, i, 26), who also share the medieval superstitious beliefs in the influence of the stars, of adverse planets or in comets importing 'change of times and states' (II, iv, 2). And yet the world they inhabit is created in time, with its variable customs, institutions and ideals. Its predominant element is change rather than continuity and

> ... changes fill the cup of alteration
> With divers liquors!
> (*2 Henry IV*, III, i, 52–3)

which excludes predictability.

History has been defined as 'the dialectic of tradition and innovation'[1] and in the plays of the first tetralogy this dialectic is manifest in the processes of change we can perceive in the relationship between the *dramatis personae* and some of their collective practices. William Camden's words are here relevant, when he writes that 'nothing has continued in its primitive state' or that 'there is a continual floating in the affairs of mankind',[2] which induces a sceptical attitude in the observer's concern with the succession of contrarieties and uncertainties in which *res gestae* – e.g. the battles, victories or defeats – are enacted. Although human nature remains fundamentally the same, yet its 'changing needs in time'[3] modify its moral, social and political motivations, which establish the context in which Renaissance historiographers like to reconstruct the movement of the past from the perspective of the present.

In the reconstruction that Shakespeare the artist is attempting, following in the steps of the chroniclers, the concept of convention plays its part. Convention (or custom, habit, fashion, manners) has the power 'to change its shape with time'.[4] That is why it is instrumental in the reconstruction of the historical or temporal setting to which men will adapt according to circumstances or contingencies.

When, fearing the civil dissension about to break out, the Duke of Gloucester (1 Henry VI, III, i, 93) calls upon his servants to set 'this unaccustomed fight aside', he is warning them against those 'ill-shapen births of time'[5] that Bacon in his essay describes as Innovations. Intestine wars, like all wars, are factors of discontinuity; they interrupt the sequence of chronological events that make up the history of the country. The unexpected skirmishes disturbing the streets of London are contrary to the normative laws of peace and mutual understanding that would normally insure the harmonious life of the Commonweal. They are contrary to customs or good manners (contra bonos mores), they are 'the viperous worm' (III, i, 72) that breeds envious discord, transforming the course of history. A similar innovation with far-reaching consequences for the whole nation takes place in the Temple Garden – a sort of game with political implications – when a few law students will pluck red or white roses according to the side they defend. Plantagenet calls this 'a fashion' as he addresses Somerset: 'I scorn thee and thy fashion, peevish boy' (1 Henry VI, II, iv, 76). The term 'fashion' stands for the convention they are starting, a convention that will mark a break with the past, the beginning of the War of the Roses:

... This brawl to-day
Grown to this faction in the Temple Garden
Shall send between the Red Rose and the White
A thousand souls to death and deadly night
                    (II, iv, 124–7)

King Henry's words sum up the folly of it all:

... What madness rules in brainsick men
When for so slight and frivolous a cause [the wearing of a rose]
Such factious emulations shall arise
                    (IV, i, 111–13)

A careful reading of the first tetralogy reveals how Shakespeare, with a few subtle hints and allusions, anonymous remarks or fictional scenes that memorialize passing moments in the experiences of men's lives, can make his audience aware of the processes of change expressing the rise of the historical consciousness of Renaissance England. 'The Janus-headed concept of convention' (or custom) – the words are Arthur Ferguson's[6] – 'at once older than memory and always up to date' serves as a challenge to stress discontinuity as opposed to continuity, the difference between the present and the past. Shakespeare's story of this difference that makes changes intelligible, implies a commentary on the moral, social or political setting of the plays in their natural historical perspective.

A few examples, while taking into account the passing away of conventions belonging to an old order that had been passively accepted, will lead us into a new world of man's own making – a world in which man instead of only conforming to customs becomes the creator of customs. Interrupted ceremonies (1 Henry VI, I, i and III, i), or the profanation of knighthood by those who, like Falstaff (IV, i, 40), usurped the name of knight, are symbols of the disintegration of the old order. The medieval trials by combat, the energies of the feudal barons, the feudal duties of vassals to their superiors are still remembered – as when the king creates Richard Duke of York – but feudalism distinctly belongs to the past.

If the ideal of chivalry is highly praised ('O Clifford ... thou hast slain / The flower of Europe for his chivalry [the Duke of York]' (3 Henry VI, II, i, 70–1)) yet the moral values associated with it are relaxed, and the sacredness of oaths and vows is losing its binding force; contracts are easily broken: Henry VI's marriage to Margaret is arranged in spite of his former betrothal to the Earl of Armagnac's daughter; and Edward's union with Lady Grey follows his former offer of marriage to Lady Bona. Salisbury's list of sinful oaths (solemn oaths for the wrong) includes the offence of wringing 'the widow from her custom'd right' (2 Henry VI, V, i, 188).[7] This refers to the foul practices that would imperil the acquired rights of the people, in this case the convention attributing to the widow 'the life-rent of part of her husband's estate'. The cavilling tone reflects the preoccupations of the times with the social context, when individuals are more and more at the mercy of dishonest men.

In the last play of the first tetralogy, Richard III, the old privilege of sanctuary, of which Queen Elizabeth has availed herself for her own protection and that of the young Duke of York is also a case in point. It has become a source of contention between the Cardinal and Buckingham, whose argument to satisfy Richard's evil intention finally succeeds. Buckingham overtly contrasts the traditional and ceremonious old-fashioned observance of past practices and what he calls 'the grossness of this age'. He pleads that with today's less refined habits the Prince, having not claimed sanctuary nor deserved it, may be taken 'from thence' (with the ominous prospect of sending him to the Tower) without breach of privilege. The forms of the past are therefore shown to be of no avail (Richard III, III, i, 44–56) in this new world where all that now counts is speed and efficiency, and where the new men are bent on making sense of their own history in the hope of reshaping the future.

Different views often confront each other. The very conduct of the war is endangered by the divergent opinions that prevail against reason:

... amongst the soldiers this is muttered –
That here you maintain several factions
... whilst a field should be dispatch'd and fought
You are disputing of your generals;
One would have lingering wars, with little cost;
Another would fly swift, but wanteth wings;
A third thinks without expense at all,
By guileful fair words peace may be obtain'd.
                    (*1 Henry VI*, I, i, 70–7)

The divided opinions will cause the death of the English hero, Talbot, and finally the loss of France. As to the several or separate factions, they are like private armies of retainers 'in livery', a custom which was to be discontinued by Henry VII's statute against maintenance and livery.[8] Thus traditional habits can be adjusted to the circumstances of time, but also of place, and this involves a certain historical relativity. It is clearly suggested in Queen Margaret's question about the government of 'Britain's isle':

My Lord of Suffolk, say, is this the guise,
Is this the fashions in the Court of England?
Is this the government of Britain's isle
And this the royalty of Albion's king?
What! Shall king Henry be a pupil still
Under the surly Gloucester's governance?
Am I a queen in title and in style,
And must be made a subject to a duke?
                    (*2 Henry VI*, I, iii, 42–9)

These lines are telling regarding the Duke of Gloucester's protectorship. 'Guise' and 'fashions' have here the meanings of 'recognized customs of a country'.[9] They announce the great dramatic moment when, in a characteristic shift of policy, the good Duke Humphrey is made to give up his staff of office, when 'Henry will to himself / Protector be' – an important change in the government of England.

It is interesting to note that in Hall's Chronicle,[10] which was the source of *2 Henry VI*, the Duke of York is presented as 'he which had brought that rude and savage nation [Ireland] to civile fashion and English urbanitie'. This implied praise of the customs of England is not repeated in the play, but in it the Duke of York is chosen by Parliament to go and pacify the uncivil kerns of Ireland (III, iii). The reference to the nobles' authority, whose decisions the king confirms ('Our authority is his consent', *2 Henry VI*, III, i, 316), together with the earlier mentions of 'the learned council of the realm' foreshadows what Sir John Fortescue will call the *dominium politicum et regale*[11] to describe the government of England in which the responsibility for the Commonweal is borne not by the king alone but by 'king and polity together'. So ruling and legislating has come to derive from the power of 'a body of men united by consent of law and by community of interest'.[12]

This community of interest is the fruit of experience and the power to rule by law is consensual. Customs which gradually become laws have been established by history and experience, associated with age and honour (*2 Henry VI*, V, i, 171: 'Why art thou old and want'st experience?') And as Thomas Aquinas[13] explains: 'When a thing is done again and again, it seems to proceed from a deliberated judgment of reason. Accordingly custom has the power of a law, abolishes law and is the interpreter of law'.

The law is the touchstone of order, and Suffolk in the Temple Garden (*1 Henry VI*, II, iv, 7–9) hints at the conflicts that may oppose the individual and the law:

> I never yet could frame my will to it [the law]
> And therefore frame the law unto my will.

The connection between the kings's power and the law is underlined in *Richard III* (III, v, 40–5). Richard, addressing the Lord Mayor gives the most specious reasons for the rash execution of Hastings. He admits – hypocritically – the importance of 'the form of law' he has dispensed with, in contradiction to the usual custom of a civilized Christian nation:

> What, think you we are Turks or infidels
> Or that we would against the form of law
> Proceed thus rashly in the villain's death
> But that the extreme peril of the case
> The peace of England and our persons' safety
> Enforc'd us to this execution?

And Buckingham evinces the same hypocrisy when (III, vii, 190) to please Richard and influence the Mayor he alleges the unlawful birth of young Prince Edward, 'whom our manners call the Prince', this time stressing the uselessness of mere convention, which he pretends to control for or against the king's own advantage, as a mere opinion.

The questioning of the law and of the control of convention are parodied in *2 Henry VI* (IV, vii) with the grotesque evocation of the lawgiver, when Jack Cade proclaims: '... my mouth shall be the parliament of England' (IV, vii, 14), while the ragged multitude of the rebels shout their *cri de guerre*, 'Let's kill all the lawyers' (IV, ii, 73). An anonymous messenger informs the king: 'All scholars, lawyers, courtiers, gentlemen / They call false caterpillars and intend their death' (IV, iv, 34–5). Already at the beginning of Act IV scene ii, a certain John Holland – probably an actor whose name may have been used for convenience – stresses the radical social levelling the rebels are hoping for when he exclaims against gentlemen: 'Well, I say, it was never merry world in England since gentlemen came up' [became fashionable]. The Commonwealth is 'threadbare' and the actor Bevis has also explained that 'Jack Cade will get a new nap upon it': the established order is threatened.

To avoid any discrimination between the noblemen representing the king's forces and himself, Cade parodies the ritual dubbing with knighthood:

> I will make myself a knight presently [kneels]
> Rise up Sir John Mortimer
>   (IV, ii, 113–14).

In the fourth play of the tetralogy, *Richard III*, Richard alludes to the inversion of social values resulting from the ennobling of the Queen's relatives, the Woodvilles. Once again the title of 'gentleman' is exposed to ridicule:

Since every jack became a gentleman
There's many a gentle person made a jack
(I, iii, 72–3)[14]

The imagery anticipates the 'troublous world' that is to follow, a world of chaos, rivalry and revenge.

In this changing world, alteration and pragmatic values present man with a challenge to which he responds by using prudence and expediency, as characteristics of a nascent individualism, of which York (2 *Henry VI* and 3 *Henry VI*) and Richard (3 *Henry VI* and *Richard III*) are good illustrations. Each of them will try and direct the movement of history according to his own will.

In his soliloquy (2 *Henry VI*, I, i), York reveals how he 'will spy advantage' to 'claim the crown', but meanwhile, as a shrewd machiavellian, he schools himself:

Then York, be still a while till time do serve
Watch thou, and wake when others be asleep
To spy into the secrets of the state
                              (I, i, 243)

This is political cunning aiming at destabilizing the king's power. Served by time, he will also serve time, and as an opportunist in *3 Henry VI* he is determined to 'take possession of his right' (I, i, 44) and 'seek occasion how to rise' (I, ii, 43). Thus with policy, he does not lose sight of occasion and of the need to be efficient in the grammar of the state. He is the prototype of Richard 'who can frame his face to all occasions' (III, ii, 185).

Richard too is resolved to catch the English crown and in order to reach his aim 'can set the murderous Machiavel to school'. Confident in none but himself ('I am myself alone', *3 Henry VI*, V, vi, 83) he tends to modify the course of history, to make it subservient to his own will, 'to impose on history his own self-perceived destiny'.[15] Crafty and self-seeking, he manipulates all the actors on the stage, as if he were free to invent his future against 'Fortune's malice'. In Bacon's words, 'the mold of Fortune is in his own hands', but as Bacon also writes in the same essay 'Of Fortune'[16]: 'those that ascribe openly too much to their own Wisdom and Policie end infortunate'. The actor Richard, whose introductory speech (*Richard III*, I, i) proclaims the change from Winter to the glorious Summer of York, commits all the murders and villainous deeds he has planned, but eventually must submit at the end 'to the rotten mouth of death' as Queen Margaret has foreseen (IV, iv).[17]

In his first tetralogy, Shakespeare measures history 'by the dylygence of men'.[18] He has reconstructed a social and political context in which an element of change confers a dynamic character to the concept of convention or custom. The same dynamic character can be found in other Shakespearean histories, when the will of individuals is seen supplanting collective habits.

We do not forget in *Henry V* the king's signifying remark to Katherine, comparing English and French customs. When Katherine declares: 'Les dames et demoiselles, pour être baisées devant leurs noces, il n'est pas la coutume de France ...' Henry replies:

> O Kate, nice customs curtsy to great kings
> You and I cannot be confined within the weak list
> Of a country's fashion: we are the makers of manners, Kate;
>   (V, ii, 273–5, 284–7)

Thus presenting the royal couple as the creators of conventions.

While weighing up the relationship with past and present practices in Shakespeare's work, it is possible to remember Erasmus's words in *Ciceronianus*:

> Wherever I turn my eyes, I see all things changed
> I stand before another stage
> I behold another play
> Even a different world.[19]

The sense of change in conventions, which subtly produces a break with the past and anticipates the future is recurrent in the Shakespearean representations of the story of man living his life in a society limited in its time and place. It produces a valuable perspective on the historical context and also on the dramatic plots of the plays. With the slight nuances of meaning implied by the different terms related to convention, custom, guise, fashion(s) and manners, it makes spectators and readers aware of the changing character of English history. Thus, even through the theatre, historical consciousness is seen gradually emerging in Renaissance England.

NOTES

All line references are to the Arden Shakespeare editions.

1.   Lawrence Manley, *Convention 1500–1750* (Harvard University Press, 1980), p. 213.
2.   William Camden, *Britannia*, 1695. Repr. (New York: Johnson Reprint Corporation, 1971). Cf. also L. Manley, ibid., p. 222.
3.   Lawrence Manley, ibid., p. 228.
4.   Ibid., p. 221.
5.   Bacon, *Of Innovations*, Essay XXIV (Paris: Aubier), p. 124.
6.   A.B. Ferguson, *Clio Unbound. Perception of the Social and Cultural Past in Renaissance England* (Duke University Press, 1979), p. 417.
7.   *The Second Part of King Henry VI* (Arden edition), note by A.S. Cairncross (ed.), p. 147.
8.   *The First Part of King Henry VI* (Arden edition), note by A.S. Cairncross, (ed.), p. 8.
9.   *The Second Part of King Henry VI*, ibid., note, p. 23.
10.   Ibid., Appendix I, p. 168.
11.   E.H. Kantorowicz, *The King's Two Bodies, A Study in Mediaeval Political*

Theology (Princeton University Press, 1957), pp. 226–7.

12. L. Manley, ibid., p. 104. (cf Sir John Fortescue, p. 31, quoting *De Laudibus Legum Angliae*, Saint Augustine, *The City of God*, 19.23.)

13. Thomas Aquinas, *Summa Theologica* I. II. xcvii. 3. and cf R. Hooker, *Laws of Ecclesiastical Polity*, IV, xiv. 1, quoted in *Clio Unbound*, p. 257: [custom] 'the weight of that long experience which the world hath had thereof with consent and good liking'.

14. *King Richard III*, The Arden Shakespeare, ed. A. Hammond, note p. 155: 'jack means not only the lower class person ..., but the 'jack' in the game of bowls ... knocked about by the other bowls'.

15. G.K. Hunter, 'The Pleasures of Renaissance history: Shakespeare's *Richard III*' in *L'Europe de la Renaissance*, Mélanges offerts à Marie-Thérèse Jones-Davies (Paris: Touzot, 1988), p. 319.

16. Bacon, 'Of Fortune', Essay XL (Paris: Aubier), pp. 208, 212.

17. G.K. Hunter, ibid., p. 320: This 'reflects back on the opening of the play and gives an answer to its proclamation of progress and achievement'.

18. Robert Whittinton, *Vulgaria*, ed. Beatrice White (London: Early English Texts Society, 1932), p. 62. Also quoted by Lawrence Manley, ibid., p. 227.

19. Lawrence Manley, ibid., p. 236.

CHAPTER SIX

Hamlet and the Dread Commandment

George Walton Williams

There is scarcely a need to emphasize the importance that Elizabethans attributed to the virtue and the doctrine of Obedience. The 'Homilie against Disobedience' concluded its opening preamble with the assurance that

> heere [in the Garden of Eden] appeareth the originall kingdome of GOD over Angels and man, ... and of man over earthly creatures which GOD had made subject unto him, and with all the felicity and blessed state, which Angels, man, and all creatures had remayned in, had they continued in due obedience unto GOD their King ... whereby it is evident, that obedience is the principall vertue of all vertues, and indeed the very root of all vertues, and the cause of all felicitie.[1]

That declaration, to be sure, was aimed specifically at quieting 'wilful rebellion', a disobedience against the civil authority, but it takes its origin and draws its confident support from the Scriptures, particularly from the Fifth Commandment:

> Honour thy father and thy mother, that thy daies maie be prolonged upon the land, which the Lord thy God giveth thee.[2]

The Geneva margin conveniently explicates 'father and mother' to mean 'all that have authoritie over us'. Obedience to parents, to all that have authority over us, and to God is a continuum, a single precept that sustains the family, the state, and the operations of the universe. The primary dutifulness of children is presented to us early in the first act of *Hamlet*: Hamlet obeys his mother (I, ii, 120), Ophelia obeys her father (I, iii, 136). These are simple instances; both children submit immediately to their parents' orders or commands or directions, and they thus present at the outset of the play examples of good behaviour. We are not asked to speculate as to what the later consequences of these responses may be. Subsequent expressions of these children's dutiful obedience are less easily interpreted (III, ii, 319; II, ii, 107, 125), but that they should obey and that they do obey are manifest.

Less simple than these responses and more central to the play are the responses to a father's commands (or a father-figure's commands) given by each of the three young men who mark the triple lines of the plot.[3] Those responses lead ultimately to the carnage at the end of the play as, for the first and only time, the three young men meet on stage. Strong in arm, Fortinbras has survived his battles; Laertes and Hamlet have not. He stands triumphant above his structural opposites and rivals; they lie dead at his feet. Each young man conceives that he has been confronted with the problem of securing retribution for his father's death, and each has gone about to find a solution to his assignment in a way that is definingly his own. The only way that the play rewards unambiguously is the way chosen by Fortinbras, for without firing a shot, Fortinbras secures at the end of the play the entire kingdom, for a little piece of which he had been contending at the opening of the play.[4] Fortinbras' days, we may say in an unexpectedly explicit vindication of scripture, will be prolonged upon the land which the Lord his God has given him.

Fortinbras receives injunctions from his uncle, his father-figure, as he prepares to march against Denmark (I, i, ii; II, ii). He has assembled a rabble to make his attack. We know that when Fortinbras' impotent uncle sent out to suppress his nephew's levies, Fortinbras obeyed, in brief, and received rebuke from Norway, submitting himself entirely to the command of his uncle who, though so weak he could not leave his bed, could nevertheless merely by speaking exert an authority to which Fortinbras was obedient (II, ii, 61–71). We know little of Fortinbras' history, but we know enough: we know this detail. This episode defines Fortinbras' character; it is of primary importance in the understanding of that character.[5]

Laertes receives injunctions from his father as he prepares to sail from Denmark (I, iii, 58–80). Of Laertes' response to many of these few precepts we have no information; but of the last and most important – 'to thine own self be true' (I, iii, 78) we have an explicit datum. Laertes disobeys. He is not true to himself; he is false to himself, and therefore false to his father's conception of him and false to every man – to Hamlet, in particular. He recognizes his failure, says that killing Hamlet is 'almost against [his] conscience' (V, ii, 285) but, overcoming that little scruple, kills him anyway. Too late he sees his error – his own 'treachery' and his 'foul practice' (296, 306). Though he restores himself before his death by giving and receiving forgiveness from Hamlet (318–21), Laertes has been false and thus disobedient. That Laertes is false to his father and to himself is perhaps best shown by the fact that he is praised by Claudius, who calls him 'a good child and a true gentleman' (IV, v, 148). He is neither: he is a disobedient child and a false gentleman. Approval by Claudius carries with it its own contamination. Praising Laertes in this way, Claudius links the two murderers: they are a pair, both guilty of 'shuffling' – Laertes of the foils (IV, vii, 136) and Claudius of the crown (III, iii, 61).[6]

Fortinbras and Laertes, one obedient and one disobedient, offer another comparison.[7] In exact parallel, they seek to execute their vengeance by force of arms and numbers. Fortinbras, in the opening scene of the play, is a threat to the safety of Denmark:

> [He] hath in the skirts of Norway here and there
> Sharked up a list of lawless resolutes
> For food and diet to some enterprise
> That hath a stomach in't: which is no other ...
> But to recover of us by strong hand
> And terms compulsatory those ... lands
> So by his father lost.
>
>   (I, i, 97–104)

In Act IV, Laertes storms the palace of the king at the head of his gang:

> The ocean, overpeering of his list,
> Eats not the flats with more impiteous haste
> Than young Laertes, in a riotous head,
> O'erbears your officers. The rabble call him lord, ...
> They cry, 'Choose we! Laertes shall be king!'
>
>   (IV, v, 99–106)

Both of these young men have assembled forces against the peace of Denmark, and both of those forces are seen on Danish soil. Fortinbras' force crosses Danish territory in Act IV scene iv; Laertes' force enters the palace in the following scene, IV, v. The juxtaposition sharpens the contrasts between the two: Laertes' force is a rabble, and its occupation of the palace fails; Fortinbras' force is an army, and its struggle against the Poles succeeds. Laertes is militant; Fortinbras is military. Fortinbras has converted his lawless resolutes into an army, an association based on law and rule, instilling in them a spirit of discipline and order. In consequence, he has succeeded in the Polish excursion. In further consequence, he will succeed in the play. He has accomplished this transformation through a single quality of his own personality: obedience, the virtue that characterizes him. He has demonstrated by his response to his bedridden uncle's command that he is capable of receiving orders; that quality has traditionally defined a person as one capable also of giving orders – the ideal soldier.[8] Fortinbras has communicated his virtue to his lawless resolutes and has transformed them into a lawful army. 'Fortinbras has only to say "Go softly on" to command their ordered and silent obedience.'[9] Obedience is the key to his command first of himself and then of his army.

Hamlet receives injunctions from the Ghost, his father-figure, kills the king, and receives from Horatio a benediction for a blameless life. If the play were as simple as that, we should not be attempting to pluck out its mystery. The application of the triangulation should be, but is not, easy: Fortinbras receives injunctions, obeys, and succeeds; Laertes receives injunctions, disobeys, and dies. Fortinbras and Laertes perceived that they had an obligation to avenge their fathers' deaths; Hamlet was directly commanded to do so. They went out and gathered gangs of armed men; Hamlet stayed at home and hired players. They made a show of force; he staged a forceful show – he indulged in metaphor, in seeming.

Hamlet receives injunctions from the Ghost, his father-figure, or, as

Horatio words it: 'a figure like your father' (I, ii, 199). He receives them
in Act I, scene v, soon after Laertes has received his injunctions from his
father (I, iii). The two scenes are linked by the same metaphor of writing:
Polonius directs his son to character these few precepts in his memory (I,
iii, 58–9); young Hamlet promises that he will set down in his tables the
commandment of the Ghost (I, v, 98–104). But, as we have seen, Laertes
does not character the most important precept in his memory, and Hamlet,
though he sets down the injunction in his tables, seems, like Laertes, not
to have recorded it in his mind.

The Ghost gives these specific commands:

[a.]   Revenge his foul and most unnatural murder;
[b.]   bear it not;
[c.]   Let not the royal bed of Denmark be / A couch for luxury and damned incest;
[d.]   Taint not thy mind;
[e.]   let [not] thy soul contrive / Against thy mother aught. Leave her to heaven.
[f.]   Remember me.

(I, v, 25–91)

Of some of these precepts, as of those to Laertes, we can say with assurance
that they do not seem by Act III to have been heeded. As to the last, (f),
the Ghost itself feels the need of reminding Hamlet – 'Do not forget' (III,
iv, 111) – by its return visit. Hamlet does not appear to have left his mother
to heaven (e); on the contrary, he proposes to speak daggers to her (III, ii,
381). Instead of sweeping to his revenge (a, b, c), Hamlet has put on a play.
But at the end of Act V we can be sure that Hamlet has not tainted his mind
(d). We can be sure because he receives a Christian benediction from Horatio,
a man whose moral integrity is beyond question. Shakespeare would not have
placed this Christian benediction in the mouth of Horatio at this point in
the play unless he had intended us to take it seriously.[10] Obedient or
disobedient, Hamlet receives at Horatio's hands a salvific dismissal; he has
committed no crime for which he is to be punished by damnation. Horatio's
pious hope is shared by the audience: Hamlet has been a man more sinned
against than sinning.

Though we may be sure that Hamlet has not tainted his mind, can we
be sure about 'his execution of the Ghost's three first commands? To pose
specifically the question of the play: 'what should [Hamlet] do crawling
between earth and heaven?' (III, i, 127–8). Or, even more exactly, what
should he have done, crawling between hell and heaven, damnation or
salvation?

If we may be reluctant to say that, like Laertes, Hamlet is disobedient,
we can scarcely say that, like Fortinbras, he has been obedient; but there
is no mean between these extremes. Still, we must acknowledge that he fails
to follow obediently each of the Ghost's few precepts. The explanation for
that un-simple response must lie in the nature of the figure giving the
command. Fortinbras has obeyed his uncle, and Laertes has disobeyed his
father; Hamlet has reacted to a ghost. We must argue backwards: as Hamlet

is blessed at his end, he must either have obeyed a spirit of health or have disobeyed a goblin damned. Much of the language describing the Ghost is honorific and elevating, figuring it a beneficent visitant; yet Eleanor Prosser has made it clear that other aspects of the language, the situation, the action, and the stage presence of the ghost almost necessitate the conclusion that it is demonic.[11] Shakespeare is having it both ways. Does Hamlet obey or does he disobey? The answer, I think, is that he does neither.

The opening question of the play, 'Who's there?' – which repeats itself at the moment of the crisis: 'Is it the King?' – requires an answer in terms also of the nature or identity of the Ghost. It is not a question that Hamlet seriously asks.

Hamlet's response to the Ghost rejects immediately the possibility that the visitant is demonic: 'O all you host of heaven! O earth! What else? / And shall I couple hell? O fie!' (I, v, 92–3).[12] But two acts and two months later he is no longer sure. Now Hamlet understands perfectly well that in his weakened state

> The spirit that I have seen
> May be a devil, and the devil hath power
> T'assume a pleasing shape, yea, and perhaps
> Out of my weakness and my melancholy ...
> Abuses me to damn me.
>   (II, ii, 584–9)

The consequence of this understanding should be a questioning of the nature of the Ghost; but though he raises here the question as to whether the spectre is a spirit of health or a devil, a goblin damned, Hamlet never seriously poses that question so as to have an answer to it. Instead, he poses the question as to whether or not the visitant is telling the truth. 'It is an honest ghost'; the success of the play-within-the-play convinces Hamlet of the veracity of the Ghost: 'I'll take the ghost's word'. That same inability to ask the proper question is evident when Hamlet asks: 'These foils have all a length?' The proper question here is directly: 'Is one of these foils unbated?'.[13] But Hamlet, free of all contriving, cannot imagine that such a question should be asked. In this second crucial matter, Hamlet fails. A question about the length of the foils is appropriate to a sporting match between friends; a question about a blunted or unblunted foil is appropriate to a duel to the death. The failure to ask this question costs Hamlet his life. A question about the origin of a ghost is appropriate to salvation and damnation; the failure to ask that specific question – or to force an answer to that question – could have cost Hamlet his soul. Why did it not?

Though the King is clearly guilty by his own confession and his actions, it is still moot before the final duel in Act V whether Hamlet would have been theologically or legally justified in killing him. The Everlasting has set his commandments against the slaughter not only of self but of anyone. Though we know – and Hamlet knows, as we have just seen – that the instruments of darkness (to borrow a phrase) tell us truths which could betray Hamlet in deepest consequence, and we see that the King's admission in his reaction to the play tells us a truth – hardly an honest trifle – yet Hamlet, aware of the prospect of damnation, is content to test only the honesty of the Ghost; he never tests the authenticity of the visitant. He is satisfied to find that the spirit tells the truth.

If for the moment, like Hamlet, we forget the Ghost and its ambiguities, we may examine the second stage in Hamlet's career of vengeance: Hamlet kills the King. On this point there is little ambiguity. The event we have been awaiting for five long acts has finally occurred; in point of fact, Hamlet commits two separate fatal acts.[14] Though some critics have objected to this double killing, it is scarcely possible to explain the dialogue or the action without arguing that the King's drinking of the potion will be fatal (as it is for Gertrude) and that the 'hurting' of the King by the poisoned sword will also be fatal (as it is for Hamlet).[15]

The motivations behind the two killings, I would submit, present some ambiguities, or are at least arguable. There should be little disagreement that the King's first death, by potion, is retribution for his having killed the Queen casually by potion – treachery falling on the inventor's head. The King who killed the Queen's first husband by poison in the ear is himself now killed, her second husband, by poison in the throat. The second killing of the King, death from the poisoned sword, however, is retribution for an offence not nearly so well defined. The normal assumption surely is that 'the hero finally achieves revenge', as Professor Harold Jenkins words it, 'with the same instrument, and the same venom ... as he suffers it'.[16] The same instrument and the same venom refer to the unbated and envenomed foil that Laertes prepared for Hamlet. Hamlet dies by these instruments and fittingly works through them his retribution on Laertes for his own death. But with this venom Claudius had nothing to do. Laertes is honest, finally, in his death throes, admitting, first, that the venom on the sword is his personal responsibility and that he is killed with his own treachery and by his own foul practice (V, ii, 296, 306–7). Laertes then goes on, however, to describe the potion as the responsibility of the King as, of course, we know that it is (308–9). Hamlet does not follow Laertes' distinction between the two. In response to 'the King's to blame' for the potion, Hamlet offers 'Then venom to thy work' – a non sequitur. Hamlet cannot know the varying degrees of blame, and the audience may be excused if, knowing better, we follow Hamlet's lead in blaming the King not only for the potion tempered by himself that killed Gertrude (V, ii, 317) but, as well, for the unction purchased by Laertes for his own vengeance (IV, vii, 140).[17] Thus, though it is apparent that Hamlet secures retribution for his own death at Laertes' hands through the instruments that are destroying him, it is not demonstrable beyond doubt that he has at the same time achieved revenge for his father's death. Though most critics, caught up in the sense of final relief and satisfaction that we all feel, agree with Professor Jenkins that Hamlet has finally avenged his father's death, others have noted that there is no mention of the death of the father in the death scene or anywhere in the concluding lines of the play.[18] Hamlet's last reference to his father occurs 250 lines earlier, in his citation of the crimes of Claudius:

> He that hath killed my king and whored my mother
> Popped in between th'election and my hopes,
> Thrown out his angle for my proper life,
> And with such coz'nage – is't not perfect conscience
> To quit him with this arm?
>
> (V, ii, 64–8)

Though in the first of these lines Hamlet mentions the death of the previous monarch – not even 'killed my father' as parallel to 'whored my mother' – in the second he has begun to talk about himself and his readiness to avenge the threats on his own proper life. Hamlet's omission of mention of his father at the end of the play contrasts with Laertes' specific reference to his father (319) and Fortinbras' reference to his ancestors (378). Hamlet has not remembered his father's Ghost.

It is undeniable that we all have a general sense of relief that, in killing the King, Hamlet has done the job he seems to have set out to do, but there is no evidence in the text that compels belief that the killing of the King fulfills the Ghost's command. The opposite would seem more likely to be true. The death of the new King has no relevance to the death of the old King. Young Hamlet, then, has not carried out the dread command: he has killed the King without reference to that command. The deaths which Hamlet administers in the final scene are manslaughters not murders, and Hamlet having not tainted his soul may properly receive the Christian benediction that Horatio speaks over him. Pledged to tell Hamlet's story, Horatio begins at the end: 'flights of angels sing thee to thy rest!' (V, ii, 349).[19]

Just as Macbeth works out his own damnation, not suffering from the control of the witches, so Hamlet, free of the influence of that ambiguous, highly dramatic, but finally ineffective ghost, works out his own salvation. He has accomplished the same thing that the Ghost wanted accomplished, but he has done so in his own way and for his own purposes. Has Hamlet obeyed the Ghost? The question is answered – with another question: should Hamlet have obeyed the Ghost? The simple responses of his opposite numbers to their fathers' injunctions set clear standards that bear only tangentially on the complex personality of the Prince. The play answers neither question clearly or without ambiguity.

NOTES

1. 'An Homilie against Disobedience and Wilfull Rebellion' in *Certaine Sermons or Homilies, appointed to be read in Churches* ... (London, 1623) (facsimile edn, Gainesville, Fla., 1968), pp. 275–76.
2. *Geneva Version.* Exodus xx, 12. See also Romans vi, 16–17; Ephesians vi, 1–3. Even Mad Tom knows this (*Lear*, III, iv, 76).

3. Claudius mentions the three in his 'inaugural' address (I, ii, 1–64); they are neatly juxtaposed in IV, iv (Fortinbras, Hamlet) and IV, v (Laertes).
4. Some critics hold that Fortinbras arranges the Polish campaign, his victory there, and his return through Denmark with such canny timing that he arrives at Elsinore at the instant that his presence will be most opportune, waiting for the moment that will deliver Denmark into his hands. Military engagements work with such precision only in critics' minds. The arrival of Fortinbras, jump at this dead hour, may be termed one of Bradley's 'accidents' – 'a prominent fact of human life' (*Shakesperian Tragedy*, p. 15). Marvin Rosenberg rightly observes: 'Fortune has conveniently brought him here at the right time' [*The Masks of Hamlet* (Newark: Univ. of Delaware Press, 1992), p. 910].
5. It has been alleged that Fortinbras was obedient because he knew that a reward from his uncle would follow that obedience. This view cannot be supported. The generosity of the uncle was, on the contrary, entirely spontaneous; the old man was 'overcome with joy'; in his surprise, he did what he had not intended to do and what, therefore, Fortinbras could not have expected. Fortinbras' sudden and surprising reformation repeats that of Prince Hal, who had a band of lawless resolutes (*1 Henry IV*, I, ii; II, i, ii), who repented – to the surprise of everyone, especially the King (III, ii) – and received 'charge and sovereign trust' (161) by which military means he defeated his and his father's enemies. Some critics, to be sure, find Shakespeare's presentation of Hal's transformation too sudden and not convincing. The accumulated legends of this hero-king did not.
    For a sympathetic appraisal of Fortinbras' character, see Rudiger Imhof, 'Fortinbras Ante Portas: The Role and Significance of Fortinbras in *Hamlet*', *Hamlet Studies*, VIII (1986), 8–29.
6. Citations are taken from the Pelican edition, ed. Willard Farnham (1969). See my "With a little shuffling", in *Fanned and Winnowed Opinions*, ed. John W. Mahon and Thomas A. Pendleton (London: Methuen, 1987), pp. 151–9.
7. The origin of this parallel has been most astutely imagined by Harold Jenkins, 'Fortinbras and Laertes and the Composition of *Hamlet*', *Rice University Studies*, vol. 60, no. 2 (Spring 1974), 95–108. Part of the interest in the parallel lies in the fact that both descriptions include references to voracious eating.
8. 'We all know the adage ... [:] ... The first duty of a soldier is obedience' (*Oxford Dictionary of Proverbs*, rev. edn, p. 585).
9. Jenkins, op. cit., p. 102.
10. Horatio survives to the end of the play, a record that demonstrates that his character constitutes an acceptable standard of moral and, indeed, religious integrity worthy of preservation. This paper assumes that the survival of Fortinbras demonstrates the same of him. Horatio is a choric figure outside the action of the play; Fortinbras, though a man of few words, nevertheless determines the outcome of the play and, more than Horatio, provides the final tone.
11. Eleanor Prosser, *Hamlet and Revenge* (Stanford: Stanford University Press, 1971), *passim*. In an article in *The Catholic World*, 'The Ghost in *Hamlet*', 162 (1946), 510–17, I.J. Semper reminds us properly that the Ghost descends not to Hell but to Purgatory, though he acknowledges that Purgatory is 'conceived – not as Dante did – but as the popular mind did – as a suburb of Hell' (p. 511).
12. Prosser has assumed that the verb here has the significance of 'coupling with'; that signification of the word, though possible, seems unlikely and, further, irrelevant here (*Hamlet and Revenge*, p. 137).
13. The unbated foil is, presumably, imagined by Claudius as a lethal weapon (as his speciality is poison, he is not aware of the unsuitability of such an instrument

for a deed that no one would notice); Laertes, on the other hand, imagines it only as an instrument that will pierce the skin and so allow the poison to enter the body.

14. See Fredson Bowers, 'Hamlet as Minister and Scourge', *PMLA*, 70 (1955), 740–9.

15. See for further comment on the double death, Michael J. Cameron, 'The Double-death of Claudius', *Renaissance Papers 1970* (1971), pp. 22–4. Cameron notes the irony in the use of the word 'chalice' by Claudius: 'that which should give life is used to kill' (p. 22). Laertes' words, 'anoint' and 'unction', both from the Service of Extreme Unction, are used with similar irony to describe the moment of death.

16. Harold Jenkins, ed. *Hamlet*, Arden edn, p. 413.

17. The King is to blame for the idea of the unbated sword, but it is clear that the mere wounding by that sword of both Hamlet and Laertes is not the cause of their deaths; Laertes' unction is the operative power at work. Bowers argues that, after Laertes' last speech, 'Hamlet recognizes the part Claudius must have taken in the unbated rapier plot against his life' (see his article cited in the next note, p. 40). Nothing in the text requires us to acknowledge that the unbatedness has significance for Hamlet (except for the probability that the point draws blood and so demonstrates that Laertes has not played the part of the sporting gentleman); he acts against the King on the basis of the knowledge that Laertes' sword is envenomed and that Laertes' venom will do its work, and he is perfectly willing to use that knowledge against the King.

    The King is always responsible for the actions of his subordinates, to be sure, but his corruption, though his natural inclination is towards poison, has not been necessary to corrupt Laertes, who bought the unction without knowing when he would be able to use it.

18. For example, Mythili Kaul, 'Hamlet and Polonius', *Hamlet Studies*, II (Summer 1980), 13–24: 'Hamlet, as he stabs the King, seems less an instrument of his dead father and much more an agent responding to the death of his mother and the treachery against himself' (pp. 23–4). So also Charles Haines, 'A Note on *Hamlet* ... "Stabs the King"' (ibid., V (1983), 87–9); Fredson Bowers, 'The Death of Hamlet: ...', in Josephine W. Bennett (ed.) *Studies in the English Renaissance Drama in Memory of Karl Julius Holzknecht* (New York: New York University Press, 1959), pp. 40–1; Lily B. Campbell, 'Bradley Revisited', *SP*, 44 (1947), 184, and *Shakespeare's Tragic Heroes* (New York: Barnes and Noble, 1952), pp. 254–5.

19. This benediction, we must believe, absolves Hamlet for the death of Polonius (as Laertes had urged (319)) and for those of Rosencrantz and Guildernstern, well-intentioned but unthinking instruments of Claudius.

PART TWO

Shakespeare and Gender

'Respects of Fortune': Dowries and Inheritances in Shakespeare, Spenser and Marvell – an Overview

John M. Steadman

In selecting an epigraph for this essay I have sought help – perhaps anachronistically – from a Victorian poet laureate instead of an Elizabethan court of chancery. In a well-known dramatic monologue Alfred Tennyson elaborated a single sentence, attributed to a Lincolnshire neighbour, into an extensive disquisition on the theme of marrying for solid profit rather than for transient beauty. In this poem the 'Northern Farmer, New Style' – who is (as we shall see later) very much the 'old style' father – is lecturing his son and heir on the advantages of choosing a rich heiress instead of a pretty, but penurious, parson's daughter:[1]

Doesn't thou 'ear my 'erse's legs, as they canters awaäy?
Proputty, proputty, proputty – that's what I 'ears 'em saäy.
Proputty, proputty, proputty – Sam, thou's an ass for thy pains;
Theer's moor sense i' one o' 'is legs, nor in all thy brains.

* * *

Thou'll not marry for munny – thou's sweet upo' parson's lass –
Noä – thou'll marry for luvv – an' we boäth on us thinks tha an ass.

* * *

Do'ant be stunt: taäke time. I knaws what maäkes tha so mad.
Warn't I craäzed fur the lasses mysén when I wur a lad?
But I knaw'd a Quaäker feller as often 'as towd ma this:
'Doänt thou marry for munny, but goä wheer munny is!'

'When I canters my 'earse along the ramper,' the old farmer had declared, 'I 'ears proputty, proputty, proputty.'[2] So did many of his social betters. The same hoof-beats echo – like the quadrupedantic thunder of Virgil's horses – over the Italian campagna and the English countryside. Petruchio's nag and the carriage horses of John Wilmot sound the same tune. And one can, perhaps, detect the same cadence in the well-timed oars that carried scores of other soldiers of Fortune to advantageous alliances with Venus.

There were, apparently, no seasonal limits on heritage-hunting. Though heiresses might seem an endangered species, sportsmen might effectively circumvent the game-warden. Like the chase of a fox or a hare, the pursuit of property might lead over convent walls, the hedges of a children's playground, the fences of the hospital or the cemetery. In real life it might result in the seduction or abduction of heiresses; in espousals at the cradle's edge, the lip of the ale-jug, the brink of the grave. In literature it pointed the way to Padua and Belmont, where (in two very different heiresses) the suitor finds the gifts of nature and fortune combined. Where a Judgment of Paris is superfluous, since wealth and wisdom and beauty are compendiously united in one highly desirable bride. And where property rights are transferred as easily and as painlessly as wedding-rings.[3]

* * *

'Proputty sticks' – outliving the successive families who owned it, and the successive marriage contracts that perpetuated family prosperity along with the family name. In literature as in life, romantic motives were often inextricably interlinked with economic and political interests: with considerations of family loyalties and (on occasion) of national welfare. The Renaissance suitor was, in effect, espousing not only a wife but a pedigree: an extended family, a substantial investment in real estate, and (in some instances) a city, a duchy, or a kingdom.

In Renaissance dramatic literature, dowries and inheritances are often subsidiary rather than central motifs, subordinated to romantic interests or sharply contrasted with them. They normally serve as aids or obstacles to the development of the central plot-line, progressing circuitously and often eccentrically toward the preordained end of a stable and happy wedlock: a felicity that will include the goods of fortune along with those of nature and character. Even in comedies like Jonson's *Volpone* and *Epicoene*, where the action does in fact center on inheritance, this motif serves primarily as a vehicle for moral satire on human cupidity and folly: on the avarice that incites prominent citizens of Venice to violate the most sacred ties of nature and personal honour – and that eventually undoes the tricksters themselves; and on the folly of the eccentric and elderly recluse who cannot abide noise and society and who proposes to wed a silent woman and thwart his nephew's expectations of an inheritance.

In some of these plays the dowry-and-inheritance theme has national and international implications; in other dramas it is essentially a private matter between middle-class citizens or between the children of country squires and minor gentry. The amours of Touchstone and Audrey, or of Fenton and Mistress Anne Page are purely private affairs, without political significance. The marriage choices of Henry V or Henry VI or Henry VIII, on the other hand, involve the peace of Western Europe, as well as the security of their respective dynasties; and the stability of the entire Mediterranean *oikoumene* hinges on Antony's relations with Octavia and Cleopatra. In *King John* the

Dauphin invades England both in the cause of the Church and in his wife's title to the realm. In contrast to private individuals, 'public' persons – like the children of sovereign princes – are, in fact, wedding an entire people (much as the Doge of Venice might espouse the sea), and embracing the sovereignty of an entire nation – England or Spain or Portugal – in the person of a single heir or heiress.

Though some of these plays preserve the traditional distinctions between comedy and tragedy and the kind of action and social class suitable to each, some of them involve frequent interplay among different social levels and literary modes. Several of them mix romance conventions with those of bourgeois comedy or explore the inherent tensions between court and city and country in marriage negotiations. They present a fairly wide range of variations on conventional stereotypes of the gentleman and the tradesman; and one encounters versions of the prodigal-son motif on a variety of social levels. One of the more striking features of these dramas is, in fact, the variety of ways in which their authors managed to manipulate traditional concepts of poetic and social decorum, to adapt themes and character-types conventional in classical and Continental drama to specifically English settings, and to achieve the illusion of contemporary scene and reference.

Inevitably the modern reader is confronted by problems of literary and social anachronisms. More than most other genres, the drama usually depends on the recognition of fairly clearly defined types or 'stereotypes', or on clearly perceptible variations from these norms. In the case of Renaissance drama one must make allowances not only for literary genre and theatre-audience, and for differences between the social categories and attitudes of our own society and those of the Renaissance, but also for the influence of types and 'paradigms' inherited from still earlier periods and societies, such as the Athens of Menander. Traditionally the concept of decorum and the alleged 'laws' of the various literary genres shaped the presentation of character, the choice of action, the quality and level of style. Comedy theoretically presented a different social class from the classes represented in tragic and heroic poetry.[4] One would not *normally* expect to see the bourgeoisie treated tragically or heroically, or kings and heroes subjected to comic treatment; and it was indeed the violation of normal expectations – the element of obvious literary unorthodoxy – that, in both instances, might provide the special pleasure afforded by mock-heroic poetry, by literary travesty, and by burlesque. Writers did not always take the 'rules' seriously, however; and there was, in fact, frequent interplay between comic and tragic elements in the same drama, or between the decorum associated with different social classes. In practice, dramatists rarely confined tragic emotions and events to 'public persons'; and the kind of doom that menaced a merchant in a hostile city might differ little from the kind of fate that threatened some star-crossed prince. Conversely, all classes of society from prince to pauper might be subjected to the distorting lenses of the comic mode, though admittedly the nature of such distortions, and the kind of vice or folly ridiculed, might vary appreciably with class and character. Despite such variations, however, the dramatist usually took for granted certain generally accepted standards of behaviour and speech appropriate to certain traditional categories of class, age, vocation, sex and the like: presuppositions in terms of which his *dramatis personae* were to be interpreted and judged.

These *attributa personarum* (as literary theorists called them)[5] were often of venerable antiquity. Derived from the character-types differentiated in Aristotle's *Rhetoric* and in the *Characters* of his successor Theophrastus, as well as from classical drama and from the *Ars Poetica* of Horace, they had been transmitted through rhetorical and poetic manuals to medieval and Renaissance writers. They conditioned the art of Chaucer and the art of Ben Jonson; and the very breadth and continuity of their influence pose yet another problem for the modern critic: the relation of the literary image to the life and society of the author's time. Since the Renaissance poet often based his images of society partly on ideas of characterization evolved in antiquity and elaborated by medieval authors, one cannot automatically assume that he was faithfully imitating the characters and mores of his own society, even if he should profess to be doing so. At the same time he was frequently committed to the principle of fashioning an image that would seem lifelike and real to his own contemporaries, faithful to the demands of probability and verisimilitude. It is worthy of note that Ben Jonson (probably the most classical of English Renaissance comic dramatists) explicitly claimed to mirror his own society and times, offering to his audience

> ... deeds, and language, such as men do use,
> And persons, such as Comedy would choose,
> When she would show an image of the times....
> (Prologue, *Every Man in his Humour*)

Although certain modes and genres (such as the romance, the Märchen, the dream-vision, and the like) might consciously sacrifice probability and verisimilitude to the marvellous and the exotic – portraying settings as remote in time as in space, and deliberately cultivating an atmosphere of unreality and fantasy – the comic dramatist was usually tied to the principles of realism and to the delineation of character-types, situations, and patterns of behaviour familiar to his own contemporaries. He could expect his audience to look for local and contemporary allusions, even though his dramatic scenes might be laid in another time and country, and though many of his *dramatis personae* might bear foreign rather than English names.

The representation of dramatic actions centred on dowries and inheritances in Renaissance literature was subject, then, to a number of variables. First and most important, literary genre and social class: the different problems that might confront royalty and nobility, bourgeoisie, and lesser artisans and peasants. Secondly, the influence of classical or foreign models. Thirdly, the background and sympathies of the author, or those of his audience.

The dowry theme itself is a conventional motif in literature as in life, from classical antiquity to the nineteenth century. It provides the occasion for a major miracle by Saint Nicholas of Bari; and it constitutes the theme of several of the principal novels by Henry James. Renaissance audiences were well acquainted with the importance of dowries and inheritances on the international level – the political implications of the various marriage alliances between Plantagenets and Tudors, between Tudors and Stuarts, or between Stuart and Valois and Bourbon; the complicated pattern of dynastic marriages which had made the Hapsburg family temporarily predominant in both Europe and the New World. On a less exalted level, many writers and their readers had engaged in lawsuits over inheritances or over marriage settlements. John Donne had experienced personally the economic hardships resulting from a hasty and clandestine marriage and from the angry opposition of the bride's family: 'John Donne, Anne Donne, Undone'. A still greater poet encountered both economic and personal difficulties in his relations with his 'in-laws'. When John Milton finally took leave of the world – and of his lawyer-brother – he was still brooding over an unpaid dowry:

> Brother, the portion due to me from Mr. Powell, my former wife's father, I leave to the unkind children I had by her; but I have received no part of it, and my Will and meaning is, they shall have no other benefit of my estate than the said portion and what I have besides done for them. ... And all the residue of my estate I leave to the disposal of Elizabeth, my loving wife.

Elizabeth Milton apparently kept a good table; and (if one may believe the testimony of a family servant) her husband offered to transfer his children's birthright to her in exchange for a mess of pottage.[4]

Before turning to Shakespeare's treatment of the dowry-and-inheritance motif, let us glance at two highly dissimilar versions of this theme in non-dramatic poems belonging to different literary genres: the one a late Elizabethan romance-epic, the other a seventeenth-century country-house poem.

* * *

Though Spenser alludes to dowries and inheritances at several points in *The Faerie Queene*, the most significant episode centered on this motif occurs in the context of equity.[7] In Canto 4 of Book V, the patron-knight of Justice (Sir Arthegall) is asked to settle a property dispute between two brethren and their fiancées. Passing along the seashore, he encounters two squires (Bracidas and Amidas) disputing over a 'Coffer strong' which seems to have been 'wreckt uppon the sands' or to have been 'carried farre from forraine lands'. When questioned as to the 'cause of their dissent', the elder brother Bracidas replies that their father had bequeathed to his two sons lands that were originally equal in size. Subsequent erosion, however, had altered the balance between them, augmenting the younger brother's portion at the expense of the elder's:

> ... Two Ilands, which ye there before you see
> Not farre in sea; of which the one appeares
> But like a little Mount of small degree;
> Yet was as great and wide ere many yeares,
>
> As that same other Isle, that greater bredth now beares.
> But tract of time, that all things doth decay,
> And this devouring Sea, that naught doth spare,
> The most part of my land hath washt away,
> And throwne it up unto my brothers share:
> So his encreased, but mine did empaire.

Besides losing much of his land, Bracidas has also forfeited the love of his erstwhile lady (Philtera), who would have brought him a 'goodly doure' upon their marriage. With the change in her lover's fortune, Philtera (whose name apparently suggests 'lover of land') forsakes her former betrothed (Bracidas) for the wealthier Amidas:

> But now when *Philtra* saw my lands decay,
> And former livelod fayle, she left me quight,
> And to my brother did ellope streight way:
> Who taking her from me, his owne love left astray.

Thus abandoned by Amidas, his first fiancee (Lucy) 'To whom but little dowre allotted was', casts herself into the ocean in despair, but chances 'unawares to light uppon this coffer'. It saves her life; and – again by chance – she and the coffer are both cast ashore on the elder brother's small island. In gratitude she bestows upon Bracidas

> The portion of that good, which Fortune gave her,
> Together with her selfe in dowry free:
> Both goodly portions, but of both the better she.

Meanwhile Philtera (now the fiancee of Amidas) disputes their right to the treasure; she has lost it by shipwreck (she claims) while bringing it to Amidas as her dowry. Arthegall finally resolves the dispute by awarding the treasure to the older brother on the very grounds whereby the younger brother had based his claims to the larger island:

> Your right is good (sayd he) and so I deeme,
> That what the sea unto you sent, your own should seeme.
>
> For equall right in equall things doth stand,
> For what the mighty Sea hath once possest,
> And plucked quite from all possessors hand,
> Whether by rage of waves, that never rest,
> Or else by wracke, that wretches hath distrest,
> He may dispose by his imperiall might,
> As things at random left, to whom he list,
> So *Amidas*, the land was yours first hight,
> And so the threasure yours is *Bracidas* by right.

This little vignette is not important for the development of Spenser's 'plot-lines'; for we do not meet Bracidas and Amidas again in *The Faerie Queene*.

On the surface the episode possesses little or no probability or verisimilitude; the remarkable coincidences and the logical patterns underlying the seemingly fortuitous operations of the sea are credible only as romance conventions, as allegory, and as moral exemplum. Nevertheless, though they are improbable, they are not irrational; and if they violate our notions of credibility, it is for the sake of greater intelligibility. For Spenser is illustrating not only the operations of equity and distributive justice (as exemplified in Arthegall's verdict), but also the operations of a sort of natural justice and covert providence in the apparent accidents of fortune and chance: a natural justice that Arthegall's judgment confirms and ratifies. The sea itself is a traditional emblem of Fortune. The names Amidas and Philtera (like the name Arthegall) involve onomastic puns appropriate to the abstract concepts they exemplify or shadow. This exemplum has been carefully contrived and structured in order to bring into juxtaposition two common types of domestic litigation – disputes over inherited lands, and suits over dowries – along with a third kind of litigation: disputes over shipwrecked goods and other maritime waifts.[8] Thus in a single episode – presented, in accordance with romance conventions, as merely one of a series of knightly adventures – Spenser introduces and combines three different legal issues common in the law-courts of his time. He has his eye fixed primarily on the universal (the abstract 'Idea') rather than the concrete particular – and he has elected precisely those particulars which will give greater clarity and intelligibility to this Idea.

*　　*　　*

From this patently 'idealized' exemplum let us turn next to a different, more complex and more elusive treatment of the dowry-inheritance theme: an episode based on family history and inserted into an encomium of the Fairfax heiress and her parents, the virtues of her remote ancestors, and the beauties of the Fairfax estate at Nun Appleton.

Andrew Marvell's poem 'Upon Appleton House' (written while he was serving as tutor to Mary Fairfax, only child of Lord General Thomas Fairfax and his wife Anne Vere Fairfax) is technically a 'topographical' or 'locodescriptive' poem – a genre normally devoted to the description of a country estate and the eulogy of its owner. Marvell begins by praising the sober and humble dimensions of the house itself; but before proceeding to a description of the grounds of the estate – its gardens, meadows, rivers, woods – he interpolates an opportune digression on 'the progress of this houses fate'. This is, in fact, the story of the sixteenth-century heiress Isabel Thwaites and her marriage to William Fairfax of Steeton (remote ancestor of the Lord General); it is family history and legend embellished with the poet's own dramatic fictions and rhetorical 'inventions'.

William Fairfax's efforts to marry the Thwaites heiress had been frustrated by her guardian Anna Langton, Prioress of the Cistercian Priory at Nun Appleton. After obtaining a legal order for Isabel Thwaites's release, Fairfax had managed to rescue her by force, and had finally married her in 1518. The property at Nun Appleton had subsequently fallen into the hands of the Fairfax family after the dissolution of the monasteries in 1542.[9] In recounting the history of the house, Marvell relates the struggle between Fairfax and the priory for possession of the Thwaites heiress and fortune, and the eventual loss of the convent lands to the Fairfax family:[10]

> Near to this gloomy cloister's gates
> There dwelt the blooming virgin Thwaites,
> Fair beyond measure, and an heir
> Which might deformity make fair.

Nearly 13 stanzas of the poem are devoted to an extended *suasoria* exhorting the heiress to take the veil:

> '... 'Twere sacrilege a man t'admit
> To holy things, for heaven fit. ...
> All beauty, when at such a height,
> Is so already consecrate.
> Fairfax I know; and long ere this
> Have marked the youth, and what he is.
> But can he such a rival seem
> For whom you heav'n should disesteem?
> Ah, no! and 'twould more honour prove
> He your *devoto* were than love.'

Religion has dispensed Isabel's 'promised faith' to her suitor (Marvell comments), and, after vain protests and entreaties, Fairfax resorts first to law and finally to force:

> What should he do? He would respect
> Religion, but not right neglect:
> For first religion taught him right.
> And dazzled not but cleared his sight.
> Sometimes resolved, his sword he draws,
> But reverenceth then the laws:
> For justice still that courage led;
> First from a judge, then soldier bred.
>
> Small honour would be in the storm.
> The court him grants the lawful form;
> Which licensed either peace or force,
> To hinder the unjust divorce.
> Yet still the nuns his right debarred,
> Standing upon their holy guard. ...
> But waving these aside like flies,
> Young Fairfax through the wall does rise, ...

Victorious at last, he bears away the 'bright and holy Thwaites / That weeping at the altar waits', and subsequently acquires the property of the convent itself:

> Thenceforth (as when the enchantment ends,
> The castle vanishes or rends)

The wasting cloister with the rest
Was in one instant dispossessed.

At the demolishing, this seat
To Fairfax fell as by escheat.
And what both nuns and founders willed
'Tis likely better thus fulfilled.
For if the virgin proved not theirs,
The cloister yet remainèd hers.

Marvell is chiefly interested in the dowry-inheritance motif for its bearing on the analogy between the Fairfax heiress and her Thwaites ancestress, but he is also keenly aware of its rhetorical possibilities. In a sense Isabel Thwaites is a 'type' of Mary Fairfax both as an heiress who will some day bring this property as a legacy into the possession of another family, and as a virgin who has experienced the happiness of the contemplative and 'retired' life in the same surroundings. The proportion of rhetoric to narrative within this digression is indicative of Marvell's primary interest and emphasis. Of the 25 stanzas, 14 are devoted to a *suasoria* addressed to the Thwaites heiress extolling the blessedness of the religious life, the *vita contemplativa* of the cloister. Only three stanzas are allotted to Fairfax's remonstrances. The remaining stanzas recount his conquest of his bride and his subsequent acquisition of the land – intermixing praise of the martial exploits of his posterity. The final stanza of this digression is devoted to Sir Thomas Fairfax, the son of Sir William Fairfax and Isabel Thwaites: a warrior 'Whom *France* and *Poland* yet does fame'.

Marvell presents Isabel Thwaites primarily from three angles: (1) as an heiress doubly desirable for her beauty and fortune – a prize to be courted by rhetoric, contested at law, and finally won by force; (2) as the worthy ancestress of the heroic Fairfax line; and (3) as a type of young Maria Fairfax – raised within the same cloistered environment and surrounded by the delights of the contemplative life; young, pure, innocent; and (perhaps more significantly) the heiress to a noble and distinguished family and possibly the future ancestress of another. As an only child, Maria will presumably emulate her Thwaites ancestress: forsaking the same rural retreat and the same maiden meditations to espouse some modern ectype of her Fairfax ancestor and raise up a second line of heroes.

Moreover, the motif of dowry-and-inheritance, as Marvell develops it, is closely interwoven with a second theme, which he elaborates sympathetically in other poems: the tension between private and public values; between the 'retired life' of contemplation and the active life; between pastoral and heroic modes. Marvell is less interested in the financial and economic aspects of inheritance than in its typological and rhetorical implications. Thus the property itself (which is the ostensible subject of his poem) is treated as a kind of topographical emblem, reflecting the private and public virtues of the Fairfax family and exhibiting the imagery of two kinds of warfare, physical and spiritual. For Maria Fairfax – and for the poet – the estate at Nun

Appleton retains something of the original meaning it had once possessed for the Thwaites heiress, as a symbol of the *vita contemplativa*.

In this pleasant retreat the young Maria 'leads her studious hours, / Till fate her worthily translates, / And find a Fairfax for our Thwaites. ...' Her legacy, as Marvell represents it, is moral as well as material; for she has inherited the virtues (along with the fortunes) of both sides of her family. From infancy she has been nursed '... Under the *discipline* severe / Of Fairfax, and the starry Vere; / ... And goodness doth itself entail / On females, if there want a male.'

*   *   *

From these two non-dramatic examples – one a theoretical model or 'construct' (so to speak), the other an historical incident adapted specifically to the encomium of a family and its country estate – let us turn to certain of the plays of Shakespeare.

I shall pass over the question of royal inheritances in the history plays – the title to crown and kingdom – though they are often of central importance. Thus the history of King Henry V opens with a lengthy discussion of the validity of the Salic law. The young king is conveniently reassured that this law, barring succession to the French crown through the female line, was not Pharamond's edict; that it applied exclusively to the region of Meissen; and that it was specifically directed against the native women of Germany by Charlemagne's French settlers.[11]

I shall also overlook the issues of primogeniture and illegitimacy in the relations between older and younger brothers in comedy (*As You Like It*); tragedy (*King Lear*); and in history plays like *King John*, where the illegitimate older son renounces his inheritance as son of Sir Robert Faulconbridge, for public recognition as the illegitimate son of the deceased King, Richard the Lion-Hearted.[12]

Shakespeare treats the motif of dowries and inheritances in a variety of social levels and dramatic contexts – though he normally subordinates this motif to other themes. In *Henry VI*, Parts 1 and 2, the king's decision to marry the almost penniless Margaret of Anjou is presented as a political disaster. In the marriage settlement Henry generously waives the customary dowry – and in fact surrenders control of the provinces of Maine and Anjou to her father Reignier. Such an act may befit the decorum of a lover but not of a monarch. The chivalric *beau geste* results in the loss of France by the English. The king himself meekly surrenders his sovereignty to his foreign wife and to her lover the Earl of Suffolk. When the dukes of Gloucester and Exeter urge a more advantageous marriage, with a 'more liberal dower', Suffolk scorns this practical, economic consideration as mean and base:[13]

SUF[FOLK]. A dow'r my lords? Disgrace not so your king
That he should be so abject, base, and poor
To choose for wealth and not for perfect love!

Henry is able to enrich his queen,
And not to seek a queen to make him rich.
So worthless peasants bargain for their wives,
As marketmen for oxen, sheep, or horse.
Marriage is a matter of more worth
Than to be dealt in by attorneyship
                    (*1 Henry VI*, V, v)

Suffolk's counsel prevails. Henry breaks his troth with another bride to espouse Margaret. The Earl of Suffolk reveals his true motives in the concluding soliloquy of Part 1:

Margaret shall now be Queen, and rule the King;
But I will rule both her, the King, and realm.

In *King Lear*, on the other hand, the motif of a dowerless princess appears in a different – and altogether favourable – light. The tragedy opens with the aged king's intent 'to publish / Our daughters' several dowers, that future strife / May be prevented now. The princes, France and Burgundy, / Great rivals in our youngest daughter's love / Long in our court have made their amorous sojourn, / And here are to be answer'd.' When Cordelia's honest but blunt and unflattering reply provokes her father to disinherit her, the Duke of Burgundy likewise repudiates her:[14]

Bur[gundy]. Royal Lear,
Give but that portion which yourself propos'd,
And here I take Cordelia by the hand,
Duchess of Burgundy.
Lear. Nothing! I have sworn; I am firm.
Bur[gundy]. I am sorry then you have so lost a father
That you must lose a husband.
Cor[delia]. Peace be with Burgundy!
Since that respects of fortune are his love,
I shall not be his wife.
                                        (I, i)

At this point the King of France takes the 'dow'rless' Cordelia, 'most rich, being poor', and invests her with greater honours as his queen:

Bid them farewell, Cordelia, though unkind,
Thou losest here, a better where to find.

Traditionally, the theme of courtship and marriage is more closely associated with comedy than with tragedy or the history-play. The economic problems which beset the middle-class, along with such domestic problems as the attempt of a father to find an advantageous match for his daughter, are the traditional staple of comedy, and it is hardly surprising, therefore, that the dowry-and-inheritance motif assumes greater importance in Shakespeare's comedies than in other genres.

Respects of fortune are not the only inducements that draw Petruchio to Padua, and Bassanio to Belmont. Nevertheless they remain a powerful incentive, and neither suitor displays any signs of embarrassment in confessing his pecuniary motives. Here, for instance, is Bassanio – in the very first scene of *The Merchant of Venice* – seeking to borrow money from a friend to whom he is already heavily in debt. Having lived beyond his means, and unable to pay his current debts, he proposes to redeem his fortunes and repay his old debts by seeking a further loan in order to court the wealthy and beautiful Portia. Such a loan (he suggests) is comparable to shooting a second arrow in order to find an arrow previously lost: his friend and creditor may (he argues) recover the sum he had already lost on Bassanio, by lending him a second sum:

> I owe you much, and, like a wilful youth,
> That which I owe is lost; but if you please
> To shoot another arrow that self way
> Which you did shoot the first, I do not doubt,
> As I will watch the aim, or to find both,
> Or bring your latter hazard back again
> And thankfully rest debtor for the first....
> In Belmont is a lady richly left;
> And she is fair, and, fairer than that word,
> Of wondrous virtues.
>
> (I, i)

Portia, in short, is the 'golden fleece' which has drawn so many Jasons to Belmont in quest of her. '... had I but the means ...', Bassanio continues, 'I have a mind presages me such thrift / That I should questionless be fortunate!'

Antonio's second arrow is, in fact, well aimed. Bassanio recoups his depleted fortunes and finances – successfully passing the casket-test and winning Portia's heart and hand. The lady herself is fully conscious of the fact that she is desirable for more than the gifts of nature and character. Here is her response to Bassanio immediately after he has opened the right casket and discovered her portrait inside:

>   Though for myself alone
> I would not be ambitious in my wish
> To wish myself much better, yet for you
> I would be trebled twenty times myself,
> A thousand times more fair, ten thousand times more rich,
> That only to stand high in your account
> I might in virtues, beauties, livings, friends,
> Exceed account. But the full sum of me
> Is sum of nothing, which to term in gross,
> Is an unlesson'd girl....
>
> (III, ii)

I am not a mathematician, and Venetian finances are beyond my comprehension. But Portia is not (I think) speaking ironically when she answers her suitor in the language of an accountant. She is, more or less, making a semi-official deed of gift. Terms like 'gross', 'full sum', 'account' sound like a broker's monthly statement; and it is perhaps significant that the desirable ratio of wealth to beauty (as she puts it) is ten-to-one. Or perhaps she is already so fair that a mere 'thousand times more fair' would be enough. One may compare this passage with Olivia's more sportive, more patently ironic catalogue of her beauties in the language of an official inventory.

Equally noteworthy is the abrupt change in the lady's status once she has accepted her suitor. While she is still an object of courtship, she is in the fullest sense the 'lady' (*domina*). She possesses the 'maistrye' (as the Wife of Bath might have put it); she is at once sovereign – 'lord', 'master', 'queen' – and Petrarchan 'mistress' – and she is to be courted in terms of the queen-and-subject, mistress–servant relationship. This relationship inevitably alters with marriage; and with it the dramatic, poetic and rhetorical relations between the suitor and the lady. In accepting Bassanio as her husband, she gives herself – and all her endowments of character, nature, and fortune – to him as 'her lord, her governor, her king'.

> But now [she declares] I was the lord
> Of this fair mansion, master of my servants,
> Queen o'er myself; and even now, but now,
> This house, these servants, and this same myself
> Are yours, my lord's. I give them with this ring ...
> (III, ii)

Portia is her own sovereign with one significant reservation – the terms of her father's will. She is not free to select a husband, and (like some enchanted heroine of folk-tales) she is hedged about with taboos. She can be attained only by a suitor who successfully passes the preordained ordeal. 'O me, the word "choose"! I may neither choose who I would nor refuse who I dislike, so is the will of a living daughter curbed by the will of a dead father.'[15] The father of Bianca and Katharina Minola, on the other hand, is still very much alive; and the decision as to their future marriages is entirely his own prerogative. His problems are altogether different from those of the deceased lord of Belmont. One daughter repels all suitors, and he is anxious to get her off his hands. Katharina's forwardness is ordeal enough, and there is no need for any further testing. The second daughter has too many suitors, and the test that Minola proposes is financial; he will bestow Bianca on the suitor who can and will make her the wealthiest. Marriage is, in effect, a business transaction between the bride's father and her suitors. (So many cattle as price for the bride, so many sheep and goats as dowry.)

Shakespeare's Padua was only a few hours' journey from his Venice. Although the Paduan society that he depicts is in certain respects less exalted than the Venetian milieu of *Othello* and *The Merchant of Venice*, it is still basically a patrician society, without a sharp distinction between bourgeoisie and gentry. Well-endowed citizens and urban merchants have as much right to the title of 'gentleman' as the country squire; and it is perhaps noteworthy that Shakespeare appears to be much less strict in his use of this term than the authors of (let us say) *Eastward Ho!* or *The Knight of the Burning Pestle* or *A New Way to Pay Old Debts*.

All the same, this is a very different world from Belmont. Portia is virtually on the same level as the Countess Olivia. Either is a suitable and desirable match for a prince or a duke. But no County Palatines or British and German noblemen or princes of Morocco and Naples and Aragon seek the hands of Minola's daughters. Bassanio can scarcely compare with these princely rivals in rank or in wealth – and the merit that wins him his bride is moral and intellectual; he proves his superior worth by the kind of choice that he makes. In no way is he Portia's social equal – any more than Sebastian is the equal of Olivia, or Viola of Duke Orsino. We are expected (I think) to regard all of these young, but distressed gentlefolk as exceptionally lucky – fortunate beyond normal expectations – if not beyond their own deserts.

The hero of *The Taming of the Shrew* – a rough, turbulent and eccentric country squire – exhibits none of Bassanio's urbanity or Venetian polish. Yet his matrimonial ambitions are similar; for he too is hunting a fortune as well as a wife. Petruchio has come to Padua after his father's decease in the interests of domestic economy: 'Happily to wive and thrive as best I may.' He is a man of some property already ('Crowns in my purse I have, and goods at home'); but (by his own confession) the chief merit he seeks in a wife is wealth. His friend Hortensio (who is courting Bianca Minola) suggests her older sister Katharina as a possibility, but frankly points out the disadvantages of such a match. Katharina is a 'very rich' woman – young, beautiful, well educated – but a nororious shrew; 'renown'd in Padua for her scolding tongue' and so 'intolerable curst, / And shrowd and froward so beyond all measure / I would not wed her for a mine of gold.'

Petruchio is of a different mind – and, like Jason and Bassanio, is willing to undergo substantial risks for sake of the golden fleece:

> ... if thou know
> One rich enough to be Petruchio's wife
> (As wealth is burthen of my wooing dance),
> Be she as foul as was Florentius' love,
> As old as Sibyl, and as curst and shrowd
> As Socrates' Xantippe or a worse,
> She moves me not, or not removes, at least,
> Affection's edge in me, were she as rough
> As are the swelling Adriatic seas.
> I come to wive it wealthily in Padua;
> If wealthily, then happily in Padua.
>
> (I, ii)

Meanwhile a youth from Pisa (Lucentio) is courting Minola's younger daughter Bianca, disguising himself as a music teacher and arranging for his manservant Tranio to assume his own persona. Between them, they manage to deceive the rival suitor Hortensio, inducing him to forsake the pursuit of Bianca for another potential bride. Disgusted by Bianca's apparent preference for a lowly music-master, Hortensio indignantly renounces her, swearing that

'I will be married to a wealthy widow, / Ere three days pass, which hath as long lov'd me / As I have lov'd this proud disdainful haggard.'

At this point the chief remaining rival to Bianca's hand is one Gremio, a rich old gentleman of Padua. While he and the feigned Lucentio are disputing their rights to Bianca's hand, old Minola cannily resolves the dispute by offering his daughter to the highest bidder:

> ... he of both
> That can assure my daughter greatest dower
> Shall have my Bianca's love.

Old Gremio promises a richly furnished house within the city, chests of treasure and a well-stocked dairy farm. The false Lucentio (i.e. Tranio) promptly raises the bid:

> *Tra*[*nio*]....I am my father's heir and only son.
> If I may have your daughter to my wife,
> I'll leave her houses three or four as good
> Within rich Pisa walls as any one
> Old Signior Gremio has in Padua;
> Besides, two thousand ducats by the year
> Of fruitful land, all which shall be her jointure.

Gremio now counters with an argosy, but his rival caps this offer also:

> *Tra*[*nio*]. Gremio, 'tis known my father hath no less,
> Than three great argosies, besides two galliasses,
> And twelve tight galleys. These I will assure her,
> And twice as much whate'er thou off'rest next.

Gremio has offered all, but still remains confident:

> *Gre*[*mio*]....Sirrah, young gamester, your father were a fool
> To give thee all, and in his waning age
> Set foot under thy table....
> An old Italian fox is not so kind, my boy.
>
> (II, i)

Since Minola has allowed Lucentio little more than a week to guarantee the dowry, a substitute father must be found to make this assurance; and the clever servant (Tranio) undertakes to find one:

> ... fathers commonly
> Do get their children; but in this case of wooing,
> A child shall get a sire, if I fail not of my cunning.

He persuades a stranger from Mantua to impersonate Lucentio's father. In the midst of the marriage negotiations the true father arrives on the scene (bringing 'a hundred pound or two to make merry withal'). Under the circumstances this generous present – a rather extravagant 'tip' for a student – seems a ridiculous trifle. While the true parent and false one are bandying accusations of imposture, the true Lucentio (now safely married to Bianca) arrives on the scene and clears up the 'counterfeit supposes'. Both fathers have been tricked; but this does not really matter, as our sympathies are with

Lucentio and Bianca. In this instance – in contrast to the Petruchio plot – the romantic interests of the lovers are pitted against the mercenary interests of Bianca's father, who is willing to auction off his daughter's hand and affection as though it were a commodity.

In *The Merry Wives of Windsor* both of the parallel plots are centred on courtship, engage persons of different social rank, and involve 'respects of fortune' as well as those of Eros. On the one hand, Sir John Falstaff (now 'almost out at heels') and compelled to 'cony-catch' for his livelihood) intends to pay court simultaneously to two middle-class housewives of Windsor. 'I am about thrift,' he declares, and 'do mean to make love to Ford's wife. ... the report goes she has all the rule of her husband's purse. He hath a legion of angels.' At the same time Sir John is also wooing Mistress Page: 'She bears the purse too. She is a region in Guiana, all gold and bounty. I will be cheaters to them both, and they shall be exchequers to me. They shall be my East and West Indies, and I will trade to them both' (I, iii).

The second plot centres on the rivalry of three very different suitors for the hand of Page's daughter Anne. To the Welsh parson Sir Hugh Evans, she seems the perfect mate for young Abraham Slender: '... seven hundred pounds of moneys, and gold and silver is her grandsire upon his death's-bed ... give when she is able to overtake seventeen years old ... and her father is make her a petter penny. ... Seven hundred pounds, and possibilities, is good gifts.' On the merits of the three candidates the Page family are divided. As a future son-in-law, Mistress Page favours Doctor Caius, a French physician with an extensive practice at court. Master Page prefers Slender – a gauche young man from the country closely related to Justice Shallow. Anne Page favours the third suitor Fenton, but this gentleman is *persona non grata* with her father, who regards him as merely a riotous and mercenary spendthrift:

> *Fen[ton]*. ... He doth object I am too great of birth,
> And that, my state being gall'd with my expense,
> I seek to heal it only by his wealth.
> Besides these, other bars he lays before me,
> My riots past, my wild societies,
> And tells me 'tis a thing impossible
> I should love thee, but as a property.
> *Anne*. May be he tells you true.
> *Fen[ton]*. No, heaven so speed me in my time to come!
> Albeit I will confess thy father's wealth
> Was the first motive that I woo'd thee, Anne;
> Yet, wooing thee, I found thee of more value
> Than stamps in gold or sums in sealed bags;
> And 'tis the very riches of thyself
> That now I aim at.
>
> (III, iv)

Like certain other suitors in Shakespeare's plays, Fenton is first attracted by the prospect of the lady's wealth, but in the course of his courtship comes to desire her for herself. She herself is the wealth he seeks, just as Cordelia and Helena are in themselves a dowry.

Dowries also play a significant, though subordinate, role in *Measure for Measure*: a role that enhances the analogies between the condemned Claudio and Lord Angelo – the severe judge who has sentenced him to death. Claudio's failure to marry Julietta hinged on the matter of a dowry – and Angelo's refusal to espouse Mariana similarly centred on considerations of property:

> *Claud*[*io*]. Thus stands it with me: upon a true contract
> I got possession of Julietta's bed.
> You know the lady. She is fast my wife,
> Save that we do the denunciation lack
> Of outward order. This we came not to,
> Only for propagation of a dow'r
> Remaining in the coffer of her friends,
> From whom we thought it meet to hide our love
> Till time had made them for us.
>
> (I, ii)

Respects of fortune – the problem of an unpaid dowry – have deferred, not prevented Claudio's marriage. In Angelo's instance, however, they have led to an actual breach of contract. Lord Angelo had previously been affianced to a Viennese lady Mariana by oath, 'and the nuptial appointed; between which time of the contract and limit of the solemnity, her brother Frederick was wrack'd at sea, having in that perished vessel the dowry of his sister. But mark how heavily this befell to the poor gentlewoman. There she lost a noble and renown'd brother ...; with him the portion and sinew of her fortune, her marriage dowry; with both, her combinate husband, this well-seeming Angelo.'

In the course of the plot, Angelo is tricked into consummating his union with Mariana (under the belief that she is actually Claudio's sister, Isabella). His case is thus essentially the same as Claudio's – although in intent he is guilty of far graver crimes: a second and more flagrant breach of contract, and the seduction of a nun.

Anne Page is more than mere 'property' in Fenton's eyes – and the same may be said of Katharina Minola and Petruchio, and Portia and Bassanio. Yet in all three cases the original object of courtship had been unabashedly economic; and it was only gradually that romantic values became paramount. None of these three suitors is so crass as to 'marry for munny' – in the words of Tennyson's farmer – but each has instinctively followed his advice to 'goä where munny is'.

Respects of fortune are rarely the central theme in Shakespeare's dramas of courtship and wedlock, however, and the economic aspects of marriage are normally secondary – dramatically as well as morally – to romantic and spiritual values. Virtue is more important than beauty, and beauty than wealth; but the ideal bride will excel in all three. In arranging a marriage, the parents of the heroine normally consult her own wishes (can she love the bridegroom whom her guardians have selected?); but in exceptional circumstances the preferences of father and daughter may be diametrically opposed – with important consequences for the development of the tragic or comic plot. Finally, in instances of inter-class marriages,[16] where wife and husband differ significantly in rank or wealth or in other goods of fortune, the poet may place primary emphasis on the contrast between virtue and fortune: on the merits of a virtuous but unfortunate heroine like Viola or Helena or Isabella, and on the correlative merits of the 'great person' who (like Duke Orsino of Illyria and the Duke of Vienna – and unlike Lord Angelo and the Count of Rousillion) chooses his wife for her virtue rather than for her material fortune.

In conclusion, I should like to re-emphasize the limited, though significant, value of literary fictions as social and historical evidence. It is only in a highly equivocal sense that art can be said to imitate nature (or vice versa); and in the Renaissance in particular the artist is often torn between the conflicting demands of reality and wish-fulfilment; between the desires and tastes of his audience and the prejudices and suspicions of his rulers and magistrates; or (as Francis Bacon might have put it) between true and feigned history, reason and imagination. Unlike reason (Bacon declared) the imagination is 'not tied to the laws of matter'; consequently poetry (or 'Feigned History') can 'give some shadow of satisfaction to the mind of man in those points wherein the nature of things doth deny it'. Because 'true history propoundeth the successes and issues of actions not so agreeable to the merits of virtue and vice, therefore poesy feigns them more just in retribution, and more according to revealed providence; because true history representeth actions and events more ordinary and less interchanged, therefore poesy endueth them with more rareness, and more unexpected and alternative variations'. Thus poetry raises and erects the mind 'by submitting the shews of things to the desire of the mind; whereas reason doth buckle and bow the mind unto the nature of things'.[17]

In theory, then, the poet presents an image of the times, a mirror of nature, a gallery of idealized or realistic portraits that are both exemplary and 'verisimilar', marvellous but also probable. His audience and readers are generally content to be simultaneously beguiled and informed by an art of deception and instruction: a craft which can make the deceived potentially wiser than the undeceived. Yet, all the same, the spectators are fully aware that the fortunes of romantic heroines like Isabella and Viola and Helena are exceptional. In real life they would no more win their respective Dukes and Counts than (in a later and different world of fiction) Richardson's Pamela, the pattern of 'virtue rewarded', would win the hand of her employer Squire B***, or Fielding's Tom Jones escape the noose of the hangman.

In both the realistic and the romantic comedy of the Renaissance, gifts of fortune are usually subordinated to those of nature and character – though these may in fact be juxtaposed, combined, or diametrically opposed.

Dowries and inheritances are generally presented as aids or obstacles to the development of the central plot-line, centred as it often is on erratic but certain progress toward a happy marriage. Economic and legal problems may complicate the plot, but for the most part they are tangential. Their treatment often varies significantly, moreover, with literary genre and style and with social as well as literary decorum. The economic and social interpretations of Renaissance literature demand, on the whole, a kind of epistemological 'slide-rule' – a sliding scale of values, ranging from patent fantasy through verisimilitude to fact, and from free invention to history. Of limited validity as historical evidence, these dramatic and poetic fictions are nevertheless potentially valuable to the social as well as the literary historian, insofar as they reflect contemporary tensions between the semi-official standards and 'public philosophy' of Tudor and Stuart society and the social realities (still vaguely and but partially understood) that were inevitably undermining them.

*　　*　　*

I began with an epigraph from Tennyson, and it is only fitting that I conclude with an epilogue from one of Shakespeare's contemporaries, the Reverend Henry Smith. 'Once women were maried without dowries,' he observed in a sermon, 'because they were well nurtured, but now if they weighed not more in golde then in godliness, many should sitte like Nunnes without husbands.'[18]

NOTES

An earlier and extended version of this essay was presented at an invitational conference on 'Family and Property in Traditional Europe' held at the California Institute of Technology and the Henry E. Huntington Library, 30 March–3 April 1981. Portions of the discussion of Shakespeare were subsequently delivered at 'Shakespeare's Renaissance: A Symposium Sponsored by USC, UCLA, and the Clark Library' on 13 November 1981. I am grateful to Professor Hallett D. Smith for reading an early version of this essay.

1. 'Northern Farmer, New Style' in *Selections from Tennyson*, ed. William Clyde DeVane and Mabel Phillips DeVane (New York, 1940), pp. 347–9.
2. Devane, p. 467. 'It was also reported of the wife of this worthy that, when she entered the *salle à manger* of a sea bathing-place, she slapt her pockets and said, "When I married I brought him £5000 on each shoulder."'
3. On dowers and dowries see the following works *passim*: Jack Goody, *The Development of the Family and Marriage in Europe* (Cambridge, 1983); Jack Goody, Joan Thirsk, E.P. Thompson (eds), *Family and Inheritance: Rural Society in Western Europe, 1200–1800* (Cambridge, 1976), especially 'Inheritance, Property and Women: Some Comparative Considerations', pp. 10–36; Alan Macfarlane, *Marriage and Love in England: Modes of Reproduction, 1300–1840* (Oxford, 1986); David Herlihy, *Medieval Households* (Cambridge, Mass., 1985); Barbara A. Hanawalt, *The Ties That Bound: Peasant Families in Medieval England* (New York, 1986); Frances and Joseph Gies, *Marriage and Family in the Middle Ages* (New York, 1987);

Christopher N.L. Brooke, *The Medieval Idea of Marriage* (Oxford, 1989), especially 'Love and Marriage in Shakespeare', pp. 228–47; Joel T. Rosenthal, *Patriarchy and Families of Privilege in Fifteenth-Century England* (Philadelphia, 1991); Suzanne W. Hull, *Chaste, Silent & Obedient: English Books for Women, 1475–1640* (San Marino, 1982), pp. 53–4, 62. See also Lawrence Stone, *The Family, Sex, and Marriage in England, 1500–1800* (New York, 1979); Marvin B. Sussman, Judith N. Gates and David T. Smith, *The Family and Inheritance* (New York, 1970); Randolph Trumbach, *The Rise of the Egalitarian Family: Aristocratic Kinship and Domestic Relations in Eighteenth Century England* (New York, 1978).

It should be noted that the distinction between *dowry* ('property or money brought by a bride to her husband') and *dower* ('a widow's share for life of her husband's estate') is not always observed in earlier periods, and that Shakespeare often uses the term *dower* in the archaic sense of *dowry*. See *The Concise Oxford Dictionary of Current English*, Eighth Edition (Oxford, 1990) and *The Shorter Oxford English Dictionary...*, Third Edition (Oxford, 1973).

Among significant studies of literature and social conventions see L.C. Knights, *Drama and Society in the Age of Jonson* (London, 1937); Arthur Sewell, *Character and Society in Shakespeare* (Oxford, 1951); John C. Loftis, *Comedy and Society from Congreve to Fielding* (Stanford, 1959); Bernice Slote (ed.), *Literature and Society* (Lincoln, Nebraska, 1964).

For the elopement of John Wilmot, second earl of Rochester, with the heiress Elizabeth Malet, see *Dictionary of National Biography*, *s.v.* Wilmot. In the opinion of literary historians Sir George Etherege may have based the character Dorimant in *The Man of Mode, or Sir Fopling Flutter* on Rochester. A scandal involving the widow Anne Elsden provided material for a lost play by Dekker, Ford, Rowley, and Webster; see Charles J. Sisson, '*Keep the Widow Waking*: A Lost Play by Dekker', *The Library*, Vol. 8 (1927–1928), pp. 39–57, 233–59; Sisson, *Lost Plays of Shakespeare* (Cambridge, 1936).

4. Traditionally, comedy dealt with the actions of the bourgeoisie; and among its central themes were love-affairs initially opposed by parents but eventually triumphant over these and other obstacles, thanks to the intrigues of some clever servant, some timely discovery of identity, or the ironies of fate. The happy ending belonged by definition to the comic genre, and in the context of the erotic plot this usually involved marriage: a contract which not only united Jack with Jill, but assured them the material support necessary for living happily ever afterwards.

'... as for tragedy are sought out piteous acts of great and illustrious men,' declared Trissino, 'so in comedy it is necessary to use jocose acts of persons of low rank and unknown, and as in tragedy there come about sorrows and deaths and it almost always ends in unhappiness, so in comedy, though there are some disturbances, they do not involve wounds and deaths, and all terminate in good, as in weddings, peaceful agreements, and tranquillity. ...' (See Allan H. Gilbert (ed.), *Literary Criticism: Plato to Dryden* (New York, 1940), pp. 224–5.). For Giraldi Cinthio, 'Comedy deals with actions that occur in the ordinary life of citizens while tragedy deals with famous and regal deeds ...' (Gilbert, p. 252). In Mazzoni's view the three principal poetic genres served three different classes in society. Heroic poetry was addressed chiefly to soldiers, spurring them on to deeds of glory. Tragedy was directed primarily to princes and magistrates and other powerful persons, encouraging them to observe law and justice. Finally, comedy had as its chief purpose 'to benefit persons of low or middle estate', consoling them for their low fortune by presenting actions that conclude happily. 'In this way the civil faculty intended to give men to understand that the humble life of the people is much more pleasant and fully satisfied than is the life of the great and regal ...' (Gilbert, p. 382). Sometimes (observed Thomas Heywood) comedy 'entreats of love, deriding foolish enamorates who spend their ages, their spirits, nay themselves, in the servile and ridiculous employments of their mistresses. ...' Sometimes 'they discourse of pantaloons, usurers that have unthrifty sons, which both the fathers and sons may behold to their instruction, sometimes of courtezans, to divulge their subtleties in which young men may be entangled, showing them the means to avoid them' (Gilbert, pp. 559–60).

Shakespeare and many of his English contemporaries tended to avoid a rigid distinction between literary genres according to class differences – sometimes mixing low and high comedy and tragic or satiric elements in the same play. Within the play, however, the *dramatis personae* might be sharply differentiated according to class decorum. The literary treatment of dowries and inheritances, like that of other themes, tended to vary, therefore, both with literary genre and (more significantly) with social class.

5. For *attributa personarum* in Cicero's *De Inventione* and other classical or medieval treatises on rhetoric or poetics, see the refrences in Steadman, *The Lamb and the Elephant* (San Marino, 1974), pp. 97–8.

6. See James Holly Hanford, *John Milton, Englishman* (London, 1950), pp. 150–1, 184–5, 70–274; and James Holly Hanford and James G. Taaffe, *A Milton Handbook*, Fifth Edition (New York, 1970), pp. 52–4.

7. For instance, in Book VI, Canto 1, of *The Faerie Queene*, Sir Calidore (the patron knight of courtesy) compels Crudor to espouse the lady Briana 'Withouten dowre or composition; / But to release his former foule condition.' Through 'high disdaine' Sir Crudor had hitherto scorned Briana's devotion, refusing to 'yeeld her love againe, / Untill a Mantle she for him doe fynd, / With beards of Knights and locks of Ladies lynd. ...' See *The Poetical Works of Edmund Spenser*, ed. J.C. Smith and E. de Selincourt (London, New York, Toronto, 1912; repr. 1942). All quotations from Spenser are based on this edition.

8. Thus the sea-nymph Cymodoce pleads for Florimell's release from Proteus' dungeon on the grounds that she is a 'waift' and that the right of disposing of her belongs legally not to Proteus but to Neptune (*FQ*, Book IV, Canto 12, stanza 31):

> ... Then it is by name
> *Proteus*, that hath ordayn'd my sonne to die;
> For that a waift, the which by fortune came
> Upon your seas, he claym'd as propertie:
> And yet nor his, nor his in equitie,
> But yours the waift by high prerogative.

Neptune thereupon issues a warrant commanding Proteus to 'enlarge the mayd, / Which wandring on his seas imperiall, / He lately tooke, and sithence kept as thrall.' Proteus reluctantly delivers Florimell to Cymodoce, and she in turn brings the maiden as a bride to her son Marinell.

Earlier in the poem (Book III, Canto 4, stanzas 21–3) Marinell's mother had induced Neptune to grant him all the treasures engulfed by the sea, thereby enriching him 'through the overthrow / And wreckes of many wretches, which did weepe, / And often waile their wealth, which he from them did keepe.' To the 'Rich strond' the sea voluntarily brings the 'spoyle of all the world,' surpassing the wealth of the East and pomp of Persian kings.

9. For the historical details concerning Fairfax's marriage with the Thwaites heiress, and their relationship to Marvell's poem 'Upon Appleton House', see the notes in Andrew Marvell, *Complete Poetry*, ed. George de F. Lord (New

York, 1968), pp. 68–88; and Andrew Marvell, *Complete Poems*, ed. Elizabeth Story Donno (Harmondsworth, Middlesex, 1972), pp. 248–55.

10. Marvell, *Complete Poems*, ed. Donno, pp. 75–99. All quotations from 'Upon Appleton House' in this essay are based on Donno's edition of Marvell's poetry.

11. In varying degrees, most of Shakespeare's history plays involve the issue of a just title to the thrones of England or France. In *King John*, for instance, the English monarch has usurped the sceptre properly due to his nephew Arthur, thereby provoking France to intervene on Arthur's behalf. To avert such a war and to seal the peace between the two countries, the Dauphin espouses King John's niece, the Lady Blanch of Spain. The plunder of church properties by John and his agents leads to his excommunication and to a French invasion of England, as the Dauphin lays claim to the crown in the right of his wife.

In *Richard II* the king precipitates his own downfall by confiscating the estates of John of Gaunt, Duke of Lancaster, after the old man's death. By thus disinheriting the rightful heir to the duchy, Richard provokes an invasion by Henry Bolingbroke and subsequently loses both his crown and his life.

Henry IV centres on the rebellion of the Percy family in an abortive effort to displace the Lancastrian king and reestablish the Mortimer line – a family with which Percy Hotspur and the Welsh leader Owen Glendower are both related by marriage. *Henry V* opens with a justification of the English king's claim to the throne of France and a rebuttal to French arguments based on the Salic Law. The Archbishop of Canterbury argues that Pharamond's edict that 'No woman shall succeed in Salique land' is no valid bar to Henry's claim to the French crown, inasmuch as the Salic land lies not in France but in Germany. Moreover, the French did not possess this territory until 421 years after Pharamond's death. The truth is that, after conquering the Saxons, Charlemagne had 'left behind and settled certain French; / Who, holding in disdain the German women / For some dishonest manners of their life, / Establish'd then this law: to wit no female / Should be inheritrix in Salique land; / Which Salique land (as I said) twixt Elbe and Sala / Is at this day in Germany called Meisen' (I, ii).

Whereas *Henry V* ends with the English king's successful vindication of his right to the French crown – a right asserted by force as well as argument and sealed by his espousal to the French princess – the three plays in the *Henry VI* cycle portray the loss of France and the outbreak of civil war in England through the dispute over the genealogical claims of the Yorkist and Lancastrian lines. *Richard III*, in turn, depicts the ultimate downfall of the Yorkist dynasty and the end of the wars of the Roses: the death of King Edward IV, the usurpation of the sovereignty by his brother, Richard of Gloucester, the murder of Edward's sons at their uncle's command, Richard's death in battle at Bosworth Field, and the triumph of the young Earl of Richmond (the future Henry VII), who will unite the two factions by espousing the Yorkist heiress:

> *Richm*[*ond*]. ... And then, as we have ta'en the sacrament,
> We will unite the white Rose and the Red. ...
> O, now let Richmond and Elizabeth,
> The true succeeders of each royal house,
> By God's fair ordinance conjoin together!
> And let their heirs (God, if thy will be so)
> Enrich the time to come with smooth-fac'd peace,
> With smiling plenty, and fair prosperous days!
>
> (V, v)

12. The issues of primogeniture and legitimacy or illegitimacy significantly affect, even if they do not absolutely determine, the relationships between brothers in several of Shakespeare's plays. In *The Tempest* and *As You Like It* a

legitimate but exiled duke recovers the title and realm usurped by his younger brother. In *King Lear* the bastard younger son of the Earl of Gloucester displaces the legitimate older son and supplants his own father – only to meet ultimate retribution at his brother's hands. In *As You Like It*, moreover, the youngest son of Sir Robert du Bois, deprived of his patrimony by the oldest son, wins a dukedom by marrying an heiress. His evil sibling, in turn – now expediently converted – makes a fortunate match with the duke's niece.

The first act of *King John* is devoted largely to a dispute between two brothers, Robert and Philip Faulconbridge, over the estate of old Sir Robert – an episode based on the anonymous play, *The Troublesome Reign of King John*. As the elder of the two sons, Philip has inherited Sir Robert's estate, but the younger brother claims the right of inheritance on the grounds of Philip's bastardy. Although Lady Faulconbridge endeavours to salvage her reputation by denying his illegitimacy, Philip proudly renounces his inheritance as old Sir Robert's son for public recognition as the bastard of King Richard the Lion-hearted – and immediately receives knighthood at the hands of his half-brother King John:

> *K. John*. Go, Faulconbridge; now hast thou thy desire;
> A landless knight makes thee a landed squire.
>
> > *   *   *
>
> *Bast[ard]*. Brother, adieu. Good fortune come to thee!
> For thou wast got i' th' way of honesty.
> A foot of honour better than I was,
> But many a many foot of land the worse!
> Well, now can I make any Joan a lady.
>
> > > (I, i)

An interesting paper on '*King John*: The Bastard and the Critics' was presented by Professor James Riddell at a symposium on 'Shakespeare's Renaissance' held at the William Andrews Clark Memorial Library on 12 and 13 November 1981.

13. All quotations from Shakespeare's plays are based on the one-volume edition by George Lyman Kittredge (Boston, 1936).
14. At this point in the scene the action centers upon the issue of the dowry. Lear demands of the Duke of Burgundy

> What in the least
> Will you require in present dower with her
> Or cease your quest of love?

But now, the king continues, 'her price is fall'n'. She is now 'Dow'red with our curse, and stranger'd with our oath'. For the King of France, in striking contrast, 'She is herself a dowry'.

In *All's Well That Ends Well* the king of France extols Helena in similar terms (III, iii):

> Vertue and she
> Is her own dower; honour and wealth from me.

Subsequently (V, iii) the king offers to pay Diana's 'dower'.

15. An interesting paper on *The Merchant of Venice*, offering a psychoanalytic approach to father–daughter relationships in this and other Shakespearean plays, was presented by Professor David Sundelson at a meeting of the Renaissance Conference of Southern California, held at the Henry E. Huntington Library on 25 April 1981. The title was 'Mourning in *The Merchant of Venice*'.
16. The variants on the theme of inter-class courtship are numerous, and in some

of these the initiative may rest with the lady. In several Elizabethan and Jacobean dramas the lady in high station is compelled to encourage a man of lower rank (perhaps legally her own servant) to seek her hand. This is the case with Silvia and Valentine in *Two Gentlemen of Verona*, with the Duchess of Malfi and her steward Antonio in Webster's tragedy, and with the Countess Olivia in *Twelfth Night*. Olivia's courtship of the Duke's page Cesareo (who is, of course, Viola disguised as a man) is counterpointed by the forged invitation to her steward Malvolio to pay court to her: 'I may command where I adore. ... She that would alter services with thee. THE FORTUNATE UNHAPPY' (II, v).

17. *The Advancement of Learning*, in *Selected Writings of Francis Bacon*, ed. Hugh G. Dick (New York, 1955), p. 244. See also Karl R. Wallace, *Francis Bacon on Communication and Rhetoric* (Chapel Hill, 1943).

18. 'A Preparative to Marriage' in *The Sermons of Maister Henrie Smith, Gathered into One Volume* (1593), pp. 55–6. For this quotation I am indebted to Professor Horton Davies of Princeton University.

CHAPTER EIGHT

Flower Maidens, Wise Women, Witches and the Gendering of Knowledge in English Renaissance Drama

Richard Levin

It should be emphasized at the outset that my argument here is tentative and speculative. I have not been able to examine all the evidence relevant to it in the drama or social history of the period, and for some steps I found very little direct evidence, so that its results must be regarded as suggestions for further investigation rather than definite conclusions. It grew out of some research on crossdressing in English Renaissance drama, which led me to question the widely held view that Beaumont and Fletcher, in contrast to Shakespeare, typically conceal the sex of their crossdressed heroines from the audience. The principal exhibit is Bellario/Euphrasia in *Philaster*, who does not reveal her secret to the other characters until the final scene; but I thought it was at least suggested to the audience early in the play when Philaster describes his first meeting with the 'boy':

> A Garland lay him by, made by himselfe,
> Of many severall flowers, bred in the bay,
> Stucke in that misticke order, that the rarenesse
> Delighted me ...
> Then tooke he up his Garland, and did shew,
> What every flower, as Countrey people hold,
> Did signifie: and how all, ordered thus,
> Exprest his griefe: and to my thoughts did reade
> The prettiest lecture of his Countrey Art,
> That could be wisht.
>
> (I, ii, 117–20, 130–5)

It seemed to me that many members of the audience would be alerted to the possibility that 'he' is not a boy, for in English Renaissance drama this kind of activity and knowledge is usually associated with young women.[1]

Shakespeare himself provides strong evidence of this association. Both Perdita and Ophelia explain at some length the 'signifying' of the flowers they distribute in *The Winter's Tale*, IV, iv, 73–129, and *Hamlet*, IV, v,

175–85, and later Gertrude reports that Ophelia fell into the brook while making 'fantastic garlands' of various flowers (IV, vii, 166–75); but the most telling passage is in *Cymbeline*, when Arviragus is describing the flowers he will place on the grave of the supposedly dead Fidele/Imogen and Guiderius exclaims, 'Prithee have done, / And do not play in wench-like words with that / Which is so serious' (IV, ii, 220–31). It is, of course, a stage convention, but like most such conventions it probably had some basis in the larger cultural conventions that we call reality. This can be inferred from other brief allusions in Shakespeare that could not depend on the drama, where we learn that young women not only know the meanings of flowers but even give them their names or nicknames: thus Oberon refers to a flower that 'maidens call ... love-in-idleness' (*A Midsummer Night's Dream*, II, i, 168); Mercutio speaks of a fruit 'as maids call medlars, when they laugh alone' (*Romeo and Juliet*, II, i, 36); and Gertrude, in her list of flowers gathered by Ophelia for her 'fantastic garlands', includes 'long purples' that 'our cull-cold maids do dead men's fingers call' (*Hamlet*, IV, vii, 171). Moreover, this connection of young women with flowers persists long after the Renaissance in romantic poetry ('My love is like a red red rose') and in the term 'flower girl', which refers either to a woman, usually young, who sells flowers on the street, like Eliza Dolittle, or to a very young one who strews flowers in a procession. And there is often a specific association with female virginity, as in our verb 'deflower';[2] indeed the bridal bouquet seems to have such a connection, since the (presumably virginal) bride carries it until the ceremony is completed and then, as she goes off to be deflowered, throws it to one of her (also presumably virginal) bridesmaids, who is thus marked as the next young woman to undergo this double defloration.

My concern here, however, is not with these associations or customs but with the fact that this was an area of knowledge and activity gendered as female.[3] It was not, of course, the only area gendered in this way. Another was the telling of stories or, rather, of a certain kind of story that Lady Macbeth characterizes disparagingly as 'A woman's story at a winter's fire, / Authoriz'd by her grandam' (*Macbeth*, III, iv, 64–5). These were fairy tales, ghost stories, and the like that were not taken seriously, as is implied in the phrase 'old wives' tale', which was used as the title of a play by George Peele, where Madge, the wife of Clunch the Smith, 'drive[s] away the time with an old wives winters tale' (95–6), and we are told that she is 'not without a score' of them (84). It is still used today in this general sense, like the similar Yiddish term *bobe-mayse* (literally, grandmother's story).[4] In Renaissance England the knowledge of these 'old wives' tales' and the art of telling them were passed down from one generation of women to the next, as Lady Macbeth says, but I found no indication that this was true of the knowledge of flowers, which girls apparently learned from their peers. It was age-specific as well as gender-specific.

It is easy to see why older women would have little interest in this knowledge of the language of flowers, or even in passing it on, since its use was so limited. It gave young women a kind of 'flower power' (and by naming the flowers they also acquired more power over them), but all they could do with it was make garlands and what Philaster calls pretty lectures. It was an adornment, a female 'accomplishment', but had no serious purpose, which is precisely why Guiderius belittles it ('do not play in wench-like words with that / Which is so serious'). We must remember, however, that these flowers included herbs, for there was no clear division between them, as can be seen in the books called 'Herbals' published in this period,[5] and that some of those herbs were believed to have very important medicinal or magical properties (which, again, were not clearly demarcated). I found no suggestion that the young 'flower maidens' made any use of these properties, or were even aware of them, but it seems to be a small step from their knowledge of the 'signifying' of flowers to the knowledge of this more potent kind of 'flower power', which was also gendered female since it was thought to be the special province of the village 'wise woman' or 'cunning woman'.

Although the literature of the period makes a number of references to this wise woman, it presents very little direct evidence of what she was like, at least in her earlier stages, and so she must be considered a missing link in my argument. It is possible, however, to construct a composite, and of course hypothetical, picture of her – or rather of the popular conception of her – through later and therefore indirect evidence by a kind of back-formation, which is how biologists construct their missing links. She was an old woman, perhaps ugly or deformed, and was usually called 'Mother', although she had no children or family. She apparently had never married and lived alone in a small house or hovel often outside the village, where she was visited by people from the village and its neighbourhood who wanted her services, which included fortune telling, finding lost or stolen articles, and dispensing herbal remedies, magical potions, and charms. (No doubt many of them were young and many of their problems centred on romance or sex – getting or keeping someone's love,[6] impotence, infertility, contraception, pregnancy and childbirth.) As I noted above, there was no clear division between her magical services and those we would now consider medical, for which there was a real need in a countryside with few doctors – indeed some of these services are still provided in Britain by licensed midwives.[7] Moreover, at least in the minds of the villagers, there would probably not have been any clear division between her legitimate knowledge of the natural properties of herbs (her 'flower power') and some possibly illegitimate or unnatural knowledge and power. Nor would we expect to find a clear division between her power to help people and her power to hurt them; she was sometimes viewed as a 'good' or 'white' witch who could detect and defeat the spells of evil witches,[8] but many also believed that it could be dangerous to cross her. In our current academic patois, she must have occupied a very ambiguous and unstable discursive and social space.

We can be sure that the wise or cunning woman was a well-known figure at this time since she is made the titular character of two plays, John Lyly's

Mother Bombie and Thomas Heywood's *The Wise Woman of Hogsdon.*
Unfortunately for my purposes, however, neither of these characters comes
very close to the hypothetical wise woman I just constructed. They both
live in a town,[9] on familiar terms with their neighbours, and neither of
them traffics in medical or magical herbs. Mother Bombie's help is sought
by young lovers, but it is limited to riddling rhymed prophecies (which of
course always come true). Heywood's Wise Woman has a much wider range
of clients and services; indeed she seems to be a jill-of-all-trades, which
include telling fortunes, curing madmen, pimping, and helping women
dispose of their illegitimate children.[10] More important, her claim to special
powers is presented as a con-game, for we are shown how she secretly gets
information about her clients before meeting them, so that she can astound
them with her 'miraculous' foreknowledge of their problems (III, i, 890–
900). And we cannot take either woman very seriously, since both plays
are fairly broad comedies. Thus if there is any truth to my reconstruction
of an earlier conception of the wise woman, these two portrayals apparently
represent a debasement of it – a debasement to which they themselves may
be contributing.

Shakespeare does not give us any wise women, unless we count Mother
Prat, the 'wise woman of Brainford', who figures in *The Merry Wives of
Windsor* only as a plot-device for disguising and punishing Falstaff (and,
unlike other wise women, she has family connections, being the aunt of
Mistress Ford's maid [IV, ii, 75]).[11] But he bestows some of the wise
woman's attributes upon another character, Friar Lawrence of *Romeo and
Juliet.* The Friar lives outside the city in an isolated cell (though other
members of his order seem to be in the area), and when we first meet him
he is gathering flowers and herbs for their 'many virtues' and 'medicin[al]
power', which he has an expert knowledge of (II, iii, 5–26). Moreover, the
young lovers come to his cell for help, and he provides it in the form of a
remarkable 'liquor' he has concocted with this knowledge, so he does seem
to be functioning like a wise woman. There is also a more distant analogue
to the wise woman in the 'old religious man' we hear of in *As You Like It,*
V, iv, 159–65, who lives in 'the skirts of this wild wood' and converts Duke
Frederick. Both of these characters, then, can be seen as taking on certain
traits and powers of the wise woman, but they of course are males (though
desexualized) and are coded as holy, which may lead us (at least it leads me)
to suspect that we are witnessing a division of her powers into good and evil
repertoires that are assigned to different vocations and to different genders.
In fact Friar Lawrence explains that the plants he is gathering also have evil
properties and so can be 'misapplied' or 'abuse[d]', but he does not identify
the people who do this (in the play it is done by his dark double, the
Apothecary in Mantua who sells poison to Romeo).

More substantial support for this suspicion can be found, however, in the
contrast set up in *Macbeth* between the pious King Edward, who uses the
powers given him by heaven to cure people (IV, iii, 141–59), and the

witches, who use their demonic powers to harm others, and in *The Tempest* between the white magic of Prospero and the black magic of Sycorax, another witch. There is a similar contrast in Jonson's *The Sad Shepherd* between the 'devout Hermit' Reuben the Reconciler and the witch Mother Maudlin the Envious, who both live in isolation in Sherwood Forest, he in a cell and she in a dreary, segregated area called 'the Witch's Dimble'. Since Jonson never finished the play we cannot be sure what role was planned for Reuben, but it seems very likely, judging from his name, that the young lovers will come to him for help with their problems and that he will reconcile them, whereas Mother Maudlin has the opposite role: the young lovers do not come to her but she goes to them and uses her witchly tricks (casting spells, changing shapes, etc.) to create their problems.[12] It would seem, then, that when a man is given some of the wise woman's powers, the powers left to her tend not only to be debased, as we saw in Lyly's and Heywood's plays, but also to be demonized. In fact this connection is made explicit in *The Sad Shepherd*: when Mother Maudlin wants to fool her victims she refers to herself as a 'cunning Woman' or 'wise woeman' (III, iv, 23, 31); and one of Robin Hood's merry men asserts that 'They call her a Wise-woman, but I thinke her / An arrant Witch' (I, vi, 62–3).

The connection between the wise woman and the witch that I am suggesting has been noted by others, especially Barbara Rosen.[13] Although hard evidence for this is not easy to come by, it seems safe to assume that some of the early victims of the witch hunts and trials were these wise or cunning women, since they were such vulnerable targets: they were isolated from the rest of the community, without a network of relatives and friends to support them; they were viewed by that community as special and different; and their knowledge and powers, as I noted above, occupied an ambiguous space between natural medicine and unnatural magic, and between good and evil.[14] There is some evidence of this relationship of the wise woman to the witch in the drama of the period, although it is seldom cited by commentators on the subject. The sequence of plays I just traced leading up to *The Sad Shepherd* seems to point toward it, and so does the fact that each of the wise women in the plays examined earlier is suspected or accused of witchcraft, even though none of them is guilty. Silena tells Mother Bombie that 'they saie you are a witch' (she answers, 'They lie, I am a cunning woman'), Serena calls her 'a weather-beaten witch', and Halfpenny and Dromio fear her demonic power (II, iii, 86–7, III, i, 50, III, iv, 86–7); the Wise Woman of Hogsdon is called a witch or sorceress several times by Chartley, Luce II, and Boyster (I, ii, 379, II, i, 442, 510, III, ii, 1043, IV, iii, 1740, V, iv, 2124, 2244); and Ford beats Mother Prat (actually Falstaff in disguise) because she is 'a witch' (IV, ii, 172–91). It is significant, I think, that these accusers are usually men, a point I will return to later.

More impressive evidence appears in *The Witch of Edmonton*, a play by Dekker, Ford and Rowley that is based on a contemporary trial and actually stages a connection between wise woman and witch. At the beginning of the play, Mother Sawyer is not really a wise woman, since she does not claim or possess any special power, but she has the external attributes of one – she is old and 'deform'd', 'like a Bow buckl'd and bent together', and lives alone in a 'ruin'd Cottage, ready to fall with age', apparently outside the village (II, i, 3–4, 106). For these reasons she is accused of being a witch by the men of the village, like the wise women discussed above, and is abused because of this, especially by Old Banks, while his son Cuddy comes to her and asks her to 'bewitch' Kate Carter into falling in love with him (II, i, 205–25). The abuse drives her to make a pact with the devil and so become a real witch, with a familiar, the dog Tom, who gives her the powers that she was accused of using earlier, and that Cuddy assumed she had when he sought her help.[15] Here then we can see the conception of the wise woman leading to and merging with the conception of the witch, so that they become indistinguishable.

The other two plays of the period that are named for witches, Middleton's *The Witch* and Heywood and Brome's *The Late Lancashire Witches*,[16] are less useful for my purpose, since their portrayals, like those in *Macbeth* and Jonson's *The Masque of Queens*, are so thoroughly interpellated into and imbricated with the more fantastic strands of witch-lore that any connection to the wise woman is virtually lost. These witches do not live and work alone, like proper wise women, but operate in a coven or 'sisterhood', which we also see in *Macbeth* and *The Masque of Queens*, and Hecat, the coven-leader in *The Witch*, even has a son.[17] And when they concoct their magic brews they make very little use of the herbs that constituted the wise woman's 'flower power' but favour instead a gruesome menu of animal and human parts.[18] In *The Witch*, which is set in an imaginary Ravenna, Hecat and her coven-sisters may be female but are not really women; they spend their time singing and dancing and flying about like naughty fairies. But they do live in an isolated locale and are visited by people asking for help – Sebastian to make a rival impotent, Almachildes to make a woman love him, and the Duchess to kill an enemy – which is their only real link to village wise women. *The Late Lancashire Witches* is based, like *The Witch of Edmonton*, on a contemporary trial, yet its witches seem just as far removed from the wise woman. Three of them are older women, Meg, Gilian and Mawd (who are called at various times 'Mother' and 'Gammer'), but they work together in a coven, as I noted, and are joined in it by Squire Generous's wife, who is not old at all, and a young woman, Mal Spencer. Moreover, no one comes to them for help – indeed no one could come, since they do not operate out of a specific place and they conceal their powers, which a wise woman would never do if she wanted to stay in business. Instead they seek out their victims, like Mother Maudlin in *The Sad Shepherd*, to play tricks on them, usually just for fun, which also is not wise-womanly behaviour.[19]

Despite their differences, however, these three witch plays share some features that support my argument. Although they all contain comic elements, they are all much more serious than the two wise woman comedies examined earlier, which suggests that while the wise woman was being devalued and trivialized, the witch was regarded as a real threat to society. Their treatment of gender is also very significant. None of them presents a 'holy man' to be contrasted to the witches, as we saw in *Macbeth*, *The Tempest* and *The Sad Shepherd*, but *The Witch of Edmonton* and *The Late Lancashire Witches* give us a much more direct gender conflict, for in both plays it is the men of the village who hunt down the witches (just as it was men who accused the wise women of witchcraft) and turn them over to the male legal authorities. In the first play Old Banks leads a group of male neighbours who first try to lynch Mother Sawyer and then have her arrested and brought to justice (IV, i); and in the second Doughty organizes some men to go 'witch hunting' and finally can report that he has 'catcht a whole Kennel of Witches' (IV, 2011, V, 2651–2), who are also put on trial. (In *The Sad Shepherd*, similarly, Alken teaches the other men 'the sport of Witch-hunting' [II, vii, 20], which would presumably have led to the defeat of Mother Maudlin if Jonson had finished the play.) Moreover, the male judicial system not only has the legal power to execute witches, but also has a kind of magical power to neutralize their magic as soon as they come under its control, for we are told in *The Late Lancashire Witches* that

> Witches apprehended under
> Hands of lawfull authority, doe loose their power;
> And all their spels are instantly dissolv'd.
> (V, 2631–3)

Thus evil female power is no match for good male power. And of course before they come under the beneficent control of the male authorities, witches are by definition under the malevolent control of the male devil and his male agents – thus in *The Witch of Edmonton* Mother Sawyer is clearly dominated by Tom, her familiar; the witches of *Macbeth* refer to 'our masters' (IV, i, 63); and in *The Witch* Hecat also speaks of 'our *Master*' (I, ii, 372), and her coven-mates remind her that '*Ther's one comes downe to fetch his dues*' (III, iii, 1344). There is no way that they can escape subjection to men.[20] That, at any rate, is what the evidence of these plays would indicate.

We should be very cautious, I believe, in drawing conclusions from this evidence, since we cannot assume any direct or simple connection between theatrical representations and the world outside the theatre. It is obvious, for instance, that the contemporary English countryside was not really teeming with religious hermits and friars and flying witches (though there were real witch hunts and trials).[21] Yet it seems reasonable to assume that these representations do point to something that was actually happening at the time, and I am suggesting that this was what we would now call a redrawing of gender boundaries, in which some of the knowledge and powers that had formerly been attributed to women (or to certain women) were divided into valuable and good components that were coded male, and devalued or demonized components that were coded female. I am certainly not implying that this was all brought about by a pervasive male conspiracy. It was in large part the result of a vast socio-economic change beyond the control of any group – the change from a traditional rural society based on agriculture to a modern urban society based on commerce. Not many young maidens raised in cities would know the language of flowers, and when the wise or cunning woman operated there she would not have access to the 'flower power' of herbal medicine and charms and would tend to be assimilated, as we saw in *The Wise Woman of Hogsdon*, to the con-men of the city and city comedy, like Subtle in *The Alchemist* (who is called 'the cunning-man' [I, ii, 8]). Even the modern derogatory meaning of 'old wives' tales' was the product of this change, not only because city wives did not tell these tales to their nuclear families by the winter fire, but also because the tales themselves lost the value they possessed in the older society where they would have been regarded as repositories of folk wisdom and so would not have been merely 'old wives' tales'.

Having paid our respects to the material 'base' and these changes occurring within it, however, I think we must still recognize that this redrawing of gender boundaries was also the result of the efforts of men and of their institutions to appropriate some of the knowledge and power of the wise woman and to condemn what remained as witchcraft. (Of course a few men were convicted of witchcraft, but in the popular conception, as in the drama, witches were women.)[22] The male-run church obviously had an interest in monopolizing all 'good' magic (remember those devout hermits and friars) and in extirpating any other kind. The male-run state obviously had an interest in policing the activity of women and ensuring that no area of this activity remained outside its control. But I believe that another factor was also at work here, one that we now call the professionalization of knowledge, which, since all the professions were also run by men, meant the masculinization of the knowledge formerly claimed by and attributed to the wise woman. Her knowledge of plants was being codified and rendered scientific in those 'Herbals' mentioned earlier, which were of course written by men.[23] And much more important, her medical knowledge was being contested by male professionals in the Royal College of Physicians (chartered in 1518) and the United Company of Barbers and Surgeons (chartered in 1540), who obviously had an interest in acquiring and maintaining a monopoly over 'real' medicine, and therefore in denigrating any competing knowledge as unscientific, unnatural and unlawful.[24] I could not find any direct evidence of this competition between doctors and wise women or witches in the plays I examined, although these plays make it very clear that doctoring is masculine – thus in *All's Well That Ends Well* we are told three separate times that Helena's medical knowledge comes from her father, a famous doctor, and so is really male (I, i, 17–27, I, iii, 220–9, II, i, 101–14).[25] I am not suggesting that this competition was something new at the time, since it goes back at least as far as the Hippocratic Oath, which draws a sharp boundary between legitimate medicine and illegitimate sorcery.

But it probably took on a new urgency in this period, as a result of the basic changes outlined above and the drive toward professionalization. And it persisted into later periods – for example, in the tensions in our hospitals between doctors and nurses in the days (not so many days ago) when virtually all doctors were men and all nurses were women, and much effort was devoted to defining and policing the limits of the nurse's medical role, which can be seen as a further development of the steps I have been tracing from flower maiden to wise woman to witch.

Readers may have noticed that I am not taking another step backward from this sequence by suggesting that it all descends from an ancient religion of the Earth Mother or Mother Goddess in an ancient matriarchal society, which some feminists have argued for recently. There are three reasons why I decline to take this step. In the first place, I am very suspicious of any form of what I call 'Edenism' – the belief in some idyllic utopia, set in the distant past, from which we have fallen (or been pushed). Secondly, I know of no evidence to support this particular form of Edenism. The pantheons of some older societies did include a Mother Goddess, but they included powerful male gods as well, and these societies, so far as we can tell, were much more patriarchal than ours. There is even some evidence that the idea of an ancient matriarchy and the related idea of an Amazon society are myths constructed by and for men.[26] And my third reason is that I disagree with the political agenda that usually underlies this argument (which is completely separate, of course, from the question of whether the argument is true), because most of the people who invoke a matriarchal Eden, like most of those who invoke the other Edens, want us to return to it, which here would mean the creation (supposedly the recreation) of a separate and superior area of female know-ledge and power.[27] It seems to me that we should not be trying to go back to this mythical past, even if we could, but forward to a better future in gender relations, and I think there is a movement in this direction, for we are now undergoing another major social change that is bringing significant numbers of women into the medical profession and the other formerly all-male professions and institutions that I said were in part responsible for the redrawing of gender boundaries in the Renaissance. And the result of this change will be, I hope, not just another redrawing of the gender boundaries of knowledge and power (even one that might carve out a special privileged domain for women), but rather the elimination of all these boundaries which would finally lead to the ungendering of knowledge and of power.

NOTES

1. There is an earlier clue near the end of the preceding scene where Philaster breaks off a discussion of state affairs to ask Dion if his daughter is still alive and is told that she 'for the penance but of an idle dreame, / Has undertooke a tedious pilgrimage' (I, i, 321–2). The exchange is so pointed because of its lack of

connection to the rest of the dialogue and her motive is so dubious that the audience would probably have been alerted.

2. Shakespeare also applies this word to the rape of non-virgins like Lucrece and Lavinia (*The Rape of Lucrece*, 348, *Titus Andronicus*, II, iii, 191, II, iv, 26).

3. In Donne's 'Elegy VII' the male speaker says to a married woman:

> I had not taught thee then, the Alphabet
> Of flowers, how they devisefully being set
> And bound up, might with speechlesse secrecie
> Deliver arrands mutely, and mutually.
>
>   (9–12)

But this flower language is a secret code for arranging assignations, which is clearly not the language exhibited by Ophelia, Perdita, or Bellario/Euphrasia.

4. The term has an added connotation in America, since *bobe* was usually raised in the 'old country' and brought with her some of its folklore and superstitions that are devalued in the new world.

5. See the list in *CBEL* vol. 1, 892; some titles use the more general term 'plants'. And the flowers distributed by Perdita and Ophelia include some herbs.

6. This is the power of the 'magic' handkerchief made by a wise woman called a 'sibyl' and given to Othello's mother by another wise woman, a Gypsy 'charmer' (III, iv, 55–75, but in V, ii, 217 Othello says his father gave it to his mother).

7. The *OED* entry includes a quotation from Scott's *Kenilworth* (1821) where 'wise woman' means 'midwife'. Barbara Rosen notes that in Renaissance England 'childbirth continued to be managed by women' who often resorted to 'magical' aids – 'Introduction', *Witchcraft* (London: Edward Arnold, 1969), p. 22.

8. In *Twelfth Night* the tormentors of Malvolio say they will 'Carry his water to th' wise woman' for diagnosis to see if he is 'bewitch'd' (III, iv, 101–2).

9. In Lyly's play this is required by his attempt to follow the model of the Roman stage, set in a single large square with all the characters' houses, including Mother Bombie's, opening on it (see Bond's introduction, p. 169).

10. See her own list of her 'many Trades' in III, i, 993–1000 and her list of other wise women with their specialities in II, i, 426–38: 'Mother *Notingham* ... was prettily well skill'd in casting of Waters: and after her, Mother *Bombye* ... Mother *Sturton* in *Goulden-lane*, is for Forespeaking: Mother *Phillips* of the *Bank-side*, for the weakness of the backe', etc. Compare the portrayal of Mother Birdlime in *Westward Ho*: she is called at various times a 'wise-Woman', 'Cunning Woman', 'witch', 'Sorceres', 'Fortune-teller' and 'Mid-wife' (II, ii, 78, 102; II, iii, 120; IV, ii, 70; V, iii, 15; V, iv, 255–67), but functions in the play simply as a bawd.

11. We also learn of plans to consult her about Slender's lost chain and his courtship of Anne Page (IV, iv, 26–48), two typical services of the wise woman. In Q1 (1602) and Q2 (1619) she is called 'Gillian of Brainford', who apparently was a real person and is accused of witchcraft in *Westward Ho*, V, i, 227. In Robert Copland's *Gyl of Braintfords Testament* (c. 1560), however, she is presented as an innocuous merry widow who bequeaths farts to various people. This testament is referred to by Sir John Harington in *Ulysses upon Ajax* (1596), B4r, and by Thomas Nashe in the Prologue to *Summer's Last Will and Testament*, 80–2, in his epistle 'To the Gentlemen Students of Both Universities' prefixed to Robert Greene's *Menaphon* (1589), A3v, where she is called 'Ioane of Brainford', and in an undated letter to William Cotton – see *The Works of Thomas Nashe*, ed. R.B. McKerrow and F.P. Wilson (Oxford: Blackwell, 1958), vol. 3, 314, vol. 5, 195. Henslowe records a payment to Thomas Dowton and Samuel Rowley on 10 February 1598/9 for a play titled 'fryer fox & gyllen of branforde' that has not survived.

12. One trick is imprisoning Earine in a tree, as Sycorax did to Ariel. And she has a magic girdle given to her by a 'Gypsan Ladie', but, unlike the Gypsy 'charmer' who gave the magic handkerchief to Othello's mother (see n. 6), this was a 'right Beldame' working with 'our Dame *Hecat*' (II, iii, 39–49).

13. See her unpublished paper on the wise or cunning woman presented to the workshop on 'Witchcraft in History and the Theater' at the 'Attending to Women Conference' in 1991.

14. We have some soft evidence in contemporary witchcraft treatises. George Gifford, for instance, in *A Dialogue Concerning Witches and Witchcraft* (1593), argues that wise or cunning women (and men) are agents of the Devil who are 'his other sort of Witches' and 'ought to die for it' (A3r, D3r, H1v–2r, K3v).

15. Old Banks later calls her 'Mother *Bumby*' (IV, i, 197), another linking of the wise woman and the witch. Cuddy visits her right after her pact with the devil, but he does not know this and would have come anyway.

16. We also have the titles of two witch plays that did not survive: *The Witch of Islington* and *Doctor Lamb and the Witches*.

17. Mother Maudlin in *The Sad Shepherd* also has children. In neither play is the father identified, but we are told in *The Tempest* that Sycorax's son Caliban was 'got by the devil himself' (I, ii, 319).

18. See the lists of ingredients collected for these brews in *The Witch* I, ii, III, iii, V, iii, *Macbeth* IV, i, 4–38, and Jonson's *The Masque of Queens* 155–203. An exception is Dipsas, the witch in Lyly's *Endymion*, who seems to work mainly with 'simples' and 'hearbes' (II, iii, 39, V, iii, 23, 29).

19. One trick is to make a man impotent on his wedding night, which is also found in *The Witch*. There is another example of the (male) tendency to blame this male failure on a female in *Thierry and Theodoret*, where Brunhalt laces her son's drink with an impotence potion at his wedding (II, i); she does not get it from a witch but that is not necessary since she herself functions as the wicked witch of the play.

20. Note also that Mother Jordan, the 'cunning witch' in *2 Henry VI*, is under the control of the conjurer Roger Bolingbrook (I, iv, 10–11). In *Endymion* Dipsas is defeated by Cynthia and in *The Masque of Queens* the twelve witches are defeated by twelve virtuous queens, but these are allegorical plays presented at court and honour Queen Elizabeth and Queen Anne, respectively.

21. In fact the dramatic hermits and friars are usually placed in Catholic countries or in pre-Reformation England.

22. Several of the people accused in the actual case that is the source of *The Late Lancashire Witches* were men, but the play does not mention them, and when Doughty begins his 'witch hunting' he assumes that 'all the Witches in *Lancashire*' will turn out to be women (V, 2206–10).

23. See note 5 and Agnes Arber, *Herbals: Their Origin and Evolution. A Chapter in the History of Botany 1470–1670*, 2nd edn (Cambridge: Cambridge UP, 1953). The first London Pharmacopoeia, one product of this evolution, was published in 1618. John Riddle notes that most of the herbal lore associated with menstruation, contraception and abortion disappears from the later and more academic Renaissance Herbals, apparently because 'this knowledge was primarily transmitted by a network of women', usually midwives, through their oral tradition (*Contraception and Abortion from the Ancient World to the Renaissance* [Cambridge: Harvard UP, 1992], p. 16). Of course not all these women were 'wise women'.

24. F. David Hoeniger cites some actual attempts by physicians and surgeons to curb the medical activities of wise women during this period in *Medicine and Shakespeare in the English Renaissance* (Newark: U of Delaware P, 1992), pp. 28–9. I am indebted to Catherine Belling for this reference.

25. The converse idea seems to underlie our popular view of a 'witch-doctor': he is male but is not really a doctor because his medicine is based on female witchcraft.
26. See Joan Bamberger, 'The Myth of Matriarchy: Why Men Rule in Primitive Society', *Women, Culture, and Society*, ed. Michelle Rosaldo and Louise Lamphere (Stanford: Stanford UP, 1974), pp. 263–80. I criticize Edenism in 'Bashing the Bourgeois Subject', *Textual Practice* 3 (1989), 76–86 (see 81–3).
27. See, for example, Mary Daly, 'Be-Witching: Re-calling the Archimagical Powers of Women', *The Sexual Liberals and the Attack on Feminism*, ed. Dorchen Leidholdt and Janice Raymond (New York: Pergamon, 1990), pp. 211–21, and Paula Gunn Allen, '"Border" Studies: The Intersection of Gender and Color', *Introduction to Scholarship in Modern Languages and Literatures*, ed. Joseph Gibaldi (New York: Modern Language Association, 1992), pp. 303–19.

PLAYS CITED

For all quotations and citations from the plays of Shakespeare, Lyly and Jonson I rely on *The Riverside Shakespeare*, ed. G. Blakemore Evans (Boston: Houghton Mifflin, 1974); *The Complete Works of John Lyly*, ed. R. Warwick Bond (Oxford: Clarendon, 1902); and *Ben Jonson*, ed. C.H. Herford and Percy and Evelyn Simpson (Oxford: Clarendon: 1925–52). The other plays discussed are listed below, with their authors, approximate dates, and the editions used.

The Late Lancashire Witches, Thomas Heywood and Richard Brome, 1634, ed. Laird Barber (New York: Garland, 1979).

The Old Wives Tale, George Peele, 1590, ed. Frank Hook, *The Life and Works of George Peele*, gen. ed. Charles Prouty, vol. 3 (New Haven: Yale UP, 1970).

Philaster, or Love Lies a-Bleeding, Francis Beaumont and John Fletcher, 1609, ed. Robert K. Turner, *The Dramatic Works in the Beaumont and Fletcher Canon*, gen. ed. Fredson Bowers, vol. 1 (Cambridge: Cambridge UP, 1966).

Summer's Last Will and Testament, Thomas Nashe, 1592, ed. Russell Fraser and Norman Rabkin, *Drama of the English Renaissance*, vol. 1 (New York: Macmillan, 1976).

Thierry and Theodoret, John Fletcher and Philip Massinger, 1617, ed. Robert K. Turner, *The Dramatic Works in the Beaumont and Fletcher Canon*, gen. ed. Fredson Bowers, vol. 3 (Cambridge: Cambridge UP, 1976).

Westward Ho, Thomas Dekker and John Webster, 1604, ed. Fredson Bowers, *The Dramatic Works of Thomas Dekker*, vol. 2 (Cambridge: Cambridge UP, 1955).

The Wise Woman of Hogsdon, Thomas Heywood, 1604, ed. Michael Leonard (New York: Garland, 1980).

The Witch, Thomas Middleton, 1615, ed. W.W. Greg, Malone Society Reprints (Oxford: Oxford UP, 1950).

The Witch of Edmonton, A Known True Story, Thomas Dekker, John Ford, and William Rowley, 1621, ed. Fredson Bowers, *The Dramatic Works of Thomas Dekker*, vol. 3 (Cambridge: Cambridge UP, 1958).

CHAPTER NINE

Transvestism in English and Japanese Theatres: a Comparative Study

Yoshiko Kawachi

In English Renaissance theatre there were no actresses. Boys played the roles of women, such as Portia, Rosalind, Viola, etc. at the Globe Theatre. In Japan, Kabuki actors called *onnagata* play the roles of women even today. In this paper, I wish to discuss the dynamics of transvestism in the theatre, comparing the English cultural tradition with the Japanese cultural tradition.

* * *

Leaving the Duke's court together with her cousin Celia and Touchstone, a fool, Rosalind makes up her mind to disguise herself as a shepherd, Ganymede, because she is afraid that a journey is too dangerous for a woman. She says:

> Were it not better,
> Because that I am more than common tall,
> That I did suit me all points like a man,
> A gallant curtal-axe upon my thigh,
> A boar-spear in my hand, and in my heart,
> Lie there what hidden woman's fear there will.
> We'll have a swashing and a martial outside,
> As many other mannish cowards have,
> That do outface it with their semblances.
> (*As You Like It*, I, iii, 113–21)

The purpose of her journey is to search for her father who was robbed of his dukedom by her uncle, Duke Frederick. He is so afraid that Rosalind, a virtuous and clever girl, will rob his daughter Celia of her name that he banishes her from his court. Celia, who sympathizes with Rosalind, resists her father and disguises herself as a shepherdess, Aliena. She says, 'Now go we in content, / To liberty, and not to banishment' (I, iii, 136–7). In this way Celia, Rosalind, and Touchstone go to the Forest of Arden, escaping from male hegemony and patriarchal power as well as the urban life.

The Forest of Arden is a timeless space, full of liberty, pastoralism and holiday humour. Northrop Frye says that the wood is 'the green world',[1] while C.L. Barber regards the wood as 'a region defined by an attitude of liberty from ordinary limitations, a festive place where the folly of romance can have its day'.[2] In this comedy almost all the scenes except Act I are laid in this forest. Therefore, the forest is a very important place.

What happens in the forest? This is a matter of concern for the audiences. In a word, it is a love game produced by a woman in male attire. Rosalind looks like a director and player of a play within a play. Her cross-dressing conceals her identity and makes it possible for her to be an actor-manager. Bernard Shaw says, 'The popularity of Rosalind is due to three main causes. First, she only speaks blank verse for a few minutes. Second, she only wears a skirt for a few minutes. ... Third, she makes love to the man instead of waiting for the man to make love to her.'[3] Rosalind lives 'in the skirts of the forest, like fringe upon a petticoat' (III, ii, 326–7) but she wears a doublet and hose, because she thinks that it 'ought to show itself courageous to petticoat' (II, iv, 6–7). She is so afraid of the gaps between her appearance and reality that she says to Celia, 'Dost thou think, though I am caparisoned like a man, I have a doublet and hose in my disposition?' (III, ii, 190–2).

Thus transvestism gives Rosalind a chance to be a person with a double personality. She is not herself; she is someone else; but someone else is her. The heroine, Rosalind/Ganymede, has an opportunity to change her personality freely as she likes it. Whenever she changes her personality, she obscures her gender. In this way, the sexual inversion by transvestism causes confusion in Shakespeare's romantic comedies. Portia in male attire goes to court and argues the law. Her cross-dressing makes it easier for her to move from Belmont, a Renaissance aristocratic and lyrical society, to Venice, a masculine, economic and realistic society. Portia succeeds in persuading Shylock, a Jew, of the importance of Christian mercy. She also succeeds in creating an imaginary cuckold of Bassanio. In *Twelfth Night*, Viola/Cesario complains that she cannot confess her love to Orsino, and she is at a loss what to do, when she is loved by Olivia.

> How will this fadge? My master loves her dearly,
> And I, poor monster, fond as much on him,
> And she, mistaken, seems to dote on me.
> What will become of this?
>
> (II, ii, 33–6)

In the Forest of Arden, Phoebe, a shepherdess, meets Rosalind/Ganymede, and she calls her/him, 'Sweet youth' (III, v, 65). She says:

> It is a pretty youth – not very pretty –
> But sure he's proud; and yet his pride becomes him.
> He'll make a proper man. The best thing in him
> Is his complexion; and faster than his tongue
> Did make offence, his eye did heal it up.

He is not very tall; yet for his years he's tall.
His leg is but so-so; and yet 'tis well.
There was a pretty redness in his lip,
A little riper and more lusty-red
Than that mixed in his cheek. 'Twas just the difference
Betwixt the constant red and mingled damask.

                                        (III, v, 114–24)

To Phoebe, Rosalind/Ganymede appears to be a graceful gallant, and Phoebe loves her/him. When Orlando sees Rosalind/Ganymede in the Forest of Arden, he calls her/him 'pretty youth' (III, ii, 325). Thus the characters except Celia believe that Rosalind is Ganymede and that she is a male, until the truth is revealed at the end of the play.

At the Duke's court, Orlando and Rosalind met and fell in love, but they each left the court. When they happen to meet again in the wood, Rosalind/Ganymede asks Orlando, 'What is't o'clock?' and Orlando answers, 'You should ask me what time o' day. There's no clock in the forest' (III, ii, 293–5). This means that in the wood there is no objective time measured by a watch.

Jan Kott says that the wood is a place where the people have a dream.[4] I think that the dream the people have in the Forest of Arden is that of sexual perversion caused by transvestism. The dream is also a love game between a Petrarchan lover and a pretty youth called Ganymede. In Greek myth, Ganymede was 'Jove's own page' (I, iii, 123). Therefore, love between Rosalind/Ganymede and Orlando appears more homosexual than heterosexual. Orlando never thinks that the youth is actually a woman. Rosalind/Ganymede suggests, 'I would cure you if you would but call me Rosalind and come every day to my cot, and woo me' (III, ii, 410–11). Orlando believes this word, and their love game starts.

When they meet next time, Rosalind/Ganymede says to Orlando, 'Come, woo me, woo me, for now I am in a holiday humour, and like enough to consent. What would you say to me now an I were your very, very Rosalind?' (IV, i, 64–7). Here Celia and the audience only know that Ganymede is Rosalind. Orlando keeps believing that Rosalind is Ganymede. It means that Orlando discourses with the boy playing the role of a woman. At last Orlando proposes to this *boy* in the *mock* marriage in which Celia plays a hedge priest.

Rosalind. You must begin, 'Will you, Orlando' –
Celia.   Go to. Will you, Orlando, have to wife this Rosalind?
Orlando. I will.
Rosalind. Ay, but when?
Orlando. Why now, as fast as she can marry us.
Rosalind. Then you must say, 'I take thee Rosalind, for wife.'
Orlando. I take thee, Rosalind, for wife.
Rosalind. I might ask you for your commission; but I do take thee, Orlando, for my husband.

                                        (IV, i, 121–31)

It is safe because this is not a real marriage. The real wedding is celebrated at the end of the play. However, it is noteworthy that this mock marriage as well as the wooing between a man and a boy must have made a great impact on the Elizabethan audiences, because in it they saw the wooing between a male player and a boy actor on the stage. I think that this was the eroticism peculiar to the Renaissance transvestite theatre.

Although there were already the professional actresses on the Continent in the sixteenth century, the public theatres in Renaissance England employed no women at all. It was not until the Restoration in 1660 that women were first seen on the London stage. On the Elizabethan and the Jacobean stage, 14- or 15-year-old boys, always of course before their voices changed, played the female roles. Hamlet speaks of the popularity of boy actors, 'little eyases' (II, ii, 339). He says, 'These are now the fashion, and so berattle the common stages' (II, ii, 341–2). Hamlet talks about the children of the private theatres, but the dramatic company of the public theatre hired boy actors to play the roles of women. All the attractive heroines of Shakespeare's romantic comedies were played by boy actors. A boy actor, who was 'not yet old enough for a man, nor young enough for a boy; as a squash is before 'tis a peacod, or a codling when 'tis almost an apple' (*Twelfth Night*, I, v, 151–3). Probably the audiences' response to the Renaissance transvestite theatre was different from that of the present-day audiences who look at both actors and actresses on the stage, because the body of a boy actor has a different impact on an audience from the body of an actress. The Renaissance audiences must have felt the special eroticism while looking at the love game between Rosalind/Ganymede and Orlando. A.M. Nagler reports about Goethe's experience when he saw male actors playing female roles.

> It was in Italy that Goethe recognized the theater as an institution dedicated to sensualism. In Rome, at a performance of Goldoni's *La Locandiera*, he was surprised to see men acting women's parts. After the initial strangeness had disappeared, Goethe experienced the unique aesthetic pleasure which Elizabethan playgoers must have felt when they watched boys playing Juliet and Cressida.[5]

Oscar Wilde also recognizes the unique beauty of the androgynous character of a boy actor playing the woman's part. He says:

> Of all the motives of dramatic curiosity used by our great playwrights, there is none more subtle or more fascinating than the ambiguity of the sexes. ... The very difference of sex between the player and the part he represented must also, as Professor Ward points out, have constituted 'one more demand upon the imaginative capacities of the spectators', and must have kept them from that over-realistic identification of the actor with his *rôle*, which is one of the weak points in modern theatrical criticism.[6]

Perhaps the male members of the audiences in the Renaissance transvestite theatre, in particular, must have enjoyed discovering the subtext of homosexuality in the love game between Rosalind/Ganymede and Orlando. It seems to me that Shakespeare described the homosexual love through the heterosexual love. His dramatic purpose must have been to let the audiences consider both kinds of love. Stephen Greenblatt writes, 'More than any of his contemporaries, Shakespeare discovered how to use the erotic power that the theater could appropriate, how to generate plots that would not block or ignore this power but draw it out, develop it, return it with interest, as it were, to the audience.'[7] Looking at the Renaissance transvestite stage, the audiences must have not only the dream of sexual perversion of sex change but also a chance to discover 'others' within themselves to undergo their mental metamorphosis. I think that this was one of the dramatic effects produced by the transvestite theatre. In a sense, Rosalind/Ganymede is a love therapist. She/he conjures not only Orlando but also the audiences.

*　*　*

In Act V, scene iv, Rosalind/Ganymede takes off the doublet and hose. In the masque, Rosalind in female attire says to Orlando, 'To you I give myself, for I am yours' (V, iv, 115). Then Orlando marries a beautiful and clever girl. This is a happy ending of Shakespeare's romantic comedy. But it is a little strange that the boy actor in female attire, who has been playing the role of Rosalind, appears on the stage to speak the Epilogue, in which he says:

> If I were a woman I would kiss as many of you as had beards that pleased me, complexions that liked me, and breaths that I defied not. And I am sure, as many as have good beards, or good faces, or sweet breaths will for my kind offer, when I make curtsy, bid me farewell.
>
> (Epilogue, 16–21)

The subjunctive mood of the first sentence is effectively used here, because it makes the audiences notice the boy actor. The Epilogue appealed especially to the male members of the audiences in English Renaissance theatre.

Philip Stubbes wrote, 'Everyone brings another homeward of their way very friendly, and in their secret conclaves they play sodomite or worse.'[8] The boy actor was sometimes regarded as the homosexual partner of an adult player. In Act I, scene i of *The Poetaster*, Ben Jonson wrote, 'What! shall I have my son a stager now? an enghle for players?'[9] According to Gerald Eades Bentley, a boy's father complained that his son would be hired by 'a company of lewd and dissolute mercenary players'.[10] The dramatic companies and the theatres in Renaissance period were not always healthy. Edmund Spenser wrote in *The Faerie Queene*, Book 4, Canto 3, stanza 37, 'Confusd with womens cries, and shouts of boyes, / Such as the troubled Theaters oftimes annoyes.'[11]

In those days, homosexuality was hated on the Continent, but it was rather generously accepted in England. We hear that Nicholas Udall, James I, Christopher Marlowe, and even Francis Bacon were homosexuals. John Marston satirizes homosexuality in his poem published in 1598.

> Behold at length in London streete he showes.
>
> ...

> How his clothes appeare
> Crost and recrost with lace, sure for some feare
> Least that some spirit with a tippet mace
> Should with a gastly show affright his face.
> His hat, himselfe, small crowne and huge great brim,
> Faire outward show, and little wit within.
> And all the band with feathers he doth fill,
> Which is a signe of a fantastick still,
> As sure as (some doe tell me) evermore
> A goate doth stand before a brothell dore.
> His clothes perfum'd, his fustie mouth is ayred,
> His chinne new swept, his very cheekes are glazed.
>   But ho! what Ganimede is that doth grace
> The gallants heeles? One who for two daies space
> Is closely hyred.[12]

While sodomy was regarded as an abominable crime, homosexual acts were not really prosecuted in Renaissance England. Stephen Orgel points out that the people did not fear homosexuality very much despite the objections of the Puritans.[13]

In his novel, *The Portrait of Mr. W. H.*, Oscar Wilde imagined that a boy actor named Willie Hughes was a dramatist's homosexual partner. Wilde wrote, 'Shakespeare found not merely a most delicate instrument for the presentation of his art, but the visible incarnation of his idea of beauty'[14] in the boy actor. This is a fiction and we do not know Shakespeare's *vita sexualis*, but Shakespeare, in his *Sonnet* 20, wrote about 'the master-mistress who steals men's eyes and women's souls amazeth'.

Concerning transvestism in the Renaissance theatre, Lisa Jardine explains,

> The boy player's female dress and behaviour kindle homosexual love in the male members of his audience. Or rather, he creates a kind of androgyny: for to the Renaissance, the sexuality associated with the effeminate boy – the 'female wanton boy' of stage cross-dressing – is that of Hermaphrodite.[15]

Hermaphrodite, a mixture of Hermes and Aphrodite, is a kind of monster. The androgynous characters such as Portia, Rosalind, and Viola are a kind of monster, too. Portia is an androgynous justice-figure in the court; Viola is a self-conscious and self-constricted female page throughout the play. When Rosalind becomes Ganymede, her gender is blurred. When Ganymede plays the role of Rosalind on the stage, his gender is more blurred. At last, when the boy actor in female attire speaks, 'If I were a woman', his gender is much more blurred. Thus the ambiguity of sex produces a dramatic confusion. Catherine Belsey asks a question, 'Who is speaking the Epilogue?' and answers, 'A male actor *and* a female character is speaking. ... Visually and aurally the actor does not insist on the femininity of Rosalind-as-Ganymede, but holds the issue unresolved, releasing for the audience the possibility of glimpsing a disruption of sexual difference.'[16] I think that the dramatist was strongly conscious of the boy actors when he wrote for the transvestite theatre.

Generally speaking, dress is a sign by which the people distinguish one sex from another. Therefore, in Deuteronomy in the Old Testament, cross-dressing is prohibited. Philip Stubbes, a Puritan, attacked cross-dressing sharply.

> Our Apparell was giuen vs as a signe distinctiue to discern betwixt sex and sex, & therfore one to weare the Apparel of another sex, is to participate with the same, and to adulterate the veritie of his owne kinde. Wherefore these Women may not improperly be called *Hermaphroditi*, that is, Monsters of bothe kindes, half women, half men.[17]

In 1620 James I issued a proclamation to admonish cross-dressing by women. For instance, Moll Cutpurse, a heroine of *The Roaring Girl* by Middleton and Dekker, wore a doublet and hose, had a sword, and smoked a pipe, according to the title-page of the printed text. Juliet Dusinberre points out that such a monster was fashionable since the 1580s and that this was a symptom of feminism.[18] From this viewpoint, Rosalind in male attire may be called the predecessor of Mary Wollstonecraft. In 1620 the anonymous pamphlets *Hic Mulier* and *Haec-Vir* were published, and both a masculine woman and a feminine man were criticised. In 1612, in *An Apology for Actors*, Thomas Heywood, however, defended boy actors' cross-dressing on the stage.

Thus cross-dressing was discussed, but it was sometimes regarded as a useful and effective means for women's social and political activity. Karen Newman says, 'The sexual symbolism of transvestism, the transgression of traditional gender roles and the figural transgression of heterosexual relations, ... all interrogate and reveal contradictions in the Elizabethan sex/gender system in which women were commodities.'[19] Jean E. Howard, however, says from the viewpoint of materialist feminism:

> I think that, often, female crossdressing on the stage is not a strong site of resistance to the period's patriarchal sex-gender system. Ironically, rather than blurring gender difference or challenging male domination and exploitation of women, female crossdressing often strengthens notions of difference by stressing what the disguised woman *cannot* do, or by stressing those feelings held to constitute a 'true' female subjectivity.[20]

Whether or not female cross-dressing was a vehicle for assuming power, it was a kind of dramatic convention.

In the Epilogue of *As You Like It*, the boy actor in female attire addresses to the women:

> My way is to conjure you; and I'll begin with the women. I charge you, O women, for the love you bear to men, to like as much of this play as please you.
> (Epilogue, 10–13)

Andrew Gurr says that there were many kinds of female audiences in the Renaissance theatre. Noble ladies and the daughters of the middle-class went to the theatre, but pickpockets, prostitutes and whores were also play-goers.[21] Probably some of them went to the theatre in order to get money or to sell themselves, as in those days the English theatre permitted men and women to sit altogether while theatres on the Continent prohibited the same. I think that the body of a boy actor must have given sexual pleasure or impulse to the female members of audiences.

Androgyny is a grotesque but beautiful monster. In Greece, Hermaphrodite was an ideal because the people thought that it had both masculinity and femininity. Therefore, I think that the audiences looking at a boy actor in female attire must have had an opportunity to reconsider the qualities and characteristics that made up femininity and masculinity. Peter Erickson says:

> This theatrical dimension reinforces the conservative effect of male androgyny within the play. ... In the boy-actor motif, woman is a metaphor for the male discovery of the feminine within himself, of those qualities suppressed by a masculinity strictly defined as aggressiveness.[22]

Transvestism itself is a performing art, and it has a dramatic effect. While looking at the transvestite stage, men and women may consider each role in their everyday life, and to rediscover their own identity. They will reconsider the sex/gender system in their society and the ideological meaning of the semiotics of dress.

The Renaissance transvestite theatre was a place where the binary opposition between a man and a woman was disrupted for a while. As a result, both sexes became free from any sexual limitations as well as religious, social and political power. In this sense, the Forest of Arden represents a *topos* of liberty. The love game between Rosalind/Ganymede and Orlando was produced at the Globe Theatre located in London's Liberties. Therefore, Celia's word, 'To liberty', was truly meaningful, because the audiences could feel free in that public theatre. Jean E. Howard points out, 'To go to the theatre was, in short, to be positioned at the crossroads of cultural change and contradiction.'[23] The title of this comedy, *As You Like It*, suggests the dramatist's message for the audiences to choose freely either being a man or a woman, or to enjoy either homosexuality or heterosexuality. Recently Jan Kott has written about the influence of the stage:

> The Forest of Arden is an initiation into eros. ... Desire and its disappointments, disguise and bodies in disguise, gender and illusions of gender are all intermingled and seem interchangeable. ... Shakespeare's Rosalind on the contemporary stage is accompanied by the shadows of all the Rosalinds who have disguised themselves as Ganymede – and by all the myths, all the obsessions, all the temptations of androgynous eros, all the ebb and flow of the ever-recurring past.[24]

*   *   *

Cross-dressing and gender impersonation are commonplace throughout history. In festivals and recreation, in particular, gender is masked and the conventional rules of society are reversed. Men are sometimes encouraged to behave like women. In Japan, there is a convention of transvestism, too, though it is not quite the same as that of English Renaissance theatre. In

Japanese traditional drama such as Noh and Kabuki, an actor plays the role of a woman. In Noh drama, the actor puts on a female mask, but in Kabuki, a professional actor called *onnagata* or *oyama* plays a female role. The word *onnagata* has two meanings, namely, 'a woman's form' and 'the woman side'. Kabuki is characterized by the *onnagata*. Recently actresses have begun appearing in Chinese traditional drama, Beijing opera; however, there are no actresses in Kabuki even today.

The word *Kabuki* comes from the verb *kabuku* meaning 'to tilt' or 'to lean'. In the Medieval Period, *kabuku* was 'to be heretic in the customs and manners'. Rogues, vagabonds or those who were indulging in eccentric behaviour such as cross-dressing or wearing strange hairstyles fell under this category. They were unorthodox, radical, but elegant and dandy. In the word *Kabuki*, *ka* means 'singing', *bu* means 'dancing', and *ku* means 'acting'. Therefore, the word *Kabuki* combines the three main arts. In early period, however, *ki* meant 'a *geisha* girl', because Kabuki was originally related to a dancing prostitute.

Kabuki dates from the beginning of the seventeenth century. Izumo no Okuni, who proclaimed herself a maiden in the service of Izumo Taisha shrine, performed a *nembutsu* dance (*nembutsu* means a prayer to Buddha) in Kyoto and acquired overwhelming popularity. Soon Noh and Kyōgen actors participated in this actress's troupe, and they became very popular because of its suggestive dance and comical skit in which, for example, a beautiful woman in male attire went to a prostitute's house. Therefore, people called this troupe *Yūjo Kabuki* (prostitute Kabuki) or *Onna Kabuki* (female Kabuki). This troupe performed Kabuki dance in Kyoto, Osaka, Edo and other cities. The *Onna Kabuki*, however, was prohibited in 1629 because it was corrupting public morals. From that year until the Meiji period, there were no actresses in the history of Japanese drama.

After the *Onna Kabuki* disappeared, the *Wakashū Kabuki*, which was mainly composed of boy actors, appeared on the stage. They danced, mimicked, and performed skits and acrobatics. They were effeminate enough to be the partners of homosexuality. As a result, their performances were prohibited in 1652. I find it very interesting that there were transvestite theatres evoking homosexuality among players and audiences in both Japan and England during the seventeenth century.

When the manager of the Kabuki company entreated the authority to reopen the theatre, only male actors were permitted to play. This is the beginning of the *Yarō Kabuki* (male Kabuki), which is considered to be the origin of today's Kabuki company. Still now the Kabuki company follows the feudal system, and the actor who plays the female role should always stand behind the actor who plays the male role. In addition, the *onnagata* cannot become the leader of the Kabuki company. Instead, *tateoyama*, the chief of the *onnagata*, supports the leader of the troupe.

The Kabuki company has a hereditary system, and regards the actor's experience very highly. Upon a famous actor's death, his son succeeds to his name, and he makes an announcement of his succession in the theatre. Whenever an actor succeeds to his predecessor's name, he bears higher responsibility and makes more efforts to become a great actor.

The Kabuki company has a system of *hanagata* (star). There are two kinds of stars of the *onnagata*; *jū no hanagata* (the weak star) who plays the role of a jealous woman, a prostitute, a *geisha* girl, etc., and *gō no hanagata* (the strong star) who plays the role of a beautiful but strong-minded woman. Each kind of star demonstrates his own ability as the *onnagata*, and he expresses the delicate feelings of a woman.

The *onnagata* is required to perform as an ideal Japanese woman who is virtuous, chaste, kind, beautiful, graceful and moralistic. Some of the actors chosen to be the *onnagata* act like women in everyday life in order to express womanliness as skilfully as possible. Ayame Yoshizawa, a famous *onnagata* in the seventeenth century, wrote *Ayamegusa*, a standard guide for actors who wanted to become the *onnagata*. In this book, he argued that the key to success was to live as a woman in everyday life.

Sometimes the *onnagata* can be a man who is 60 years old or older, and still can play the part of a 16-year-old girl on the stage. It is fundamentally unnatural and perverse that a man should play the role of a woman, but the *onnagata* tries to express the beauty of a woman artificially and artistically, however manly he is in real life. Unless a man lives and thinks as a woman, his inherent masculinity will unconsciously appear on the stage. Therefore, he behaves himself like a woman in everyday life. In addition, the *onnagata* should have sex appeal on the stage. Generally speaking, the seductive *onnagata* commands popularity in Kabuki theatre.

Usually the *onnagata* of the first rank is more beautiful and effeminate than a woman because he studies womanhood and possesses a special training to *become* a woman. His actions are so feminine that the audiences sometimes believe that he is a female. The *onnagata*, a treasure of Kabuki, is the acme of make-believe.

Kabuki plays are fully stylized performances. Men actors play the roles of women better than boy actors, because the former knows about sexuality better than the latter. The *onnagata* in Kabuki does not have the squeaky voice of the boy actor in English Renaissance theatre. I remember that a drama critic argued that Lady Macbeth is basically a man's role rather than a boy's role. In Japan, Tamasaburō Bandō, a famous *onnagata*, successfully played the role of Lady Macbeth a few years ago.

It is very interesting that transvestism is a phenomenon common in English Renaissance theatre and Japanese Kabuki theatre, but there are several differences between them. Jan Kott says:

> The boy actor must have been like the *onnagata* in the traditional Kabuki. In the Japanese theater the convention is never bared onstage or the illusion abruptly suspended. In Shakespeare's theater, however, at least on two occasions the convention is suddenly unveiled for a brief moment; dramatic illusion is transformed into 'theater in the theater', and as in Brecht's alienation effect theatrical time for

that moment becomes audience time, and the performer who represents the role is not the he, or, rather, the she, whose role is being played.[25]

I quite agree with Jan Kott's point of view. In Kabuki theatre the *onnagata* plays the female role from the beginning to the end. He speaks and acts as womanly as possible on the stage during the performance. The audiences enjoy seeing his transformation from a male to a female and appreciate his proficiency in acting.

Generally speaking, Kabuki theatre is not radical but conservative. It shuts the doors to the actresses and it is full of dramatic conventions. The story of a Kabuki play is not up-to-date, and the dramatists write about the feudal society or the tragic women suffering from male hegemony or patriarchal power. Anyway, the *kimono* is not as helpful for emulating feminism as a doublet and hose which Shakespeare's heroines wear. There are different cultural paradigms between Kabuki theatre and English Renaissance theatre.

One of the notable features of Kabuki theatre is the use of *hanamichi* (flower walkway) running along the left-hand wall of the auditorium to the stage at the level of the spectators' heads. Along this walkway the actors make their entrances and exits, or withdraw for an aside. When the actors pass through the *hanamichi*, the audiences feel that they have participated in the dramatic world. In this way, the *hanamichi* is a very useful piece of equipment for the close communication between the actors and the audiences.

In Kabuki, there is a technical term, *sekai*, which means 'the world' or 'the cosmos'. The *sekai* is the dramatic world including dramatic time, place, story, characters, and their names and actions. The Kabuki play takes its subject from many sources – history, myth, daily life, even from Noh drama, or from the puppet-theatre or *bunraku*. The idea of the *sekai* reminds me of Jaques's speech, 'All the world's a stage, / And all the men and women merely players' (*As You Like It*, II, vii, 139–40) or Hamlet's speech, 'the purpose of playing ... is to hold as 'twere the mirror up to nature' (III, ii, 20–2).

We find that the theatre, then and now, Occidental and Oriental, is the place of our metamorphosis as well as our entertainment. Drama tells us how to live and how to dream. The transvestite theatre makes it possible for us to change not only our ordinary life but also our personality. In *Orlando*, Virginia Woolf describes the beauty of androgyny.

> The sound of the trumpets died away and Orlando stood stark naked. No human being, since the world began, has ever looked more ravishing. His form combined in one the strength of a man and a woman's grace.[26]

This is what the audiences see in a transvestite performance.

Transvestism on the stage makes it easier for the players and the audiences to reconsider the sex/gender system and to discover 'others' in themselves. Such experience may have been common to the audiences in Shakespeare's theatre and in the Japanese theatre. The present-day audiences of Kabuki plays enjoy looking at transsexualism as well as transvestism on the stage just as the audiences in Shakespeare's day did.

NOTES

All quotations from Shakespeare's works are cited from *William Shakespeare: The Complete Works*, eds Stanley Wells and Gary Taylor (Oxford: Oxford University Press, 1986).

1.   Northrop Frye, *Anatomy of Criticism: Four Essays*, 3rd edn (Princeton: Princeton University Press, 1973), p. 182.
2.   C.L. Barber, *Shakespeare's Festive Comedy: A Study of Dramatic Form and its Relation to Social Custom*, 2nd edn (Princeton: Princeton University Press, 1972), p. 223.
3.   G.B. Shaw, 'Toujours Shakespear', in *Shakespeare's Critics: From Jonson to Auden: A Medley of Judgment*, eds A.M. Eastman and G.B. Harrison (Ann Arbor: The University of Michigan Press, 1964), p. 161.
4.   Jan Kott, *Shakespeare Our Contemporary*, trans. Boleslaw Taborski (New York: Doubleday, 1966), p. 342.
5.   A.M. Nagler, *A Source Book in Theatrical History* (New York: Dover Publications, Inc., 1952), p. 433.
6.   Oscar Wilde, *The Portrait of Mr. W. H.* (London: Methuen, 1958), pp. 52–3.
7.   Stephen Greenblatt, *Shakespearean Negotiations* (Berkeley: University of California Press, 1988), p. 88.
8.   Philip Stubbes, *The Anatomie of Abuses* (London: 1585), sig. L8ᵛ.
9.   *Ben Jonson: The Complete Plays*, ed. Felix E. Schelling (London: J.M. Dent and Sons, 1964), I, 237.
10. Gerald Eades Bentley, *The Profession of Dramatist in Shakespeare's Time, 1590–1642* (Princeton: Princeton University Press, 1971), p. 48.
11. *Spenser: Poetical Works*, eds J.C. Smith and E. de Selincourt, 22nd edn (London: Oxford University Press, 1966), p. 228.
12. *The Works of John Marston*, ed. J.O. Halliwell (London: John Russell Smith, 1856), III, 223–4.
13. Stephen Orgel, 'Nobody's Perfect: Or Why Did the English Stage Take Boys for Women?', *The South Atlantic Quarterly*, vol. 88, 1 (Winter 1989), 18.
14. Wilde, op. cit., p. 47.
15. Lisa Jardine, *Still Harping on Daughters: Women and Drama in the Age of Shakespeare* (New York: Columbia University Press, 1989), p. 17.
16. Catherine Belsey, 'Disrupting sexual difference: meaning and gender in the comedies', in *Alternative Shakespeares*, ed. John Drakakis (London: Methuen, 1985), pp. 181–3.
17. Stubbes, op. cit., sig. F5ᵛ.
18. Juliet Dusinberre, *Shakespeare and the Nature of Women*, 3rd edn (London: The Macmillan Press, 1985), pp. 232–3.
19. Karen Newman, 'Portia's Ring: Unruly Women and Structures of Exchange in *The Merchant of Venice*', *Shakespeare Quarterly*, XXXVIII (Spring 1987), 32.
20. Jean E. Howard, 'Crossdressing, The Theatre, and Gender Struggle in Early Modern England', *Shakespeare Quarterly*, XXXIX (Winter 1988), 439.
21. Andrew Gurr, *Playgoing in Shakespeare's London* (Cambridge: Cambridge University Press, 1988), pp. 59–64.
22. Peter Erickson, *Patriarchal Structures in Shakespeare's Drama* (Berkeley: University of California Press, 1985), p. 34.
23. Howard, op. cit., p. 440.

24. Jan Kott, *The Gender of Rosalind: Interpretations: Shakespeare, Büchner, Gautier*, trans. Jadwiga Kosicka and Mark Rosenzweig (Evanston: Northwestern University Press, 1992), pp. 21–37.
25. Ibid., p. 11.
26. Virginia Woolf, *Orlando: A Biography* (New York: Penguin Books, Inc., 1946), p. 85.

CHAPTER TEN

Entertaining the Offered Phallacy: Male Bed Tricks in Shakespeare

Raymond B. Waddington

Reflecting on the uneasy resolutions of *All's Well That Ends Well* and *Measure for Measure*, Anne Barton observes that 'the comedy ends by using the folk-motif of the bed-trick to force a clash between those opposing elements of fairytale and realism, of romance motivation and psychological realism' to achieve 'a kind of pyrrhic victory' by 'blatantly fictional' means.[1] This from an acute modern reader, trying to feel her way into comprehension of a now-dead convention. Yet the most celebrated of Renaissance bed tricks comes to us not from theatre but from life.

Arnaud du Tilh assumed the identity of Martin Guerre, carrying off a successful impersonation that convinced the villagers of Artigat, Martin's two sisters, and his wife, Bertrande de Rols. Eventually charged with being an imposter by Martin Guerre's uncle, whose motives seem to have been governed as much by financial self-interest and spite as by a concern for truth, Arnaud du Tilh was at the very point of vindication by the tribunal, who considered that, having slept with the defendant for more than three years, 'during which long interval it is not likely that the said de Rols would not have recognized him for a stranger if the prisoner had not been truly Martin Guerre'.[2] But, as the Criminal Chamber was ready to pass judgement in the case, a man with a wooden leg appeared at the Parlement and, in a *coup de théâtre* not unworthy of Shakespeare, announced that he was the real Martin Guerre. Even though Guerre expressed contemptuous disbelief at Bertrande's protestations that she had been deceived by du Tilh's role-playing, the justices, themselves witnesses to the uncanny power of the defendant's acting, sympathized to the extent of declaring legitimate the daughter resulting from this extended bed trick, 'deciding to accept Bertrande's claim that she thought she was having intercourse with Martin Guerre when the child was conceived'.[3] Almost a refraction of Diana's riddle in *All's Well* – 'one that's dead is quick' – the success of this bed trick, verified by impregnation, ordains the death of the husband's respect.

From the real-life bed trick, we may infer two characteristics consistent with the theatrical deceptions in Barton's realm of folk-tale, romance, and improbable fiction. First, the necessary complicity between participants, tricker and trickee. Despite the complicated ambivalences and outright contradictions of Bertrande's behaviour and testimony, it seems fair to conclude that Arnaud du Tilh could not have pulled off the impersonation without her collusion, however spontaneously decided upon; and that the remarkable stranger would have seemed to her a more attractive bed-partner than the coldly disapproving, sometimes impotent husband who had deserted her years before. Second, the inherent theatricality of the situation itself. The distinguished jurist Jean de Coras, who had been recorder of the court proceedings, published his *Arrest Memorable, du Parlement de Tolose, Contenant une histoire prodigieuse* (1561), a popular book that continued to engross him as much as it did his readers. To the 1565 edition he added the annotation, 'It was truly a tragedy for this fine peasant, all the more because the outcome was wretched, indeed fatal for him. Or at least it makes it hard to tell the difference between tragedy and comedy.'[4] Responding to this authorial cue, the printer of the 1572 edition elaborated:

> The Protasis, or opening, is joyous, pleasant and diverting, containing the ruses and cunning tricks of a false and supposed husband. The Epitasis, or middle part, uncertain and doubtful because of the disputes and contention during the trial. The Catastrophe or issue of the Morality is sad, pitiful and miserable.[5]

Although responsive to the drama of the story, the printer's description falsifies this by tidying it into a consecutive pattern, thereby missing the oxymoronic simultaneity that Coras, more accurately, projects. Any Shakespeare critic can sympathize with Coras's difficulty in telling the difference between tragedy and comedy; the label 'problem comedy' was invented to dodge it. Montaigne, having read the *Arrest Memorable*, marvels that Jean de Coras presumed to pass judgement on Arnaud du Tilh and muses on the lameness of human reason: 'Truth and falsehood are alike in face, similar in bearing, taste, and movement; we look upon them with the same eye.'[6]

Theatrical convention parts from life in one crucial respect, however; Natalie Davis argues that Bertrande de Rols's complicity in the bed trick should be understood as a form of liberation, a woman of hitherto limited resource empowering herself. On stage, however conscious or unconscious the complicity, the bed trick works to exalt its operator's authority and control while conversely denigrating the victim. Male bed tricks put down women.

The pattern is crystalline in the dramatic imagination of the next age. Otway's *The Orphan* (1680) imparts the travails of Monimia, ward to Acasto, whose two sons, Castalio and Polydore, are rivals for her affections. Castalio makes the mistake of concealing the depth of his attachment from the frankly lustful Polydore, denying that he would ever marry Monimia. Thus, when Polydore overhears Castalio making an apparent assignation with Monimia, he has no reason to suspect that the secretly married couple are planning to consummate their wedding vows; arranging to have Castalio detained, in the darkness and silence Polydore substitutes for his brother. The pleasure that he enjoys – 'posted / To more advantage on a pleasant hill / Of springing joy, and everlasting sweetness' (IV, 382–4) – is succeeded by horror at the primal offence:

> ... thus let's go together,
> Full of our guilt, distracted where to roam,
> Like the first wretched pair expelled their paradise.
> Let's find some place where adders nest in winter,
> Loathsome and venomous; where poisons hang
> Like gums against the walls, where witches meet
> By night, and feed upon some pampered imp,
> Fat with the blood of babes. There we'll inhabit. ...
> (IV, 450–7)[7]

Polydore provokes a quarrel with Castalio and runs on his brother's sword; Castalio stabs himself; Monimia, concurring with her brother-in-law's assessment of her guilt, drinks poison, apologizes to her husband for her 'pollution' and betrayal, and dies: 'Tis very dark: good night.'

Rather chillingly, the brothers, while convinced that she is tainted, bear Monimia no ill will for her unwitting transgression; that surfaces in Restoration comedy. *The Plain Dealer* (1677) depicts the situation of Manly, who trusts only two mortals, his mistress Olivia and his friend Vernish. Returning from an unfortunate expedition in the Dutch War, Manly is rebuffed by Olivia, who is attracted only to his 'little volunteer', the disguised Fidelia. Through Fidelia's surrogate courtship, Manly discovers that Olivia is married secretly (to Vernish it eventually emerges), has always despised him (not without reason) as a boorish lout, and has pretended to love him only to obtain his jewels (which she refuses to return). Convinced of Olivia's duplicity, Manly commands Fidelia to arrange an assignation at which he will substitute for the volunteer, assuring Fidelia that he no longer loves Olivia but must revenge himself on her honour. Fidelia, who is endearingly innocent of worldly ways, obeys, protesting, 'But are you sure 'tis revenge that makes you do this? How can it be?' (IV, ii, 286–7).[8] The revenge is so satisfactory – 'Thou wouldst laugh if thou knewest but all the circumstances of my having her' (V, ii, 154–5), he assures Vernish – that he arranges a repeat performance with an audience to interrupt them. Manly worries that Olivia 'hast impudence enough to ... make revenge itself impotent, hinder me from making thee yet more infamous, if it can be' (V, iii, 15–17). But, although the second encounter does not reach sexual consummation, his revenge is potent enough; Manly publicly humiliates Olivia: 'Here, madam, I never yet left my wench unpaid' (V, iii, 125). In this play 'Manly' behaviour is that which degrades a woman; and Fidelia's fidelity is sorely tested through the humiliations that she, too, endures – the unwanted, amorous attentions of both Olivia and Vernish and the necessity of becoming Manly's pander. She earns Manly's love by her successful impersonation of a male.

The Restoration taste for male bed tricks betrays a sensibility different from that of the earlier dramatists, with whom – when they occur at all – there is an element of sheer sensationalism or of legerdemain qualitatively distinct from the plausible degradations conceived by their successors. Samuel Harding's *Sicily and Naples* (1640) hinges on a double bed trick: on Calantha's wedding night, she substitutes Felicia, who is pregnant by the bridegroom, Ferrando, little knowing that in a simultaneous bed trick Zisco has been employed to ravish and murder Calantha. On completing his assignment, Zisco discovers that his victim is actually Felicia; and, in horror, unmasks as Frederico, Felicia's brother.[9] Finding in this farrago any concerted motive other than shameless exploitation is difficult, although it does make more comprehensible the Puritans' drive to close the theatres.

Far more seriously intended, *The Widow's Tears* (ca 1605), Chapman's riposte to *Measure for Measure*, rescripts his Petronian source, the Widow of Ephesis story, with elegantly chiselled cynicism about human nature. Whereas Petronius has his mourning widow seduced by a soldier in her late husband's tomb, here the disguised Lysander cuckolds himself, seducing his mourning wife, Cynthia. His complacent assurance of his wife's virtue shaken by his brother Tharsalio's crowing confidence that all women are fallible, Lysander determines to test Cynthia's vow of constancy by faking his own death and wooing her in another identity. In his humourless, Baconian experimentalism, Lysander reveals a spiritual kinship with the priggish virtuoso Alsemero, whose vials, potions and virginity tests set him up for the deception of another bed trick in *The Changeling*. Cynthia holds firm to her widow's vows, earning even Tharsalio's grudging admiration, until, worn down by her five days' fast and the blandishments of her waiting woman, she finally succumbs to the persuasions of the disguised Lysander.

Appalled by his own success, Lysander just manages to escape the final humiliation: 'This mirror of nuptial chastity, this votress of widow-constancy, to change her faith, exchange kisses, embraces, with a stranger, and, but my shame withstood, to give the utmost earnest of her love to an eight-penny sentinel; in effect, to prostitute herself upon her husband's coffin!' (V, ii, 39–44).[10] But, of course, as with his pretended death, Cynthia's offences are only imaginary, her virtue intact; Chapman frames Lysander's obsessive, self-destructive curiosity with allusions to the myth of Actaeon and Diana. Jackson Cope observes, 'His happiness has been killed by an adultery which does not exist any more than the corpse exists in the coffin. He wears only the horns of a would-be self-cuckold who has not even succeeded in this except in spirit.'[11] As Cynthia is pleased to inform her husband, she is the 'Ill-destined wife of a transformed monster, / Who, to assure himself of what he knew, / Hath lost the shape of man!' (V, v, 82–4). The offences committed are, like the missing body, non-existent, 'A mere blandation, a *deceptio visus*' (V, v, 154); appropriately, the concluding line by the peacemaker Tharsalio ironically emphasizes the human capacity for self-deception: 'And think you have the only constant wife' (V, v, 340). Unlike the consummated male bed tricks of his Restoration successors,

Chapman's avoids dishonouring the female victim – Cynthia is the most sympathetically presented of the main characters – while, like Otway's, having the plot rebound on its perpetrator's head.

When Shakespeare's mind runs to male bed tricks, he thinks of twins; and, as with Chapman, there is an element of obliquity, puzzle, and *deceptio visus*. In *The Comedy of Errors* Antipholus of Syracuse determines to 'entertain the [offer'd] fallacy' (II, ii, 186); but we are to understand that the entertainment consists only of his brother's board, not his bed.[12] The more intimate communion is displaced to his servant Dromio, who is terrified by the demands of Luce-Nel-Dowsabell, 'one that claims me, one that haunts me, one that will have me' (III, ii, 82–3). Amused by the 'beastly' demands of Luce, Antipholus puts Dromio through a catechism of anatomical–geographical analogy, an erotic topos most familiar from Donne's Elegy XIX, 'On Going to Bed'. But Dromio is no conquistador or new-world colonist. 'Where stood Belgia, the Netherlands?' 'O, sir, I did not look so low' (III, ii, 138–9). Although we appreciate Dromio's last-act relief that 'She now shall be my sister, not my wife' (V, i, 417), we are not meant to know just what having him 'as a beast' did entail.

Similarly elusive is the bed trick in *Twelfth Night*. Sebastian, mistaken by Olivia for Viola–Cesario, agrees to be ruled by her, vanishes into her house, and, as is later attested by the priest, plights troth to her. We do not know for certain but might infer that the newly betrothed couple occupy themselves during the time following the ceremony in the same manner as did Claudio and Juliet in *Measure for Measure*. When Olivia, frustrated by Cesario's denial of the marriage, commands the priest to unfold what he knows, 'though lately we intended / To keep in darkness what occasion now / Reveals' (V, i, 152–4), she establishes an associative link with the intervening dramatic episode, Malvolio's imprisonment in the dark house of ignorance, a victim of his solipsistic delusions about love and social mobility. If Olivia does bed her espoused in the belief that he is Cesario, the action involves illusion, not harm, with nature correcting the bias of artifice resulting from Viola's deception (V, i, 259–63).

In both instances, whether countess or cook, love or lust, feminine aggressiveness seizes on the wrong half in a set of twins. The comedy, and the ultimate harmlessness, is twofold, lying equally in the reversal of gender stereotypes, dominant women and yielding men, and in belying the romantic myth of the unique love object, convulsively insisting on duplication where only singularity can be perceived – insisting on, as Bob and Ray once titled it, 'The Two and Only'. Yet, in their appeal to the 'reality' of biological twinning, these comedies retain a grain of real-world misogyny by mocking, however good-naturedly, female assertiveness.[13]

Some plays obtain a greater imaginative freedom by reversing the modality, presenting a psychic twinning in the face of physical distinction. The bed trick in *Much Ado* is a *deceptio visus* in more than one sense: Margaret both is not and is Hero, so Borachio is not and is Claudio. Borachio contrives the plot:

... to see me at her chamber-window, hear me call Margaret Hero, hear Margaret term me Claudio; and bring them to see this the very night before the intended wedding – for in the mean time I will so fashion the matter that Hero shall be absent – and there shall appear such seeming truth of Hero's disloyalty, that jealousy shall be call'd assurance. ...

(II, ii, 42–9)

and springs it, 'court[ing] Margaret in Hero's garments' (V, i, 238) and wooing her 'by the name of Hero' (III, iv, 146). As the deformed thief who fashions what he will, stealing and altering reputations, Borachio produces a demonic parody of the benevolent comedic action, the refashioning of the perceptions, the 'seeming truth' that Beatrice and Benedick have of each other. Like Don Pedro, he has wooed 'Hero' in Claudio's name; similarly his extenuation of Margaret's character – she 'always hath been just and virtuous / In any thing that I do know by her' (V, ii, 302–3) – seems to mimic Claudio's shifting and over-positive assessments of Hero's worth, the 'drunken' and rudderless aspect of Claudio's perception. Margaret's character, in fact, is one of the minor puzzles of the play. It cannot be only to a late twentieth-century audience that her willingness to receive her lover in her mistress's underwear and enact the postures of love by an assumed name seems either selfless to a fault or sexually bizarre. Even to the dimmest of ladies-in-waiting it must be apparent that this charade at this of all times rudely degrades the impending ceremony. Don John urges, 'Go but with me to-night, you shall see her chamber-window ent'red, even the night before her wedding-day' (III, ii, 112–14). Putting aside psychosexual speculations, Margaret's behaviour is difficult to reconcile with the 'just and virtuous', except insofar as her malleability, passiveness and suggestibility shadow those frequently remarked qualities in her mistress. Borachio and Margaret impersonate aspects of Claudio and Hero, elements that must be distanced, recognized, and repudiated before their union can be whole, their marriage a forecast of happiness.

Cymbeline reprises the *Much Ado* situation of the male protagonist tricked into accepting the 'evidence' of an imagined sexual betrayal and expressing his rage by imagining the death of the heroine. Whereas Hero apparently is killed by Claudio's denunciation, Posthumus believes that Imogen has been murdered by his command. But *Cymbeline* ventures even further into the territory of psychic 'twinning' or doubling; Posthumus has not just one but two secret sharers in Cloten and Iachimo, who reveal to us the things he would rather not know about himself. 'It could be said that *Cymbeline* involves the realization of double images', Geoffrey Hill has postulated; and he illuminates the 'natural and partly unconscious collusion between the deceived and the deceiver' through Bacon's description of the vice that

... brancheth itself into two sorts; delight in deceiving, and aptness to be deceived, imposture and credulity; which, although they appear to be of a diverse nature, the one seeming to proceed of cunning, and the other of simplicity, yet certainly they do for the most part concur ... (*Advancement of Learning*).[14]

In this symbiosis of victor and victim, the complicity of deceiver and deceived, Shakespeare finds a dramatic agon to exemplify the warring impulses within the individual psyche. The bed trick itself, daringly conceived as coitus interruptus, is suspended over two acts and represented in two of the most spectacular and hauntingly evocative scenes that he created.[15]

The alacrity with which the banished Posthumus sets himself up for a fall in the wager on Imogen's chastity contrasts jarringly with the opening scene's extravagant praise of his character, so much so that it is explained away as the survival of an earlier convention or as the imperfect assimilation of disparate sources.[16] But, in performance if not in the study, his behaviour in Rome – no more noble than that of the Count of Rossillion in Florence – has obvious affinities with Cloten's braggadocio and with Iachimo's confident egotism.[17] Suggestively, both of Posthumus's doppelgängers assault Imogen's chastity on the same night, Cloten from without and Iachimo from within. Complementing Iachimo's penetration of Imogen's bedchamber, the aubade performed by Cloten's musicians declaredly has the same purpose: 'Come on, tune. If you can penetrate her with your fingering, so' (II, iii, 14–15). Iachimo penetrates Imogen's defences by the trick of the treasure chest, in which she rightly believes 'My lord hath interest' (I, vi, 195), that she offers to keep in her chamber. The visual image of the 'trunk' in her bedchamber, the product of Iachimo's 'Italian brain', would be that of a cassone, the bridal chest commissioned by her husband-to-be which became bedroom furniture after the wedding.[18] The erotic and mythological motifs with which cassoni were decorated here are displaced to the bedchamber itself, with its tapestry of Cleopatra meeting Mark Antony at Cydnus, the chimney-piece of Diana bathing, the golden cherubim and winking cupids (II, iv, 66–91).[19] Since cassoni invariably came in pairs and exclusively were used as furniture for married couples, the image both affirms Imogen's marital status and suggests its vulnerability; the companion chest, like Posthumus himself, is missing. As Iachimo's comparison of himself to Tarquin and Imogen's bedtime reading make clear, her honour as a married woman is particularly at stake.[20]

But the violation of Imogen involves more than her reputation. Posthumus is a Leontes who creates his own Polixenes; Iachimo can penetrate the sanctity of Imogen's chamber only with Posthumus's complicity. Emerging from the bridal chest (a visual action not without its own sexual symbolism), Iachimo's unerring choice of convincing evidence reveals his understanding of his co-conspirator's mind:

> On her left breast
> A mole cinque-spotted, like the crimson drops
> I' th' bottom of a cowslip. Here's a voucher,
> Stronger than ever law could make; this secret
> Will force him think I have pick'd the lock and ta'en
> The treasure of her honor.
>
> (II, ii, 37–42)

Posthumus does indeed conclude that Imogen has opened her chaste treasure to this unmastered importunity,[21] and his soliloquy exposes a festering sexual imagination worthy of Othello:

> Me of my lawful pleasure she restrain'd.
> And pray'd me oft forbearance; did it with
> A pudency so rosy the sweet view on't
> Might well have warm'd old Saturn; that I thought her
> As chaste as unsunn'd snow. O, all the devils!
> This yellow Jachimo, in an hour − was't not? −
> Or less − at first? Perchance he spoke not, but
> Like a full-acorn'd boar, a German [one],
> Cried 'O!' and mounted ...
>
> (II, v, 9−17)

As with the suddenness of Leontes's conviction of betrayal in which the fuel is his embittered recollection of Hermione's long resistance in courtship, so here the phantasy of an instantaneous coupling − the grunting Iachimo, a boar in rut, simply mounting speechlessly the receptive Imogen − generates compensatively from the grievance of rejection. Since Imogen and Posthumus seem not to have concealed their marriage from Cymbeline, it is reasonable to assume that the banishment followed hard on the ceremony. Posthumus falsifies his recollection. If Imogen 'pray'd [him] oft forbearance', she must have done so in their courtship, not depriving him of a 'lawful pleasure' after the very recent marriage.[22] Everything about these two proclaims that they know each other as little as do Claudio and Hero.

Iachimo removes the cover from the cistern of Posthumus's sexual imagination; and the grossness of what emerges, that ruttish German boar, attests to his kinship with Cloten. That kinship is exposed in the second nightmare scene, the completion of the bed trick. In both scenes Imogen has fallen into a heavy sleep, the first induced by three hours of Ovid and the second by the queen's drug. She is so still as to make Iachimo think of death (II, ii, 31−3); and Belarius, Guiderius and Arviragus actually believe that she is dead. In the second scene Imogen fancies that she is asleep in bed (IV, ii, 294−5); in the first she is in her bed. The crucial difference is that the second time she awakens:

> A headless man? The garments of Posthumus?
> I know the shape of's leg; this is his hand,
> His foot Mercurial, his Martial thigh,
> The brawns of Hercules, but his Jovial face −
> Murther in heaven? How? 'Tis gone.
>
> (IV, ii, 308−12)

'A headless man' is not a bad description of Posthumus at this point in the play; and the wakening dream that Imogen experiences is his as well. By awakening, Imogen reverses her role from the earlier scene, becoming Iachimo to Cloten's Imogen. Like Iachimo, she is now the intruder on another's death-like stillness; like Iachimo, she passionately catalogues the beauties of that other's body. Whereas Iachimo had kissed the sleeper's ruby-tipped breast (II, v, 136–8), Imogen embraces passionately the headless corpse. Michael Taylor has commented:

> When Imogen clutches the decapitated body to her, daubs herself with its blood, and falls into an exhausted, dreamless sleep – the sleep of an emotional satiety – the coital sequence suggested by these responses supplies an equivocal, parodic answer to the earnest prayer of Guiderius and Arviragus: 'Quiet consummation have, / And renowned be thy grave' (IV, ii, 280–1).[23]

This overtone of sexual aggressiveness in an active, dominant Imogen embodies the nightmare imaginings loosed through Posthumus's acceptance of Iachimo's pretended bed trick, that belief as much the product of his fear of Imogen's sexuality as was his authorization of Iachimo's attempt. Imogen believes that she is a Briton Juliet, awakening from a drug-induced, death-like sleep beside her husband-lover's body, and the final, erotic oblivion in his arms is a consummation devoutly to be wished. Both images, of course, are illusory; Cloten is not Posthumus, nor is Imogen a female Iachimo.

Shakespeare has given us the ghostlier demarcations of a double bed trick with both substitutions as insubstantial as Iachimo's pretended conquest. Michael Taylor dwells on the 'nightmare degradation', the 'humiliation', the 'literal and symbolic besmirching' that Imogen is forced to endure in embracing Cloten's mutilated corpse.[24] But the humiliation, and the discomfort it engenders is something of which only the audience is conscious; Imogen does not become aware of the substitution until after her joyous reunion with Posthumus. Only retrospectively does she learn Montaigne's lesson, that she has looked on truth and falsehood with the same eye. By this time Posthumus already has 'disrobe[d himself] / Of these Italian weeds and suit[ed him]self / As does a British peasant' (V, i, 22–4), re-established his nobility, and acknowledged his fault. The most obvious meaning of his name is that of a man reborn after death.[25]

Considering the action as a spectrum of possibilities between the 'realistic' or 'naturalistic' on one end and the symbolic or emblematic at the other, it is evident that Shakespeare engages most fully with the conventions of the male bed trick at the latter point, the farthest from Wycherley. The single exception in the Shakespeare canon of the consummated male bed trick in *The Two Noble Kinsmen* itself operates at such a remove from the Restoration norm that it helps illuminate the strategy of the symbolic tricks.[26] Conceiving a passion for the imprisoned Palamon, the Jailer's Daughter releases him and, consumed by guilt and the loss of her love object, succumbs to madness. The Doctor, who recognizes the sexual frustration underlying her illness, cures her by having her devoted Wooer impersonate Palamon, even in the act of love-making. Here, untypically, the instigator of the trick is not the consummator; both male agents are benevolently motivated, the Doctor by professional concern and the Wooer by affection, rendering the deception harmless, positive and eventually moral.[27] By the end of the play, the Jailer's Daughter is 'well restor'd, / And to be married shortly' (V, iv, 27–8).

That the symbolic tricks are illusory, with no actual sexual violation of the woman, goes even farther to ameliorate the usual misogyny of the male bed trick; Hero and Imogen suffer a temporary loss of reputation, not a permanent awareness of rape. In this transformation, the male trick becomes one in purpose with its sororal complement, the benevolent, female bed trick.[28] As well as fully exploiting both the theatricality and the element of complicity between deceiver and deceived that are characteristic of the trick, Shakespeare's modification permits the deceived women to escape the category of victims. Rather than undergoing the small deaths of sexual climax, Hero and Imogen deceive their deceivers by going underground and pretending to be dead, thereby regaining some control over themselves and authority over the men they love. For them, as for Bertrande de Rols, the bed trick is a means to liberation. The life of theatre and the theatre of life here enact the same meaning.

NOTES

1.   *The Riverside Shakespeare*, ed. G.B. Evans *et al.* (Boston: Houghton Mifflin, 1974), p. 502. The plays will be quoted from this text.

2.   Translation quoted from Natalie Zemon Davis, *The Return of Martin Guerre* (Cambridge, MA, and London: Harvard Univ. Press, 1983), p. 79. For the parallel instance of an actual, female bed trick, see Pedro Mexia, *The foreste or Collection of Histories*, trans. Thomas Fortescue (1571), Part III, Chapter 13, 'Of a pretie guile practised by a virtuous and good Queene, towards her husbande, by meanes whereof Iames Kyng of Aragon was begotten, and of his birthe, and death' (pp. 138v–139). I am indebted to Winfried Schleiner for this example.

3.   Davis, p. 89.

4.   Davis, p. 111.

5.   Davis, pp. 111–12.

6.   *The Complete Essays of Montaigne*, trans. Donald M. Frame (Stanford: Stanford Univ. Press, 1958), p. 785. Davis, pp. 118–22, makes the appropriate caveat: Coras's book reveals an uncertainty as deep as Montaigne's own.

7.   Thomas Otway, *The Orphan*, ed. Aline Mackenzie Taylor (Lincoln: Univ. of Nebraska Press, 1976).

8.   William Wycherley, *The Plain Dealer*, ed. Leo Hughes (Lincoln: Univ. of Nebraska, 1967).

9.   For a full plot summary, see William R. Bowden's helpful study, 'The Bed Trick, 1603–1642: Its Mechanics, Ethics, and Effects', *Shakespeare Studies*, 5 (1969), 112–23. Writing a quarter-century ago, Bowden does not think to differentiate male and female substitutions for commentary; and, despite his minority evidence, tends to treat them all as female: 'The basic bed trick formula is essentially irreducible, since, by definition, the bed trick must involve the victim, the person he thinks he is sleeping with, and the person he is actually sleeping with' (p. 113). In contrast, see Marliss C. Desens, *The Bed-Trick in English Renaissance Drama: Explorations in Gender, Sexuality, and Power* (Newark: Univ. of Delaware Press / London: Associated University Presses, 1994).

10. Quoted from *Drama of the English Renaissance II: The Stuart Period*, ed. Russell A. Fraser and Norman Rabkin (New York: Macmillan, 1976).

11. Cope, *The Theater and the Dream: From Metaphor to Form in Renaissance Drama* (Baltimore: Johns Hopkins Univ. Press, 1973), pp. 55–75; quotation, p. 69.

12. On the implications of meals, missed and shared, in this play, see Joseph Candido, 'Dining Out in Ephesus: Food in *The Comedy of Errors*', *Studies in English Literature*, 30 (1990), 217–41.

13. I owe this point to Helen Ostovich.

14. Geoffrey Hill, '"The True Conduct of Human Judgment": Some Observations on *Cymbeline*', in *The Lords of Limit* (New York: Oxford Univ. Press, 1984), pp. 55–66; quotations, pp. 57, 60. On the doubling of Posthumus and Cloten, see particularly Homer D. Swander, '*Cymbeline* and the "Blameless Hero"', *ELH*, 31 (1964), 259–70; and '*Cymbeline*: Religious Idea and Dramatic Design', in *Pacific Coast Studies in Shakespeare*, ed. Waldo F. McNeir and Thelma N. Greenfield (Eugene, Oregon, 1966), pp. 248–62. See p. 251 of the latter for the argument that one actor should take both parts. For the similarities between Posthumus and Iachimo, see Hill, pp. 58–9.

15. In *Shakespeare's Other Language* (New York and London: Methuen, 1987), Ruth Nevo makes a similar argument: 'Imogen is the victim, twice, of a species of (unconsummated) bed-trick, once with a slanderer sent by her husband to test her, and once with the dead body of her rejected suitor whom she takes to be her husband ...' (p. 63).

16. See, for example, Hallett Smith in *The Riverside Shakespeare*, p. 1518, and Robert M. Adams, *Shakespeare: The Four Romances* (New York and London: Norton, 1989), pp. 64–5.

17. Nevo comments, 'They are clearly antithetical doubles. ... significantly related to Posthumus himself' (p. 73).

18. On cassoni, see Diane Hughes, 'Representing the Family: Portraits and Purposes in Early Modern Italy', *Journal of Interdisciplinary History*, 17 (1986), 7–38; and Rona Goffen, 'Renaissance Dreams', *Renaissance Quarterly*, 40 (1987), 700–1 and n. 30.

19. For a rather heavy-handed iconographic commentary on the bedchamber, see Peggy Muñoz Simonds, *Myth, Emblem, and Music in Shakespeare's* Cymbeline: *An Iconographic Reconstruction* (Newark: Univ. of Delaware Press, 1992), pp. 95–135.

20. For the implications of these allusions, see Ann Thompson, 'Philomel in "Titus Andronicus" and "Cymbeline"', *Shakespeare Survey*, 31 (1978), 23–32; Coppélia Kahn, 'The Rape in Shakespeare's *Lucrece*', *Shakespeare Studies*, 9 (1976), 45–72; and Simonds, pp. 70–5.

21. Given the Italianate brainwork here, it may be relevant to recall John Florio's definition of *chiavare*: 'to locke with a key. ... but now a daies abusively used for Fottere'. See Florio, *Queen Anna's New World of Words, 1611* (Menston: Scolar Press, 1968), s.v. *chiavare*. For the English parallel, see Robert Herrick, 'Corinna's Going a Maying', lines 55–6: 'Many a jest told of the keys betraying / This night, and locks picked, yet we're not a Maying.'

22. Nevo, p. 70, plausibly assumes that the marriage was not consummated before their enforced separation.

23. Taylor, 'The Pastoral Reckoning in "Cymbeline"', *Shakespeare Survey*, 36 (1983), 99.

24. Taylor, pp. 97, 98, 99.

25. See Douglas L. Peterson, *Time, Tide and Tempest: A Study of Shakespeare's Romances* (San Marino, CA: Huntington Library, 1973), p. 111.

26. I do not wish to enter into the argument over who wrote what in the collaboration with Fletcher. I would maintain, however, that a successful collaboration would seem to require a shared conceptualization. For a thorough review

of the question by the play's most recent editor, see Eugene M. Waith, *The Two Noble Kinsmen*, The Oxford Shakespeare (Oxford: Clarendon Press, 1989), pp. 4–23, 62–5. Waith, who tentatively credits Shakespeare with three scenes in the subplot, observes, 'The work of the two playwrights is tightly interlaced' (p. 62), but concludes that 'it seems reasonable to guess that Shakespeare's was the vision that determined the meaning and the predominant tone' (p. 63).

27. Hallett Smith has commented, 'The extended sentimentality of the daughter's situation and the coarseness of the doctor's suggested cure by seduction are far more characteristic of Fletcher than of Shakespeare' (*Riverside Shakespeare*, p. 1640). My examination of gender attitudes in Shakespeare's bed tricks would point to the opposite conclusion. For a perceptive and sympathetic discussion of the Jailer's Daughter, see Mary Beth Rose, *The Expense of Spirit: Love and Sexuality in English Renaissance Drama* (Ithaca: Cornell Univ. Press, 1988), pp. 224–8. The Doctor's behaviour has been placed in its historical context by Winfried Schleiner, 'Ethical Problems of the Lie that Heals in Renaissance Literature', in *Eros and Anteros: The Medical Traditions of Love in the Renaissance*, ed. D.A. Beecher and Massimo Ciavolella (Ottawa: Dovehouse, 1992), pp. 167–74.

28. Bowden finds that 'the bed trick is a morally neutral device used by the dramatists in an essentially moral context' (p. 118). Peggy Muñoz Simonds interestingly relates Shakespeare's handling of female bed tricks to providential interpretation of a biblical locus classicus, the episode of Tamar and Judah in Genesis 38. See 'Overlooked Sources of the Bed Trick', *Shakespeare Quarterly*, 34 (1983), 433–4; and 'Sacred and Sexual Motifs in *All's Well That Ends Well*', *Renaissance Quarterly*, 42 (1989), 55–9. In the latter essay, p. 36, n. 4, she attributes gender bias to 'a long line of male critics' who object to Helena's behaviour.

PART THREE

Shakespeare and Staging

CHAPTER ELEVEN

'All … trouble, wonder, and amazement': Shakespeare's *The Tempest* and the New Courtly Hieroglyphics

John G. Demaray

In those years just before and after *The Tempest* was composed and twice presented at court, first on 'Hollowmas nyght' in 1611 and then for a royal marriage in 1613, certain seventeenth-century 'moderne' theatrical writers spoke out emphatically against the tyranny of an excessive reliance upon classical themes and images.[1] These were reformist authors of court masques, writers who in part rejected the classicism of Ben Jonson and who sought to produce new imaginative works suitable for specific social occasions and known individual performers. These authors favoured original inventions, unique images, and literary components functioning in harmony with a novel 'hinge'. And they defined a kind of theatrical work to which Shakespeare, making central use of masque elements in what appears to be his final work, gave expression in *The Tempest*.

Shakespeare's play has long been recognized as embodying a range of traditional classical and Renaissance theatrical conventions and characters. The allusions to Dido and Carthage in Act II, i; the appearance of Ariel like a harpy in Act III, iii; and the wide emphasis upon themes of 'storm' and 'wandering' have been revealed as reflecting motifs in Virgil's *Aeneid*.[2] The familiar classical dieties in the fourth-act betrothal masque – in which Juno, Ceres and Iris appear as characters, and Venus and Cupid are mentioned – are immediately identifiable as character-types of a kind Ben Jonson introduced into court masques such as *Hymenaei* (1606), *The Haddington Masque* (1608), and *Love freed from Ignorance* (1611).[3] Vestiges of a classical Latin-play structure modelled on the dramas of Terence have been found as components of form in Shakespeare's work.[4] And throughout the play, dramatic confrontations between Prospero and his enemies culminate in a traditional fifth-act 'comic catastrophe' of reconciliation, a reconciliation growing in part from the Magus's inner transformation from fury to nobler reason and virtue. But because the play is largely centred upon a Magus who

135

uses magic to control events, and because conflicts are therefore rendered through imaginative antic and harmonious masque-like visionary episodes as well as through dramatic confrontations, *The Tempest* can be seen as also influenced by overlooked early masque theories, different from those of classicist Ben Jonson, that give priority to fancy over reason and that stress unique symbolism.

It should be recalled that in Act IV of *The Tempest* Prospero announces that the betrothal masque is an enactment, not of his reason, but of his 'present fancies' (121) – notably fancies of 'virtue' as distinguished from his contrasting fancies of 'furie' that are in part represented in antic spectacles (V, i, 26–8).[5] For at climactic points in the main and subplots, *The Tempest* contains six of Prospero's magical, fanciful 'spectacles of strangeness' that mirror masque conventions. Three of the spectacles interspersed in Acts III and IV – the magical banquet, the appearance of Ariel like a harpy, and the attempted theft of Prospero's *'glistering apparel'* – are disruptive antic visions that serve as dramatic fulcrums turning the play from possible tragic denouements of revenge and murder. Abruptly, evil usurpers are startled, exposed, restrained or punished; and the usurpers' hidden obsessions and natures are symbolically suggested through fleeting apparitional temptations and chastisements, the products of Prospero's unleashed magical fury. Three other largely harmonious and counterbalancing spectacles at the end of Act IV and in Act V – the broken-off betrothal masque, the release of corrupt nobles from charms, and the 'discovery' of Miranda and Ferdinand playing chess – are limited and fanciful theatrical 'triumphs' that through their symbolism generally emphasize themes of reconciliation.[6]

It is through these varied theatrical masque-like visions, as well as through dialogue and dramatic action, that the deepest unfolding desires and conflicts of characters come to light. Insofar as *The Tempest* is a Renaissance play with Latin-play derivations, such fancies in harmony or tension with reason are acted out directly by the protagonists through speeches and encounters fostering dramatic conflict. But insofar as *The Tempest* is a masque-like drama, the fancies in themselves are objectified in the iconographic spectacles which serve as partial revelations of the motivations and desires of the central figures.

Over the years critics have focused on Ben Jonson as the author whose masque spectacles, with their anti-masque main masque structure and their largely classical iconography, most directly influenced Shakespeare.[7] But attention also needs to be called to those reformist masque writers whose neglected speculations, printed in the introductions to their masques, can be related to *The Tempest*.

As early as 1604, Samuel Daniel in the Preface to *The Vision of the 12 Goddesses* pointed out that the masque 'Shewes' were dependent upon the original 'intentions' of the authors. The shows, moreover, were seen to point to the evanescent inner imaginative, affective, and dream life of figures, with this inner dream life often at variance with waking action and frequently disclosing inner error.

in such matters of Shewes, these like Characters (in what forme soeuer they be drawne) serue vs but to read the intention of what wee would represent: ... for that these apparitions and shewes are but as imaginations, and dreames that portend our affections, and dreams are neuer in all points agreeing right with waking actions: and therefore were they aptest to shadow whatsoeuer error might bee herein presented.[8]

The 'Shewes' thus represented in external dream-iconography the disordered inner 'affections' of man as a microcosm, affections that were believed to correspond to and influence the elements of the earth and universe, the wider macrocosm. The theatrical dream world of the antic *intermezzos* in masques were indeed disordered, but the main masque dream world could and did contain ideal, if evanescent and insubstantial, visions of harmony and delight. Even the names of some of Jonson's masques – masques, it should be noted, with strong neoclassical elements – capture this ideal imaginative realm: *Oberon, the Faery Prince* (1611), *Love Restored* (1612), *The Vision of Delight* (1617), and *Pleasure reconciled to Virtue* (1618).

What spurred the invention of original 'hinges' and dream-like hieroglyphic figures were unique pressures and restraints upon masque authors: the need to write on command for a particular social occasion and for particular masque performers often in a particular indoor or outdoor setting. 'Hinges' were often produced following the orders of a royal or noble patron. At court the masques were then staged under the control of the Office of the Revels. As Thomas Heywood states in his *Apology for Actors* published within a year of the first production of *The Tempest*, it was a current practice of the Office at St John's Gate, Clerkenwell – where the scenery, costumes, and revels 'mechanicks' were accommodated – to take a hand in the rehearsal and 'perfection' of dramas presented at Whitehall so that they might be suitable for the king and the nobility, not to say free from possibly treasonous implications.

> And amongst vs, one of our best *English* Chroniclers records that when *Edward* the fourth would shew himselfe in publicke state to the view of the people, hee repaired to the Palace at *S. Johnes*, where he accustomed to see the Citty Actors. And since then, that house by the Princes free gift hath belonged to the office of the Reuels, where our court playes haue beene in late daies yearely rehersed, perfected, and corrected before they come to the publike view of the Prince and the Nobility.[9]

Under these various constraints, reformist masque writers, moving beyond Jonson's neo-classicism, frequently altered or even abandoned classical conventions and characters. They needed to form their materials to social and practical requirements, and this necessity produced artistic 'intentions' that were indeed new. 'And though these images haue oftentimes diuers significations,' declares Samuel Daniel in the introduction to *The Vision of the 12 Goddesses*, 'we tooke them only to serue as Hierogliphicqs for our present intention, according to some on property that fitted our occasion ...' (unnumbered page). So muddled and contradictory are the mythographers interpretations of hieroglyphics, Daniel argues, that he simply ignores them. By contrast, Ben Jonson generally stressed the precise, traditional meaning of classical 'Hiergliphicqs' and characters in his early masques by appending notes with citations and explanations of classical sources. Taking a different position, Daniel maintains that he will use the 'Hierogliphicqs'

> without obseruing other their misticall interpretations, wherein the Authors themselves are so irrigular & confused, as the best Mytheologers, who wil make somwhat to seeme any thing, and so unfaithful to themselues, as they haue left vs no certaine way at all, but a tract of confusion to take our course at aduenture. And therfore owing no homage to their intricate obseruations, we were left at libertie to take no other knowledge of them, then fitted our present purpose. ... then they fell out to stand with the nature of the matter in hand. (unnumbered page)

'Modernist' Thomas Campion, in the introduction to *Somerset's Masque* (Dec., 1613), went so far as to claim that in what he called 'ourdays', as distinct from the days of the past, conventional iconographic figures, though of some 'use', were no longer basically appropriate to the new inventive purposes of the writer. Campion, possibly even with a copy of *The Tempest* 'in hand', argued that modern fictions needed to feature new imaginative figures of power.

> In ancient times, when any man sought to shadowe or heighten his Inuention, he had store of feyned persons readie for his purpose As *Satyres, Nymphes &* their like: such were then in request and beliefe among the vulgar. But in our dayes, although they haue not vtterly lost their vse, yet finde they so litle credit, that our moderne writers haue rather transferd their fictions to the persons of Enchaunters & Commaunders of Spirits, as that excellent Poet *Torquato Tasso* hath done, and many others.
> In imitation of them (having a presentation in hand for Persons of high State) I grounded my whole Inuention vpon Inchauntmens and severall trans-formations:[10]

In his introduction to *Tethys Festival* (1610), Samuel Daniel went further in urging writers, when necessary, to break with the 'tyrannie' of classical conventions and to create original images in harmony with their inventions:

> And for these figures of mine, if they come not drawn in all proportions to the life of antiquity (from whose tyrannie, I see no reason why we may not emancipate our inuentions, and be as free as they, to vse our owne images) yet I know them such as were proper to the busines, and discharged those parts for which they serued, with as good correspondencie, as our appointed limitations would permit.[11]

But the new freedom of Daniel as a creator of masques, unlike that of Shakespeare as a playwright, was in one respect curtailed in performance by the authority of the court architect. For Daniel meekly acceded, in deferential politic fashion, to what in effect was the possible artistic 'tyrannie' of Inigo Jones over the details of the actual, performed show.

> But in these things wherein the onely life consists in shew: the arte and inuention of the Architect giues the greatest grace, and is of most importance: ours, the

least part and of least note in the time of the performance thereof, and therefore haue I interserted the discription of the artificiall part which only speakes M. *Inigo Jones* (E 2).

Clearly the theatrical outlook to which Shakespeare in *The Tempest* was very deeply indebted was that advanced by Thomas Campion and Samuel Daniel, stressing novel inventions and imaginative iconography of open suggestiveness, an outlook allowing the fancy of the poet to create original shows and character-types. Shakespeare's general movement away from the Jonsonian masque iconographic tradition, centred on classical or conventional 'hieroglyphics' with mostly established meanings, has accordingly made *The Tempest* a critically elusive work. The classical allusions and echoes that do appear throughout the play – some admittedly with definite meanings such as the references to the gods and their actions in the betrothal masque – are ultimately subsumed by the wider 'moderne' masque-like symbolism of the magical island; the tempestuous storm; the mysterious 'maze' in which enchanted nobles wander; the overall strangeness of the apparitions, spirits and visionary shows; and the suggestiveness of the powerful and controlling Magus himself with his '*glistering apparel*', apparel apparently sparkling in masque-like fashion with 'orbes' and 'spangs'.

Because throughout the play magical spectacles of strangeness objectify something of the inner fancies, desires and compulsions of the involved characters, figures in *The Tempest*, though symbolically significant, lack profound complexity or depth. The passions and obsessions of the characters are to a degree dramatically acted out, but they are also to a considerable degree symbolically represented in the visionary shows. As a result, a character such as Prospero can be seen to be partly a dimensional human figure, partly a 'Magus' archetype, and partly a symbolic creation. Prospero gives relatively limited emotional, acted-out, human expression to his deepest inner life: to his stated 'fury' at the treason of his enemies, and to his obviously profound imaginative delight at the impending bounteous marriage of Ferdinand and Miranda. He rather fancifully projects his unrestrained anger and idealized hopes for the marriage into the original but formalized action and iconography of spectacles of strangeness, and in doing so, reveals his own desires and feelings in both typal and symbolic ways.

The Magus thus emerges as a new kind of magical 'moderne' theatrical figure of the sort praised by Campion in his preface to *Somerset's Masque*, an enchanter and commander of spirits who replaced formally defined classical types and who appeared on stage on portentous 'Hollowmas nyght', 1611. The two antic, elemental attendants of Prospero – the airy spirit Ariel, and the lumbering Caliban whom Prospero calls 'Thou earth' – also emerge as newly minted, partially individualized theatrical figures, although ones still somewhat reflecting formal typal patterns. In *Somerset's Masque*, for example, there appears the traditional, strictly typal antic figure the '*Ayre*' who dances 'in a skye-coloured skin coate, with a mantle painted with Fowle, and on his head an Eagle. ...' Another typal antic spirit, the '*Earth*', dances as well dressed 'in a skin coate of grasse greene, a mantle painted full of trees, plants, and flowers, and on his head an oke growing' (unnumbered page opposite B). And if in Act I scene ii of *The Tempest* Prospero tells how using his magic 'art', in a situation imaginatively differentiated from and yet mirroring traditional theatrical types, he caused a tree to 'gape' and so released Ariel from a 12-year imprisonment, so too in Campion's *Lord Hayes Masque* (1607) the magician Night magically releases performers from trees but in ways accommodating the formal, typal iconography of court stagecraft. After Night touches the trees three at a time, they sink into the stage by means of a trap-door arrangement, and then rise and open to reveal nine Knights garbed in 'false' woodland garments which are later changed for their 'principall' heroic apparel.

> When the trees had sunke a yarde they cleft in three parts, and the Maskers appeared out of the tops of them, the trees were sodainly conuayed away, and the first three Maskers were raysed againe by the Ingin. They appeared then in a false habit, yet very faire, and in forme not much vnlike their principall, & true robe. It was made of greene taffetie cut into leaues, and layed upon cloth of siluer, and their hats were sutable to the same.[12]

But it is Caliban, the figure associated with earth, who in his composite uniqueness can in particular be seen to transcend the explicit types most likely influencing his characterization. Although the monster is often said to be moulded after New World natives including the 'natural' noble savages of Michel de Montaigne's famed sixteenth-century essay 'Des Cannibales', Caliban has also rightly been found to have affinities with the threatening part-human, part-monstrous beings of the largely fictitious late medieval travel volume *The Book of Sir John Maundeville* (c. 1322), a work recounting strange wonders that was published in many editions throughout the sixteenth century. But Caliban in his alternately wrathful, menacing, mentally dull, pitiable, drunken, idolatrous, and finally accepting individuation, like the antic but very different Bottom in *A Midsummer Night's Dream*, appears as the antic figure who through contrast gives significant dimension to the ideal projected fancies and the imperfect realities experienced by the play's central characters.

Reflecting speculative theories and some practices of masques, the visionary shows in *The Tempest*, in presenting the fancies and so the dream life of characters, give final configuration to themes long present in Shakespearean drama. It will be remembered that in earlier years in *Romeo and Juliet* such imaginative dream life is dismissively mocked by Mercutio as the product of 'vain phantasie, / Which is as thin of substance as the ayre, / And more inconstant then the wind'.[13] And in *A Midsummer Night's Dream*, a play rendering seeming objective reality to dream-like events and figures, the soldier-ruler Theseus similarly mocks the reveries of lovers and the creations of poets as the 'tricks' of 'strong imagination':

> That, if it would but apprehend some joy,
> It comprehends some bringer of that joy.

Or in the night, imagining some feare,
How easie is a bush supposed a bear![14]

Yet 'strong imagination' is forcefully if somewhat enigmatically defended by Hippolyta, Theseus's future bride. When imaginative stories are witnessed by many with 'minds transfigured', she insists, then there 'grows something of great constancy'.

Although in *The Tempest* the fanciful enchantments depicted in the visionary spectacles, especially the visionary betrothal masque, have sometimes been considered digressive 'inserts', they in fact serve as deeply emotive, thematic climaxes of the main and sub-plots. Each spectacle of strangeness, in objectifying through iconography the inner drives of the involved characters, provides symbolic insight into the wider unfolding conflicts underlying the entire play. Each spectacle evokes from the characters, at crucial turning points, exclamations of deep astonishment or fear. And as presented indoors at Whitehall, each spectacle appearing from shadows in flickering candle or oil light – 'speaking' to the audience through the masquing arts of music, speech, choreographic movement, and possibly scenic iconography – would doubtless have had a strong impact upon aristocratic spectators familiar, in ways foreign to many modern readers, with the conventions of court masque staging.

In *The Tempest* Shakespeare captured in the spectacles' strangeness and in the reactions of characters to them, not only revelatory meanings, but also the wonder that was evidently stirred by these magical dream visions. And he captured too, in Prospero's fabric-of-a-vision speech, the jolting recognition that the spectacles were composed from a base stage materiality. Still, it is the sense of the miraculous that remains pervasive throughout the drama. In the final act when spells are dissolved and Prospero is finally 'unmasked' as the true Duke of Milan, Gonzaga's words about the island's magic would appear to convey something of the early experience of both the spectacles and of the entire extraordinary masque-like drama: 'All torment, trouble, wonder, and amazement / Inhabits here. Some heavenly power guide us' (V, i, 104–5).

NOTES

1.   E.K. Chambers, *William Shakespeare* (Oxford, 1930), vol. 2, pp. 342 (*Revels Account*) and 343 (*Chamber Account*). The *Revels Account* of 1611 notes that on 'Hollowmas nyght was presented at Whitehall before the Kinges Maiestie a play Called the Tempest'. Two years later, a *Chamber Account* contains an 'Item paid to John Heminges ... dated att Whitehall xx die Maij 1613, for presentinge before the Princes Highnes the Lady Elizabeth and the Prince Pallatyne Elector ... The Tempest'.
      Evidence suggests the 1611 presentation was in the Banqueting House. The Audit Office Declared Accounts for October 1611 note a payment 'To James Maxwell gentleman usher ... for making ready ... the Banqueting House there three severall tymes for playes ...' (Bundle 389, Roll 49, fol. 10b in the British

Public Records Office); and in late October and early November, the King's Men were paid for Whitehall performances of three plays: *The Tempest*, *The Winter's Tale*, and a third drama.

2.   See Donna B. Hamilton, *Virgil and The Tempest: The Politics of Imitation* (Columbus, Ohio, 1989), for a recent interpretation of Shakespeare's use of the *Aeneid*.

3.   R.C. Fulton discusses the traditional classical iconography in the betrothal masque in '*The Tempest*: The Masque of Iris, Ceres, and Juno', in *Shakespeare and the Masque*, gen. ed. Stephen Orgel (New York and London, 1988), pp. 120–78. Garland Publishing Company. Gary Schmidgall, *Shakespeare and the Courtly Aesthetic*, (Berkeley, Los Angeles, and London, 1981), has helpfully called attention to elements in *Hymanaei* that suggest 'more than a casual relation' with *The Tempest*; namely, 'contentious music' reflecting 'confused noise' in Act IV of Shakespeare's play; the descent of Juno and Iris in Jonson's masque and in Act IV of *The Tempest*; comments by Caliban and Prospero on sounds and sights comparable to those found in Jonson's masque; and a dance circle in the masque that reflects the circle Prospero draws in Act V. Schmidgall notes too that 'In both *pietas* crushes *furor*; in both, potent virtue render vice impotent. Magic was a common theatrical mean of effecting the representation of this bias' (pp. 224–5). An authoritative account of the iconography in *Hymanaei* appears in D.J. Gordon, 'Jonson's Masque of Union', *The Renaissance Imagination*, ed. Stephen Orgel (Berkeley, 1975), pp. 157–84. See also an analysis of Jonson's employment of iconography from masque to masque in my *Milton and the Masque Tradition* (Cambridge, Mass. and London, 1963), pp. 59–82; and of the large patterns of court masque iconography in my 'The Temple of the Mind: Cosmic Iconography in Milton's *A Mask*', *Comus Contexts*, ed. Roy Flannagan (Athens, Ohio, 1988), pp. 59–76.

4.   See Frank Kermode on the influence of Terence's Latin play structure on Shakespeare's drama in *The Tempest: The Arden Edition*, 6th edn, Kermode (London, 1988), pp. lxxiv–vi.

5.   All line references to *The Tempest* are from the Arden edition, 6th edn, Frank Kermode (1988). This Arden edition of the play was first published in 1954, with the 6th edition printed in 1988.

6.   In a footnote to his introduction to *The Tempest* in the Arden edition, Frank Kermode records a perceptive comment by D.J. Gordon, apparently made in conversation, about the climactic nature of the four masque-like visions in just Acts III and IV:

> Prof. D.J. Gordon makes the interesting suggestion that at the climax of each plot there is a spectacular contrivance borrowed from the masque: thus the rapacity of the 'men of sin' is confronted with its own image in the Harpy; the disorderly desires of Caliban and the rest are chastised by hounds who, in the Actaeon story, typify such desires; and the betrothal of Miranda is conventionally signalized by a courtly mythological entertainment (p. lxxxiv, n.2).

Surprisingly left out of these remarks, however, are the climactic fifth-act contrivances 'borrowed from the masque': the nobles' emergence from Prospero's spells and the symbolic 'unmasking' of various figures; and the 'discovery' of Ferdinand and Miranda playing chess.

7.   Because recent masque structural interpretations of *The Tempest* turn for reference simply to what was then the new Jonsonian anti-masque and main masque form that Ben Jonson first explained only in May of 1609; and because the interpretations ignore the older and more episodic intermezzo masque forms upon which Shakespeare also drew, these interpretations seem to me unduly

limited. Glen Wickham in 'Masque and Anti-masque in "The Tempest"', *Essays and Studies* (1975), pp. 1–14, for example, writes solely of the disruptive 'antimasque' banquet vision in Act III, scene iii and then of the harmonious main masque of Ceres in Act IV, scene i, arguing that the two visionary shows, separated by what is termed some 80 lines of 'dialogue', manifest Jonsonian anti-masque main masque structure. This argument leads Wickham to insist that Shakespeare, unlike Thomas Campion in his original and imaginative masques, followed Ben Jonson and Inigo Jones in giving structure and very specific allegorical meaning to the play. On the other hand, Ernest B. Gilman in '"All Eyes": Prospero's Inverted Masque', *Renaissance Quarterly* 33 (1980), 214–30, turns such an approach to the drama entirely around. By concentrating selectively upon the orderly but broken-off masque of Ceres in Act IV, and the supposed 'antimasque' of 'dogs and hounds' that follows in the same act, Gilman makes the contrary claim that Shakespeare 'inverted' Jonsonian masque structure. In both readings, additional masque-like episodes, particularly in Act V, having an impact on the play's overall structure are overlooked or given insufficient attention. Consequently, the Jonsonian influence is, in my view, exaggerated.

8. *The Vision of the 12 Goddesses, presented in a Maske the 8. of Ianuary, at Hampton Court* (London, printed by T.C. for Simon Waterson, 1604), unnumbered page.
9. Thomas Heywood, *An Apology for Actors*, Containing three briefe Treatises (London: Printed by Nicholus Okes, 1612), p. E1.
10. Campion, *The Description of a Maske: Presented in the Banqueting roome at Whitehall. ... At the Mariage of the Right Honourable the Earle of Somerset* (London, printed by E.A. for *laurence Li'sle*, dwelling in Paules Church-yard, at the signe of the *Tyger*shead, 1614), pp. A2, verso A2.
11. Daniel, *Tethy's Festival* (London, printed for John Budge, 1610), p. E2.
12. *The Discription of a Maske, Presented before the Kinges Maiestie at White-Hall, on Twelfth Night last, in honour of the Lord Hayes* (S. Dunstones Churchyeard in Fleetstreet, London, 1607), pp. C3, D2. See also *The Description of a Maske* in *Campion's Works*, ed. Percival Vivian (Oxford, 1909), pp. 70–1.
13. *Romeo and Juliet: The Arden Edition*, ed. Brian Gibbons (London, 1988), p. 112, 98–9.
14. *A Midsummer Night's Dream: The Arden Edition*, ed. Harold Brooks (London, 1979), p. 104, 18–22.

CHAPTER TWELVE

How Many Ways Portia Informs Bassanio's Choice

S.F. Johnson

Many comedies, including most of Shakespeare's, resolve their plot conflicts by the repeal, suspension or outwitting of a local law, edict or compact. As Berowne explains to his fellow academicians,

> Young blood doth not obey an old decree.
> We cannot cross the cause why we were born;
> Therefore, of all hands must we be forsworn
> (*Love's Labour's Lost*, IV, iii, 212–14)[1]

Portia says something remarkably similar to Nerissa in her first substantial speech:

> The brain may devise laws for the blood, but a hot temper leaps o'er a cold decree.
>
> > (*Merchant of Venice*, I, ii, 17f)

The speech begins in the 'What is to be done' vein of Macbeth's 'If it were done' and ends lamenting that 'the will of the living daughter is curb'd by the will of the dead father'. This conflict of 'wills' is the first statement of a theme that will unfold in five variations, accounting for much of the action of the play: (1) Lancelot Gobbo trying confusions with his sand-blind father in Act II, ii, where his 'it is a wise father that knows his own child' may be taken as retroleptic of the 'good inspirations' of Portia's dying father in devising the lottery (I, ii, 27); (2) Jessica's o'erleaping of her father's will in her elopement with Lorenzo; (3) Portia's multiple hints to Bassanio in the first 70 lines of the third casket scene, which will be the main subject of this paper; (4) Portia's o'erleaping the legal knowledge of the Venetian authorities themselves to deliver Antonio from Shylock's taking his forfeiture; (5) Portia's o'erleaping the marital authority of Bassanio and rebonding Antonio as surety for Bassanio's future faith in the resolution of the ring plot.

In his brilliant recent book, Graham Bradshaw points out how such 'rhyming' actions in different parts of a play 'bear on each other' as 'variation developments and perspectival complications'.[2] Overreaching the restrictive wills of fathers and authority figures brings the comedy to its harmonious conclusion. (Shylock's enforced 'Will', the 'deed of gift', provides the last touch – 'after his death'.) The last three variations add up to Portia's triumph in attempting to control her conditions of existence. Some critics want Bassanio's wit, or Fortune, to intervene. She (that is, Shakespeare) cannot trust to these, nor can she be sure of Bassanio's educational attainments. That is, Shakespeare cannot count on most of his audience comprehending the hints he plants in her speeches and the song. He makes Portia say, 'lest you should not understand me well' (III, ii, 7) and then speak equivocally about teaching him and about being forsworn or not (10–14). We should remember the commonplace of the Latin Elegiac poets: 'At lovers' perjuries, / They say, Jove laughs' (*Romeo and Juliet*, II, ii, 92). When Bassanio feels himself on the rack, he exclaims:

> O happy torment, when my torturer
> Doth teach me answers for deliverance!
> (*Merchant of Venice*, III, ii, 37f.)

When she says, 'If you do love me, you will find me out' (41), she is challenging him to understand her well, to unriddle what she will say. The next 21 lines, the rest of the speech before the song, are crucial. She orders Nerissa and the servants to stand aloof. She calls for music which will begin at line 63, after her speech. She stands alone for these lines, Bassanio having moved to the 'shrine' of the caskets, the servants to their aloof position. Is she addressing them? She no longer refers to Bassanio in the second person but in the third, as 'he, him' (seven times, lines 44–53). Unless this is performed in an aside, it is to be heard by Bassanio, even as if overheard by Bassanio – listening to all he can hear from her for more teaching. The music 'while he doth make his choice' will even be appropriate if he loses, occasioning imagery of death: the dying swan and Portia's 'eye' the deathbed (to be resumed in the song). At line 53,

> Now he goes ...
> [like] young Alcides when he did redeem
> The virgin tribute paid by howling Troy
> To the sea monster. I stand for sacrifice.
> (53–7)

The servants are watching 'The issue of th' exploit' (60). She concludes, shifting to the intimate second person 'thou':

> Go, Hercules!
> Live thou, I live. With much, much more dismay.
> I view the fight than thou that mak'st the fray.
> (60 ff.)

The allusion is to the even younger Hercules at the crossroads making his choice of Virtue over Pleasure in the legend devised by the moral sophist, Prodicus, as told to Xenophon by Socrates. 'It was extremely popular and, by the time of the Renaissance, was considered the most significant part of the story of Hercules.'[3] It is a frequent subject of sixteenth-century woodcuts and paintings, known in England notably by Geoffrey Whitney's

Choice of Emblems (Leyden, 1586). It was used by grammar school masters as a corrective for the stories of misbehaviour of those other youths, Icarus and Phaeton. The usual visualization is of a moment in the 'story of how Hercules as a young man came to a place where two paths branched off. ... At the dividing point two fair women met him, one modest and sober, urging him to take the steep path; the other meretriciously seductive, using her arts to attract him to the other path.'[4] Prodicus's legend is of the rite of passage from adolescence to young manhood.

Bassanio may read the epigraphs during at least the last nine lines of Portia's speech, and whatever preliminary music precedes the song proper, but he also listens to what is being said and later sung. Is it possible that Portia herself sings the song? Boy actors were likely to be good singers, notably those who played Ophelia and the Folio Desdemona. The original music for the song is lost; it could tell us much about the stress given particular syllables or words. And performance would have been all important, with Shakespeare indicating the desired phrasing and accentuation in 1597. We simply do not know what effect(s) it could have had. But the five '-ed' rhymes are there, and some members of any audience may have noticed them, perhaps more in a court audience than in the playhouse. Something else resonates in the second half of the song, where 'fancy dies / In the cradle where it lies' (68 f.) echoing the 'swanlike end' (44) and Portia's eye as 'the stream / And wat'ry deathbed for him' (46 f.). And 'the eye' is indeed where fancy is engend'red and fed with gazing. It is in fact singular to rhyme with 'reply' in the Quarto; it becomes plural to rhyme with 'dies' and 'lies' in the Folio. Not only is fancy dead lying in the cradle (the deathbed) but a death bell or funeral knell is rung for it. This would suggest lead itself to those audience members who might remember any of five other recent poetic links between funerals and lead. Three of these occur in Spenser's *Shepheardes Calendar* (1579):

Nowe dead he is, and lyeth wrapt in lead.
                    (June, 89)

But ah Maecoenas is yclad in claye,
And great *Augustus* long ygoe is dead:
And all the worthies liggen wrapt in leade,
That matter made for Poets on to play:
                    (October, 61–4)

Dido my deare alas is dead,
Dead and lyeth wrapt in lead:
                    (November 58f.)

Another occurs in a popular pre-Shakespearean play by his coeval, Marlowe. It is near the end of Act II of *Tamburlane* Part 2 just after the death of Zenocrate:

Where ere her soule be, thou shalt stay with me
Embalm'd with Cassia, Amber Greece and Myrre,
Not lapt in lead but in a sheet of gold ...

The fifth occurs earlier in the *Merchant of Venice* itself, perhaps noticed by attentive members of an audience. It is where the Prince of Morocco, making his choice, reconsiders the caskets:

> Is't like that lead contains her? 'Twere damnation
> To think so base a thought; it were too gross
> To rib her cerecloth in the obscure grave.
> (2.7.49–51)

The New Arden (J. Russell Brown) comments: 'Corpses were normally wrapped in lead during this period'. Surely such wrappings of lead foil were too rich for the average man. Most were, like Ophelia, laid in earth in their winding sheets (cerecloths if waxed); and the bier was taken away for re-use. But the very rich did use lead wrappings, and the lower classes knew it.

After the song, Bassanio's comments on the caskets to himself take the form of an aside (III, ii, 73–107). The first eight lines, however, do not take off from the song or Portia's teaching but from a lesson taught him by Antonio during the bargaining over the terms of the bond with Shylock:

> Mark you this Bassanio,
> The devil can cite Scripture for his purpose. ...
> O what a goodly outside falsehood hath!
> (I, iii, 97 ff.)

Bassanio ponders false 'outward shows' in a world 'deceived with ornament' (74), and heresy being blessed and approved 'with a text', another 'fair ornament' (79 f.). Then he considers other ways in which vice pretends to be virtue: cowards wearing 'the beards of Hercules' and beauty (the famous Venetian courtesans?) using cosmetics and wigs or tires of hair from corpses: 'the dowry of a second head, / The skull that bred them in the sepulchre' (95 f.), almost an exact echo of Sonnet 68. He links Hercules and death-and-burial by images of head hair: the beard of the former and 'crisped snaky golden locks' that make 'wanton gambols with the wind' (92 f.), very different from the 'golden mesh' that is Portia's hair in her portrait (122), though both the snaky and the mesh were designed 'to entrap' (101, 122). Are they the two ladies at the crossroads offering Hercules his choice?

NOTES

1. Shakespearean citations are to G.B. Evans text in *The Riverside Shakespeare* (Boston: Houghton Mifflin, 1974).
2. Graham Bradshaw, *Misrepresentations* (Ithaca, NY: Cornell UP, 1993), p. 147. See also Harry Levin, 'Shakespeare's Themes, with Variations', in *The Return of Thematic Criticism*, ed. Werner Sollers (Cambridge, Mass.: Harvard UP, 1993).
3. Hallet Smith, *Elizabethan Poetry* (Cambridge, Mass.: Harvard UP, 1952), p. 293. See Erwin Panofsky, *Hercules am Scheidewege* (Leipzig: Tübner, 1930).
4. Eugene M. Waith, *The Herculean Hero* (New York: Columbia UP, 1962), p. 18.

CHAPTER THIRTEEN

The Evil of Play and the Play of Evil: Richard, Iago and Edmund Contextualized

Tom McAlindon

One of the most idiosyncratic and fascinating aspects of Renaissance drama in England is the representation of wickedness as sportive and histrionic. It is a tradition with deep roots in the past; and although it has attracted much attention from medieval and Renaissance scholars, something remains to be said about its origins and manifestations.

In the first place, the character of the jocular, histrionic villain derives from the devil and not, as has generally been thought, from the Vice of the moralities; as the playwrights themselves well knew, the Vice was himself an obvious derivative of the archetypal figure of evil in the Christian mythos. Furthermore, the comic and ludic conception of demonic behaviour does not originate in the medieval drama, nor (*pace* G.R. Owst) in medieval sermon literature.[1] It was far more abundantly exhibited in the lives of the saints, in other-world legends such as *St. Patrick's Purgatory*,[2] and in ascetical treatises dealing with the ways in which Satan seeks to ensnare the devout. It can be traced in religious literature as far back as such seminal monastic texts as Athanasius' *Life of St. Antony* (fourth century) and Cassian's *Collatio* (sixth century).[3]

That grave spiritual authors should treat demonic evil in this way constitutes a provocative paradox. Several scholars (beginning with C.S. Lewis) have concluded that comic devilry originates in the metaphysical conception of evil as non-being, a conception which logically reduces the threats of Satan to the level of ludicrous pretence.[4] This explanation, however, ignores the fact that there were two distinct, though often overlapping, kinds of such comedy in the Middle Ages, one emanating from, and the other directed at, the demon or demonic character. There is the simple, farcical ridiculousness of the type whose inglorious role in the given story-pattern demonstrates the power of divine grace and of those who have recourse to it in time; and there is the cunning playfulness and cruel wit of the type who is credited with intelligence, success and *de facto* control over his victims. The 'privative' conception of evil probably helped to underpin the first kind of comedy, and may in some sense account for it. But it does not account for the second; and it is that which bears rich fruit in drama and narrative, giving us the terrifying playfulness of characters as different as the tormenting soldiers in the Wakefield *Buffetting of Christ*, Gawain's Green Knight, and Othello's 'ancient'.

The association of evil with game, play and laughter has, I would suggest, a much less abstract origin than the privative conception of evil. Although it was subsequently affected by a diversity of cultural forms, such as folk plays and carnivalesque rituals, its origin lies in the fierce hostility of the early church to the pagan spectacles. Embracing plays, games, athletic and gladiatorial contests, dancing and music, the *spectacula* were intimately associated with the worship of the old gods and had a riotous and orgiastic character antithetical to the Christian ideals of calmness and chastity. They constituted a major threat to the new religion. Thus just as the gods were dismissed as demons, magicians or devilishly inspired fictions, so the plays and games were classified as a primary means by which Satan lured mortals into the worship of false gods and all the sins associated with it.[5]

Because of this early association with evil entertainment, athletic as well as histrionic, the tempter and accuser of biblical tradition quickly developed into a creature of boundless energy, the energy of disordered passion; and he became too a theatrical artist who specializes in presenting fictions as reality.[6] Patristic authors fleshed out this conception by transferring to the devil (patron of plays and games) the satirical portrait of the poet, orator and dramatist drawn by Plato in his attacks on rhetoric and imaginative literature: that of a glib manipulator of language and image, an imitator with a treacherous talent for giving probability to lies and fancies, making evil seem good, stirring up men's passion at will and providing them with the semblance of knowledge and wisdom without the reality.[7] The patristic axiom that the devil was the inventor of magic facilitated this development of his character in the direction of artful illusion.[8]

The intensity and subtlety with which the playfulness of evil is projected on the Renaissance stage owes much to the fact that the dramatists were fully acquainted with the arguments which gave rise to it. As a student of theology, Marlowe would have had direct access to such arguments in Augustine's *De Civitate Dei*; but he and everyone else would also have encountered them in Puritan diatribes against the drama. In these writings and sermons, patristic authorities are repeatedly cited to the effect that actors, magicians and conjurers are all of a kind; that the plays were devised by Satan to ensnare men in idolatry and stir up base passions; that theatres are schools of deceit and dishonesty of every kind.[9] Such arguments could not be ignored as religious antiquarianism, since they provided the ideological basis for a political movement which was threatening the livelihood of the dramatists.

By fully endorsing in their work the theological identification of play with evil, the dramatists evolved an artful strategy for disarming the Puritan attack. Marlowe, as one would expect, deploys the theological argument with notable exactness. Gaveston, the 'sly inveigling' seducer (*Edward II*, I, ii, 57), is a 'Proteus, god of shapes' (I, iv, 410), who lures the King from his responsibilities by means of 'Sweet speeches, comedies, and pleasing shows' in which lascivious mythological tales are re-enacted (I, i, 50–71).[10] Once Faustus renounces divinity in favour of magic he devotes himself to 'shadows, not substantial things' and is encouraged to believe that he is like Jove and Apollo, 'a mighty god'. To distract him from thoughts of repentance, the devils entertain him with shows and then give him the book of transformations so that he can become a performer himself: 'Then in this show let me an actor be' (III, i, 76). He 'play[s] Diana' (IV, i, 98) in jest and the lover of 'heavenly Hellen' [old spelling] in earnest: 'I will be Paris' (V, i, 91, 104). When he is carried off to Hell Lucifer's earlier promise that 'in Hell is all manner of delight' (II, ii, 105) should be recalled, since it echoes a mocking assurance regularly given to their victims by medieval demons (both narrative and dramatic): that Hell is the home of everlasting play and dance.

In the manipulation of the play–evil equation, however, Kyd precedes Marlowe. And his example was the more influential. This is partly because he exploited the tradition of terrifying comedy, whereas Marlowe veered towards farce, and partly because of the thoroughness with which he integrated the theatrical conception into the whole structure and texture of his play. Lorenzo is the first villain of note in the tragedies whose wickedness is enhanced by a grimly elaborate sense of humour. The 'quaint device' and 'jest' (IV, v, 5, III, v, 13–17) by which he directs his unwanted accomplice to go laughing to the gallows made a deep impression.[11] It is echoed in *Richard III* when Hastings laughs and jests triumphantly before being despatched to the block, charged by Richard with involvement in 'devilish plots' (III, iv, 62).[12] Much later, it is imitated exactly by no less a master of demonic comedy than the author of *The Revenger's Tragedy* (I, ii, 89ff.).[13]

But it is the protagonist and not the villain who is the focus for the play of evil in *The Spanish Tragedy* (as in *The Revenger's Tragedy*). Hieronimo's transformation from a grave man of law into a violent, indiscriminate revenger is marked by a lethal jocularity and a conspicuously theatrical delight in the execution of his murderous 'plot'. The note of grim irony and metadramatic self-consciousness which this conception of the hero's character transmits to the play as a whole is exquisitely refined by the continuous presence on stage of the figure of Revenge as spectator to the drama which he has scripted himself, and whose unexpected outcome he awaits with smiling assurance. Having been dispatched from the underworld by Pluto, Revenge is something like a classicalized devil; as such he is a pointer to the unstable relationship between the righteous desire for justice and a passion which is integral to the character of Satan ('Revenge' was the name of the Vice in Pickering's *Horestes* [1567]). The mocking, self-satisfied aloofness with which Revenge views the victims of his play is ultimately shared by Hieronimo, and is prototypical. It can be traced in the demons who enter aloft to mark how Faustus 'doth demean himself' (V, ii, 10) in his last desperate attempt to escape reality by playing Paris to the succubous Helen; in Barabas as he views from 'above' the enactment of his device – 'So neatly plotted and so well performed' (III, iii, 2) – to make his daughter's two suitors dispose of each other; in the way Richard, and the other leading actors in his 'violent tragedy', respond to the engineered misfortunes of their rivals ('I shall ... laugh to look upon their tragedy' [III, ii, 57–91], 'English woes shall make me smile' [IV, iv, 115]); in Hamlet's 'hoisting' of Rosencrantz and Guildenstern; in Iago's gloating over the fallen Othello ('Work on my medicine, work'); and in Bracciano and the conjuror as they watch the dumb shows in which the murders commissioned by the duke are represented: the murderers 'depart laughing' and the two spectators are quietly pleased: 'Excellent, then she's dead', ''Twas quaintly done' (II, ii, 23ff.).[14]

Kyd's conception of evil as treacherously playful is reinforced by his constant punning on words like 'show', 'act', 'plot', 'play', 'device', and 'perform'. It was remembered no doubt that the morality Vice loved to moralize two meanings in one word; but Kyd's practice probably did more than all the morality plays to ensure that the words of play and the play on words would become a major element in Renaissance presentation of tragic confusion and contradiction. Marlowe emulated Kyd's word-play in *Faustus*, where a key pun is on the word 'perform' – 'the miracles that magic will perform' are a mere performance, shadow not substance (I, i, 31). But only Shakespeare (in *Hamlet* and *Othello* especially) and Middleton (in *Women Beware Women*) surpassed it.

However it was Kyd's device of the play-within-the play which most impressed his contemporaries and did most to perpetuate the play–evil equation. With this device Kyd gave rise to that most conventionalized and popular scene in Renaissance drama: the treacherous entertainment wherein play, game, friendly contest, masque or banquet cloaks the climactic outburst of violence. The Treacherous Entertainment of Renaissance tragedy owes something to the bloody rituals of Senecan tragedy (and perhaps something to contemporary chronicles of Italian feuding and assassinations). But it is essentially a Renaissance elaboration of Satanic game and play: white devilry in its most spectacular form.

Because of the humanist conviction that speech is the most powerful instrument for evil as well as good available to humankind, the theological conception of the devil as a genius of persuasion, a corrupt orator, was enthusiastically appropriated by the dramatists (as it would be by Milton).[15] Shakespeare rather than Kyd is the pioneer figure here. His interest in sinister persuasion is evident from the outset in *Titus Andronicus*, where the 'siren words' of the barbarian queen bewitch the emperor and precipitate the decline of Rome into a wilderness of tigers. The demonic matrix of such art is indicated in the portrait of Sinon in *The Rape of Lucrece*: Sinon is 'a constant and confirmed devil' who deludes 'credulous old Priam' with an 'enchanting story', so that 'His words like wildfire burnt the shining glory / Of rich-built Ilion' (lines 1513–24). What Sinon does to credulous Priam and to Troy,

Edmund does to his brother and father, and Iago (the 'demi-devil') to Othello and also, in a sense, to Cyprus, that outpost of Christianity which fell to the Turk immediately after the presumed date of the dramatic action. The villainized hero of *The Revenger's Tragedy* is a graduate of the same school as this group. When asked to corrupt his sister and mother with his 'smooth enchanting tongue' – to 'cozen' them 'out of all grace' – he is initially horrified (I, iii, 112–13); such however is his pride in his persuasive skills that he throws himself into the task with unholy fervour. It is obvious, of course, that the verbally persuasive and the (equally impressive) theatrical skills of such characters are aspects of one and the same 'Satanic' genius for deception and transformation.

Another, and related, aspect of the Satanic myth which Shakespeare rather than Kyd or Marlowe (among the major dramatists) was the first to exploit is the notion of 'the noon-day fiend', the false 'angel of light' who can delude even the saintly by presenting himself as his prospective victim's best friend, the voice of wisdom, moderation and compassion. Richard III plays this role with engaging melodramatic success (poor Clarence!). In Iago it is fully naturalized and all the more insidious; but still the demonic matrix is explicit: 'Divinity of hell! / When devils will their blackest sins put on, / They do suggest at first with heavenly shows, / As I do now' (II, iii, 339–42). In *Women Beware Women*, Livia's blend of worldly wisdom with a benevolence which is part genuine as well as false makes her an exceptionally realistic and compelling version of the friendly fiend. In the art of making evil seem good she surpasses all her predecessors in the drama; concerning her apt pupil Bianca, Leantio aptly says, 'Damnation taught thee that wisdom' (III, iii, 134).[16]

The strategic purpose of this general endorsement of the play/evil equation was never emphasized, but attention was drawn to it from time to time. For example, the conspicuous contrast between the entertainments presented by Hieronimo in Acts I and IV of *The Spanish Tragedy*, and between the dissembling, plotting and persuasiveness of Edgar and Edmund in *King Lear*, points to a distinction between play which works in the service of truth and concord and play which feigns in order to confuse, divide and destroy. Perdita, most charming of puritans, has come to understand just such a distinction when she punningly concedes: 'I see the play so lies / That I must bear a part' (*The Winter's Tale*, IV, iv, 645–6).

If the play of evil was a tradition which could be used to counter Puritan criticism of the drama by way of appropriation, it was also a phenomenon which exposed the plays to condemnation by classical purists, who allowed no place in tragedy for laughter and jest. Webster seemed to be of this mind when in the Preface to *The White Devil*, and again in the text, he complained about the necessity of having to please 'ignorant asses' who would never accept 'sententious tragedy ... observing all laws as height of style and gravity of person' – 'tragedy must have some idle mirth in't / Else it will never pass' (IV, i, 119–20). This complaint was unnecessary if not disingenuous, a token gesture perhaps to the likes of Ben Jonson. Webster should have had enough confidence to point out that he had thoroughly integrated the laughter of evil to the design of his tragedy and that it could be justified in terms of agreed aesthetic norms. In this (as I have claimed elsewhere), Kyd and Shakespeare led the way; in plays such as *The Spanish Tragedy*, *Othello* and *King Lear*, as in *The White Devil*, the conjunction of mirth and horror is implicitly justified by the underlying conception of the tragic world as a place where things decline to their confounding contraries and something like primal chaos comes again. In such tragedies, the ring of laughter is part of a whole system of clashing oppositions, an artistic *discordia concors*.

But of course Renaissance critics never changed their tune to the extent of advancing a theoretical rationale for jesting tragedy. Far worse, the Puritans finally did what Tertullian, Augustine and Cyprian told them to do: shut the playhouses. But as I began with a large paradox, so I must end with one. Ancient and modern hostility to the drama had proved to be one of the richest sources of inspiration for Shakespeare and his contemporaries. Defensiveness and the strategies of self-defence enhanced (if they did not generate) the metadramatic complexity of their work; and the play of evil gave their tragedies a range, subtlety and theatrical power unrivalled before or since.

NOTES

1. See L.W. Cushman, *The Devil and Vice in English Dramatic Literature before Shakespeare* (Halle: Niemeyer, 1900), pp. 33–4; J.B. Moore, *The Comic and Realistic in English Drama before Shakespeare* (Chicago: 1925); A.P. Rossiter, *English Drama from Early Times to the Elizabethans* (London: Hutchinson, 1950), pp. 68–70; G.R. Owst, *The Pulpit in Medieval England* (Oxford: Blackwell, 1951), pp. 194–206; Bernard Spivak, *Shakespeare and the Allegory of Evil* (New York: Columbia University Press; London: Oxford University Press), 121–3, 193–6. Irena Janicka, *The Comic Elements in the English Mystery Plays Against the Cultural Background* (Poznan, 1962), pp. 23–4, 38–40, 52–4, stresses the connection between the demonic comedy of the stage and the grotesque style in medieval art and sermon literature, where the good/evil antithesis is regularly figured in terms of the sublime and the grotesque. Charlotte Spivack, *The Comedy of Evil on Shakespeare's Stage* (Cranbury, New Jersey, and London: Associated University Presses, 1978), pp. 32–46, also emphasizes the prominence of demonic humour in medieval art, especially architecture.
2. For the *St. Patrick's Purgatory* legend, see *The Early South-English Legendary* [c. 1290], ed. Carl Horstmann, *EETS*, 87 (1887), p. 204; *The South English Legendary* [early fourteenth century], ed. C. D'Evelyn and A.J. Mill, *EETS*, 235 (1956), p. 92; ed. E. Kölbing, *Englische Studien*, I (1877), pp. 97–112 (a superior, late thirteenth- or early fourteenth-century version, in which the sadistic playfulness of the demons is finely imagined).
3. *Vita S. Antonii*, 24, 39–40, 42 (J.P. Migne, *Patrologia Graeca*, XXVI, 879, 899–906); Cassian, *Collatio*, VII, xxi, IX, vi (Migne, *Patrologia Latina*, XLIX, 696, 777). The author of the early Middle-English ascetical treatise the *Ancrene Riwle* articulates clearly the two conceptions of demonic comedy

inherited from the early church, one of which makes the defeated tempter, and the other the ensnared sinner, an object of ridicule: 'Laugh the old fool loudly to shame and he will flee: spit in his beard' (ed. M. Day, EETS. OS, 225 [1952], pp. 130–1; cf. pp. 110, 121); 'The fiend beholds all this game: laughs till he bursts' (pp. 93–5).

4.   Charlotte Spivack, *The Comedy of Evil on Shakespeare's Stage*, pp. 13–30.
5.   Tertullian, *De Spectaculis*, cap. x, xv, xvii (Migne, *PL*, I, 716–18, 721–2, 733–4)); Cyprian, *De Spectaculis*, cap. iv–vi (PL, IV, 813–15); Augustine, *De civitate Dei*, II, viii–xiv, IV, i, xxvi, VII, xiii–xiv, xviii, VIII, xviii (Migne, *PL*, XLI, 53–60, 111, 132–3, 205, 243).
6.   The devil's cunning and malevolent playfulness is emphasized in early ascetical writing by habitual use of the verbs *ludere*, *deludere*, and *illudere* (and their derivatives) in describing his attempts to ensnare the soul: (1) *ludere*: Cassian, *Collatio*, IX, vi (*ludificatio*), (Migne, *PL*, XLIX, 777); Bernard of Clairvaux, *Epistola*, LXXXVII, 12 (*PL*, CLXXXII, 217); Gregory the Great, *Moralia*, XXXIII, ii (*PL*, LXXVI, 670) ('Ludus daemonum est humanas mentes de vitio in vitium rotare. ... ludunt cum reprobi spiritus humana corde in illicitas cogitationes pertrahunt'); (2) *deludere*: Cassian, *Collatio*, II, v (*PL*, XLIX, 529); Isidore of Seville, *Sententiae*, III, v, 22 and vi, 2 (Migne, *PL*, LXXXIII, 664, 668); (3) *illudere*, *illusio*: Cassian, *Collatio*, I, xx, VIII, xvii (*PL*, XLIX, 516, 749); Gregory, *Moralia*, VIII, xxiv, 42 (*PL*, LXXV, 827). On the semantic and theatrical implications of these three terms in relation to Marlowe's demonic theatricality, see my *Doctor Faustus: Divine in Show* (New York: Twayne, 1994), ch. 7, 'Lusion, Illusion, Delusion'.
7.   I summarize *Phaedrus*, 258–79 (cf. *The Republic*, bk. X). Christian apologists took particular pleasure in quoting the pagan philosopher in their diatribes against pagan drama, literature, and gods: see Tertullian, *Ad Nationes*, 1, iv and II, vii, *Apologeticus*, cap. xiv (*PL*, I, 403, 633, 667), and Augustine, *De civitate Dei*, 11, xiv, VIII, xxi (*PL*, XLI, 58–60, 245–6).
8.   Augustine, *De civitate Dei*, VIII, xviii.
9.   John Northbrooke, *A Treatise against Dicing, Dancing, Plays and Interludes*, Shakespeare Society Reprint (London, 1843), pp. 85–104; Phillip Stubbes, *Anatomy of Abuses in England*, ed. F.J. Furnivall, New Shakespeare Society (London: Trubner, 1877), pp. 142–3; Thomas Beard, *The Theatre of God's Judgements* (London, 1597), pp. 374–6. See also, Russell Fraser, *The War Against Poetry* (Princeton: N.J.: Princeton University Press, 1970), 93–5; Jonas Barish, *The Antitheatrical Prejudice* (Berkeley, Los Angeles, and London: University of California Press, 1981), pp. 91–2.
10. Marlowe citations are from Roma Gill's edition of *The Plays* (London: Oxford University Press, 1971).
11. *The Spanish Tragedy*, ed. Philip Edwards, The Revels Plays (London: Methuen, 1959).
12. Shakespeare citations are from *The Complete Works*, ed. Peter Alexander (London and Glasgow: Collins, 1951).
13. Ed. R.A. Foakes, The Revels Plays (London: Methuen, 1966).
14. Webster, *The White Devil*, ed. John Russell Brown, The Revels Plays (London: Methuen, 1964).
15. On Milton, see Douglas Wurtele, '"Persuasive Rhetoric": the Techniques of Milton's Archetypal Sophist', *English Studies in Canada*, 3 (1977), 18–33.
16. Ed. J.R. Mueryne, *The Revels Plays* (London: Methuen, 1975).

CHAPTER FOURTEEN

The Staging of *A Midsummer Night's Dream*, 1595–1895

Jay L. Halio

Where and when *A Midsummer Night's Dream* was first performed no one
certainly knows. Editors assume, rightly, that on stylistic grounds the play
belongs to Shakespeare's so-called lyric group, which includes *Romeo and
Juliet* and *Richard II*. Together with other indications, stylistic evidence puts
the date of composition at 1595–6. The play was definitely known by
1598, since Francis Meres mentions it among Shakespeare's comedies in
Palladis Tamia, registered in September that year. And Titania's reference
to foul weather suggesting the seasons' inversion (II, i, 82–114) may reflect
the bad, wet summers of 1595 and 1596 (Brooks, pp. xxxvii–viii). But for
what occasion the play was written and where its first performances were
held remain a mystery.

The mystery inevitably has aroused much speculation. The 'hymeneal'
aspect of the play suggests that the *Dream* was written expressly for a noble
wedding, then transferred to the public theatre. Chambers lists six late
sixteenth-century weddings scholars have advanced as possibilities, beginning
with the wedding of Robert Earl of Essex and Frances Lady Sidney in April
or May 1590 and ending with Henry Lord Herbert and Anne Russell's
wedding at Blackfriars on 16 June 1600 (Chambers, 1930, vol. I, p. 358).
The former is of course too early, unless one accepts the conjecture that the
Dream reveals several layers of composition, a theory put forward by John
Dover Wilson but now largely dismissed. The latter remains a possibility for
a revival of the play, although no hard evidence exists to prove that the *Dream*
was in fact performed then. Queen Elizabeth's presence at the wedding is
inconclusive, since she was present at other weddings, earlier ones more
consistent with the agreed-on dates of composition.

The weddings at which the queen was present to receive Shakespeare's
elegant compliment – Oberon's description of the 'fair vestal thronèd in the
west' (II, i, 148–64) – those which fall within the accepted time of composition, are (1) the wedding of William Stanley, Earl of Derby, and Elizabeth
Vere at Greenwich on 26 January 1595; and (2) that of Thomas Berkeley
and Elizabeth Carey at Blackfriars on 19 February 1596. After due consideration, E.K. Chambers (1944, pp. 61–9) remained unconvinced the

Dream actually was performed at the Stanley–Vere wedding. He was more inclined to believe it was performed at the Berkeley–Carey wedding, about which unfortunately less is known. Elizabeth Carey was one of the Queen's god-daughters and granddaughter of her first cousin and Lord Chamberlain, Henry Lord Hunsdon. Shakespeare's company, Lord Hunsdon's Men, subsequently passed under the patronage of Sir George Carey, who in turn became Lord Hunsdon after his father's death in 1596. Although it is not certain that Queen Elizabeth attended the wedding, she very likely did. It is also possible that the Lord Hunsdon's men were asked to perform a play, one resembling the increasingly popular masques, suitable for the occasion.

The reason behind the speculation also has much to do with the dramatis personae of the *Dream*. Absent any obviously starring roles, the play emphasizes ensemble acting. Moreover, the number of parts that might be assumed by boys suggests that family also performed in the play, particularly in the roles of fairies who attend Titania. The ending of the play further suggests two different conclusions, one for the public stage (Puck's epilogue), the other (the fairy masque, V, i, 349–400) for a private performance, such as a wedding feast. But as Stanley Wells has argued persuasively, the episodes are well integrated and together suitably conclude the play. There is no compelling reason, furthermore, to believe the *Dream* was not originally intended for the public stage. For example, if Shakespeare's company could at any time muster enough boys for public performance, surely they could do so from the start (1967, pp. 12–15; 1991, pp. 14–22). Moreover, arguments favouring a large cast fail to consider that in Shakespeare's company (as in others) doubling of parts was commonplace (Ringler, pp. 110–34).

In the most extensive, theoretical discussion of the play's original productions, Ronald Watkins and Jeremy Lemmon centre mainly on the public performances of the *Dream*. They are doubtless right in supposing that even if the play was originally commissioned for private performance, Shakespeare would have kept in mind transfer to the public stage. Recall what public theatres were like then: large, open structures, with a thrust stage around which those who paid their penny stood. Seating in tiers of galleries was available for another penny, and a few exceptional members of the audience might be seated in the Lord's Room above the stage, or on the stage itself. Actors and audience thus enjoyed an intimacy fostered by close proximity and the absence of the kind of artificial lighting that tends to distance modern theatre audiences from characters and action.

Entrance to the stage from the tiring-house was usually from one of two doors (both noted in the Folio stage directions at the beginning of Act II, i), although it is likely that Puck occasionally sprang through a trap door from underneath the stage to make a more startling entrance (Watkins and Lemmon, p. 17). The stage was largely bare and action continuous, although the Folio direction at the end of Act III, ii, 'They sleepe all the Act', indicates that in a later adaptation for the Blackfriars private theatre, intervals were instituted ('Act' here refers to an intermission between acts). The stage was strewn with rushes, and scenery was kept to a minimum. Perhaps the fairy who enters first in Act II, i hung a few leafy boughs on the pillars that held up the canopy, or 'heavens', above the stage, and possibly some kind of apparatus was used for Titania's bower in Act II, ii or the hawthorne brake in Act III, i (Watkins and Lemmon, pp. 52, 64). Otherwise, scenery and lighting were largely supplied through dialogue, as in the night-time forest scenes or the details of Oberon's speech, 'I know a bank where the wild thyme blows' (II, i, 249 ff.). The literalistic mind, lacking imagination, is thoroughly mocked in Peter Quince's comic concern about moonlight and a wall for Pyramus and Thisbe's meeting (III, i, 36–55).

Costumes could be and often were elaborate. The finery Theseus and Hippolyta wear as Duke and Duchess of Athens was doubtless Elizabethan with perhaps a bit of classical embellishment, and Oberon and Titania, as their counterparts in the forest world, dressed similarly. Watkins and Lemmon believe that Puck was dressed as a king's jester, complete with coxcomb and motley (p. 25), but the more traditional costume of Robin Goodfellow seems to fit the character better, despite his relationship to Oberon. Watkins and Lemmon are closer to the mark when they remind us (p. 22) that the fairies were not gauzy ballet dancers dressed in tutus, and they were not female: Bottom refers to one as 'Monsieur Cobweb', another as 'Monsieur Mustardseed', and a third as 'Cavalery [i.e. Cavalier] Cobweb' (IV, i, 8–22). Cutting into these two levels – the mythical–historical and the supernatural – is the downright realistic. Called 'hard-handed workmen of Athens', the 'rude mechanicals' were actually Warwickshire craftsmen: Peter Quince the carpenter, Bottom the weaver, Snug the joiner, and the rest, all dressed as we should expect them to be in Shakespeare's time.

The young lovers were also dressed in Elizabethan fashion, though not so elaborately as Theseus and Hippolyta. The men carried swords, as required by their attempted duel (III, ii, 401–12). Few other props were necessary, but of course Bottom needed his (removable) ass's head, and for the play within the play Starveling as 'the man i' th' moon' had to have his lantern, his bush, and his dog (V, i, 242–4). Music was supplied by musicians sitting in the gallery directly above the stage, while the choristers who sang the lullabyes and other songs were boys who played the fairies (Watkins and Lemmon, pp. 26–7).

As T.W. Baldwin argued in *The Organization and Composition of Shakespeare's Company* (p. 197; cited by Watkins and Lemmon, p. 13), Shakespeare's creative method was to fit the play to his company, not the company to his play. Will Kemp must have played Bottom and Thomas Pope was Peter Quince. But if the satire were further self-directed, why not Shakespeare as Peter Quince? (Curiously, though an actor too, he is not listed in Baldwin's cast list. But Glynne Wickham, *Early English Stages 1300 to 1660*, II, 183, believes the satire is directed to James Burbage, the carpenter-turned-actor, builder of the Theatre, and father of Richard and Cuthbert; cited by Watkins and Lemmon, p. 145.) Pope might then have played

Theseus, whose role Baldwin assigns to Phillips. Richard Burbage and Henry Condell played Demetrius and Lysander; Ned Shakespeare (the dramatist's brother), Hippolyta; Goffe (whose roles included Juliet), Oberon; Tooley, Puck; and the other boys in the company – Eccelston, Cooke and Gilburne: Hermia, Helena and Titania (Watkins and Lemmon, pp. 19–21, 45).

Beyond these outlines and surmises it is perhaps unnecessary to try to recreate a production of the *Dream* at the Globe (1599 and afterwards) or the Blackfriars (1609 and afterwards). Watkins and Lemmon believe that the specific detail with which Shakespeare introduces the mechanicals in the stage direction to Act I, ii carries over to typical behaviour. Supposing the men's daily occupations are marked by visible properties, they imagine that 'Bottom, for instance, fingers with professional interest the cloth upon which Starveling is plying his needle and thread; Flute uses a pair of bellows, which he is mending, to blow down the neck of Snug, whose strident saw is drowning Quince's attempts to draw the attention of "all our company"' (p. 46). They may be right in their suppositions and imaginings, but alternative kinds of action were also possible. Nor will everyone accept that Quince and his fellows first appear in the inner stage from behind a curtain (Quince's carpenter shop), though again that is a possible staging (p. 45). More convincing is the imagined use of the trap door for some of Puck's quick entrances and exits, as at II, ii, 89, III, i, 60, III, ii, 463 (ibid., pp. 68, 74, 102).

Shakespeare's achievement in *A Midsummer Night's Dream* of course goes well beyond its stagecraft, although clearly the dramatist was seriously interested in the relationship between illusion and reality. Through the workmen's staging of 'Pyramus and Thisbe' and their literal-minded concerns, for example, that the lion's roaring should frighten the ladies in their audience, the playwright takes direct aim at this issue. Nor should its farcical treatment blind us to it. The creation of a unique fairy world and the interplay of several complementary levels of reality are also relevant: fairies and humans, dukes and rude mechanicals, young lovers and old all meet and intermingle in the world, or worlds, of Shakespeare's play. Dream-sequences, which the forest scenes resemble, are nicely framed by scenes in Athens and Theseus's court. Agents of providence – Oberon in the forest, Theseus in the city – play a direct and beneficent role in the lives of others, as befits hymeneal comedy. Only Pyramus and Thisbe are tragically deprived of such beneficence; but, as represented by Quince & Co., their fate scarcely appears disruptive – only a veiled reminder of yet another, more sombre reality. And just as the natural and supernatural worlds are connected, so are the worlds of animate and inanimate nature, as Titania's long speech on the seasons' upheaval emphasizes (II, i, 81–121). This complex, colourful, comic world of powerful interrelatedness is among Shakespeare's supreme achievements.

Not that it was always perceived thus. While we have no concrete, first-hand reports of the play's reception in Shakespeare's time – or indeed any time before the Restoration in 1660 – we can infer that it was revived fairly often and was therefore quite popular. It was probably one of the first plays chosen for performance before King James I on New Year's Day, 1604, if the play 'of Robin goode-fellow' reported by Dudley Carlton refers in fact to *The Dream* (Chambers, 1923, vol. III, p. 279). In the Folio text, which contains some revisions as well as new stage directions and was probably printed from a copy of the second quarto marked up from a theatrical manuscript (very likely the promptbook; see Greg, p. 246), an actor named Tawyer, who did not join the King's Men until later on, is mentioned by name in a stage direction at V, i, 125: 'Tawyer with a Trumpet before them'. Other variants between the first edition (the Fisher quarto of 1600) and the Folio also suggest revision for stage revival (Greg, pp. 243–5). Chambers suspects that, curiously, an amateur performance in 1631 was held 'for the Sabbath delectation of Bishop Williams' (1930, vol. I, p. 362; vol. II, pp. 348–9).

The King's Men apparently revived the play for their patron again on 17 October 1630 at Hampton Court Palace, according to a document printed in G.E. Bentley's *Caroline and Jacobean Drama* (vol. I, p. 27). How often it had been revived between 1604 and 1630 for the sovereign's pleasure or others' is not known. Some parts of it remained popular even during the period when the theatres were officially closed (1642–60); the comic interludes involving Bottom and his friends tended to separate from the main body of the play and develop a life of their own under such titles as *The Comedy of Pyramus and Thisbe* and *The Merry Conceits of Bottom the Weaver* (Salgādo, p. 116). A 'droll' called *Bottom the Weaver*, published in 1661, maintains on the title page that 'It hath been often publickely Acted by some of his Majesties Comedians, and lately, privately, presented, by several Apprentices for their harmless recreation, with Great Applause', but no details of these purported performances have come down to us.

Bottom the Weaver is the earliest published adaptation of the play after the Restoration and preserves all the episodes involving Quince, Bottom, and the rest taken from the text of the Second Folio (1632; Stanley Wells, Introduction to the Cornmarket facsimile, 1970). The young lovers are omitted, and the roles of Titania, Oberon and Puck severely cut. A few brief additions, based on Shakespeare's lines, are included to provide continuity. The printed list of actors indicates that a number of parts may be doubled, especially the roles of Theseus and Oberon. The doubling probably reflects earlier stage tradition – one that recent productions have revived with interesting effects. *Bottom the Weaver* was reprinted in 1673 in a collection of short plays (*The Wits*, Part II) and is the longest play in it.

Other adaptations indicate how the play caught the imagination, if not as Shakespeare wrote it, then as current taste dictated he might have or should have written it. By 1660, when the theatres reopened and productions were heavily influenced by French neo-classicism, a more 'refined' stage decorum prevailed. Shakespeare's plays were mined by other dramatists, such as Davenant and Dryden, who rewrote them to meet the tastes of their age (see, for example, Dobson, pp. 17–61). Samuel Pepys saw the *Dream* acted on

29 September 1662. Although we don't know what version he saw or who performed in it, it was among Shakespeare's plays assigned to Thomas Killgrew and the King's Company after the Restoration (Odell, vol. I, p. 23). Probably the text was close to that of the Folio, for Pepys did not like what he saw. His remarks, often quoted, say more about the taste of his time than the actual production: 'Then to the King's Theatre, where we saw 'Midsummer Night's Dream', which I had never seen before nor shall ever again, for it is the most insipid ridiculous play that I ever saw in my life. I saw, I confess, some good dancing and some handsome women, which was all my pleasure' (Odell, vol. I, pp. 40–1).

Dancing indeed. By this time, of course, following the French lead, women had taken the female roles hitherto usually played by boys. Under Continental influences, too, Elkanah Settle transformed Shakespeare's *Dream* into an opera called *The Fairy Queen* with music by Henry Purcell. Thomas Betterton produced it in 1692 at Dorset Gardens Theatre. It was revived the next year with additional music and songs by Purcell. However, he did not set a single line of Shakespeare's to music. The Shakespearean parts in this severely mangled version are all spoken and acted. The lovers, the fairies, the rude mechanicals are there, but so are new characters: Coridon, Mopsa, nymphs, 'a Chorus of *Fawns*, and *Naids*, with *Woodmen*, and *Hay-makers* Dancers'. In addition, allegorical figures – Night, Mystery, Secrecy, Sleep – and their attendants appear, as well as Spring, Summer, Autumn and Winter with Phoebus for a 'Dance of the Four Seasons'. The opera has still more for the delight of the age: Juno, a chorus of Chinese men and women, a dance of six monkeys, and 'a Grand Dance of 24 *Chineses*' (as recorded in 'The Names of the Persons' in Jacob Tonson's edition of 1692, reprinted by Cornmarket Press, 1969).

Tonson's edition does not give Purcell's music, which is now available (in a form adapted for modern voices) among Edwin F. Kalmus's vocal scores (No. 6868, New York, n.d.) that includes the augmentations of 1693. Therefore, to reconstruct the productions of 1692–3 one must consult both the Tonson edition and Kalmus's score. With origins in Italy and France, opera was a relatively recent art form in Britain that Sir William Davenant had introduced. The Preface to *The Fairy Queen* calls his *Siege of Rhodes* 'the first Opera we ever had in England' and bemoans the lack of financial support from the crown that would make English opera a true rival to the Continental. Perhaps the enormous expense in mounting such a production – £3000 – is the reason the complete opera was not revived after 1693, when the opera just barely broke even, despite its highly successful staging, which definitely catered to the taste of the times, debased though it may appear to us (Milhous, pp. 48, 58, 178; Odell, vol. I, p. 195).

A good deal of cutting of Shakespeare's text was obviously necessary to make room for the songs, instrumental music, dancing, and spectacle that were now inserted. Some omissions were doubtless concessions to contemporary taste, for example, the deletion of Titania's description of the

games she played with the pregnant Indian princess (II, i, 124–35). Diction
was also altered for much the same reason: to satisfy the 'refinements' of
the age. Hence, Lysander and Hermia's dialogue in Act I, i is not only
abbreviated, but transformed in part as follows:

Ly. O my true *Hermia*! I have never found
By Observation, nor by History,
That Lovers run a smooth, and even course:
Either they are unequal in their Birth –
Her. O cross too high to be impos'd on Love!
Ly. Or if there be a Simpathy in choice,
War, Sickness, or pale Death lay Siege to it,
Making it momentary as a sound,
Swift as the Lightning in the blackest night ...

Such changes invariably flattened the poetic effect. But in an age that saw
– and preferred – Nahum Tate's *King Lear* (1681) to Shakespeare's, that
is hardly surprising.

Aided by advances in theatrical machinery and movable stage sets, spectacle
became increasingly important on the Restoration stage (as it has done these
days in Broadway and West End musicals), and *The Fairy Queen* was 'second
to none for mechanical marvels' (Summers, p. 235). At the end of Act III,
for example, Titania summons her elves to prepare 'a Fairy Mask' to entertain
Bottom and orders her bower to become an 'Enchanted Lake'. At once '*The
Scene changes to a great Wood; a long row of large Trees on each side: A
River in the middle: Two rows of lesser Trees of different kind just on the
side of the River, which meet in the middle, and make so many Arches: Two
great Dragons make a Bridge over the River; their Bodies form two Arches,
through which two Swans are seen in the River at a great distance*'. Then
'a Troop of Fawns, Dryads and Naides' enter, and a soprano and chorus
sing a song of 12 lines, not Shakespeare's ('If Love's a Sweet Passion, why
does it torment?'; No. 20 in Kalmus's score). '*While a Symphany's Playing*
[Kalmus, No. 21], *the two Swans come Swimming on through the Arches
to the bank of the River, as if they would Land; there turn themselves into*
Fairies *and Dance* [Kalmus, No. 22]; *at the same time the Bridge vanishes,
and the Trees that were Arch'd, raise themselves upright*'; whereupon '*Four
Savages Enter, fright the* Fairies *away, and Dance an Entry*' [Kalmus, No.
23]. In the 1693 version, a soprano sings another song, 'Ye Gentle Spirits
of the Air' [Kalmus, No. 24], but both the early and the later versions then
introduce the quite unShakespearean dialogue and duet by Coridon and his
coy Mopsa. As if not satisfied by this intrusion of conventional pastoralism
into Shakespeare's more interesting one, Settle and Purcell conclude the act
with 'A Dance of Hay-Makers', another choral song, and (not until then)
Titania's ardent wooing of Bottom with his ass's head.

But this is only a precursor to what followed. Making room for the
spectacular ending of the opera, the playlet 'Pyramus and Thisbe' was
transferred from the last act to the rehearsal in the forest – a transposition

that some later versions of the *Dream* in the eighteenth and nineteenth centuries would also adopt. For the conclusion, Oberon and Titania appear before Theseus, Hippolyta and their assembled guests, and show them Juno 'in a Machine drawn by Peacocks'. 'While a Symphony Plays, the Machine moves forward, and the Peacocks spread their Tails, and fill the middle of the Theater'; then Juno sings a song to the lovers. As Oberon and the others depart, the machine ascends, the scene darkens, a symphony plays, and the scene is suddenly illuminated, revealing a Chinese garden. Before the final curtain comes down, a Chinese man and woman sing, six monkeys come from between the trees and dance, and two sopranos sing 'in parts' a song summoning Hymen, who appears and responds with a song of his own [Kalmus, Nos. 52–53]. The Chinese man and woman dance, and then all the dancers join in after 'The Grand Chorus'. Finally, after Oberon and Titania briefly bless the newly-weds, they end the opera with satirical verses directed at 'Wits, and Criticks'; 'Sharpers, Beau's, the very Cits' – altogether different in both substance and style from Puck's epilogue in Shakespeare's original.

The Fairy Queen was not restaged again until 1946, at Covent Garden jointly with the Sadler's Wells ballet company, after its score – lost for two centuries – had been recovered (Williams, 1973, p. 42). Nevertheless, Settle and Purcell's opera seems to have influenced later revivals and adaptations of Shakespeare's *Dream*, such as Garrick and Colman's in the next century. Interspersing the text with additional songs and dances as well as spectacle apparently appealed to audiences then more than a 'straight' production would have done (recall Pepys's reaction). While not nearly as spectacular as *The Fairy Queen*, these later adaptations also drastically altered Shakespeare's original, which presumably did not suit theatrical taste, though parts of it did and were accordingly mined for the stage. Indeed, *The Fairy Queen* heralded a prolonged period in which *A Midsummer Night's Dream* was adapted for a variety of purposes without itself ever being staged.

* * *

The first known eighteenth-century adaptation was *The Fairies* (1755), an opera by David Garrick and Handel's pupil, John Christopher Smith. Before that, bits and pieces of *A Midsummer Night's Dream* appeared in such afterpieces as Richard Leveridge's *Comick Masque of Pyramus and Thisbe*. A spoof of Italian opera that was then popular in London, in which even Wall sings (Williams, 1973, p. 43), it had nine performances in Lincoln's Inn Fields from 11 April 1716 to 9 September 1723 (Stone, p. 467). Twenty years later, in 1745, Leveridge's adaptation was revived and expanded as 'a Mock Opera, set to Musicke by Mr. Lampe' at Covent Garden (Odell, vol. I, p. 347). Earlier, on 2 January 1723, some of the Pyramus and Thisbe material was adapted for presentation (without singing) in Charles Johnson's redaction of *As You Like It* called *Love in a Forest*. Appropriately or not,

it was played before the Duke and his co-mates in exile for their entertainment in the forest (Odell, vol. I, pp. 244–5). Thus Shakespeare's text
continued to be used for whatever purposes a dramatist or theatre manager
deemed suitable, and it was a long time before anything like his original
Dream found its way to the stage again. Entertainment, not authenticity,
became the criterion governing theatrical representation, certainly as regards
Shakespearean comedy (compare Dobson, pp. 186–98).

Garrick and Smith's opera contains songs from Shakespeare, Milton,
Waller, Dryden, Lansdowne and Hammond. Several Italian singers were in
the cast along with the Drury Lane company and 'Savage's Boys' (*London
Stage*, Part 4, vol. I, p. 467). Garrick's witty, self-deprecating Prologue, which
defends English opera against Italian, mockingly attributes this 'awkward
Drama', 'guilty ... of Poetry and Sense', to one 'Signor Shakespearelli'. The
courtiers, lovers and fairies were all retained, but Peter Quince & Co. are
gone. Other cuts were also required 'to reduce the Performance to a proper
length', as the 'Advertisement' to the printed edition says. Though listed
among the dramatis personae, Hippolyta has nothing at all to say, and the
speeches of many other characters are sharply curtailed to make room for
airs to be sung. Unlike Purcell's opera, however, some of Shakespeare's
verses – however altered or shortened – are set to music (e.g. Helena's
lines, 'O happy fair!', I, i, 182–4, 192–3, and Hermia's, 'Before the time
I did Lysander see', 204–7). Twenty-one songs by others are interspersed
within the dialogue as well, along with 'Sigh no more, ladies, sigh no more'
from *Much Ado About Nothing*, Ariel's 'Where the bee sucks, there lurk
[*sic*] I' from *The Tempest*, and two other songs from Shakespeare's plays
(Stone, p. 471).

The Fairies' simplified plot is essentially that of Shakespeare's *Dream* minus
Act V. Although Bottom's role is cut, Puck reports to Oberon how Titania
woke from her sleep and straightaway loved a 'patch'd fool' that had come
into the forest with others to rehearse a play for Theseus's wedding day.
Omitting 'Pyramus and Thisbe', the opera ends with Helena's air, 'Love's
a tempest', Theseus's summons to the altar, and a chorus, 'Hail to love, and
welcome joy!' instead of Shakespeare's fairy masque. The production was
well received at its first staging at Drury Lane on 3 February 1755 and ran
for ten more performances. It was the first of four such 'entertainments'
Garrick adapted from Shakespeare's plays; its success led to similar adaptations of *The Winter's Tale*, *The Taming of the Shrew* and *The Tempest*
(Odell, vol. I, pp. 358–9; see also Stone, pp. 469–72).

Not ten years later, in 1763, Garrick (who was actually a staunch admirer
of Shakespeare) attempted to stage something closer to the original text,
something actually called *A Midsummer Night's Dream*. The eighteenth
century, after all, was the first great age of Shakespeare editing, and complete
texts of the plays became increasingly available after Nicholas Rowe's edition
of the *Works* appeared in 1709. But Garrick's efforts to restore Shakespeare's
original were in large measure stymied by his colleague, George Colman,

and the result was a fiasco. Garrick was by then living abroad, having fallen temporarily into disfavour after the riots instigated by Thaddeus Fitzpatrick at Drury Lane. Colman therefore supervised rehearsals at the Lane; he also frequently and abundantly altered the playscript. Garrick's version (Shattuck 3; Folger MND, 6) shows much more of Shakespeare's verse retained than Colman's, which cut an additional 561 lines that Garrick had retained (Stone, p. 474; see pp. 475–7 for some illustrative comparisons of the two versions). Colman's largest excision was the omission of almost all of Act V. But he also added lines; for example, 18 inserted at the end of Act I, ii, which turn the first meeting of Quince and his friends into what G.W. Stone calls 'a glee club rehearsal' (p. 474). These are followed by four eight-line stanzas sung consecutively by Quince, Starveling, Bottom and Flute intended for an 'epilogue' before the Duke, although of course the playlet was never performed despite Garrick's intention to retain it.

Given the quality of performance by the leading actors, Garrick's longer version probably would not have been any more successful than Colman's, which closed after a single night, 23 November 1763. The *St. James Chronicle* maintained that however 'admirable' the children's performance was, the acting of the adults was 'execrable' (see Stone, p. 480). The sleeping scene particularly displeased, as reported in the *Diary* of William Hopkins (the prompter): 'The Performers first Sung the Audience to sleep, & then went to sleep themselves' (*London Stage*, Part 4, vol. II, p. 1021). Three of the four vocal performers could not adequately deliver blank verse, except in recitative, and quite destroyed whatever good effect the children playing the fairies produced (Stone, p. 480).

In an attempt to recoup some of his losses, Colman produced *A Fairy Tale* three days later as an afterpiece to his *Jealous Wife* (Stone, p. 481). Unlike *The Fairies*, this two-act skit of 400 lines and 13 songs includes the Athenian workmen and the fairies but omits all the *Dream*'s lovers and courtiers. It begins with Shakespeare's second scene almost unaltered until the end, where Colman inserts a shorter version of his 'glee club' rehearsal. The scene then shifts to the fairies, includes several airs and a duet between Oberon and Titania, and then shifts to Titania's bower and a good deal more singing, including the fairies' lullaby. The first act ends as Oberon places the magic potion on Titania's eyes and the First Fairy sings another air. Act II opens with the workmen in the forest about to rehearse their play and proceeds to Puck's mischief. But instead of imposing an ass's head on Bottom, he simply scares everyone else away with thunder and lightning, leaving Bottom to be discovered and wooed by the Fairy Queen. The business continues much as in the *Dream*, but very abbreviated, as Titania and Oberon become reconciled, Puck removes a sound-asleep Bottom from the stage, an air is sung about Orpheus, and a lark heralds daybreak and the end of the play.

Colman's afterpiece seems to have been popular, with numerous performances in 1763–6 and one in 1767 (Hogan, vol. II, pp. 471–2). Years later, on 18 and 23 July 1977, *A Fairy Tale* was revived at the Haymarket as an afterpiece following *The Sheep-Shearing* (Colman's adaptation of *The Winter's Tale*) and *The Merchant of Venice*, respectively. But the seven performances of *A Fairy Tale* that summer were the last of the eighteenth-century adaptations and revivals (Hogan, vol. II, p. 473). We know of no others until Frederick Reynolds's operatic version in 1816 for John Philip Kemble, one that held the stage in some form or another for many years.

*   *   *

The nineteenth century saw a continuation of the depredations and borrowings, or adaptations, of Shakespeare's *Dream*, as it did for many other plays in the canon. In this great age of theatrical spectacle, text was often sacrificed for historical or technological display, as in the extravangazas of Charles Kean at the Princess's Theatre in mid-century. Scene painting had surpassed anything ever seen before and was consequently thoroughly utilized for productions. The advent of Mendelssohn's great score for an overture and incidental music to *A Midsummer Night's Dream* also had its impact on productions of that play as the century wore on. Garrick's rather abortive attempts to restore Shakespeare's texts nevertheless began to gather momentum, and eventually redactions such as Nahum Tate's *King Lear* disappeared from the stage. At the same time, romantic criticism and theory proclaimed that many of Shakespeare's plays could only be distorted or corrupted – certainly not properly realized – in performance. Granted, much of that criticism was grounded, in part, on plays performed in mutilated versions as compared with printed editions. But romantic critics held that the *Dream* was so highly imaginative a work of art, that *any* representation was bound to fall far short of what the language of the play itself could convey to an active intelligence.

Typical is William Hazlitt's comment on the first performance of Reynolds's *Dream* at Covent Garden on 17 January 1816: 'All that is fine in the play, was lost in the representation' (Salgādo, p. 117; see also Odell, vol. II, pp. 111–12). This view continued to dominate much thinking about Shakespeare in performance during the Romantic period in England.

What Hazlitt saw, however, was yet another adaptation of Shakespeare's play. Reynolds criticized Colman's 1763 version as 'inefficient' and attributed its failure on the stage to two main causes: (1) the omission of many of Shakespeare's 'poetical' passages, particularly those by the fairies, and (2) the excision of all of 'Pyramus and Thisbe', though the audience had been led to expect it. He claims to preserve more of the original 'beauties', admitting nevertheless that Shakespeare's name may be 'degraded', perhaps, insofar as his lines are 'interwoven with those of a modern Dramatist'. The modern dramatist is of course Reynolds, who confesses he was 'compelled to alter, transpose, introduce new Songs, and new Speeches' and even to compose a whole new scene and part of another. He insists, nevertheless, that he has made 'some atonement' for his own 'defects', by 'restoring to the Stage, the lost, but divine Drama, of *A Midsummer Night's Dream*' ('Advertisement' in the 1816 edition).

A careful collation of Reynolds's adaptation with any modern edition will show that his claims are overstated. As the promptbook in the Folger Shakespeare Library demonstrates (Folger, MND 18), Kemble went still further in deleting more of the original script, as did Edmund Kean, who followed him, using the Reynolds text (Folger, MND 9). Reynolds deleted or revised many lines, adding new ones along with songs, 'quartettos', choruses, and even a 'Bird Symphony' near the end of Act II, i. Most of the lovers' dialogue (III, ii, 188–344) is omitted, and a new 'finale' ends the scene (although this is crossed out in pencil in the Folger promptcopy). A new 'Hunting Scene' appears at IV, i, 100, and afterwards Reynolds transposed a good deal, so that 'Pyramus and Thisbe' occurs earlier, and the play ends with the discovery and awakening of the young couples in the forest, an air by Hermia, and a rousing recitative, 'Warriors! march on!'; whereupon, instead of Shakespeare's fairy masque or Puck's epilogue, '12 or 20 warriors enter in procession in their way to the Hall of State' in a Grand Pageant proclaiming Theseus's triumphs. Finally, Hermia sings 'Now pleasure's voice be heard around' to conclude the action (see Odell, vol. II, pp. 75–7, 113). No wonder Hazlitt reacted as he did!

Spectacle and operatic adaptation thus continued to overwhelm Shakespeare's fairy play (see Williams, 1973, pp. 49–50). Describing the set designs and scenery, Odell admits that they must have been 'very pretty pictures', alluring in their way (II, 113), as the designs of *The Fairy Queen* once had been. Audiences of all periods seem to be attracted by spectacle; 'designer's theatre', bemoaned by some critics today, is not a new phenomenon. Reynolds adapted more of Shakespeare's plays, but by 1833 his version of the *Dream* had been reduced to an afterpiece of merely two acts, whose only distinction is that it was the first to use Mendelssohn's great 'Overture' (Odell, vol. II, p. 147; Williams, 1973, p. 52). Not until the end of the nineteenth century, which witnessed the experiments of William Poel and Harley Granville-Barker, did reaction against extravagant display begin in earnest. Meanwhile, Madame Vestris's production at Covent Garden in 1840, Samuel Phelps's at Sadler's Wells in 1853, and Charles Kean's at the Princess Theatre in 1856 are major productions of the *Dream* at mid-century.

Although we can credit the Italian contralto and theatrical manager Madame Lucia Elizabeth Vestris with restoring Shakespeare's language to *A Midsummer Night's Dream*, it is also true that her production, staged at Covent Garden in 1840, continued the tradition of spectacle, song and dance that *The Fairy Queen* began a century and a half earlier. The promptbook used for the production is lost, but the edition published by James Pattie in 1840–1 was taken from it and gives a reasonably accurate picture of what it was like (Williams, 1977, p. 4, who notes that the text in *Lacy's Acting Plays* is really based as much on Charles Kean's 1856 production as on Vestris's and is thus unreliable). To make room for musical interludes and dances, and to provide time for scene shifting, Vestris cut nearly 400 lines, or about 18 per cent, of Shakespeare's text, mostly from the lovers' dialogue in Act III, ii (ibid., p. 5; Griffiths, pp. 390–1). Still, Vestris's production retained a good deal more of Shakespeare's language than theatre audiences had heard for over two centuries – and more than they would hear in Charles Kean's celebrated production 16 years later. Vestris, furthermore, tended to keep major passages, such as Titania's 'forgeries of Jealousy' (II, i, 81–117) and Puck's epilogue, relatively intact. In this respect, she was ahead of her time, as later nineteenth-century productions did not quite follow her example (Williams, 1977, pp. 5–6). Mid-Victorian taste, moreover, soon dominated poetic decorum. Although Vestris's production omitted the metaphors of 'big-bellied' sails and 'wanton wind' (II, i, 128–9, 131; Griffiths, p. 390), Hermia still spoke of giving up her 'virgin patent' (I, i, 80); and at the end Theseus could say, 'Lovers, to bed'. In later Victorian productions Hermia refers to her 'maiden heart' and Theseus cries, 'Lovers, away' (Williams, 1977, p. 6).

Madam Vestris's colleague, James Robinson Planché, deserves much of the credit for such integrity as the script retained (Williams, 1977, p. 6). He was also the scenic and costume supervisor and devised the elegant staging of the last scene which, unlike earlier productions, such as Reynolds's, was developed from a reading of Shakespeare's lines rather than a disregard for them. It was none the less spectacular, with more than 50 fairies flying or dancing through architectural galleries, up and down palace stairs, carrying blue and yellow lanterns (Griffiths, p. 394; Williams, 1973, p. 55). Vestris also used music differently – to set off Shakespeare's words, not to replace them, and to develop a dramatic purpose. The 14 songs, all taken from Shakespeare's text, are sung by fairies to distinguish them further from the mortals (Williams, 1977, p. 6). Mendelssohn's great overture raised the curtain, as it had for Tieck's production in Berlin 13 years earlier (Salgãdo, p. 118); but thereafter Vestris tended to stay with one composer, Thomas Simpson Cooke, instead of a hodgepodge of others, as her predecessors had done (Williams, 1977, p. 7).

Costumes were 'classical' for the Athenians, sandals and tunics for the mechanicals, and variations on Greek themes for the wingéd fairies (Griffiths, p. 392). Vestris herself played Oberon and sang nine of the songs, while a girl played Puck – traditions that originated earlier and continued throughout the nineteenth century (Williams, 1977, p. 9); even today an actress sometimes assumes the role of Puck. A woman playing Oberon seemed in the nineteenth century to convey better than a man the 'ephemeral idea' of fairyland consistent with the taste of the age (recall that it was a woman who posed for the famous portrait of Sir Galahad). This consideration outweighed whatever 'impotence' or contradiction the casting of women for both Oberon and Titania might bring to the quarrel between the fairy king and queen (Williams, 1974, p. 77).

Covent Garden required spectacle, and spectacle there was, as noted;

but it was not quite so extravagant as before. Vestris employed Reynolds's excellent scene painters, and she took full advantage of their talent. The first scene, for example, disclosed a view of Athens from Theseus's palace – a long perspective of fanes overlooking the Acropolis towering in the distance (Williams, 1977, p. 11). Of the forest scenes, one reviewer remarked: 'all is sylvan and visionary; the wood scenes change like the phases of a dream' (*The Spectator*, 21 November 1840; cited by Williams, 1977, p. 15). In Act III the lovers lose their way in 'a mist of descending gauzes', a device that influenced many later productions of the play (Williams, 1977, p. 17). One delightful touch (used again by eight-year-old Ellen Terry in Charles Kean's production) was Puck's first appearance, not as Shakespeare introduces him – the text was altered slightly for the effect – but rising up centre stage sitting on a mushroom at II, i, 31 (Griffiths, p. 390; Williams, 1977, p. 18).

Except for the difficulty conveying the subtleties of Shakespeare's poetry through the vast spaces of Covent Garden – a defect of the production many commentators remarked – Vestris's *Dream* was artistically successful, though not financially. With an enormous payroll to cover, Vestris and her husband, James Matthews, found (like Betterton in 1692–3) that receipts could not cover costs, and the production consistently lost money even as it made history. Others might enchant their audiences more completely, but Vestris's *Dream* set the pattern for the century (Williams, 1977, pp. 16–19).

Foremost among those who thoroughly enchanted their audiences was Samuel Phelps at Sadler's Wells a dozen years later. His production was a culmination of much Romantic theorizing, which maintained that Shakespeare's *Dream* had to be ethereal, truly dreamlike, to succeed in performance – if it could be actualized on stage at all. Thus Henry Morley begins his review in 1853 by stating: 'Every reader of Shakespeare is disposed to regard the *Midsummer Night's Dream* as the most essentially unactable of all his plays. It is a dramatic poem of the utmost grace and delicacy; its characters are creatures of the poet's fancy that no flesh and blood can properly present. ... The words they speak are so completely spiritual that they are best felt when they are not spoken'. No wonder, then, that Madame Vestris's 'spectacle ... altogether wanted the Shakespearean spirit' (p. 56).

But predisposed as Morley was, even he recognized Phelps's accomplishment. Both the acting and the set design conspired to realize in the theatre something closely approximating Shakespeare's ideal, because Phelps understood that he had to present 'merely shadows'. To persuade the audience, therefore, that they but slumbered on their seats, that what appeared before them were merely visions, Phelps subdued everything to this 'ruling idea'. 'There is no ordinary scene-shifting, but, as in dreams, one scene is made to glide insensibly into another' (Morley, p. 57). To achieve this effect, Frederick Fenton, Phelps's scene designer, used a diorama and a piece of greenish-blue gauze let down in front of the stage for Acts II to IV (Foulkes, pp. 57–8).

The acting was something else again, and here Morley rather misses an important point in the play when he complains that the four lovers 'could not fancy themselves shadows' (p. 59). Of course they could not – and should not have done. The 'arguing and quarrelling and blundering', which Morley says should be 'playful and dreamlike and poetical', are, if anything, harsh and discordant and nightmarish, as more recent critics have insisted (e.g. Kott, p. 212–18; Halio, pp. 137–41). Morley's sympathies, typical of his time, favour Hermia in Act III as 'a gentle maid forlorn ... not at all meant to excite mirth', but here again he misconstrues the action of the play and its point. He is closer to the mark in praising Phelps's Bottom, especially as he moved from the violently gesticulating clown of Act I to the quieter, accepting dream-figure in Act IV. But Morley goes too far in regarding Bottom 'as unsubstantial, as airy and refined as all the rest' (p. 60).

If dreaminess is what the audience wanted, dreaminess is mainly what they got in Phelps's production. It was the greatest triumph of his career, and Bottom his most notable role (Odell, vol. II, p. 322). Gas lighting, which Fenton introduced for the first time at Sadler's Wells, along with the diorama and gauze curtain, helped produce the desired effect (Foulkes, pp. 57–8). Costumes also contributed and harmonized with the scenery. The fairies 'were none of your winged, white-muslin fairies with spangles and butterfly wands, but were real, intangible shadowy beings that ... would infallibly at the first cockcrow melt into thin air' (Douglas Jerrold; cited by Odell, vol. II, p. 324). In keeping with the 'ruling idea', quiet movement and, where appropriate, a bright, full moon also characterized the production (Morley, p. 58; Odell, vol. II, p. 324). Music there was, and dancing, although which music has not as yet been discovered for either this production or its revival in 1855–6. For the 1861 revival, however, Mendelssohn's score (arranged by W.H. Montgomery) and new scenery were featured (Williams, 1973, pp. 57–8).

Whether Phelps used it or not, by mid-century Felix Mendelssohn's music was becoming a fixture in many stage productions. Williams (1973, pp. 58–9) records the use of nine pieces and the overture, with additional pieces 'by Beethoven, T. Cooke, Horn, Levey, &c.', at the Theatre Royal, Dublin, in November 1852; and in February 1854 two New York productions, one by William Evans Burton and the other by Thomas Barry and E.A. Marshall, advertised the whole of Mendelssohn's score, Burton claiming its use for the first time anywhere. If this was the first time Mendelssohn's music was used in America, it was not the first production of the play across the Atlantic. There had been an operatic version in 1826; and in 1841, possibly inspired by Vestris's success, Charlotte Cushman played Oberon in a non-operatic version (Shattuck, *Hallams to Booth*, p. 89).

The competing New York productions of 1854 were likewise probably inspired by a British success – Phelps's – although Burton insisted that, as he had never seen the *Dream* performed, all the stage business and spectacular effects were new and original (ibid., p. 111). He also claimed that both scenery and costumes were historically correct. The warriors were attired, for example, as pictured by 'Willemin, in his Costumes des Peuples d'Antiquité', Hermia and Helena wore 'the long sleeveless tunic, the caladris or stole, with the rich and varied peplum over the bust, and the crepida sandal', etc. (ibid., p. 113). In Act II, Oberon and Titania descended in aerial cars, and in Act IV at sunrise, mists rose from the valleys and the sun rose in powerful splendour. This was, after all, an age that emphasized archaeological verisimilitude, and for once, as Shattuck says, 'New York was served as fulsomely with erudition as Charles Kean served his audiences at the Princess's in London' (ibid.). Burton scored a resounding triumph as Bottom and was led shortly afterwards to introduce another Shakespeare play, a spectacular *Tempest*. But Barry's production, if more spacious, was less successful and even occasioned negative comments on the play itself. Shakespeare in America was gradually coming of age, but for a long time would still follow British leads.

A watershed for nineteenth-century productions of the *Dream* was surely reached in Charles Kean's version, which opened on 15 October 1856. Kean heavily cut more than 800 of Shakespeare's lines to keep performances under three hours, despite a great deal of music, dance and spectacle. Not only Mendelssohn's music, but many other pieces were used – the promptbook is studded with music cues – although the orchestra at Kean's Princess Theatre did not do justice to them (Williams, 1973, p. 60). Nevertheless, the production was immensely successful, running for 150 performances. Once again, a woman, Fanny Ternan, played Oberon, but the fairies were all full-grown adults, not children. Morley generally admired the production but criticized some aspects, particularly the famous May-pole ballet that ended the third act. Complaining that 'we miss a portion of the poem most essential to its right effect – the quarrel between Hermia and Helena', he comments on its substitute: 'a ballet of fairies round a maypole that shoots up out of an aloe, after the way of a transformation in a pantomime, and rains down garlands. Fairies, not airy beings of the colour of the greenwood, or of the sky, or robed in misty white, but glittering in the most brilliant dresses, with a crust of bullion about their legs ...' (Morley, p. 134). Evidencing the 'depraved taste' of the audience, in Morley's view, the ballet was encored.

Although Kean here eschewed historical authenticity, representing Athens in the Age of Pericles rather than of Theseus (explained in the Preface to his edition), his set designs were greatly admired. Even Morley remarked on 'the exquisite scenery' of the play, for which the original water-colour paintings are still extant. Then as now, however, set designs could – and in Morley's view did – detract from the poetry of the play. Instead of letting the verse provide the scenery, the designers foreclosed abruptly on the audience's imagination (p. 133). Thus, instead of an unspecified room in Theseus's palace, an elaborate painted set filled the stage. The scene location in the edition (as in the playbill) hardly conveys what the audience actually saw: '*A terrace adjoining the Palace of Theseus, overlooking the City of*

Athens'. Kean's biographer more fully describes the vista: 'We saw, on the hills of the Acropolis, the far-famed Parthenon, the Erichtheum, and the statue of the tutelary goddess Minerva, or Athena; by its side the theatre of Bacchus; in advance, the temple of Jupiter Olympus, partially hiding the hall of the Museum; and on the right the temple of Theseus' (Cole, vol. II, p. 198). Even the summit of Mars Hill appeared (Kean, p. vi). The setting of course recalls Madame Vestris's production, but Kean outdid even hers, as did the final spectacle of 'some ninety fairies tripping up and down the stairs of Theseus's palace, waving bell-like lanterns while the fairy chorus sang Mendelssohn's "Through this house give glimmering light"' (Williams, 1973, p. 60).

Just as Vestris's production had inspired Edmund Simpson's and Phelps's had inspired both Burton's and Barry's, so Kean's inspired Laura Keene's in New York in 1859 at the Olympic Theatre. She used both his text and the Maypole ballet with still greater dollops of Mendelssohn's music, and the opera singer Fanny Stockton as Oberon (ibid., p. 61). On 8 October 1867 at the same theatre but under different management and with a different cast the play was revived, but its chief claim to fame was its scenic splendour (Odell, *Annals*, vol. VIII, pp. 280–1). In 1873, Augustin Daly went further yet with spectacle and extended pantomimes using 'the famous Golden Quartette of California, in the dress of Satyrs' to sing the lullabye to Titania in Act II (ibid.). Daly again staged the play in 1888, with John Drew, Otis Skinner, and Ada Rehan; Isadora Duncan in papier-maché wings was one of the dancing fairies. But this time Weber's *Oberon* overture opened the performance and more of Bishop's 1816 score than Mendelssohn's was played (Williams, 1973, pp. 61–2).

Daly once again staged the play in 1895. On 9 July, George Bernard Shaw reviewed the performance at Daly's Theatre and remarked how Daly had fitted up all his fairies 'with portable batteries and incandescent lights, which they switch on and off from time to time, like children with a new toy' (vol. I, p. 169). He is especially harsh on Lillian Swain as Puck and on Daly's casting a woman as Oberon, although he has the highest praise for Ada Rehan's Helena (vol. I, pp. 173–6). Above all, he criticizes Daly for his persistent illusionism, which destroys rather than complements the effect of Shakespeare's verse. The time was ripe, if not overripe, for reaction, and in Granville-Barker's productions early in the twentieth century, reaction indeed began.

WORKS CITED

Bentley, Gerald Eades, *The Jacobean and Caroline Stage* (Oxford, 1941–68), 5 vols.

Brooks, Harold (ed.), *A Midsummer Night's Dream*, New Arden edn, (London, 1979).

Chambers, E.K., *The Elizabethan Stage* (Oxford, 1923), 4 vols.

————, *Shakespearean Gleanings* (Oxford, 1944).

————, *William Shakespeare* (Oxford, 1930), 2 vols.

Cole, John William, *The Life and Theatrical Times of Charles Kean, F.S.A.* (London, 1859), 2 vols.

Dobson, Michael, *The Making of a National Poet* (Bloomington, Indiana, 1992).

Foulkes, Richard, 'Samuel Phelps's *A Midsummer Night's Dream*: Sadler's Wells – October 8th, 1853', *Theatre Notebook*, XXIII, 1968/9, 55–60.

Greg, W.W., *The Shakespeare First Folio* (Oxford, 1955).

Griffiths, Trevor, 'A Neglected Pioneer Production: Madame Vestris' *A Midsummer Night's Dream* At Covent Garden, 1840', *Shakespeare Quarterly*, XXX, 1979, 386–96.

Halio, Jay L., 'Nightingales That Roar: The Language of *A Midsummer Night's Dream*, in *Traditions and Innovations*, ed. David G. Allen and Robert A. White (Newark, Del., 1990), pp. 137–49.

Kean, Charles (ed.), *A Midsummer Night's Dream* (London, 1856).

Hogan, Charles Beecher, *Shakespeare in the Theatre, 1701–1800* (Oxford, 1957), 2 vols.

Kott, Jan, *Shakespeare Our Contemporary*, trans. Boleslaw Taborski (Garden City, NY, 1964).

London Stage, 1660–1800, The, ed. William Van Lennep *et al.* (Carbondale, 1960–68), 5 parts. Part 1: 1660–1700, ed. William Van Lennep, 1965; Part 4: 1747–1776, ed. George Winchester Stone, 1962, 3 vols.

Milhouse, Judith, *Thomas Betterton and the Management of Lincoln's Inn Fields, 1695–1708* (Carbondale and Edwardsville, 1979).

Morley, Henry, *Journal of a London Playgoer, from 1851 to 1866* (London, 1891).

Odell, George C.D., *Annals of the New York Stage* (New York, 1927–49), 15 vols.

————, *Shakespeare from Betterton to Irving* (New York, 1920), 2 vols.

Ringler, William, 'The Number of Actors in Shakespeare's Early Plays', in *The Seventeenth-Century Stage*, ed. G.E. Bentley (Chicago and London, 1968), pp. 110–34.

Salgādo, Gāmini, *Eyewitnesses of Shakespeare*, New York, 1975.

Shattuck, Charles, *Shakespeare on the American Stage: from the Hallams to Edwin Booth* (Washington, DC, 1976).

————, *Shakespeare on the American Stage: From Booth and Barrett to Sothern and Marlowe* (Washington, DC, 1987).

Shaw, George Bernard, *Dramatic Opinions and Essays* (London, 1906), 2 vols.

Stone, George Winchester, '*A Midsummer Night's Dream* in the Hands of Garrick and Colman', *PMLA*, LIV, 1939, 467–82.

Summers, Montague, *The Restoration Theatre* (New York, 1934).

Watkins, Ronald, and Jeremy Lemmon, *In Shakespeare's Playhouse: 'A Midsummer Night's Dream'* (Totowa, NJ, 1974).

Wells, Stanley (ed.), *A Midsummer Night's Dream* (New Penguin), (Harmondsworth, 1967).

————, '*A Midsummer Night's Dream* Revisited', *Critical Survey*, III, 1991, 14–29.

Williams, Gary Jay, '"The Concord of this Discord": Music in the Stage History of *A Midsummer Night's Dream*', *Yale/Theatre*, IV, 1973, 40–68.

————, 'Madame Vestris' *A Midsummer Night's Dream* and the Web of Victorian Tradition', *Theatre Survey*, XVIII, 1977, 1–22.

————, 'Our Moonlight Revels: *A Midsummer Night's Dream* on the English-Speaking Stage, 1662–1970', Yale University diss., 1974.

Shakespeare and Language

CHAPTER FIFTEEN

U and Non-U: Class and Discourse Level in *Othello*[1]

T.H. Howard-Hill

In general, a play is a collection of speech acts accompanied by gestures and actions. The priority of the speech acts is determined by the progress of the play from the playwright's pen to the stage. In the classical or neo-classical style of writing the quality of the speech acts must be appropriate to the social status of the characters as well as the genre of the play: decorum must be observed. And, of course, as Hamlet knew from his humanistic studies at Wittenberg, the players should suit the actions to the words. For *Othello*, then, Olivier was correct to demand for his Iago (as Berry reports) 'a solid, honest-to-God N.C.O'.[2] The basis of Olivier's choice was not, as Berry claims, Iago's rank as Ensign because in the Elizabethan military code his rank was only one step below Cassio's. Iago is identified as a 'non-commissioned officer' (in modern terms) by the properties of his speech acts. If this needed to be made clearer than it seems in the first scene of the play, Shakespeare provided as a contrast to Iago a gentleman and a different style of speech. The linguistic differences between Cassio and Iago are the focus of this essay.

Drama is a special kind of discourse in which speeches are directed from speaker to hearer and to an attendant audience at the same time. In drama such as Shakespeare's the speakers of the play and the listeners in the audience inhabit different linguistic milieus. M.H. Short has shown convincingly that the text rather than performance provides suitable material for discourse analysis, which rescues 'dramatic criticism from the variability of performance analysis on the one hand and the inadequacy of traditional textual analysis on the other'.[3] Nevertheless, while he recognizes 'the general *embedded* nature of drama, because features which, for example, mark social relations between two people at the character level become messages *about* the characters at the level of discourse which pertains between author and reader / audience' (p. 188), his analysis takes little account of the playwright's obligation to convey information to the audience, and neglects to consider that the audience may lack information that is ostensibly implicated by the dialogue that would enable them to complete the circuit of communication. The application of discourse theory to drama has, therefore, a complexly

double function: to describe the properties of the utterances between characters in the play, within that special communicative context, and then, to
identify the information that the audience should receive from the communicative exchange. This last function falls within the scope of the traditional
literary criticism.

Moreover, since a play is an artificially constructed complex of conversations controlled by the playwright's design for the work, one may
possibly identify quite readily the 'cooperative principle' that H.P. Grice
suggested was involved in conversations, and note the application of the
accompanying regulative conventions that he called 'maxims'.[4] I can summarize them briefly. The maxim of *quantity* (1) relates to parsimony: speeches
should supply neither too little nor too much information. The maxim of
quantity (2) requires speakers to believe that their contributions to conversations are true. The maxim of *relation* (3) requires relevance, and the
maxim of *manner* (4) suggests the avoidance of prolix, obscure, ambiguous
and disorderly speech. Fortunately for the sake of linguistic variety and the
fictions of drama, the maxims are frequently broken. Sites of dislocation can
point to significant variations in the relationships of dramatic characters, as
the ensuing discussion shall reveal.

In apparently the only monograph devoted to the subject, *Shakespeare
and Social Class*, Ralph Berry declares that 'class as motivation is the principle
of *Othello*. In the relations between military rank and social class lie the causes
of the tragedy' (p. 112). In Cinthio's story, the Moorish Captain, the Ensign
and the Corporal operate on the company level and the spread of social
class is not great, nor is it insisted on. The Ensign lusts after Disdemona
and it is on account of his rejection that he plots against the Corporal and
Disdemona. (The Moor is his confederate, not the object of his hate.) In
Othello, as is well known, the situation is remarkably different. Although
his military relations with his officers seem to be those of a captain of a
company, the Moor is also the commander of the Venetian forces. His
lieutenant, Cassio, besides his immediate responsibilities within the company,
has capabilities as an officer that warrant his appointment from Venice to
succeed Othello as the military governor of Cyprus. By enlarging the military
dimension of the play, Shakespeare thickened the motivational texture of
the source in a manner that makes the class relationships of the principal
characters freshly significant.

Declaring that 'Rank goes with class', Berry elaborates the distinction
that Iago himself draws in the opening of the play: 'this counter-caster
(accountant)' Michael Cassio,

A fellow ...
That never set a squadron in the field,
Nor the division of a battle knows
More than a spinster — unless the bookish theoric,
Wherein the toged consuls can propose
As masterly as he.
                                        (I, i, 21–6)[5]

Iago's words can elicit surprising sympathy amongst naïve readers and listeners. He voices the common antipathies between doers and thinkers, men of affairs and mere scholars, workers and bosses, common soldiers and their officers, and frontline soldiers and base staff in a speech directed to the 'silly gentleman', Roderigo. Iago's complaint is motivated by hatred and fed by envy and resentment and is therefore intrinsically unreasonable. Even in our egalitarian society it is not expected that soldiers who have fought 'At Rhodes, at Cyprus, and on other grounds, / Christen'd and heathen' (I, i, 29–30) even with distinction[6] are thereby qualified for command positions, or that staff officers should possess all the experience and military expertise of the men under their command. To serve and to command entail different abilities and responsibilities.

If Berry is correct to assert that the causes of the tragedy lie in the relations of rank and class, then we must believe that Iago's initial and foremost motivation is to secure military promotion. Then it follows that Iago would discredit Cassio to obtain the promotion he was denied originally, or he would seek to destroy Othello to punish him for choosing Cassio in his place. Iago does indeed succeed to Cassio's place and Othello is indeed destroyed, but these events do not occur for the reasons Berry's statement suggests. It seems to me that he neglects Bradley's warning about the intrinsic unreliability of Iago's communications and ignores the circumstances that influence his speeches in Act I, i.[7] The play opens at a crucial and stressful point for Iago. He has cultivated the wealthy young gentleman, Roderigo, on the pretext that he can further his courtship of Brabantio's daughter, Desdemona. (Why he believes that Iago has access to her the play does not explain.) Their relationship is that of Sir Toby Belch and Sir Andrew Aguecheek in *Twelfth Night*. Indeed, the first thing that Shakespeare tells us about the two is that Iago has had Roderigo's purse as if the strings of it were his, that is, at command (I, i, 2–3). As well, we learn later that Iago has been pocketing the gifts Roderigo has given him to deliver to Desdemona. In short, Iago has found the gullible Roderigo a rewarding source of undeclared income:

> Thus do I ever make my fool, my purse;
> For I mine own gain'd knowledge should profane
> If I would time expend with such a snipe
> But for my sport and profit.
>   (I, iii, 383–6)

On Desdemona's elopement with Othello this profitable arrangement seems about to be ended.[8] Unless Iago is to forfeit it, Roderigo must be persuaded first, to persist in his courtship of the now-married Desdemona, and second, to continue to employ Iago as his agent. In Bertrand Evans's words,

> Seizing on Roderigo's convenient cue ... 'Thou told'st me thou didst hold him in thy hate,' he assures his victim that such is indeed the case, for has not the Moor unjustly passed him over in favour of the incompetent Cassio? ... Reconsidering the circumstances in which these protestations are made – Iago's dire need of sudden, dramatic speech and action if he is to keep his fish now

that Desdemona has married – we are obliged to question the truth of everything spoken by the villain.[9]

In particular, we may suspect the truth of Iago's statement that 'Three great ones of the city, / Off-capp'd to him [the Moor]' (I, i, 8–10) for his promotion because there is no other evidence in the play for the event. However, we cannot doubt the priority of Iago's hatred of Othello to his attempt to be promoted (if in fact that occurred at all) because Roderigo refers to an earlier occasion when Iago 'toldst me thou didst hold him in thy hate' (I, i, 7). Cassio's promotion is brought in to provide a circumstance that will assure Rodrigo that he hates Othello for a good reason and therefore may be trusted to work against his commander for Roderigo's benefit.[10]

It is clear from Iago's self-serving speeches that he is deeply hostile towards Cassio; the hostility is driven by class antagonism. Setting aside the prior questions about Iago's chances of promotion and the expedience of his statements to Roderigo, Shakespeare in quite few words has prepared us to meet a Cassio who is substantially distinguished from Iago. From Iago's own words we have learned that Cassio is the kind of man who achieves high staff rank, and Iago is not.[11] Shakespeare has reversed the relative military standing of the two from his source and widened their class differences in a number of crucial passages. Noticing that 'relations between Cassio and Iago are continuingly tense', Berry maintains that Cassio knows 'perfectly well that his subordinate has in some respects a better claim to the post' (p. 113). The play gives no sign that Cassio knows anything of the kind nor would any Elizabethan suspect it. Elizabethans knew well from campaigns in Ireland, the Netherlands and at Cadiz the hazards of inexperienced gentlemen being appointed to command positions. However, that did not lead to widely experienced common soldiers being put over their social superiors but only to pleas for the appointment of more competent gentlemen: 'Rank goes with class' (Berry, p. 113) or more clearly, class governs rank.[12] Gentlemen volunteers may have been expected to trail pikes in Elizabethan armies,[13] but they remained gentlemen, with different expectations and opportunities than the likes of Bates, Williams, Bardolph, Pistol, Bullcalfe and Shadow. The play does not present, as Berry has it, a Cassio 'naturally wary and also compensatory' (p. 113) but rather, a Cassio who acts like the gentleman he is and on that count unsuspectingly gets into very deep trouble with the one character in the play whose ungentleman-like qualities are insisted on. *Othello* is not about class nor otherwise are motivations closely related to class. Nevertheless, it is the singlemost important and defining aspect of the relationship between Iago and Cassio. The truth of this is revealed by examination of the language of their exchanges in the play.

Berry gets close to the point when he notes in Cassio's 'address a scarcely veiled policy of putting Iago down' (pp. 113–14) in social situations. Nevertheless, Cassio does not act from 'policy': that is Iago's forte. He acts according to his status as a gentleman: simply the thing he is makes him live. Shakespeare discloses the clear-cut difference between them in a passage that seems to have been neglected by commentators, including Berry. In Act I scene ii Iago, apparently professing ignorance of Othello's marriage, asks him about it (I, ii, 11).[14] Iago was not in Othello's confidence in the business, a situation that contrasts forcefully with what we later learn of Cassio's role. Then Cassio enters, bearing an urgent summons to attend the Duke. Othello enters the house, presumably to say farewell to Desdemona, leaving Cassio and Iago together on the stage at Cassio's first entrance. Because Othello could well have gone to the Senate immediately without attracting our attention, or occupied Cassio and Iago with other business, Shakespeare must have had some special purpose in mind for the ensuing exchange between Iago and Cassio.

> *Cas.*   Ancient, what makes he here?
> *Iago.* Faith, he to-night hath boarded a land carract.
> If it prove lawful prize, he's made for ever.
> *Cas.* I do not understand.
> *Iago.*   He's married.
> *Cas.*   To who?
>
>   (I, ii, 49–52)

The first point of observation is that Cassio initiates an exchange in which he pretends not to know that Othello is married, flouting Grice's maxim of quality. He first asks what Othello is doing in that place, which may appear to be an innocent request for information. But, the question that ends the conversation ('To who') reveals rather more than a shaky grasp of verb/object agreement. At III, iii, 96 we learn that Cassio went between Desdemona and Othello in his courtship 'from first to last', and, in the historic rather than the dramatic time of the play, was Othello's confidante. We could take Cassio here to be respecting confidentiality, not knowing that at the start of the play Iago knew of the elopement and had since had it confirmed by Othello himself. However, the overall tenor of the passage and its consistency with other exchanges between Othello's two officers indicates that Cassio is purposefully reticent. In fact, because he initiated the exchange we can call this a deliberate prevarication: Cassio pretended to seek information about Othello when he was privy to Othello's actions and whereabouts all the time.[15]

However, the most significant feature of this passage is that it reveals that Cassio and Iago have a communication problem: 'I do not understand,' Cassio replies to Iago's first speech. Iago has breeched the maxim of quantity; instead of the simple 'He's married' of line 52, he shrouds his communication in metaphor, thus flouting the maxim of manner as well. Cassio's response is an almost inevitable response to Iago's failure to cooperate in their conversation. It provides Cassio's second prevarication or, if one prefers, downright lie. In fact, he responds with those words simply *because* he understands Iago. Once commentators learned that a 'carract' was 'a large trading ship' (Evans), no one found any difficulty with Iago's words. Cassio understands Iago very well but he rejects the register of the discourse and

its attempt to situate Cassio within Iago's linguistic milieu. 'Unless I am
mistaken,' Bradley wrote '[Iago] was not of gentle birth or breeding. ... for
all his great powers, he is vulgar' (p. 213–14). It is as a vulgarian, a charter
member of the 'nudge nudge, wink wink' school of barrack-room raconteurs
that Iago talks about Othello's marriage-night. Besides suggesting that the
marriage is Othello's opportunistic move to better himself ('he's done all right
for himself, hasn't he?'), the metaphor of a rich merchant ship taken as a
prize by pirates barely conceals the suggestion of despoliation. It 'debases
Othello's marriage', in Norman Sanders's words: he points out that '"Boarded"
has a sexual connotation', which Iago intends to convey.[16] This language
is, of course, characteristic of Iago's part throughout the play. Citing this
passage, Ifor Evans remarks that 'Instead of beauty there is a continuous and
emphatic imagery that renders gross and contemptible the sexual act on whose
contemplation the action of the play depends.'[17] When Cassio claims not to
understand Iago's communication, he rejects the offensive code employed
by someone of a lower social status. Not only do gentlemen not use such
language; they do not allow themselves to be addressed in such a manner.
Iago simply does not know how to talk to a gentleman, and the well-born
Cassio feels no obligation to accommodate himself to his vulgar colleague.
We may suspect that Iago adopted that tone deliberately, as an assault on
the sensibilities of a man he despises, but that is not important. The main
point is that Cassio and Iago employ different speech codes based on social
class, a fact that Shakespeare established in the play as early as he could.

   Cassio takes the social offensive when next we see him in Iago's company,
in an exchange where it is almost possible to sympathize with Iago. In Act
II scene i Cassio's is the first of the ships to arrive at Cyprus, followed by
Desdemona and Emilia, with Iago and Roderigo. Cassio greets Iago with
unexceptional words, and then Emilia:

> Let it not gall your patience, good Iago,
> That I extend my manners; 'tis my breeding
> That gives me this bold show of courtesy.
>   (II, i, 97–8)[18]

Shakespeare confirms Cassio's social superiority to Iago by making him
act like a boor. It is one thing to extend gentlemanly courtesies to the wife
of a colleague of lower social class; it is another to comment on the gaping
social gulf between them, as if Iago were incapable even of understanding
the basis of Cassio's attention to Emilia. Then, significantly, Cassio is
silent during Iago's rather clumsy foolery with Desdemona until he answers
her question:

> How say you, Cassio? is he not a most profane and liberal counsellor?
> *Cas.* He speaks home, madam. You may relish him more in the soldier than in
> the scholar.

This is the second time Cassio has distinguished his class superiority to
Iago, the third if the opening passage (I, ii, 44–52) be counted. In fact,

that is all that he has done with Iago to this point in the play. After this speech Iago is left isolated on the stage, well placed for his extended aside:

> *Iago.* He takes her by the palm; ay, well said, whisper. With as little a web as this will I ensnare as great a fly as Cassio. Ay, smile upon her, do; I will gyve thee in thy own courtship. You say true, 'tis so indeed. If such tricks as these strip you out of your lieutenantry, it had been better you had not kiss'd your three fingers so oft, which now again you are most apt to play the sir in. Very good; well kiss'd! an excellent courtesy! 'Tis so indeed ...
>
> (II, i, 167–77)

Iago here is observing Cassio with Desdemona. Berry remarks that 'Behaviour appropriate to rank looks like bad acting to those of lesser station, placed as audience' (p. 115) but 'the concentrated viciousness of his commentary', as Berry describes it, draws fundamentally on Cassio's 'put down' and is merely fuelled by Cassio's further demonstration of his breeding. His 'well kiss'd' refers to the earlier occasion with Emilia as well as Cassio's present behaviour with Desdemona.[19] 'Courtesy' is a term picked out of Cassio's speech, to which he twice refers directly: ''tis so indeed'. Iago's intention announced at the conclusion of Act I, 'To get his place and to plume up [his] will / In double knavery' (I, iii, 393–4), is now invested with emotional justification: within the same scene Iago will move directly against Cassio – for Cassio's own sake, not simply as a step towards the destruction of Othello's marriage – conspiring with Roderigo to provoke Cassio to strike him and be discredited.

Iago's long speech to Roderigo at II, i, 221–47 contains his second characterization of Cassio:

> who stands so eminent in the degree of this fortune as Cassio does? a *knave* very voluble; no further conscionable than in putting on the mere form of civil and humane seeming, for the better compass of his salt and most hidden loose affection? Why, none, why, none – a slipper and subtle *knave*, a finder-out of occasion; that has an eye can stamp and counterfeit advantages, though true advantage never present itself; a devilish *knave*. Besides, the *knave* is handsome, young, and hath all those requisites in him that folly and green minds look after; a pestilent complete *knave*. ...

So many of these lines before Iago describes Cassio's person are more appropriate for Iago himself that it is not surprising that he gives Cassio the designation that is his in the play. Iago calls Cassio 'knave' no fewer than five times in ten lines of text, a degree of repetition that must be significant. (He uses the word in *Othello* only six times.) 'Knave' had its origin in class, being often used in contrast with the word 'knight', and developed to mean 'a *base* and crafty rogue' (O.E.D.). The context indicates that craftiness is not the issue; rather, Iago is concerned to impugn the gentlemanliness that so clearly distinguishes Cassio from him. He brings Cassio to his social level first in words, only secondly in deeds.[20]

Within a short time Iago is positioned to work his plot: in Act II scene iii he and Cassio meet to set the watch. As if to emphasize the social difference between the two, as indicated by their speech, Shakespeare stages a reprise of the situation I first commented on (I, ii, 44–52). Here, however, instead of rejecting Iago's inferior linguistic codes, Cassio rephrases Iago's comments about Desdemona – who is now enjoying a second wedding-night, in Cyprus – in a different register. This is analogous to the kind of code-switching among multilingual speakers described by such linguists as Carol Myers-Scotton: speakers shift between languages as part of 'negotiations of personal rights and obligations relative to those of other participants in a talk exchange'.[21]

> [*Iago.*] Our general cast us thus early for the love of his Desdemona; who let us not therefore blame. He hath not yet made wanton the night with her; and she is food for Jove.
> *Cas.*   She's a most exquisite lady.
> *Iago.* And I'll warrant her, full of game.
> *Cas.*   Indeed she's a most fresh and delicate creature.
> *Iago.* What an eye she has! Methinks it sounds a parley to provocation.
> *Cas.*   An inviting eye; and yet methinks right modest.
> *Iago.* And when she speaks, is it not an alarum to love?
> *Cas.*   She is indeed perfection.
> *Iago.* Well – happiness to their sheets! ...
>
> (II, iii, 14–29)

In this stichomythic passage Iago makes four statements about Desdemona designed to draw attention to her physical attractiveness in a context of love-making. Cassio responds with four statements that translate Iago's into a different code/register. For Iago's 'sport for Jove', 'full of game', provocative 'eye' and speech, Cassio returns 'exquisite lady', 'fresh and delicate creature', 'right modest', and 'indeed perfection'. The content of this exchange again exposes the social distance between the two; the contrived parallel structure of the passage reveals that Shakespeare intended it to provide a significant element in the play.[22]

Another small exchange between Cassio and Iago deserves small attention. Because Cassio has a weak head for drink, Iago's plot succeeds: Cassio is dismissed as Othello's lieutenant. Citing his reputation as 'an honest man', Iago describes the reputation that Cassio has lost as 'an idle and most false imposition; oft got without merit, and lost without deserving' (II, iii, 268–70). Although these words are ironic when applied to the reputation for honesty Iago has cultivated, from Iago's standpoint they are literal truth. Cassio's reputation as a worthy lieutenant to Othello was indeed 'got without merit' as Iago had claimed earlier ('Preferment goes by letter and affection, / And not by old gradation, [I, i, 36–7]) and, as the contriver of Cassio's misfortunes, Iago *knows* that Cassio lost his reputation 'without deserving'. Eventually, after accepting Iago's advice, offered 'in the sincerity of love and *honest* kindness' (II, iii, 327–8), Cassio leaves: 'Good night, *honest* Iago' (334). This second of three 'honest's in 26 lines is the first occasion on which Cassio swells the chorus testifying to Iago's honesty. Iago repays him in the same language: Cassio becomes 'this *honest* fool' in Iago's concluding soliloquy. So much for honesty, and gentlemen.

At this point having discovered that necessity makes strange bedfellows, Cassio has become the third of Iago's gulls in the play. However, Iago does not yet have complete control of the situation, as he learns in Act III, iii when the focus of the spectators' attention turns to Iago with Othello. Pleading for Cassio's reinstatement in Iago's presence, Desdemona refers to Cassio's part in Othello's courtship:

> What, Michael Cassio,
> That came a-wooing with you, and so many a time,
> When I have spoke of you dispraisingly,
> Hath ta'en your part — to have so much to do
> To bring him in!
>
> (III, iii, 70–3)

Shakespeare supplies only one small point of illumination of Iago's reaction to the knowledge that Cassio had deceived him in their first conversation (I, ii, 44–55). Iago himself had been duped: Cassio had known very well why Othello was at the scene of Act I, ii.

> *Iago.* My noble lord —
> *Oth.*   What dost thou say, Iago?
> *Iago.* Did Michael Cassio, when you woo'd my lady,
> Know of your love?
> *Oth.* He did, from first to last. Why dost thou ask?
> *Iago.* But for a satisfaction of my thought,
> No further harm.
> *Oth.*   Why of thy thought, Iago?
> *Iago.* I did not think he had been acquainted with her.
> *Oth.* Oh yes, and went between us very oft.
> *Iago.* Indeed!
> *Oth.* Indeed? ay, indeed. Discern'st thou aught in that?
> Is he not honest?

And so it goes. Desdemona's revelation of Cassio's dishonesty inspires Iago's very first speech after her departure; it, rather than her persistence in urging Cassio's reinstatement, now feeds his practice. The knowledge of Cassio's involvement in the courtship gives Iago all the ammunition he needs to pursue his design against the three principals. Because Iago is almost continuously on stage with Othello during this part of the play, there is no occasion for Shakespeare to inform us how Iago reacted to learning of Cassio's deliberate reticence. It can only have strengthened his resolve to gull the only character in the play who had gulled the guller — but in the following scenes the arch-gentleman Cassio dwindles into a pallid pawn in Iago's diabolic game. Only the unanticipated rebellion of the 'silly gentleman' Roderigo brings Iago into conflict with his social superiors. Hereafter Cassio's speeches with his ally Iago are not socially coded. But in the early half of the play Shakespeare has made the first demonstration of Iago's ability to persuade others to 'speak his language'; in the second half of the play his pupil is Othello.[23]

NOTES

1.   The title refers to a classic article on the distinctive properties of upperclass
     British speech by Alan S.C. Ross, 'Linguistic class-indicators in present-day
     English', *Neuphilologische Mitteilungen*, 55 (1954), 20–56, abridged in
     Noblesse Oblige, ed. Nancy Mitford (London, 1956), pp. 11–36.

2.   Ralph Berry, *Shakespeare and Social Class* (Atlantic Highlands, N.J.: Humanities
     Press International, 1988), p. 113.

3.   M.H. Short, 'Discourse analysis and the analysis of drama', *Applied Linguistics*
     11 (1981), 180–202, p. 183.

4.   H.P. Grice, 'Logic and conversation', *Syntax and Semantics*, ed. Peter Cole and
     Jerry L. Morgan (Academic Press, 1975), pp. 41–58.

5.   Shakespeare's text is quoted from G.B. Evans's New Riverside edition (Boston,
     Mass., 1974).

6.   This speech gives the main information about Iago's military career. Even though
     the words are his own, it is not necessary to doubt them. He is described as
     'the bold Iago' (II, i, 75), 'brave Iago' (V, i, 37) and 'a very valiant fellow' (V,
     i, 52), terms consistent with his function as Ensign. However, there is no certain
     indication that he has held any higher position than Ensign or that anyone (other
     than himself) in the play thinks he merits one.

7.   'One must constantly remember not to believe a syllable that Iago utters on
     any subject, including himself, until one has tested his statement by comparing
     it with known facts and with other statements of his own or other people, and
     by considering whether he had in the particular circumstances any reason for
     telling a lie or for telling the truth', A.C. Bradley, *Shakespearean Tragedy;
     Lectures on Hamlet, Othello, King Lear, Macbeth* (London: Macmillan, 1904),
     p. 211.

8.   The play does not explain how Iago knew of the elopement. It is somewhat
     surprising that he does at this point in the play considering that he knew nothing
     of Cassio's serving as Othello's go-between. Roderigo could not have learned
     of Desdemona's flight from Brabantio because, as this scene shows, he was
     ignorant of it himself.

9.   B. Evans, *Shakespeare's Tragic Practice* (Oxford: Clarendon Press, 1979),
     pp. 120–1.

10. We don't have to believe that Iago was ever a candidate for the lieutenantship
     even in his own mind. An argument designed to persuade the gullible Roderigo
     cannot easily withstand rational examination.

11. Paul A. Jorgensen (*Shakespeare's Military World*, Berkeley: University of
     California Press, 1956) notes that 'Accelerated promotion, in an army of any
     period, is bound to cause resentment in anyone victimized by it' (p. 110), a
     view that Barry quotes in support of his argument. However, the play gives
     no evidence that Cassio's promotion was accelerated. He has known Othello
     for some time (Desdemona: 'You have known him long', III, iii, 11) and fought
     alongside him: (Desdemona to Othello: 'A man that all his time / Hath founded
     his good fortunes on your love, / Shared dangers with you', III, iv, 93–5).
     Only by accepting the literal truth of Iago's characterization of Cassio's military
     experience in Act I, ii can we believe that it was inferior to Iago's.

12. Berry justly observes that 'Othello has rightly appointed Cassio for the very
     qualities he lacks – the social skills, excellent connections with the Venetian
     Establishment, a general worldly savoir faire' (p. 166). Having these good
     attributes, why should Cassio feel that he holds his position unfairly? Nothing
     in the text suggests he does. These qualities, too, are not those practical men-
     at-arms are expected to show and display Iago's lack of qualifications for the
     appointment.

13. J.W. Fortescue, 'The Soldier', *Shakespeare's England* (Oxford: Clarendon Press, 1916), p. 115.

14. The reservation comes from doubt whether 'Are you fast married' should be read as Iago's request for information he did not have before then (which I incline to believe), or as his query about the status of the marriage. The New Cambridge edition glosses 'fast' as 'firmly'. Iago then is asking Othello in effect whether he has consummated the marriage, which would make it indissoluble. However, although this interest fits some of Iago's other speeches, it doesn't seem appropriate to the circumstances of this scene.

15. Incidentally, 'The Senate [having] sent about three several quests / To search [Othello] out' (II, ii, 46–7), Cassio's was the successful party. This suggests Cassio's prior knowledge of Othello's whereabouts.

16. New Cambridge Shakespeare edn (Cambridge: CUP, 1984), p. 66.

17. Ifor Evans, *The Language of Shakespeare's Plays*, 2nd edn (London: Methuen, 1959), p. 150.

18. E.A.J. Honigmann, whose sensitivity to gradations of the English class speech code is greater than mine, identifies condescension in Cassio's 'good Iago'. 'Between that condescending "good Iago" and the word "Sir", with which the ancient replies, an Elizabethan audience must have recognized a common speech barrier' (*Shakespeare's Seven Tragedies; The Dramatist's Manipulation of Response*, New York: Macmillan, 1978, p. 83). However, such monosyllables were useful for the metre and are not reliable social indicators. (Iago says 'good Cassio' at V, i, 87, in circumstances that do not suggest irony or sarcasm.) Nevertheless, a class difference may be indicated by the fact that whereas Cassio addresses Iago by his name (before they become 'friends' in Act II, iii), Iago does not use Cassio's name to his face until IV, i, 48, by which time Cassio has become his client, and he uses Cassio's rank (V, i, 56) even after he has taken his place. A context for these comments is given by Roger Brown and Albert Gilman, 'Politeness theory and Shakespeare's four major tragedies', *Language in Society* 18 (1989), 159–212, and Carol Replogle, 'Shakespeare's salutations: a study in stylistic etiquette', *Studies in Philology*, 70 (1973), 172–86, Peter J. Gillett, 'Me, U, and non-U: class connotations of two Shakespearean idioms', *Shakespeare Quarterly*, 25 (1974), 297–309, and Joan Mulholland, '"Thou" and "you" in Shakespeare: a study in the second person pronoun', *English Studies*, 48 (1967), 1–9, all reprinted in *A Reader in the Language of Shakespearean Drama*. Essays collected by Vivian Salmon and Edwina Burness (Amsterdam: J. Benjamins, 1987).

19. Iago's reference to 'her lips' (II, i, 101) shows how Cassio kissed the married Emilia in the 'bold show' of his manners. On the other hand, it hardly seems likely that the conventions of Elizabethan society permitted Cassio to lollygag around frequently kissing his general's wife on the lips. (Further, for actors to do so would give too great support to the suspicion that Desdemona and Cassio were over-friendly.) It seems from Iago's references to 'fingers' that her hands marked the limits of his liberties. Then, it would be possible for Iago and the audience to compare Cassio's treatment of married women of different social classes.

20. I do not mean that Cassio ever loses his gentility but rather, by stripping Cassio of his lieutenantry, Iago produces at least a symbolic class inversion. From the end of Act III, iii onwards, Iago – at least in terms of rank – is the gentleman.

21. Carol Myers-Scotton, 'Code switching as indexical of social negotiations', *Codeswitching: Anthropological and Sociolinguistic Perspectives*, ed. Monica Heller (Berlin: Mouton de Gruyter, 1988), pp. 151–86, p. 178. I am grateful for the advice and help my colleague provided during the writing of this paper. Code-switching among languages in plays is discussed by Esme Grobler,

'Varieties of dramatic dialogue', *South African Theatre Journal*, 4 (1990), 38–60, pp. 41–8.

22. Cassio's insistence in his drunkenness that 'the lieutenant is to be sav'd before the ancient' (II, iii, 109–10) strikes Berry as 'something Cassio has been saying all the time to Iago' (p. 114). It seems, however, that by his mention of 'the general, nor any man of quality' (106), Cassio is referring foremost to the military hierarchy (rather than to social class) and that here, by virtue of his rank, Iago is included among men 'of quality'. In brief, Cassio's modest quip here should not be read as another put-down, though of course Berry's comment that 'Shakespeare uses [Cassio] to get at Iago' (p. 114) is amply demonstrated elsewhere.

23. This point is too widely recognized to need documentation.

CHAPTER SIXTEEN

Etymology in Shakespeare
Marvin Spevack

Whatever else it may be, etymology is not simply a linguistic or rhetorical or lexicographical pursuit. It may be all of these, of course, but it is more. It is most importantly, in the words of Ernst Robert Curtius, a 'Denkform'. Curtius's characterization, it must be remembered, is a rendition of a well-known rhetorical concept: etymology as a special form of 'interpretatio'.[1] That interpretation is connected with definition, arrived at through etymology, which, as conceived by Quintilian and others, seeks the 'basic truth' believed to be inherent and reflected in the form or shape of the word.[2] Although this relationship between meaning and form may be arbitrary, it was the rule and the practice until modern times. And it still exists in popular etymologizing, as in the view that the London interchange Elephant and Castle is derived from Infanta of Castile or that Alzheimer's disease is somehow Old Timer's disease.

It would be a mistake, however, to regard this kind of etymologizing as primitive or irrational (even if occasionally applied ludicrously, as in the type *canis a non canendo* or *lucus a non lucendo*). It may belong to the dubious tradition of the pictogram, arbitrary and limited, hardly compatible with the real and factual. Yet in its emphasis on truth based on observation, on the stability of meaning, as evidenced in the authorities down the ages who have proposed and championed it, it has interesting implications. For one thing, it resembles the mode of thought called figura, illustrating patterns which are multi-dimensional and omnipresent.[3] To call it 'false' etymology is to miss the point, much as artistic anachronism, another inflection of figura, is (mistakenly) derided in literature (but not, tellingly, in painting). For another, it is a pendant to history in that it connects the past with the present. The interpretation which is etymology is, further, a way of coming to terms with the present and may have important socio-political ramifications. In the Renaissance it reflected the uses of the past in the present and served, *inter alia*, to bolster the definition of self and social order and, if properly applied, to foster social stability. Socio-political reflections of popular etymologizing, too vast for adequate treatment here, are apparent in the powerful Elizabethan interest in genealogy, which resembles etymology in its tracing of origins.[4] They are also to be seen in such activities as the etymological analysis of the names of the ranks of society. William Harrison's treatment of the 'degrees of people in the commonwealth of England' is based on the premise that the etymology of the name 'expoundeth the efficacy of the word'. Accordingly, Roman or Latin sources of such names as *prince* or *duke* are appropriate to 'gentlemen of the greater sort', as opposed to those of the third 'sorts of persons' by which England is 'governed and maintained', the 'yeomanry ... and their sequel, the laborers and artificers', who are 'not called masters and gentlemen but goodmen'.[5] William Camden uses political personages to illustrate the much-admired and widely found practice of visual renditions of popular etymologies. As examples of 'Rebus, or Name-devises', also labelled 'painted Poesies', he indicates that '*Morton*, Archbishop of *Canterbury* ... was content to vse a *Mor* vpon a Tunne; and sometime a Mulberry tree called *Morus* in Latine, out of a Tunne' and that 'The Abbot of *Ramsey* more wisely sette in a Seale a Ramme in the Sea'. And it is hard to deny the socio-political subtext of other devices he uses which in method if not in essence are related, directly or indirectly, to popular etymologizing. As an instance of an 'Allusion ... as it were a dalliance or playing with words, like in sound, vnlike in sence, by changing, adding, or subtracting a letter or two; so that words nicking and resembling one the other, are appliable to different significations', he mentions that 'in the beginning of her late Maiesties raigne one alluded to the name *Elisabetha*, with *Illæsa-Beata*, that is, *Safe without hurt, and happy*'. Similar are his examples of anagrams, 'the onely *Quintessence* that hitherto the *Alchimy* of wit could draw out of names ... which is a dissolution of a Name truly written into his Letters, as his Elements, and a new connexion of it by artificiall transposition, without addition, subtraction, or chang of any letter into different words, making some perfect sence applyable to the person named': for example, Thomas Egerton (Lord Ellesmere): *Gestat Honorem*; *D'evreux* (Earl of Essex): *Vere dux*; Edwardus Somerset (Earl of Worcester): *Moderatus, sed Verus*.[6]

A further support for the persistence of the 'truth' inherent in the over-lapping of meaning and form was the practical view that etymology, in essence an audio-visual experience, was also the criterion for the correct spelling, pronunciation and usage of words.[7] It is no wonder that the time of Shakespeare, which witnessed the marshalling of energies into what has come to be called the modern state, was likewise a period of concentrated didacticism, of a striving – in all the activities and strata of society – for order. This was especially true in the area of letters, in which the emergence of Early Modern English was marked by an astounding increase in the recorded vocabulary and in book production, with the attendant appearance of mono-, bi- and polylingual dictionaries, of school books, of orthoepist tracts, and other forms of educational prescriptiveness devoted to 'true' writing, speaking, living – much of it addressed to an ever-widening audience in a bustling and changing world. So the addressees of the hard word dictionary of Robert Cawdrey (*A Table Alphabeticall*, 1604) 'gathered for the benefit & helpe of Ladies, Gentlewomen, or any other unskilfull persons'; so those of Henry Cockeram (*The English Dictionarie*, 1623):

'Enabling as well Ladies and Gentlewomen, young Schollers, Clarkes, Merchants; as also Strangers of any Nation, to the understanding of the more difficult Authors already printed in our Language, and the more speedy attaining of an elegant perfection of the English tongue, both in reading, speaking, and writing.'[8]

*   *   *

Within the main stream and addressing a popular audience, Shakespeare was a traditional etymologist. But though he accepted the norm, he was, as was his wont, both conservative and innovative. Etymology was for him a rhetorical device and a pattern of thought. Because it predicated the inter-dependence of the audio-visual and the essential, the concurrence of sound, form and meaning, it had interesting dramatic applications. Certain of them are well known. Naming is the most obvious example. Telling names, nicknames, assumed names, attributive and metaphoric names, direct and indirect, ironic and symbolic names: all have been discussed in detail and require little more than mention.[9] They serve as a quick and efficient means of delineating persons and collectively of providing local colour and atmos-phere. Naming is Shakespeare's favourite device for establishing character and scene. Falstaff's recruits – Mouldy, Feeble and friends – need only be named (and Shakespeare always makes a point of having their names said aloud) and the scene is complete. It should be noted, however, that many of such applications are reserved in the main for relatively few 'real' or 'historical' characters, being largely employed for characters in fictional contexts – i.e. comedies – where there is a greater latitude in naming, both for the characters on stage and, it is interesting to add, for those who do not appear in the dramatis personae at all. Of the 124 obvious telling names in Shakespeare, for example, only Hotspur is non-fictional. For 'normal' names – especially British names, which constitute the largest group in Shakespeare – the exact etymological connections are so embedded or established, like sunken metaphors, as to be unrecognizable or irrelevant. The characterizing 'nomen est omen', a standard feature of Shakespearean critical practice, has yet to be applied to surnames like Blunt ('blond, fair-headed'), Bolingbroke ('brook of the family / folk of [as AS called] Bull'), Gloucester ('bright / splendid Roman site'), Lovell ('wolfcub, little wolf'), Mortimer ('dead sea [in the sense of stagnant lake]'), Stafford ('ford by a straithe / landing-place'), Vaughan ('little').[10] Or to first names like George ('from Old French, from Latin *Georgius*, from Greek Georgios [from *georgos* farmer, a compound of *ge* earth + *ergein* to work]'), Malcolm (Anglicized form of the Gaelic name *Mael Coluim* 'devotee of St Columba' whose name means 'dove' in Latin'), Oswald ('Old English personal name composed of the elements *os* god + *weald* rule'), Stephen (from the Greek word *stephanos* 'garland, crown'), William ('composed of the elements *wil* will, desire + *helm* helmet, protection').[11]

More dynamically, popular etymologizing serves characterization and dramatic situation. It identifies and defines in an assertive, if not aggressive, manner. Requiring wit and imagination, it is the inevitable weapon of critical characters like Mercutio mocking Romeo 'without his roe, like a dried herring' (*Romeo and Juliet*, II, iv, 37) or Edmund ironically yoking *bastard* and *base* (*Lear*, I, ii, 6) or Dick the Butcher deflating the ancestral claims of Jack Cade: Mortimer, 'a good bricklayer'; Plantagenet, 'a midwife'; Lacies, sellers of 'many laces' (2 *Henry VI*, IV, ii, 39–46). What is noteworthy is the method: the selective interpretation of names in a way that suits the purposes of the etymologizer in the immediate situation. For Mercutio (*Romeo*, III, i, 77) Tybalt (from Theobald, 'composed of the elements *theud* people + *bald* bold, brave') is King of Cats (alluding to Tibert, the cat in *Reynard the Fox*); for Talbot (*1 Henry VI*, I, iv, 107) Joan la Pucelle (from the late Latin *pulcella*, deriving from the Latin *puella*) is a pucelle (drab, slut); in self-mockery the dying Gaunt (a variant of Ghent) is indeed gaunt (*Richard II*, II, i, 82). Such nonce formations dynamize the moment and the person, the inventor as well as the subject, who becomes the object. Indeed the object may, albeit unconsciously at times, turn the weapon against himself. That is Shakespeare's way with pedants, malapropists and various other blunderers. So the laborious Holofernes is self-exposed in his insistence on the pronunciation 'abhominable' for *abominable* (*Love's Labour's Lost*, V, i, 24); so Constable Dull's interpreting the Latin *haud credo* as 'awd [old] gray doe' (*Love's Labour's Lost*, IV, ii, 12); so Mistress Quickly's invention of *honeyseed* for *homicide* (2 *Henry IV*, II, i, 52).

The interplay of such etymologizing and punning – especially paronomasia and antanaclasis – is self-evident. Not simply indulging in a form of amusement, punning etymologizers – be they the warring – wooing lovers of the romantic comedies or the brooding discontents of the tragedies – embody or seek or achieve superiority and domination. And their opposites – the witless, the pedantic, the pretentious – are undermined and deflated not only by the attacks on them but also by their own occasional attempts at etymologizing. At any rate, what results is a tension between individuals, men and women, and indeed social classes. Comic or serious in intent and effect, popular etymologizing is at its core neither neutral nor impartial. Unlike historical or scientific etymology, which is factual and objective, popular etymology is personal and interpretive, often reflecting psychological and social needs and pressures. In effect, where there is an overlapping or at least compatibility of etymologizing and objective, as in the 'gaunt' example, the result is concentrated emphasis. Where there is a discrepancy, the result is stress, the effect ranging from comic idiocy, as in *honeyseed*, to irony, as in *pucelle*. In either case the ideal of suiting the action to the word, the word to the action, is implemented, modified, underscored or even subverted by the acceptance or non-acceptance, by the recognition or non-recognition, of the respective claims of appearance (i.e. popular etymology) and reality (i.e. historical etymology). Etymologizing in Shakespeare is thus still another inflection of this ever-present, central, and of course much-discussed theme.

*   *   *

Etymologizing as a way of thinking, as a method of imaginative interpretation, is not restricted to the internal workings of Shakespearean drama. It is, and always has been, a ready tool of editors of Elizabethan texts since 'true' writing and 'true' speaking were aims rather than realities, as the abundance of prescriptive and self-help works indicates. What makes the deciphering of Elizabethan texts, written or printed, so enticing is their inherent instability. The vagaries of Elizabethan spelling, the confusions arising from homophones or homographs like *travel/travail* or *metal/mettle* or *deer/dear* or *hart/heart*, the difficulties attributable to careless or carefree handwriting (leading to a school of editorial activity devoted to minim errors), even the now discredited theory of aural dictation to a compositor: all have contributed to the founding and perpetuation of the editorial establishment. Not surprisingly, for what solves the problem, settles the reading, is the interpretation of the visual image, what it looks or sounds like and seems to suggest or, conversely but simultaneously, how the image may correspond to and reinforce an interpretation already arrived at. Whichever the case, choosing is irrelevant. For both procedures use the same means: each attempts to justify the interpretation by analysing the core of the visual image – in short, by identifying and defining on the basis of a preferred etymology.

Cruxes in Shakespeare offer abundant evidence. Cleopatra's apostrophe 'An *Anthony* it was / That grew the more by reaping' (the Folio reading, 1. 3305–6) has been amended by practically every editor since Lewis Theobald (1733) to 'An Autumn 'twas ...' Etymologically, both readings have much in common. For one thing, they are perfect for speculative reasons since scholarship has concluded that their etymologies are not at all clear. The *Oxford English Dictionary* regards *autumn* as being of 'doubtful etymology'; *The Dictionary of First Names* identifies *Anthony* as 'the usual form of the old Roman family name *Antonius*, which is of uncertain (probably Etruscan) origin'. For another, both readings can be supported by the interpretations – i.e. popular etymologizing – of Renaissance authorities. Thus John Minsheu (*Ductor in Linguas*, 1617), following a long tradition, derives *autumn* from the Latin *augeo*, 'to increase, because at that time fruits and corn are increased'. Shakespeare's contemporary, William Camden, derives (p. 43) *Anthony* as coming from '*Antheros*, flourishing, from the greeke *Anthos*, a floure' (while admitting 'there are yet some that drawe it from *Anton* a companion of *Hercules*'). And finally, if both etymological interpretations have been defended as being logical for the same reason, so both have been rejected by a line of critics as being illogical for much the same reason. To the first, Hiram Corson (1873): 'It could hardly be said that an autumn *grows* the more by reaping.' To the second, Theobald (1733): 'How could an *Antony* grow the more by reaping?' Similarly, editors, unable to detect the 'true' meaning of the Folio reading *An-heires* (*Merry Wives of Windsor*, 1. 749) and yet able to assert that it is 'a form of a non-extant but then understood word' (Arden, ed. H.J. Oliver, 1971) or that the later Folios were 'prepared to print a nonsense-word' (Oxford, ed. T.W. Craik, 1989) have proposed a spectrum of possibilities ranging from *on here* to *Ameers* (or emirs, the Turkish title) but settling in the main (perhaps out of frustration) for Theobald's conjecture *myn-heers* (or modern spellings of the Dutch expression), the 'required word'. Oddly enough, no one seems to have realized or recognized the etymological potential of the Folio spelling – i.e. the possible connection with the German *Ahnherr*, literally ancestor, but a not unlikely term of respect.[12]

Not only the resolving of cruxes but most efforts by editors and critics to establish the 'true text' are connected, in one way or another, with popular etymologizing. In a not so strange way they may resemble the procedures of characters in the plays. Certainly it is hard to deny that some emendations and interpretations result from the heat of competition. John Payne Collier, apparently restless with the uncontroversial explanation of *foison* (*Anthony*, 1. 1357), suggests in his fourth edition (1877) the etymology 'Possibly, from Fr. *fois*, because it is *timely, seasonable*'. How else to explain Franz's (*Die Sprache Shakespeares*, 1939) considering *Triumpherate* (*Anthony*, 1. 1781) a Shakespearean blending of *triumvirate* and *triumph*, while J. Dover Wilson (ed. 1950) finds the Folio spelling an excellent example of a Shakespearean spelling of *triumvirate*? Or can it be the frustration by the lack of a reasonable alternative that accounts for the *OED* joining Minsheu, who finds *Sirra* (1. 3475) '*A contemptuous word, ironically compounded of* Sir, *and* a, ha, *as much as to say*, ah sir, *or* sir boye, *&c.*'

*   *   *

Etymology, as this brief outline suggests, is a far-reaching and elusive process, perhaps as much the province of philosophy, where the study began, as of historical linguistics. In essence, both popular and historical etymology seek truth arrived at through a chain of correspondences, a process of development. But whereas the orientation of historical etymology is multilingual and chronological, dealing with many languages over many years, popular etymology is mainly monolingual and immediate, an instantaneous and indelible reaction or interpretation. The former is leisurely and expansive; the latter is compressed and restrictive. It may seem contradictory to hold that popular etymology is consistent with stability when it is the product of ad hoc interpretation. But that interpretation is finite and fixed, is not always bound by established syntax and semantics, admits no modification or change. It is ahistorical and thus permanent, well suited to Shakespeare's art, ever creating ever-fixed marks.

NOTES

1. See Edmond Faral, *Les arts poétiques du xiie et du xiiie siècle* (Paris, 1924), p. 65, who modifies Cicero's placing etymology under *inventio*.
2. See Heinrich Lausberg, *Handbuch der literarischen Rhetorik*, 2 vols (München, 2nd edn, 1973), I, 76–7, 255.
3. See the classic treatment by Erich Auerbach, 'Figura', *Archivum Romanum*, 22 (1938), 436–89.
4. See my 'Beyond Individualism: Names and Namelessness in Shakespeare', *Huntington Library Quarterly*, 56:4, Autumn 1993, 383–98.
5. *The Description of England* [1587], ed. Georges Edelen (Ithaca, 1968), pp. 95, 113, 120.
6. *Remaines of a Greater Worke, Concerning Britaine* (1605), pp. 145–56.
7. See Lausberg, op. cit., I, 255. Tellingly, Cicero used the term *veriloquium*. Using popular etymology as a support, the orthoepist John Hart (*An Orthographie*, 1569, p. 20v) would pronounce and write herald 'Herralt', 'wholy a Dutch [i.e. German] word compounded of Herr, and Alt, which is olde Maister' and not 'Herault', a French word 'signifying a high Maister'.
8. Self-help books enjoyed a noteworthy popularity. According to R.C. Alston, *A Bibliography of the English Language from the Invention of Printing to the Year 1800: A Corrected Reprint of Volumes I–X* (Ilkley, 1974) even books on the English language reached a total (including editions and issues) of 471 to the year 1640.
9. For a summary, see 'Beyond Individualism', pp. 386–7. To the studies of names cited in fn. 15 of that article may be added two wide-ranging ones in *Shakespeare Jahrbuch (West) 1988*: Dale B.J. Randall, 'A Glimpse of Leontes through an Onomastic Lens', pp. 123–9, and Inge Leimberg, '"The Image of Golden Aphrodite": Some Observations on the Name "Hermione"', pp. 130–49.
10. Etymologies from Basil Cottle, *The Penguin Dictionary of Surnames* (Harmondsworth, 1967).
11. Etymologies from Patrick Hanks and Flavia Hodges, *A Dictionary of First Names* (Oxford, 1990).
12. This could apply as well to the crux often discussed along with *An-heires*, its likely homophone *Oneyres* (*1 Henry IV*, II, i, 76), whose pairing with *Burgomasters* reinforces the Germanic etymology.

CHAPTER SEVENTEEN

'My tongue-tied Muse': Inexpressibility in Shakespeare's Sonnets

Werner Habicht

The sigh at the beginning of Shakespeare's Sonnet 80 – 'O, how I faint when I of you do write' – along with repeated references to the poet-lover's exhausted Muse in the surrounding sonnets – 'my sick Muse' (79, 4); 'my tongue-tied Muse' (85, 1); 'forgetful Muse' (100, 5); 'resty Muse' (100, 9); 'O truant Muse' (101, 1)[1] – are extraordinary uses of what E.R. Curtius has identified as an 'unspeakability topos' (*Unsagbarkeitstopos*) that traditionally adorns rhetoric of praise.[2] That topos also occurs in Petrarchan love poetry, where the predictable reason for a poet's self-declared speechlessness or writer's block is, of course, his admiration of the beloved person's beauty – when 'onely my loke declareth my hert' (Wyatt, 25, 14) – and perhaps his diffidence, when 'her presence does astonish me / and strikes me dumb' (Griffin, 18, 9). Beauty, idealized by the loving thoughts and lofty fantasies it inspires, can cause a lover's desperate silence, as, for example, in Spenser's *Amoretti*, 3, 7ff.:

> But looking still on her, I stand amazed
> At wondrous sight of so celestial hew.
> So when my toung would speak her praises dew,
> It stopped is with thoughts astonishment;
> And when my pen would write her titles true,
> It ravisht is with fancies wonderment.
> Yet in my hart I then both speake and write
> The wonder that my wit cannot endite.

Spenser's concluding couplet also points to the paradox inherent in any use of that rhetorical device: even what is inexpressible must somehow be expressed; the silence must be performed with words that reveal its substance or betray its lack of substance. Nor will the poet desist from writing sonnets vowing his love and praising its object, for all the subjective problems posed by its verbalization. Hopefully the beloved person will not only be pleased by the 'leaves, lines, and rymes' that are offered (*Amoretti*, 1, 13), but also appreciate that 'they love indeed who quake to say they love' (Sidney,

Astrophil and Stella, 54, 14). The ideal may be a delicately balanced interaction between awe-struck silence and verbal praise – a poetic ideal to which Petrarch himself had alluded, even if admitting that it might be beyond a human poet's ingenuity:

> ivi l'parlar che nullo stile aguaglia
> e 'l bel tacere, e quei cari costumi,
> che 'ngegno uman non pò spiegar in carte.
>   (*Canzoniere*, 262, 11)[3]

If Petrarchan love sonnets examine the validity of both their silence and their speech, the necessity of exploring the paradoxical interaction of inward love and its outward manifestation presents itself.[4] What is implied – more or less tangibly – is a metapoetic concern with the expression of inexpressibility and, as a consequence, an exploration of the power of love poetry and its limitations. Petrarchan poetry, in that it strives to spiritualize, to idealize and to eternize the love-inspiring experience of beauty – for all the poet's physical frustration and inner strife that are involved – is necessarily about the nature of poetry as well as about the nature of love.[5]

Seldom, however, are the implications of inexpressibility dealt with as fiercely and as dramatically as in Shakespeare's *Sonnets*, especially in the rival poet group (78 to 87), on which the following remarks will chiefly concentrate. Here the poet-lover is 'silenced' not by his perception of the friend's beauty, but by the intrusion of a competitive 'other' – the rival who, by writing the friend's encomium more effectively and in a prouder and more progressive style, appears to be more successful in winning the desired favour (note the sexual innuendo in 'spends all his might'):

> O, how I faint when I of you do write,
> Knowing a better spirit doth use your name,
> And in the praise thereof spends all his might
> To make me tongue-tied speaking of your fame.
>   (80, 1–4)

We need not concern ourselves with the autobiographical triangular 'story' that may or may not underlie the experience reflected here, let alone with the much-debated identity of the rival, in order to notice that the drama of a poetological crisis is unfolding, with Sonnet 80 as a sort of climax. After all, the rival poet could also be, as Th.P. Roche has recently argued, a projection of the fictional poet's alter ego that up until then had too proudly claimed to conquer time by immortalizing the friend's beauty.[6] In any case the lead-up to that climax is compellingly consistent. In fact the poet's awareness of the redundancies, limitations and reductions of his own power of writing has manifested itself before the actual rival poet dauntingly enters the scene. As long as that awareness was dealt with in a more general and perhaps hypothetical fashion, positive consolations and justifications were not overly hard to come by. In Sonnet 26, for instance, the poet's devotion ('duty') may 'seem bare, in wanting words to show it'; but the friend will

remedy the deficit by putting 'apparel on my tattered loving'. And if Sonnet
32 imagines that 'these poor rude lines' will 'be outstripped by every pen'
after the poet's death, they still deserve to be treasured for the love they
contain; had the poet lived longer, he (and his Muse) would no doubt have
participated in 'the bettering of the time'.

But Sonnet 76, whose initial question 'Why is my verse so barren of
new pride' resumes the idea, exposes it to the pressure of present time and
so eliminates the consolations provided by prophecized future memories of
the past. In these circumstances the poet's repetitiveness, 'barren of new pride',
and his reluctance to 'glance aside / To new-found methods and to com-
pounds strange' (76, 1ff.) finds its sole justification in the conviction that
his love is an enduring reality:

> O, know, sweet love, I always write of you,
> And you and love are still my argument;
> So all my best is dressing old words new,
> Spending what is already spent.
>
> (76, 9–12)

If, then, the poet's power of expression becomes barren, repetitive and
predictable, one obvious conclusion is that he might as well stop writing
altogether. Indeed this conclusion is, in the following sonnet (77), exhibited
emblematically, with the help of a glass, a dial and an empty book; and it
will be resumed in Sonnet 103. The friend need only project his mirrored
likeness (which also bears his 'mind's imprint') directly onto the vacant leaves
of the book, while the dial will record the beauty-impairing passage of time
which the poet's writing has so far dwelt upon with persistent emphasis.
'These waste blanks'[7] of the book, then, could be the complete silence to
which the loving, but outwritten, poet is reduced. But Shakespeare does not,
of course, end here as Samuel Daniel ends the last sonnet of his cycle – 'I
say no more, I feare I said too much' (*Delia*, 50, 14). In fact Shakespeare's
Sonnet 77 is the very central item in his sequence of 154 poems, at least if
one accepts, as well one may, the Quarto order. Hence the 'blanks' of the
book also forestall its as yet unwritten but ineluctable second half.[8] In
Sonnet 78 the poet immediately recalls his necessary role as a mediator who
must channel into his verse the inspiration received from the friend, his only
'Muse' – the 'tenth Muse' already invoked in sonnet 38 (and by other
Elizabethan sonnetteers as well)[9] and identical with 'Thine eyes, that taught
the dumb on high to sing' (78, 5).

And yet it is at this point that the silencing effect of the 'others'' poetic
activity begins to intervene more incisively. The 'others' are no longer what
they often are in Petrarchan sonnets – those more or less conventional and
unoriginal poetic predecessors responsible for some sort of 'anxiety of
influence', from whose 'pre-text' a poet will emancipate his own heart-felt
writing (sometimes with no small degree of self-assurance), as, for instance,
in Sidney's *Astrophil and Stella* ('And others' feete still seem'd but strangers
in my way' [1, 11]; 'You that do search for everie purling spring' [15, 1];

'You that with allegorie's curious frame / Of other's children changelings use to make' [28, 1f.]), or in Daniel's *Delia* ('Let others sing of Knights and Palladines' [46, 1f.]), or in Drayton's *Idea* ('Some when in ryme they of their Loves doe tell' [18, 1]).[10] In the middle of Shakespeare's sequence, by contrast, 'others' (and one 'other' in particular) are usurping the lover-poet's own writing, along with his own Muse – the friend, the only source of his poetry: 'As every alien pen hath got my use / And under thee their poesy disperse' (78, 3f.), with extra ornament and learning being added ostentatiously. Even so a comforting distinction can still be made – that the poet-lover, despite his 'rude ignorance', offers a pure, genuine and exclusive reflection of the friend ('But thou art all my art'), whereas 'In others' works thou dost but mend the style'. But that consolation, too, will explode in the ensuing Sonnet 79 (which is tightly linked with its predecessor) and so cause the lover-poet's desperate and dumb reticence:

> But now my gracious numbers are decayed,
> And my sick Muse doth give another place.
>   (79, 3f.)

Significantly, the poet's 'sick Muse' is, unlike the 'Muse' in Sonnet 78, severed from the friend (from 'thy lovely argument', which is now projected by 'a worthier pen' [79, 5f.]); the Muse that remains is his own poetic capability, and that is fading. Even apparent inconsistencies such as this, which can be detected within the argument of Sonnets 78 and 79,[11] would seem to express a dumb-stricken bewilderment.

What is entirely consistent, however, is the way all this leads up to the opening of Sonnet 80 and its sigh of inexpressibility: 'O, how I faint when I of you do write'. However, Sonnet 80 also marks a turning point in the poet's attitude. He begins to accept the challenge, to see and to grapple with the paradox of inexpressibility, to consider and weigh the relative value of speech and silence, to defend actively the virtue that resides in his dumbness and in the humble plainness of his silence-like words. The sea-and-ship image evoked for this purpose may as such be conventional enough, but it affirms his intention not only to cling to his love, but also to persevere in its expression, even at the risk of utter failure; he will 'wilfully appear' on the ocean as a 'saucy bark' beside the grand vessel that represents the rival; he will do so despite the possibility, if not the likelihood, of his foundering:

> But since your worth, wide as the ocean is,
> The humble as the proudest sail doth bear,
> My saucy bark, inferior far to his,
> On your broad main doth wilfully appear.
> Your shallowest help will hold me up afloat
> Whilst he upon your soundless deep doth ride;
> Or, being wrecked, I am a worthless boat,
> He of tall building and of goodly pride.
>   If then he thrive and I be cast away,
>   The worst was this: my love was my decay.
>   (80, 5–14)

The lover-poet's gesture of desperate determination encapsulated in this image, however risky and dangerous and 'saucy', derives its strength from being supported by an increasingly critical attitude to the rival's grand style and rhetoric, which is opposed to his own humble love and seems to decimate his power of expression. Though at first the rival – 'a worthier pen' (79, 6); 'a better spirit' (80, 2) – appears to command intimidating authority, the lover-poet's respect for it is increasingly undermined: first by subtly ironical references to the rival's pride veiled in the ship metaphor of Sonnet 80 itself – 'the proudest sail' (80, 6, to be resumed with overt sarcasm in Sonnet 86: 'Was it the proud full sail of his great verse ...'); 'He of tall building and of goodly pride' (80, 14). Then, in the ensuing sonnets (up to 86), the initial irony gradually and by dint of intensified repetition of the main metaphors builds up into the bitter satire that exhibits the rival's (and rivals') use of 'what strained touches rhetoric can lend' (82, 10) and of 'their gross painting' (82, 13); their verbal cosmetics (which refers back to Sonnet 21) will be more explicitly denounced in Sonnet 83. Their 'modern quill', the poet now realizes, 'doth come too short' (83, 7), and their 'golden quill / And precious words' (85, 3f.) add up to no more than 'polished form of well-refined pen' (85, 8). The rival is 'making worse what nature made so clear' (84, 10) – urged, it seems, by grotesquely sinister powers, 'the compeers by night' and 'that affable familiar ghost / Which nightly gulls him with intelligence' (86, 9f.), whoever may be alluded to here. The friend may well be haunted to death by the 'others'' excessively flattering rhetoric; 'they would give life and bring a tomb' (83, 12; cf. 86, 4). It is surely no mistake (as re-arrangers of the sequence tend to assume) that the argument developed in the rival poet group should be interrupted by a version of the tomb-and-monument motif and the concomitant immortalizing claim in Sonnet 81, which looks considerably more conventional and is certainly less explorative than Shakespeare's previous treatments of this theme (as, for instance, in Sonnet 55);[12] for at this point it would seem to expose the rival's proud and lethal self-confidence.

It will, however, be noticed that the negativity (pride with its overtones suggesting affectation, public display, insincerity, flattery) thus inflicted upon the rival(s) is in practically every instance linked syntactically with positive values that the poet comes to attach to his own silence – to his 'tongue-tied Muse', which is explicitly distinguished from the traditional nine Muses, on whose rich compilation of speech-adorning material the rival's 'precious phrase' depends (85, 1–4). Unlike the latter, the lover-poet by his silence proves his good manners (and doubtless the decorum required by his lower social status as well): 'My tongue-tied Muse in manner holds her still', with an allusion, perhaps, to Petrarch's 'cari costumi', even though these comprised 'parlar' as well as 'tacere'. Silence also attests to plain truth (82, 12), pure glory (83, 10), natural clarity (84, 10) and expansive thought (85, 10f.). Hence the lover-poet comes to convince himself that 'I think good thoughts whilst others write good words' (85, 5) and, thus fortified, turns to the beloved friend: 'Then others for the breath of words respect, / Me for my dumb thoughts, speaking in effect.' In short, the poet's dumbness, whose value is postulated *ex negativo*, is to prove itself to be superior to others' speech. And, conversely, the ironical criticism levelled at 'others'' polished verbosity argues *ex silentio*:

> This silence for my sin you did impute,
> Which shall be most my glory, being dumb;
> For I impair not beauty, being mute,
> When others would give life and bring a tomb.
> (83, 9–12)

This intimate linkage of the vindication of silence and the derision of utterance would seem to prevent the two from being neatly polarized, let alone the opposition from being resolved. Silence cannot be justified conclusively; utterance cannot be condemned outright. Silence will not be love's ultimate manifestation; the poet will continue to write both his love and his silence – 'for who's so dumb that cannot write to thee?' (38, 7). And his writing will need the 'breath' of future generations to exist and prove its virtue (81, 14). The poet, for all his critique of affable 'others', in a sense continues to be in awe of and even shares their pride in utterance. The paradox is reflected in metaphorical complexities such as the ones affecting the tomb image. The friend, who (in Sonnet 81) is to be immortalized by the 'monument' of the poet-lover's verse, will be 'entombed in men's eyes' (81, 8; note the pun on 'tomb' and 'tome'), and 'tongues to be' will 'rehearse' the poem (81, 11; note the pun coupling live performance and funeral rite, supported by 'inhearse' in 86, 3). And if instead of giving life the rival 'bring[s] a tomb' (83, 11), the memorial tomb itself (including its epitaph) will remind us of the poet's own verse, which in more than one sonnet is compared with sepulchral monuments. The pointed development of the paradox again leads to Sonnet 86, where the poet speaks of the rival 'That did my ripe thoughts in my brain inhearse, / Making their tomb the womb wherein they grew' (86, 3f.). What is 'inhearsed' by the rival's 'great verse' (86, 1) is, of course, the lover-poet's silence; but that is pregnant with a poetry yet to be born – in accordance with what poets, Shakespeare himself included, usually say about the way poetry comes into being (Sonnets 59, 2; 76, 8; 77, 11).[13] In short, Shakespeare, even while he strives to establish that love is served better by thoughtful silence than by studied utterance and that private inwardness is superior to public (and courtly) display, nevertheless senses that the struggle between being in and writing about love is a complicated and persistent one.[14]

   The most critical stage of that struggle is reached when, at the end of the rival poet group, the poet is forced to realize that the friend's beauty, since the 'lines' of the rival have usurped it, threatens to leave him, the lover-poet, without a worthy subject, as the couplet of Sonnet 86 announces ('But when your countenance filled up his [i.e. , the rival's] line, / Then lacked I matter; that enfeebled mine'). Separation from the friend – from the *raison d'être* of his poetry – seems unavoidable: 'Farewell, thou art too dear for my possessing' (87, 1). But ironically, the necessity of that separation may to some extent be self-inflicted; it may be because of the poet's unexpressed love that the friend withdraws favour, esteem and fidelity, and that the time-defying ideality which the poet's loving thoughts have conferred on the friend appears to be tainted and temporal. And yet at the same time the valedictorian admission of finite temporality – 'My bonds in thee are all determinate' (87, 4) releases its own retraction; the phrase plays on the meanings of both 'bond' (which also suggests 'bounded') and 'determinate' ('terminated'/'determined') and thus elicits, as Stephen Booth notes, an 'extra pathos in overtones of "my soul is circumscribed by you", "you are all my world"',[15] and in this way prepares the theme for the next sonnet group (88 to 99), which will both reveal and conceal the absent friend's blemishes with a passionate determination to reassess the relationship.

As soon as the poet emerges from this crisis of love, however, he returns, especially in Sonnets 100 to 103, to the crisis of expressibility that had absorbed him in the rival poet group and once again addresses the precarious shortcomings of his 'Muse'. But he now does so in a new, reactivated strain, unoppressed by the rival's intimidating intervention – even if some of the by now worn-out arguments justifying his silence recur. The Muse, once again clearly identifiable as the poet's subjective poetic capability, is chided for being forgetful and reminded of her appropriate office: 'Rise, resty Muse, my love's sweet face survey' (100, 9). Even if love's ideal beauty has been impaired by time, it is still possible to write 'a satire to decay, / And make Time's spoils despised everywhere' (100, 10–12) and so to redeem the friend's excellence. The repetitive arguments of the 'truant Muse's' imagined defence of the inexpressibility of 'beauty's truth' are rejected both through the wordplay on 'truant'/'truth' and by the explicit reminder that the memorial furnished by poetic utterance outdoes that of material monuments, an idea persuasively established in Sonnet 55 and elsewhere:

> Excuse not silence so, for't lies in thee
> To make him much outlive a gilded tomb,
> And to be praised of ages yet to be.
>   (101, 10–12)

A standard of poetic manners comprising utterance as well as silence, comparable to the effectively interrupted song of the nightingale, is restored: 'like her [Philomel] I sometime hold my tongue, / Because I would not dull you with my song' (102, 13f.), albeit the imperfect mimesis achieved by 'my verse' has to be conceded too (103). And in Sonnet 106, the balance between expressive and inexpressible praise is confirmed even by an evocation of the poetic predecessors' 'antique pen', which, though unable to express fully the friend's beauty, has the power to prefigure it prophetically.

In the rival poet sonnets, however, the drama of the lover-poet's involvement with inexpressibility is presented in its most acute phase. At that stage, the poet's predicament in a way resembles that of Cordelia at the beginning of *King Lear* and could be read as a preliminary study of what is to go on in Cordelia's mind. Old Lear expects a panegyric display of his daughters' love in exchange for his favours – not dissimilar to what the (aristocratic) young man of the *Sonnets* seems to expect from his poets. Significantly, Goneril's speech that opens the love contest, indeed her first utterance in the play, parades a conventional use of the inexpressibility topos – 'Sir, I love you more than word can wield the matter'; 'A love that makes breath poor and speech unable' (I, i, 55; 60)[16] – whose rhetorical amplification betrays its emptiness, which Regan ironically calls 'metal' (69) and 'nam[ing] my very deed of love' (71). Cordelia, on the other hand, under the impression of such rhetoric becomes aware of the 'true' reality of love's unspeakability, as does the sonnet poet when daunted by his rival's success: 'What shall Cordelia speak? Love and be silent' (62); 'I cannot heave / My heart into my mouth' (91f.). Hence when called upon to be more 'opulent' than her sisters, her speech is reduced to 'Nothing'. And when advised to 'Mend your speech a little', she feels that 'My love's more ponderous than my tongue' (77f.). All she can cite is her 'bond' (93), which will, as in Sonnet 87, soon be 'determinate', that is, ended and yet retained. Again in analogy with the sonnet poet, Cordelia discovers the value of the unspoken and of true, plain words (reminiscent of Sonnet 82) while recognizing and, supported by Kent, exposing the 'flattery' (148), the 'hollowness' and 'that glib and oily art' in the large speeches of her sisters (224), to whose 'professed bosoms' (272) she is forced to commit her beloved father, albeit well knowing them what they are (269). And when Cordelia is urged (by France's inquiry) to explain the cause of her silence in so many words, these words are, again like those of the sonnet poet, 'a constant *argumentum ex silentio*', as William Elton has pointed out.[17] Similar parallels could be drawn between banished Cordelia's loving effort to vindicate the King despite his manifest faults and the lover-poet's comparable concern in the group of absence sonnets; and also between the reconciliation scenes, which include a reconciliation of Cordelia's silent sorrow and 'verbal question' (IV, iii, 25), and Sonnets 100 to 103. And in more incidental ways the relative values of speech and silence are, of course, touched upon in many plays, even if as lightly as when in *The Merchant of Venice* Gratiano's garrulous speech that questions the wisdom behind Antonio's sadly 'saying nothing' is in turn mocked for uttering 'an infinitive deal of nothing'. Paradoxical complexities resulting from interactions of unexpressed substance and insubstantial expression are a constantly recurring phenomenon in Shakespeare, 'Where every something being blent together / Turns to a wild of nothing, save of joy / Express'd and not express'd', as dumb-struck Bassanio aptly puts it (*Merchant of Venice*, III, ii, 181–3).

The emphatic treatment of such paradoxes at the very centre of Shakespeare's sonnet sequence amply reveals the irritations of poetic productivity that are involved. Once brought into the foreground, these irritations would seem to question in retrospect the apparent confidence with which the poet – and poets in general – have previously claimed a time-conquering and immortalizing power of their verse. When that claim is first put forward in Sonnet 18, the approach to it is tentative ('Shall I compare thee ..') and the conclusion, the repetition of the simple demonstrative pronoun, is like a speechless gesture pointing to the poem that has made such a daring attempt ('... So long lives this, and this gives life to thee'). That 'this', poetic utterance and the material poem, has a brittle and vulnerable existence is remembered often enough.[18] And when at last, in Sonnet 74, a neat distinction between the material poem and its spiritual substance is arrived at, its summing-up is like a complicated echo of the cold gestic conclusion of Sonnet 18 (and also of the monument Sonnet 55):

> The worth of that is that which it contains.
> And that is this, and this with thee remains.
>   (74, 13f.)

It is almost immediately thereafter that, in Sonnet 76, the lover-poet's drama of inexpressibility begins. After having been exposed to it, he will avoid invoking the immortality of his verse and, perhaps, be better prepared for the less idealistic emotional involvement in the dark lady sonnets.

NOTES

1.   Shakespeare's *Sonnets* are quoted from John Kerrigan's edition (Harmondsworth: Penguin, 1986).
2.   E.R. Curtius, *Europäische Literatur und lateinisches Mittelalter*, 2nd edn (Berne: Francke, 1954), pp. 168ff.
3.   'Here is the speech which no style equals / and the lovely silence, and those dear manners / which human wit cannot display on paper.'
4.   On the larger context of this theme see Anne Ferry, *The Inward Language: Sonnets of Wyatt, Sidney, Shakespeare, Donne* (Chicago: University of Chicago Press, 1983).
5.   On this point see, for instance, Hugo Friedrich, *Epochen der italienischen Lyrik* (Frankfurt a.M., 1964), pp. 220ff.
6.   Thomas P. Roche, Jr, *Petrarch and the English Sonnet Sequences* (New York: AMS, 1989), p. 403.
7.   There is little reason not to assume that the Q reading 'black' is a printer's error, despite the argument to the contrary advanced by Katherine M. Wilson, *Shakespeare's Sugared Sonnets* (London: Allen & Unwin, 1974), p. 250. See also Stephen Booth's note in his edition of *Shakespeare's Sonnets* (New Haven: Yale University Press, 1977), p. 268.
8.   Roche, p. 405.
9.   Examples in Christian Enzensberger, *Sonett und Poetik*, Diss. (Munich, 1962), pp. 29–31.
10.   See also K.M. Wilson, *Shakespeare's Sugared Sonnets*, p. 252. Wilson's exclusive emphasis on the parodistic nature of Shakespeare's response to earlier love poetry, however, hardly does justice to the seriousness and complexity of his involvement with inexpressibility and silence.
11.   See also Gerald Hammond, *The Reader and Shakespeare's Young Man Sonnets*

(Totowa, NJ: Barnes & Noble, 1981), p. 99f.

12. Hammond, p. 101, finds good reasons to defend the Quarto position of Sonnet 181.
13. See Enzensberger, pp. 54–63.
14. For these implications see Ferry, *The Inward Language*, p. 195.
15. Booth (ed.), p. 290.
16. Shakespeare's plays are quoted from the [New] Arden editions.
17. William R. Elton, *King Lear and the Gods* (San Marino, California: Huntington, 1966), p. 75.
18. Cf. my essay '"This": Poetic Gesture and the Poem', in *Shakespeares Sonette in europäischen Perspektiven*, ed. D. Mehl and W. Weiß (Münster: Lit, 1993), pp. 116–28.

PART FIVE

Shakespeare, Art and Music

CHAPTER EIGHTEEN

The Original Music for the French King's Masque in *Love's Labour's Lost*

Andrew J. Sabol

In *Shakespeare: 'the lost years'* (1983), E.A.J. Honigmann presents in Chapter 6 a relatively recent review of the evidence from the early 1590s about the activities of the dramatic company sponsored by the fifth Earl of Derby known as Lord Strange's Men. Here readers of today may comfortably refamiliarize themselves with those formative years when both Shakespeare and Robert Greene served as two of the dramatists writing for a company seeking to establish itself in the midst of the plague years of 1592–3, if not late in the 1580s. At the later time each perhaps engaged in a rivalry which prompted Greene's allusion to his fellow dramatist in a now famous quotation appearing in a pamphlet of 1592 entitled *Greene's Groat's Worth of Wit* as 'the absolute Johannes factotum' who is 'in his own conceit the only Shake-scene in a Country'.

What further emerges from the Honigmann account is that in the early months of 1592 Lord Strange's Men produced three of Greene's plays – *Friar Bacon, Orlando Furioso* and *A Looking Glass for London and England,* – and that 'by 1592 Shakespeare already enjoyed a very special social position in Lord Strange's circle, and that could explain why Greene sought him out, maliciously, as the central figure amongst "those puppets"'.[1] Honigmann also regards *Love's Labour's Lost* as one of the more important as well as the most allusive and topical of the plays written for this troupe and, to do so, had to part company with E.K. Chambers and other more recent critics who had tried to date the play in the late 1590s at the earliest. For them 1598 was the year in which it first appeared in quarto 'As it was presented / before her Highness / this last Christmas / Newly corrected and amplified'. The second quarto title page of 1631 adds that it had also been acted 'at the Blacke-friers and the Globe'. He further sees Shakespeare as having served Lord Strange for eight or more years – the critical years of his apprenticeship in the theatre, and he also reminds us that Greene died as early as 1592. It should also be noted that the fifth Earl of Derby died in 1593.

Shakespeare's frequent allusiveness in *Love's Labour's Lost* to matters involving Lord Strange – also known as Ferdinand, Earl of Derby – has suggested to some commentators that the play may even have been intended as a kind of private theatrical piece to be enacted at his own court, which was an establishment 'little inferior to the Queen's'. Honigmann continues thus: 'A dramatist who wished to put Lord Strange into a topical comedy, but preferred not to do it openly, could copy the Derby household in his play and call it by a different name.' Noting that there never was a Ferdinand who was King of Navarre (as named in Shakespeare's play), but only a Henri of Navarre who became King of France in 1589, he goes on further to show that Henri could suggest an apt likeness to Lord Strange in his brilliance by including witty word-plays on 'change' and 'strange', which encourage such speculation. Some echo his mottos 'Dieu et mon foy' and 'Sans changer ma vérité', while others deck out emphatic closing couplet rhymes. Here is one of a few similar examples from the play, when the King entreats the disguised Rosaline – whom he takes to be the Princess – thus:

> Then in our measure do but vouchsafe one change,
> Thou bid'st me beg; this begging is not strange.
> (V, ii, 209–10)

Much of Honigmann's information had already been anticipated by scholars such as Richard David, whose editions of *Love's Labour's Lost* had appeared in the Arden Shakespeare in 1951 and 1956. After a detailed survey of the facts David convincingly concluded that

> Henri's popularity in England was at its height in August 1591 (when Essex played a flamboyant but not very effective part in the campaign for the capture of Rouen), but was forfeited in July 1593 when, coming to terms with the [Catholic] League, Henri renounced his Protestantism and was received into the Catholic church, and that the English troops supporting him were finally withdrawn in November 1593. A playwright would therefore be most tempted to write a play about Navarre in 1591–3, when Englishmen were fighting with his troops as allies in a popular cause.[2]

Included among the brief notes appearing at the close of H.H. Furness's *A New Variorum Edition of Shakespeare, Love's Labour's Lost*, is one small item retrieved from Joseph Ritson's *Remarks, Critical, or Illustrative* of 1793, where on p. 40 Ritson had noted that the following extract from Edward Hall's 'Henry VIII' (fo. 6.b) conveyed an idea of the dress worn by the king and his lords when they appeared disguised as Russians:

> In the first year of King Henry the Eighth, at a banquet made for the foreign ambassadors in the parliament chamber at Westminster, came the lorde Henry, Erle of Wiltshire and the lorde Fitzwater in twoo long gounes of yelowe satin, trauarsed with white satin, and in every bend of white was a bend of crimosen satin after the fashion of Russia or Ruslande, with furred hattes of grey on their hedes, either of them hauyng an hatchet in their handes, and bootes with pykes turned up.[3]

Much later Fred Sorensen, in a brief article, 'The Masque of the Muscovites in *Love's Labour's Lost*', calls attention not only to Ritson's early identification, but adds to it the significant fact that Hall's account was printed with some amplification by Raphael Holinshed in 1587. He quotes the following passage from the section on Henry VIII appearing in Holinshed's *Chronicles*:

> On Shrouesundaie the same yeare [1510], the king prepared a goodlie banket in the parlement chamber at Westminster, for all the ambassadors, which then were here out of diuerse realmes and countries. The banket being readie, the king leading the queene, entered into the chamber, then the ladies, ambassadours, and other noble men followed in order.
>
> The king caused the queene to keepe the estate, and then sate the ambassadours and ladies, as they were marshalled by the K. who would not sit, but walked from place to place, making cheare to the queene and the strangers: suddenlie the king was gone. And shorlie [*sic*] after, his grace, with the earle of Essex, cam in apparelled after the Turkie fashion, in long robes of baudekin, powdered with gold, hats on their heds of crimsin veluet, with great rolles of gold, girded greene, like two swords called cimiteries, hanging by great bauderiks of gold. Then next came the lord Henrie earle of Wiltshire, and the lord Fitzwater, in two long gownes of yellow sattin, trauersed with white sattin, and in euerie band of white was a band of crimsin sattin, after the fashion of Russia or Rusland, with furred hats of graie on their heads, either of them hauing an hatchet in their hands, and boots with pikes turned up.
>
> ... The torchebearers were apparelled in crimsin sattin and greene, like Moreskoes, their faces blacke; and the king brought in a mummerie.
>
> ... After them entered six ladies, whereof two were apparelled in crimsin sattin and purple. ... Their faces, necks, armes, and hands, couered in fine pleasants blacke; some calle it Lumbardines, which is maruellous thin; so that the same ladies semed to be Nigers or blacke Mores.[4]

On the basis of this passage Sorensen finds that everything necessary to inspire Shakespeare's Masque of Muscovites in *Love's Labour's Lost* is present: the king and nobles disguised as Russians accompanied by servants with black faces, and these are followed by ladies apparelled in crimson and purple satin. Here also are the words 'black Mores'.

Other more recent investigators have added further important details emerging from their awareness of these sources in Hall and Holinshed, many of them noting that in the early 1590s Shakespeare himself was making extensive use of Holinshed for his earliest history plays. Notable work in listing other similar accounts has been accomplished by C. Edward McGee and John Meagher in their series entitled 'Preliminary Checklist of Tudor and Stuart Entertainments', begun in *Research Opportunities in Renaissance Drama* [henceforth *RORD*], XXV (1982), where the section for the years 1485–1558 appeared. For 28 February 1510, they provide a brief summary of what has been termed by Hall in the foregoing account as a disguising 'led by the King, of lords costumed as Turks, Russians, and Prussians; then a mummery, dancing, music, and a banquet'.[5]

What they have shown to be of equal importance among their listings is that over the decades of the late fifteenth and early sixteenth centuries the fifth Earl of Derby's progenitors – as well as many other nobles – were frequently hosts if not participants in a number of private entertainments. In November 1489 (see *RORD*, XXV, p. 37) a Lord Strange had sponsored an entertainment at Chester entitled 'The Assumption of Our Lady', which was either a pageant or a play, and on February 12 1555, at the marriage of his predecessor the fourth Lord Strange and Lady Cumberland (see *RORD*, XXV, p. 109), the festivities included 'jousts and a tourney on horseback, and after dinner, a play, music, and bankett after supper'.

Among the more recent contributors to the studies of the music in the plays is John H. Long, who also provides new details unnoted by his predecessors in discussing the Masque of Muskovites. In Holinshed he finds 'a masked dance given by the English noblemen at the French Court in Ard in 1520', and here too 'certeine young honourable lords of England' were 'apparelled after the manner of Russland or farre Eastland'.[6] This is also important as an early example of a French court entertainment which featured a visit of a group of elaborately costumed English courtiers.

When it comes to dealing with the nature of the actual music performed in *Love's Labour's Lost* by the Blackmores for the entry of the masqued Muscovites and the aborted dance which follows, Long quotes the long passage from Arbeau's *Orchesography* (in the translation by Mary Steward Evans)[7] describing one of several alternative ways that the galliard may be danced, and noting its many and various complex movements he chooses this triple metre dance to show how these complex movements may appropriately prefigure the mimed procedures of the courtiers in their subsequent encounters with the ladies. Long, however, did not have the music to turn to for the entry of the Muscovites – the original music for that scene not yet having been reported as discovered – and was forced to fall back on what appeared to be the best choice, the galliard, as a type of social dance significant for describing the ensuing activities in the scene. However, since the item entitled 'The Earle of Darbyes coraunta' – which appears in the Ballet Manuscript preserved in the Library of Trinity College, Dublin, and is the first of several cognates discussed at some length below – specifies and includes as the second of its two parts a setting of the courante, or coranto, as the dance which actually was performed, it is of course fitting to note that on pp. 123–24 of Arbeau (in Evans' translation) a considerably lengthy alternative description of the way of dancing the courante is carefully supplied. An account of what transpires after the masquers' entry is discussed later in this essay.

A recent study of Shakespeare's use of the masque in plays early and late is that of Robert C. Fulton who, in treating the significance of the Masque of Muscovites, not only provides the fullest account to date with respect to the source material but demonstrates in several examples[8] how that masque 'gathers together and concentrates the various tensions of the play'. Like his predecessors, he cannot cite the specific music used for the entry of the masquers, but his penetrating analysis of the courtiers' interaction with the ladies shows how 'The Lovers' hyperbolic flattery – the product of a debased and superficial Petrarchism – dribbles past its object, unregarded. … Moreover, the courtiers have entrapped themselves through a new set of oaths – love vows which will have to be broken because they have been sworn to the wrong persons (see ll. 181–85)'. All ends in that play in irresolution and postponement. In his later treatment of Prospero's masque in *The Tempest*, on the other hand, what is revealed is how 'seasonal changes coalesce in an eternal and abundant spring'. To these observations we may add that a character named Ferdinand appears in each masque, the King of Navarre in the former, and Prince Ferdinand, son of the King of Naples and the betrothed to Miranda, in the latter. A coincidence this is, and most likely not intended, and while not of any importance when one views each of the plays separately is nevertheless interesting for those concerned with the whole canon as it may invite questions about the overtures and closures which it evokes. What is, however, most fortunate in the music resources for *The Tempest* is that, in addition to the recovery of two well-known settings of Ariel's songs by John Wilson there has also been an instrumental item found entitled 'The Tempest' (from British Museum Additional MS 10, 444) which is presumed by some to have been used for the reapers' dance in Prospero's masque.

Among the many music manuscripts of late Elizabethan and Jacobean times containing collections of popular songs and dances are five surviving in various British and Continental repositories which have a relevance to the drama of the day and especially for one of Shakespeare's early plays. Each of these five manuscripts,[9] which have been compiled largely by various choristers and instrumentalists (mostly lutenists), contains an item of no little importance for *Love's Labour's Lost* as well as an additional and unmistakable piece of similar import for Greene's *The History of Orlando Furioso* (editions in 1594 and 1599), both plays in the repertory of Lord Strange's Men. These five have been carefully examined and commented upon by musciologists of the present century, as noted below, and some of these have readily identified the Greene item entitled either simply 'Orlando' or 'Orlando sleeping' as music for a dance near the end of the play intended for a group of satyrs encircling the sleeping Orlando drugged by the wine of the enchantress Melissa.

But the identification of the two-part item (noted earlier in this essay and now appearing at its close as Music Example 1) entitled 'The Earl of Darbyes Coraunta' in the Ballet Lute Book of Trinity College, Dublin, as no less significant for *Love's Labour's Lost* as for those shorter cognate versions appearing in other manuscripts of the period, seems to have eluded virtually all investigators. In these four cognates only the first part of two appears in each of these subsequent manuscripts, each chiefly to be distinguished from the other cognate versions in their divisions. These four are variously entitled 'The french Kings Maske' (on two occasions), 'King's Maske', or simply 'Ballet'. Many of the commentators probably regarded the Trinity College item as a dedicatory piece to a patron without any special dramatic significance, if not as a masque entry for a French *ballet de cour*. Certainly no one has attempted to identify any of the four additional cognate versions which survive as versions of the original item intended for Shakespeare's play until the present writer had done so for two of them: first in 1978, in a brief note citing the Holmes consort cognate at the close of *Four Hundred Songs and Dances from the Stuart Masque* (see item 231),[10] and then again in the supplement of the reprint of 1982, the Board Lute Book version (see item 436). These two identifications – reproduced at the end of this essay as Examples 2 and 3, the former the Holmes consort ensemble for four instruments preserved in Cambridge University Library manuscripts and the latter a lute setting from the Board Lute Book, now in private hands – were lost for most Shakespeareans among the dozens of music items for the court masque of the seventeenth century included in *The Songs and Dances*. Examples 2 and 3, both anonymous cognate versions of the Ballet Lute Book item, are clearly intended for Shakespeare's play, as their titles jointly confirm. A brief discussion of each of these five manuscript versions follows, with full information about the most significant of them – the Ballet Lute Book containing the item entitled 'The Earle of Darbyes caraunta' – together with additional observations about the slight differences in the four varied cognate versions of the same piece appearing in each of the remaining manuscripts, all presumably transcribed from an earlier version of a later date.

The first and perhaps the earliest of these – the so-called Ballet Lute Book – is a manuscript in two parts preserved in Trinity College Library, Dublin, which had been analysed and commented upon as early as 1967 by John M. Ward, who dated it as having been gathered together in the early 1590s.[11] He reports that William Ballet's hand – his identity remains unknown – is visible in Part I, and that of the three distinct hands discernible in Part II his is also the third hand which transcribes the last few items appearing on p. 111, and these in Ward's numbering are items 53 and 56, entitled 'Orlando' and 'The Earle of Darbyes coraunta' respectively. The latter of these lute tablatures is in two parts, the first consisting of two brief strains in binary measure, and the latter also consists of two strains, but these are in triple metre. Its two opening strains present the tune (in the key of F major) which was doubtless used for the masquing entry of the King of Navarre and his associates as they appear to the Princess and her train in the middle of Act V scene ii of *Love's Labour's Lost*, while the two latter (in the related key of C major/minor) presumably served to introduce a revels dance in which the lovely Rosaline refuses to take part. Here in these latter two strains appears the 'coraunta' of the item's title as an example of a well-known triple-metre social dance of the period. One may be tempted to regard the term 'coraunta' to be used informally here to suggest liveliness in general for these frigid Muscovites absorbed in their self-imposed philosophical asceticism, but as shall be shown in the ensuing paragraphs its significance emerges in its providing what is virtually a detailed step-by-step diagram wherein the mimed balletic movements of the participants are carefully spelled out in a kind of 'ballet d'action'. In its usual English spelling a coranto refers to a popular Renaissance dance in triple-metre – rather than in the duple-metre in which the two strains of this item are obviously presented – which as a vehicle for dancing evokes in general terms a kind of animation in the quick running steps demanded of its participants. A photofacsimile of p. 111 of this manuscript appears on p. 22 of Ward's article, and my transcript of the lute tablature of this item for keyboard – the first two strains for the entry of the masquers, and the latter two for the invitation to the dance – appears as Ex. 1 (as noted) at the close of the present account.

What should be noted about this item is that the simple melody of the opening two strains, of the sort that may be easily and endlessly varied in divisions, is presented in two four-measure duple-metre strains set to simple harmonic progressions utilizing chiefly the tonic, subdominant and dominant chords, much in the style of similar short items of the period for comedians variously entitled 'The Antic', 'Buffoons', 'Bergamask', and 'Pantalone', as one may see in items 214–218 in *Four Hundred Songs and Dances from the Stuart Masque*.[12] Although the Masque of Muscovites of Act V, ii is planned as a formal masque – William Carroll, who has written most extensively and penetratingly on *Love's Labour's Lost*, reminds us that 'actors are given parts to memorize, rehearsals are held, ... and an array of masks and disguises is worn'[13] – their music (and it is likely that this item in its first two strains was played for their entry in V, ii, 157 as well in its latter two strains as for the dance later described in line 220) indeed suggests that the Muscovites are geared to present a sort of informal antic, for they plan, says the Princess in line 139, to do it 'in mockery merriment'. They may have indeed expected that their entry was to be accompanied by appropriate introductory music in duple metre and that the attending consort of Blackamoors would have been directed to prepare contrasting music for their first social dance in triple metre as well.

Of special interest is the use of the term 'coraunta' in this music title, and a full account of that dance (courante) as it appears in Thoinot Arbeau's *Orchésographie* of 1588, where it is noted as in duple metre ('mesure binaire legière'), as Mabel Dolmetsch reports.[14] In Cyril W. Beaumont's translation of the Arbeau passage it is described as 'danced to a light duple time, consisting of two *simples* and a *double* to the left, and the same to the right, going forwards or sideways and sometimes backward as it pleases the dancer. And note that the steps of the Courante must be *sauté* (literally *jumped*). ...'[15] Here Arbeau's description rehearses the standard way of dancing the courante in the 1580s. Putnam Aldrich also describes it as 'a rapid dance performed with little hops and light springs between most of the steps', but he further notes, significantly, that 'the main intent is apparently centered on the movement of the dancers around the room and the changing of partners rather than on the patterns of the individual steps'.[16]

What is of special significance is that Arbeau (in Beaumont's translation)

goes on to describe in picturesque detail a variant manner in his early years
– he was born in 1519 – of dancing the courante, where he treats the dance
as a mimed ballet thus:

> In my young days there was a kind of game and ballet arranged to the Courante.
> For three young men would choose three girls, and having placed themselves in
> a row, the first dancer would lead his damsel to the end of the room, when he
> would return alone to his companions. The second would do the same, then the
> third, so that the three girls were left by themselves at one and making all manner
> of amorous glances, pulling his hose tight and setting his shirt straight, went to
> claim his damsel, who refused his arm and turned her back upon him; then, seeing
> the young man had returned to his place, she pretended to be in despair. The two
> others did the same. At last all three went together to claim their respective damsels,
> and kneeling on the ground, begged this boon with clasped hands, when the damsels
> fell into their arms and all danced the *Courante* pell-mell.[17]

What is specially to be noted in this description of an alternative manner
of dancing the courante is that it provides – with a few slight variations –
a detailed account of what happens on the stage when, in V, ii, 158ff, the
King of Navarre and his associates Berowne, Longaville, and Dumain –
each masked and disguised – make their entrance to the music played by
a consort of blackamoors. The stage direction at line 158 as it appears in
both Quarto and Folio is this: '*Enter Blackmores with musicke, the Boy with
a speech, and the rest of the Lords disguised.*' The music apparently ceasing
after their entry – and this obviously would have consisted of the first two
strains of the piece entitled 'The Earle of Darbyes coraunta' – the quartet
masqued as Muscovites individually then proceed to take part in a series of
encounters, and these clearly are not danced to music but are made up of
words and action paralleling in what is virtually a literal stage enactment
(episode by episode) of Arbeau's description of the alternate procedure of
dancing the courante, finally ending at line 483. In a résumé delineating the
description already provided by Arbeau we see here each of four characters,
rather than only three, who two by two go up to their damsels, presumably
walking, not dancing, but as they proceed, they were very likely accompanied
by the repetition of the tune of the triple-metre coranto strains subtly varied
in divisions. Such repetitions of a melody broken up with rapid figurations
were frequently extemporized by instrumentalists if not by a composer eager
to provide inventive variety. The two strains of the coranto of Ex. 1 could
easily have been subjected to a kind of amplification surrounding the skeleton
of the melody in its first simple statement to evoke distinct responses ranging
from the amusingly sardonic to the blatantly derisive in order to underscore
the unexpected movements if not the mocking words of the visitors from
Moscow who are masters of conspicuous irresolution.

The first two are the King and Berowne, each in succession confronting
respectively the visored ladies Rosaline and the Princess. These latter two,
having been apprised of their coming visit, have also donned masks to confuse
their would-be partners. Each of the young men pay their respects in genteel
terms, but are quickly made sport of by a barrage of sharp-tongued retorts,

and they continue conversing apart, as the stage direction notes, each masquer in turn with the lady he addresses. When the King begs Rosaline to join in a measure, she at first assents, and then quickly changes when he hesitates. These are her words:

> Play music, then: nay, you must do it soon.
> Not yet? – no dance – thus change I like the moon.
> ...
> Since you are strangers, and come here by chance
> We'll not be nice: take hands – we will not dance.
>   (V, ii, 211–12, 218–19)

Alexander Leggatt observes thus on this refusal: 'Were this to happen in a real masque, the result would likely be an international scandal.'[18] Yet not to be overlooked at this point is the relevance of Fulton's citation of the account of a 1512 epiphany masque in which 'six gentlemen disguised in silke, bearing staff torches, entered and desired the ladies to dance; some were content and some refused' (*RORD*, XIV, 66).[19] It is at this juncture in Shakespeare's play that the King renews his invitation to the Princess and Rosaline, noting that 'The music plays; vouchsafe some motion to it' (line 216). Then the next two, Dumaine and Longaville, address Maria and Katharine, also visored, in mistaken order, and are similarly rebuffed. After a few conversational barbs, each of these pairs similarly converse apart. Then the Princess wishes the frozen Muscovites 'twenty adieus' and the Lords and Blackamoors exeunt. After devising a plan to their own advantage, the ladies unmask and superciliously await the return of the lords, and soon the gallants are back at hand 'in their proper habits' to address their ladies – now properly identified – with new delicately phrased words of compliment as each advances his suit, only finally agreeing, once the sudden sad news of the death of the Princess's father is announced, to postpone resolving their courtship for a twelvemonth and a day.

From noting the similarity of the mimed ballet movements of the alternate way of dancing the courante as described by Arbeau to what actually transpires through most of Act V scene ii of *Love's Labour's Lost*, one can only conclude that Shakespeare had been apprised of its dramatic possibilities either through having seen it or heard of its being performed at some ball or having read of it himself in Arbeau's *Orchésographie*.

The first cognate of the music appears in the Holmes consort books preserved in the Cambridge University Library, and these consist of an incomplete set of pieces for violin, flute, base viol, cittern, lute and bandora; of this set the violin part and the bandora part are missing. These part books have been carefully analysed by Ian Harwood in 'The Origin of the Cambridge Lute Manuscripts'.[20] Noting that they are in the hand of Matthew Holmes, who was a singingman and Precentor at Christ Church from 1586 to 1597, and a chanter and singingman at Westminster Abbey from 1617 till his death in 1621, Harwood suggests that its items were probably copied in Oxford c. 1595. This consort set is of special importance for containing in four of the six parts of each item unmistakable identifying titles, and particularly so for the item which seems clearly intended for use in *Love's Labour's Lost*. In Cambridge U. L. MS Dd.2.11, f.61r the item is headed 'The Kings Maske', for lute; in MS Dd.5.21, f.4v, the item is headed 'The french Kings maske', for flute; in MS Dd.5.20, f.4r, the item is headed 'The french Kings Maske', for bass viol; and in MS Dd. 14.24, f.23r, the item is headed 'The French King's Mke', for cittern. A violin part, missing, can easily be reconstructed from the melody line of the lute part, and a bandora part, also missing, can be based on the bass viol part which may serve as a guide to enriching the harmonic texture of these two short strains of the consort by a doubling of the tonic, dominant, and subdominant chords already intoduced in the lute part.

One may find a dozen additional items of music from the Holmes consort set transcribed and edited by Warwick Edwards in *Music for Mixed Consort*, in *Musica Britannica*, 40 (1977),[21] pp. 97–127. What is especially significant in this cognate version of 'The French King's Masque' is its six-part consort setting which provided parts for the Blackamoors – and there would have had to be six of them – accompanying the masqued King of Navarre and his associates as they meet the Princess and her attendant ladies. The growing popularity of such part-settings for a consort eventually resulted in the publication of Thomas Morley's *First Book of Consort Music* in 1599, [22] which comprises a collection of contemporary consort items arranged for six instruments: violin, flute, bass viol, and lute, cittern and bandora. One can well imagine that this sophisticated play which late in either 1597 or 1598 was exhumed for performance before Queen Elizabeth and then later before Queen Anne in 1604 at the residence of the Earl of Southampton would have required similar gatherings of instrumenalists for what would evidently have been full-dress performances.[23] The four surviving parts from this Cambridge University consort set have been transcribed and scored in *Four Hundred Songs and Dances from the Stuart Masque* (item 231, p. 309). This transcript is transferred here as Ex. 2, the first cognate to the first two strains of the 'The Earle of Darbyes coraunta' of the Ballet Lute Book setting.

A third source is the lute book of Victor de Montbuysson, dating from the early seventeenth century, which is presently housed in the Gesamthochschul–Bibliothek Kassel (Landesbibliothek und Murhardsche Bibliothek der Stadt Kassel) as 4to MS Mus. 108 (1). It contains a miscellany of assorted songs and dances, variously for the French *ballet de cour* and the English court masque, and on f. 23v appears the item entitled 'Orlando Furioso' and on f. 3v the item entitled 'Ballet' (in a cognate version of 'The Earle of Darbyes caraunta') containing a striking division in each of its two strains. A fourth cognate survives in Cambridge University Library MS Dd.2.11, f. 61v, dating from the early 1590s. It is entitled 'King's Maske', and like the third source it consists of two duple metre strains which are briefly ornamented in ingenious divisions. Neither of these two cognates, however, is otherwise sufficiently distinctive to merit inclusion in this compact account.

Yet neither of these two cognates are as richly embellished with divisions as is the fifth and final source, the Margaret Board Lute Book, which, presumably assembled as late as the 1620s, contains a miscellany of various popular songs and masque dances. Of these, several of the latter had been introduced in masques performed at court during the first two decades of the century. The manuscript is at present in the private library of Robert Spencer, who provided extensive commentary for the facsimile edition of the lute tablatures published by the Boethius Press in 1976. Here on f. 8r the item for *Love's Labour's Lost* is entitled 'The French Kinges Maske', and on f. 1v the item for Greene's play is again simply noted as 'Orlando'. Not only are all four versions of the item so titled cited in the Notes to the Music, but as many as 11 cognate versions are noted of the item for *Orlando Furioso*.[24] A transcript of the lute tablature of this item for keyboard appears in *Four Hundred Songs and Dances from the Stuart Masque* (reprint with Supplement, 1982, item 436, p. 679).

It is not essential to think that all five cognate versions were performed only in productions of *Love's Labour's Lost*. After its earliest appearance in the Ballet Lute Book, the music item in its various cognate forms entered a broad general repertory and could have been used for a variety of non-dramatic as well as dramatic occasions in later decades. Its divisions, or variations, often composed of clusters of notes of increasingly smaller time values in the melody line, could readily have been improvised by successive performers or copyists.

In his treatment of the episodes of Act V, ii of *Love's Labour's Lost* in his book, *Shakespeare and the Dance*, Alan Brissenden emphasizes that the theme of the comedy stresses the unfinished, the broken and the incomplete, which is an aspect of a larger concern with 'the recurrent Shakespearean theme of illusion and reality'. He continues, noting that the pattern of the play as a whole is one where 'Planned events which represent a turning away from reality are disrupted and foiled by the intrusion of reality'. And at the end of the play he observes that the concluding song is 'one of warning to the married and finishes with winter rather than spring, an indication of the hibernation of love before the springtime of its fulfilment. There is the sense here of life not incomplete any longer, but in suspension.'[25] The masquers' plan conceived 'in mockery merriment' has meant turning aside from a genuine masque entry dance, but the 'coraunta' taking its place, however, does spell out a longer range plan in Arbeau's alternate description of performing it which leads ultimately – in dialogue and comportment if not in dance – to a virtually happy resolution of their matches, even if courtship proceedings are to be held in abeyance for a twelvemonth and a day.

NOTES

1.   E.A.J. Honigmann, *Shakespeare: 'the lost years'* (Totowa, NJ: Barnes & Noble Books, 1983), chapter 6, pp. 71 and 67.

2.   William Shakespeare, *Love's Labour's Lost*, Arden Shakespeare, 5th edn, ed.
      Richard David (Cambridge, MA: Harvard University Press, 1956; reprinted,
      1960). Intro., xxviii. All quotations in this essay from the play are derived from
      this edition.
3.   H.H. Furness, *A New Variorum Edition of Shakespeare's Love's Labour's Lost*
      (Philadelphia, Lippincott, 1904), pp. 377–8 and Edward Hall, *The Lives of
      the Kings of England: Henry VIII*, Intro. Charles Whibley, 2 vols (London:
      T.C. and E.C. Jack, 1904), vol. 1, pp. 15–17.
4.   Fred Sorensen, 'The Masque of the Muscovites in *Love's Labour's Lost*', *Modern
      Language Notes*, L (1935), 499–501, and Raphael Holinshed, *Chronicles of
      England, Scotland, and Ireland*, 3 vols (London, 1587).
5.   *Research Opportunities in Renaissance Drama*, XXV (1981), 31–114.
6.   John H. Long, *Shakespeare's Use of Music* (Gainesville, FL: University of Florida
      Press, 1955), p. 67.
7.   Thoinot Arbeau [Jehan Tabourot], *Orchesography*, translated by Mary Stewart
      Evans, with introduction by Julia Sutton and labanotation by Mireille Backer
      and Julia Sutton (New York: Dover Publications, Inc., 1967), pp. 76–7.
8.   Robert C. Fulton, *Shakespeare and the Masque* (New York and London:
      Garland Publishing Inc., 1988), pp. 31, 32, and 152. For the music surviving
      for *The Tempest*, see the Arden edition edited by Frank Kermode, (Cambridge,
      MA: Harvard University Press, 1954), pp. 159–61. See also the concluding
      chapter in Peter Seng, *The Vocal Songs in the Plays of Shakespeare* (Cambridge:
      Harvard University Press, 1967), and John P. Cutts, *La Musique de scène de
      la Troupe de Shakespeare the King's Men sous le règne de Jacques Ier* (Paris:
      Éditions du Centre Nationale de la Récherche Scientifique, 2nd revised edn,
      1971), pp. 24–6.
9.   (a) Trinity College Library, Dublin. Manuscript 408/2 (*olim* D1.21), the so-
      called Ballet Lute Book inablature in two parts, 1590–1610; a few items
      of the latter are for lyra viol. The second part, consisting of pp. 81–113,
      is now usually referred to as the 'Ballet' book and was joined to the former
      (cited as Ballet book) at a later time.
          See *Répertoire international des sources musicales* (RISM), B VII;
      *handschriftlich überlieferte Lauten- und Gitarrentablaturen des 15 bis 18.
      Jahrhunderts, beschreibende Katalog von* Wolfgang Boetticher, (Munich,
      1978); p. 96, for a compact description of both parts. Much of the
      information in B VII on the Trinity College Dublin manuscripts has been
      summarized in John M. Ward, 'The Lute Books of Trinity College, Dublin
      II: MS. D.1.21 (the so-called Ballet Lute Book)', *Lute Society Journal*, 10
      (1968), 15–32. Ward's article includes a photofacsimile of p. 111 of the
      second part, which now has been assigned a new shelf-mark, MS 408/2.
      The last of the five lute pieces on p. 111, entitled 'The Earle of Darbyes
      coraunta', is transcribed for keyboard in this essay as Example 1.
      (b) Matthew Holmes Consort books, c. 1595. Below are four of ten part books
      in Holmes's hand, variously for the instruments cited in the four books below
      which contain 'The Kings Maske'. These are the only four surviving for a
      mixed consort of six. Violin and bandora parts are missing. (The remaining
      six books appear in John M. Ward's bibliography, cited below.)

      Cam. U.L.   Dd.2.11, f. 61r: 'The Kings Maske'; lute.
      Cam. U.L.   Dd.5.21, f. 4v: 'The french Kings maske'; recorder.
      Cam. U.L.   Dd.5.20, f. 4r: 'The french Kings maske, The Base Vyall pte.'
      Cam. U.L.   Dd.14.24. f. 23r: 'The French King's Mke.'; cittern.

      (c) Cam. U.L.   Dd. 3.18: 'The Kings Maske'; a second lute part presumably
      for the Holmes consort set.

(d) Gesamthochschul–Bibliothek Kassel (Landesbibliothek und Murhardsche Bibliothek der Stadt Kassel): 4to MS Mus. 108, vol. 1. Victor de Montbuysson's Lute Book; early seventeenth century.

(e) Margaret Board Lute Book: a repository of lute pieces of the Jacobean period in tablature; c. 1620–30; in the private library of Robert Spencer. 'The french Kinges Maske' appears on f. 8r.

The preceding group of five manuscript sources are cited in an extensive bibliography in vol. 1 of John M. Ward's *Music for Elizabethan Lutes*, 2 vols (Oxford: Clarendon Press, 1992), which lists more than a hundred manuscript items, chiefly of lute music for gatherings of the popular song and dance repertory of the late sixteenth and early seventeenth centuries. See pp. 134–7.

Permission to reproduce in transcript the items from manuscript sources in their repositories has been kindly granted by the governing bodies of the following institutions: Trinity College Library, Dublin, for Ex. 1, and Cambridge University Library for Ex. 2. Example 3, is transcribed from the Margaret Board Lute Book in the library of Robert Spencer, who has also granted permission for its reproduction. The lute tablatures in Exs. 1–3 are transcribed for keyboard.

10. A.J. Sabol, *Four Hundred Songs and Dances from the Stuart Masque* (University Press of New England, 1978) 2nd edn with Supplement, 1982. A full account of 'antic' music is presented in John M. Ward, *Music for Elizabethan Lutes*, vol. 1, pp. 123–7. Although Bryan N.S. Gooch and David Thatcher, in *A Shakespeare Music Catalogue*, 5 vols (Oxford: Clarendon Press, 1991), do list the 1978 edition of the *Four Hundred Songs and Dances* in their bibliography in vol. 5, the section on music for *Love's Labour's Lost* in vol. 1 cites only the music specially composed or devised for the dozens of productions of that play in every century since – but not of – Shakespeare's day.

11. See John M. Ward, 'The Lute Books of Trinity College, Dublin', *Lute Society Journal* 10 (1967), 15–32. See also note 9 above.

12. See A.J. Sabol, *Four Hundred Songs and Dances*, pp. 295–7, and annotation on pp. 593–4.

13. William C. Carroll, *The Great Feast of Language in 'Love's Labour's Lost* (Princeton: Princeton University Press, 1976), p. 72.

14. Mabel Dolmetsch, *Dances of England and France from 1450 to 1600* (London: Routledge and Kegan Paul Ltd, 1945). See Chapter 8, pp. 129–43, and especially p. 135.

15. Thoinot Arbeau [Jehan Tabourot], *Orchesography*, translated by Cyril W. Beaumont, with a preface by Peter Warlock (London, 1925; New York, 2nd printing, Dance Horizons, Inc. 1968), p. 107.

16. Putnam Aldrich, *Rhythm in Seventeenth-Century Italian Monody, with an Anthology of Songs and Dances* (London: J. M. Dent, 1966), pp. 94–6.

17. Thoinot Arbeau [Jehan Tabourot], *Orchesography*; see edn. cited in footnote 15 above, p. 108.

18. Alexander Leggatt, *Shakespeare's Comedy of Love* (London: Methuen & Co Ltd, 1973), p. 69.

19. For R.C. Fulton's citation of a 1512 Epiphany masque, see op. cit., pp. 12–13.

20. Ian Harwood, 'The Origin of the Cambridge Lute Manuscripts', *Lute Society Journal*, V (1963), 32–48.

21. *Music for Mixed Consort*, edited and reconstructed by Warwick W. Edwards, *Musica Britannica*, 40 (London, Stainer & Bell, 1977), pp. 97–127.

22. See *The First Book of Consort Lessons*, collected by Thomas Morley (1599 and 1611). Reconstructed and edited by Sydney Beck (New York: C.F. Peters Corporation for the New York Public Library, 1959).

23. See Richard David, op. cit., Introduction, li.

24. See the *Board Lute Book*, facsimile edition with an introductory study by Robert Spencer, (Leeds: Boethius Press, 1976). Citations for both the items — 'Orlando' and 'the french Kings Maske' — appear in the notes to the music for f. 1r and f. 8r. For the latter of these two I am further obliged to Professor Spencer for supplying a list of four Continental cognate versions, each dating from the first quarter of the seventeenth century in manuscripts which are briefly described in Wolfgang Boetticher's *Handschriftlich überlieferte Lauten- und Gitarren- tabulaturen des 15. bis 18. Jahrhunderts* (RISM. B VIII), Munich, 1978. See especially RISM. B VIII, p. 15, for an account of the Van den Hove MS (Berlin), which on f. 161v contains the cognate entitled 'La Masque du Roy'; also RISM. B VIII, p. 18, for an account of MS Druck 13.4⁰.85 (Bautzen) which contains on p. 69(2) the cognate entitled 'Intrada'; also RISM. B VIII, p. 95, for an account of MS M. 297 (Dresden), which contains on p. 149 the cognate entitled 'Chorea Anglica'; and finally RISM. B VIII, p. 244, for an account of MS 33748/1 (Nürnberg), which contains on ff. 53v–53r the cognate entitled 'Intrada Mauritij'. This last title is especially significant as it mirrors Shakespeare's stage direction in *Love's Labour's Lost*, V.ii at line 158: 'Enter Blackamoors with music.' For a modern transcription of this last title see *Die Tabulatur*, heft 25, 1979, ff. 52v–53r; it appears here displaying several attractive divisions and fittingly placed in the midst of a half-dozen corantos.

25. Alan Brissenden, *Shakespeare and the Dance* (Atlantic Highlands, NJ: Humanities Press, 1981), pp. 41 and 36. It is regrettable that a careful search through all of these manuscripts for the original settings for the play's concluding songs of Winter and Spring has not proved fruitful.

Example 1 'The Earle of Darbyes coraunta', from the Ballet Lute Book,
Trinity College Library, Dublin (Lute)

Example 2 'The french Kings maske', from the Matthew Holmes Consort
Part Books, Cambridge University Library (consort in four parts)

Example 3 'The french Kinges Maske', from the Margaret Board Lute Book.
Private Library of Robert Spencer (lute)

CHAPTER NINETEEN

Perspective in
Troilus and Cressida
François Laroque

Troilus and Cressida[1] has long been regarded as one of Shakespeare's most disconcerting plays. This may be because it is both in perspective and about perspective. Yet its design is far from identifiable with the baroque palaces of illusion which Inigo Jones, a disciple of the Italian architect Palladio, built in the masques and pageants presented at the court of James I. But with its *trompe l'oeil* plot interweaving ancient epic and legend (Boccacio, Caxton, Chaucer, Henryson), it immediately leads one to address the question of its sources. Indeed the textual mosaic of *Troilus and Cressida* is not only a simple reworking of the Homeric legend through the filter of Chaucer's own interpretation of it. The introduction of several perspectives allows its pluri-dimensional nature to show through. Moreover the characters of the play seem themselves bent on the rather perverse course which consists of destroying the mimesis of theatrical illusion to emerge as types rather than as real people with whom the spectators might identify. The games played with perspective do not serve their ordinary function in this play – they tend to demystify, to run down, to depreciate the legendary characters of antiquity as well as to introduce unexpected correspondences thanks to odd, intriguing or emblematic angles.

Indeed, the most prominent thing here is first and foremost the *eye*: the word, in association with numerous verbs of perception, happens to recur 51 times in the course of the play both in the singular and in the plural. The characters add up as a sum of points of view that diverge, overlap or exclude one another. Everything in the play is either reflection, image or, on the contrary, darkness, invisibility. The importance of perspective may be due to an overemphasis on looks and looking (and of the speeches that refer to them) at the expense of action itself, so that reality appears as what constantly evades people. That supernumerary eye may be that of the voyeur or that of woman, since it is she who is at the origin of all that happens in the play, that is according to Thersites for whom 'All the argument is a whore and a cuckold' (II, iii, 74–5).

The difficulty of perspective also comes from the multiple meanings of the word: an illusionary rendition of reality, through geometry and the artist's skill, it has the power to transform a flat space into a three-dimensional one. But the term also designates a form of deceptive illusion, a decoy, the source of errors and of lies.[2] However, the notion of pictural artifice, which leads us to a form of visual realism since it integrates the point of view of the spectator, is then combined with that of an optical game in the technical sense of the word perspective in Shakespeare[3] (in *The Sonnets*, *Richard II*, *Twelfth Night* and *All's Well That Ends Well*), namely that of anamorphosis, i.e. an image that can change into another when the points of view are changed.

These different meanings reflect the kaleidoscope of the play, that can in turn be understood as a parody, as a means of calling attention to the gap between appearance and reality, and as a lesson on the relativity of things and points of view; in short it amounts to a putting in perspective of present time and to a *mise en abyme*[4] of the text through the interplay of sources, rhetoric and dramatic specularity. I shall here successively consider four types of perspective in *Troilus and Cressida* – formal or parodic perspective, dramatic perspective, spatio-temporal perspective and 'perverted' perspective, i.e. anamorphosis.

* * *

The question of parody or of travesty poses the problem of the way Shakespeare treats his sources. He generally prefers to use stories from various origins rather than to invent his own subject matter. Now what characterizes *Troilus and Cressida* is not only the absence of originality of his topic but the fact that what is being borrowed is so ostensibly revealed. Rare words appear as such (like 'orgulous' for instance, borrowed from Caxton), proverbs and mythological clichés, sententiae or instances borrowed from scholastic or judicial rhetoric witness to the presence of many visible twists of expression in the play.

Shakespeare takes his inspiration from the story of Troy ('In Troy, there lies the scene') as it is told by Homer in Chapman's translation, then re-interpreted by Boccaccio, Chaucer, Caxton and Henryson. The love affair which he borrowed and expanded from Homer's *Iliad* is rendered through the successive filters of provençal *fin amor*, of the medieval code of knightly honour and of fifteenth century chronicles. Shakespeare engaged in a complex rewriting that shortened (as in the case of Chaucer's *Troilus and Criseyde*), transposed or integrated in another context the episodes, data or textual elements borrowed from his predecessors. Such amalgamation of the old with the new is precisely what parody consists of, provided the model is well known, which was indeed the case with Chaucer's *Troilus and Criseyde*.[5] By the same token, the unusual warning to 'the eternal reader' that precedes the prologue looks like a winking at the well-read audience of the 'Inns of Court' (where the play was probably performed for the first time) whose alleged wit and ingenuity allowed them to enjoy its subtle complexity.

Shakespeare's use of *Troilus and Criseyde*, a poem which is put in perspective within a sophisticated drama should not, however, lead us to believe that Chaucer's romance, which does emphasize the values of courtly love, gives an image of the walled city of Troy as primitive or naïve as its graphic representations are in medieval illuminations. Chaucer had already reworked the ancient legend and his interventions in the narrative draw the reader's attention to the gap between the time of the legend and that of the narrative; while praising romantic love, he added a number of ironical touches to reveal that this love is not without dangers or drawbacks.[6] Chaucer thus allows for a subtlety of vision at a dual level where sympathy for his characters nicely combines with the distance that is taken from them. If *Troilus and Criseyde* may indeed be regarded as the equivalent of the cities that fade away at the back of a painting to suggest distance, one must then consider that this medieval city is not only stylized but that its details also give a miniature image of Shakespeare's Troy. This would then amount to a perspective of perspective, to a game of mirrors, defining the relationships between the two texts. To quote only one example, I will take Criseyde's expression in Book II, stanza 61, to designate the specious nature of her uncle's speech – 'peynted process'. In *Troilus and Cressida*, Pandarus makes the phrase his when he ironically addresses his fellow procurers in the end: 'Good traders in the flesh, set this in your painted cloths' (V, x, 46–7). One can see how Shakespeare translated poetic images into stage language with, as is the rule in this play, a strong emphasis on alienation effect.[7] In *Troilus and Cressida*, we never have the slightest doubt that we are attending a play.

By staging two secondary characters from Homer's epic, one could say that, in *Troilus and Cressida*, Shakespeare used the *Iliad* in a way that may be compared with Stoppard's use of *Hamlet* in his parody of it, *Rosencrantz and Guildenstern Are Dead*, where Shakespeare's tragedy is entirely seen from the point of view of Hamlet's so-called friends, the two flat characters of the title. This amounts to a revolution in the point of view, but Chaucer also served him as a precedent for this. It is Chaucer who invented Pandarus, whom Shakespeare will only make into an older figure, but the idea of giving him a counterpart in the Greek camp, the misanthropic buffoon Thersites, is entirely Shakespeare's invention.

Derision also undermines love and war, the great human values of the Middle Ages. Up to a certain extent, the chivalric ideal is kept up with the characters of Troilus and Hector, but Shakespeare also stresses the gap between their illusions or their ideal and a sordid reality which Pandarus and Thersites cynically gloat over in their bitter asides. The very fact that the commentaries are more important than action in the play reveals that the observers take precedence over the protagonists of the drama and that reality only exists in the way it is rendered and distorted by the prism of their imprecations and of their salacious or gloomy remarks. Whereas Troilus metaphorically links the losses of the war to the ravages of a somewhat vampirical beauty ('Helen must needs be fair / When with your blood you daily paint her thus', I, ii, 90–1), Thersites sees things as a grotesque satirist whose point of view constantly stresses the seamy and the sexual, as when he contemptuously refers to 'those that war for a placket' (II, iii, 21). Chaucer had already sketched out the idea of a gap between reality and the courtly and chivalric ideals, offering a run-of-the-mill version of the war and love epic, or taking up through the pretended *gaucherie* of the narrative the theme of the humble condition of medieval man presented as caught up in day-to-day problems and dwarfed by those moral giants, the heroes of antiquity. Shakespeare introduces a contrast between tones and a great diversity of points of view while re-examining the ancient myth in a new light against which the drabness and the disillusions of the modern age easily stand out.

What could be called Shakespearian revisionism works through his almost systematic debunking of the great speeches and by pricking the bubble of his heroes' pride (Achilles and Hector mainly) as well as by his mock-heroic rendition of love and war. On the one hand there is the pompous rhetoric of glorious phrases, in the Greek camp as behind the ramparts of Troy. These noble speeches, on the other hand, whether they be Ulysses' 'degree' soliloquy (I, iii, 75–137) or Troilus's lyrical outburst when he affirms that Helen 'is a theme of honour and renown, / A spur to valiant and magnanimous deeds, / Whose present courage may beat down our foes, / And fame in time to come canonize us' (II, iii, 200–3), cannot stand the confrontation with the facts. All this, once again, reveals the gap between practical attitudes and verbal poses.

In *Troilus and Cressida*, the putting in perspective of antiquity is also achieved through the use of the burlesque that belittles or ridicules the great characters in the various stinging images or formulae invented by the foul Thersites. Patrocles is '[Achilles'] masculine whore' (V, i, 16); Menelaus, whom Diomedes had already called a 'puling cuckold' (IV, i, 62), becomes 'the primitive statue and oblique memorial of cuckolds' (V, i, 54) in the parlance of the grotesque satirist, who further stigmatizes 'that stale old mouse-eaten dry cheese Nestor and that same dog-fox Ulysses' (V, v, 10–11). As to Ajax, whom he had already called 'a very land-fish, languageless, a monster' (III, iii, 262–3), he is later described as swollen with a pride superior to that of Achilles: 'now is the cur Ajax prouder than the cur Achilles' (V, v, 14–15). The very name of Ajax, in Thersites' heap of insults, harks back to John Harrington's pun in *The Metamorphosis of Ajax*, with its allusion to 'a jakes', that is to say a privy. The bestiary of impure beasts, obscenity and scatology are all part of this general satire, where perspective is systematically perverted, but the insults are so biting that they all seem part of the mad world of Sebastian Brant's *Ship of Fools* (1509) or the engravings of the world upside down. The satirist's levelling humour makes him see the world through a darkening and distorting prism so that the heroes of olden time are reduced to beasts and monsters. Indeed, Thersites' range depends on teratology as much as on zoomorphy, it is fantastic rather than simply fanciful. Pandarus's style is quite different:

incapable of understanding the movements of the heart, he reduces everything to the level of sexual and material interests. His particular function is to serve as a cynical and grotesque counterpoint to Troilus's bashful love lyrics. Just before the arrival of Deiphobus, Antenor and Diomedes, who have come to fetch Cressida, it is Pandarus who exclaims at the sight of the young lovers: 'What a pair of spectacles is here!' (IV, iv, 13). Cressida's salacious uncle refers both to the charming spectacle of the young lovers and to his voyeuristic spectacles, in a pun that slyly punctures the dignity of the characters while indirectly stressing the importance of perspective. To this burlesque effect must be added a process of ironical focus due to the fact that neither of the two has guessed the misfortune which is just about to plague them.

Shakespeare also uses perspective in *Troilus and Cressida* in order to stress the importance of intertextuality in the play. The subtleties of this sophisticated text summon the attention, right from the unusual foreword to the 'eternal reader', on the part of an author who seems very much aware of the parallels with other works dealing with the same theme as well as with mythological references, mostly derived from Ovid.[8] The quotations, allusions, montages or verbal echoes have not been woven into the text as they normally are in Shakespeare: they are deliberately allowed to jar with the whole like so many variegated pieces in a patchwork.[9] This is true of the pagan gods invoked by the characters in a context that gives them a daily or even ordinary look.[10] The images and the names associated with the mythological figures enrich the range of caricature, as in the description which Alexander, Cressida's servant, gives of Ajax: 'he is a gouty Briareus, many hands and no use, or purblind Argus, all eyes and no sight' (I, ii, 29–31). Mythological invocation introduces a distortion that is one of the bases of irony in the play. Incapable of greatness, the protagonists of the drama deconstruct the ancient world and then rebuild it at their own Lilliputian scale so that the giants of the past are now looked upon as grotesques or monsters. Besides, Shakespeare invites the reader to play a game of self-reference insofar as he had before alluded to the Troilus and Cressida story in comedies like *The Taming of the Shrew*, *Much Ado About Nothing*, *1 Henry IV*, *As You Like It* and *Twelfth Night*, all plays where the history of the two lovers is evoked in a facetious style. Their misfortune may also be regarded as a bitter parody of the earlier tragedy of *Romeo and Juliet* in which Pandarus would replace the Nurse and Calchas old Capulet.

The last level of these games of formal perspective is that of rhetoric which has such a visible role in the play. The sudden shifts in dramatic tone from one scene to the next, from one character to the other, contribute to a constant reversal of perspectives. One passes from the martial and epic tone of the Prologue to the effeminate lamenting of a 'hero' who exclaims 'I am weaker than a woman's tear' (I, i, 9), to the pompous and mannered style of the Greek chiefs while Pandarus's vulgarity is echoed by Cressida's mischievous vivacity, which itself differs from the suave and languorous repetitions found in Paris and Helen's conversation (III, i). As to Thersites' venomous barbs, they are the true reflection of his idiosyncratic humour that tackles reality from a somewhat marginal perspective, steeped in dark melancholy but which serves to question all ready-made assumptions and to puncture illusions. Besides the more visible rhetorical effects like paradox, oxymoron, hypallage, or antimetabole, the frequent resorting to linguistic artifice, underlined by the creation of many nonce-words ('protractive', 'oppugnancy', 'scaffoldage') gives the impresion of a stylistic mannerism which is the dramatic equivalent of the conceits of the Metaphysical poets with which *Troilus and Cressida* has obvious affinities. Thersites' commentary on Cressida, who allows Diomedes to seduce her without openly acknowledging it ('A juggling trick: to be secretly open', V, ii, 24), might be used to describe the verbal and mental juggling of the characters. The meandering syntax of the play bears witness to the bafflement of the hearts or to the casuistry of sexual desire which works its way through ambiguous phrases or innuendoes. Perspective amounts here to a rhetorical game exploiting amphibologies or the superimposition of stylistic figures. Language becomes inscribed within a game of mirrors and is a reflectivity that favours ulterior motives and the dispersion of meaning at the expense of spontaneity and sincerity. In addition to the cunning prevarications of the army's commanders or of the lovers, proverbs and gnomic formulations are underlined in the verse soliloquies. The abuse of clichés, of sententiae, of sayings or of the instance of scholastic logic tends to make the characters rather mediocre human beings, addicted to imitation with no substance in history or originality in their handling of style. This applies to Pandarus, Nestor, Agamemnon, Achilles, even to Ulysses and perhaps also to Troilus who, in his most inflamed praises of Cressida, can only capitalize on adjectives and images borrowed from Petrarchan codes. The effect of those hackneyed phrases works contrary to a high-lighting of differences in the prism of the various points of view. It leads to a flattening out and to a levelling of situations, i.e. to a suppression of perspective. But Shakespeare makes up for this by skilfully adjusting his dramatic structure, so that the points of view of the characters, baffling or meaningless when seen isolated, reach their true significance by being compared with one another.

'Skiagraphy', or the science of perspective, is said to have been invented by Apollodorus at the end of the fifth century BC and this technical term, like that of 'skenographia', also served to designate the art of painted settings for the theatre.[11] From a dramatic point of view, perspective in *Troilus and Cressida* first and foremost concerns characters and plot.

The absence of a hero or of a dominant point of view in the play has often been remarked.[12] The eponymous characters are standing curiously back in view of the overall plot, where they hold but a fairly limited part. When compared to the other plays of Shakespeare whose title is provided by the names of one or two characters, like *Romeo and Juliet* or *Antony and Cleopatra*, *Troilus and Cressida* appears to occupy a marginal situation.

Some critics have seen in Ulysses or in Hector the true heroes of the play, without realizing that these two characters are themselves highly focused: this contributes to reducing their stature insofar as what they say seems limited to their own viewpoint and cannot be considered as the statement of some synthetic or even universal truth. If Ulysses presents himself like a philosopher and a strategist, it should also be pointed out that his acts are not in conformity with his speeches. He has no qualms about loading the dice and rigging the lottery to designate Hector's adversary in single combat ('[...] make a lott'ry, / And by device let blockish Ajax draw / The sort to fight with Hector', I, iii, 374–6), so as to 'pluck down Achilles' plumes' (I, iii, 386). More seriously, he organizes the scene in which Cressida is kissed by the whole Greek camp, in order to demonstrate that she too is part of the 'daughers of the game' (IV, iv, 63). As to Hector, alternatively qualified as 'brave' and 'manly', he ironically feels 'i' th' vein of chivalry' (V, iii, 32) on the morning of the very day when he is butchered by Achilles' Myrmidons. He is both a kind of Socrates, an ironist who lucidly judges war (particularly in the debate about Helen when he claims that 'pleasure and revenge / Have ears more deaf than adders to the voice / Of any true decision', II, ii, 172–4) and a quixotic figure engaged in the pursuit of the fanciful schemes of another age. As he is to learn at his own expense, the ideals of chivalry have become outdated and must now be regarded as a dangerous and destructive illusion. The victim of an error of parallax, he no longer understands the gap between the mythical time of origins and the daily realities making war an enterprise as dangerous as it is absurd. The characters are caught up in a highly deceptive drama as they are still inspired by chivalric and courtly models that no longer correspond to contemporary realities. Transcendental ideas have become myths and the often bitter irony of the plot contributes to placing the play under the sign of the relative.

Such relativism appears in the fact that all the characters are constantly compared to one another and in that they can be judged mostly thanks to the accumulation or the difference of the points of view coming from their own camp or from that of the adversary.[13] From the very beginning, the beauty of Cressida is compared to Helen's, the courage of Troilus to Hector's then to Achilles'. The constant to-and-fro movement from one camp to the next, from one warrior to the other, is a constant process in a world where the words flow and paralyse action. There is no absolute, only a series of differences which forms the basis for social distinction and degree. Simply, contrary to the cosmos described in Ulysses's soliloquy (I, iii,) the various echelons and proportions separating men are no longer governed by a strict hierarchy. The main problem of the play is that everything boils down to a question of perspective and that things and beings have no price of their own. They only have a fiduciary value so that, like money, they depend on the trust placed in them or in the credit they have acquired (reputation). Hector, who criticizes his brother's idolatry, will himself fall victim to it when he goes to the fight in spite of the repeated warnings of Cassandra, Hecuba, Andromache and Priam.

This is reinforced by the internal contradictions of the characters. Thus Troilus is deeply mistaken about the real nature of his love: he thinks it is ideal when it is only sensual. But he behaves in a realistic manner in the war, while Hector still follows obsolete rules of conduct. He will learn too late that modern war is neither a game nor a sport (Aeneas had spoken of 'good sport' in I, i, 115) but a terrifying reality that may cause an unarmed man to be slaughtered. Troilus is mistaken about Cressida when he sees in her a 'pearl' on the bed of India and the imaginary 'wand'ring flood' (I, ii, 100–2) that is supposed to separate them gives an idea of his error of perspective.[14] Pandarus resorts to a more down-to-earth image, that of a cake to be baked in the oven (I, i, 23–4). Cressida herself is characterized by a fundamental uncertainty as to what she wants without being at all an idealist as we can see from her very straightforward repartees to Pandarus and Troilus. She is aware of the power of her charms and her answers waver between the declaration of love ('I love you now', III, ii, 119) and the confession that she loves to seduce ('Perchance I show more craft than love / [...] to angle for your thoughts', III, ii, 151–3). Above all she knows by experience that charms last only as long as one hides one's real feelings ('If I confess much you will play the tyrant', III, ii, 118) and also as long as she refuses to yield to the desire of the other: 'You men will never tarry' (IV, ii, 16) is the comment she makes after her night with Troilus.

The games with perspective are not absent in the bouts of pride that affect Achilles and Ajax in turn. Ulysses' stratagem consists in giving Achilles an impression analogous to the one he has on others when he withdraws under his tent with Patroclus or when he refuses to fight. It is for Ulysses a matter of 'reflection' (III, iii, 99) so as to lead him to contemplate himself in his true light. This is the theme of the mirror of pride which will be the occasion of long exchanges between Ulysses and Achilles in Act III, iii. This scene itself is placed in the reverse order of the one in which Troilus and Hector engage in a debate about Helen and where Ulysses seems to echo Troilus while Achilles echoes Hector. Structurally, all this looks like the inversion of images seen in a mirror.

But perspective is also present at the level of theatricality in the little sketches where Achilles and Patroclus burlesque the generals of the Greek army. These are a series of distorting miniatures, of small portraits in the manner of Theophrastus that parody Ulysses's speech of which they offer a comic counterpart. As in Hal's and Falstaff's 'play extempore' in *1 Henry IV* (II, iv, 276), they present us with examples of travesty in Ulysses' own speech before turning, a little later, to a parody of characters and of situations which we have already seen (Nestor and Agamemnon in their roles as grave and sententious old men). Ulysses uses 'pageant' (I, iii, 151) as a verb to designate these irreverent imitations of which Ajax will be a victim later when Thersites says to Achilles 'You shall see the pageant of Ajax' (III, iii, 270–1). Ulysses relates in detail Achilles' and Patroclus's 'scurril jests' (I, iii, 148) before he compares them to 'strutting players' on the 'scaffoldage'

(I, iii, 156), a fertile anachronism which allows a double alienation of the Trojan scene while putting it in relation with the contemporary Elizabethan stage in the background. This ridiculous discrepancy between reality and image may be rendered in Achilles' description of great Agamemnon's voice ("Tis like a chime a-mending', I, iii, 159) while Patroclus causes 'Sir Valour' to 'split [his] spleen' and to die with laughter as he mimics 'the faint defects of age' and counterfeits the coughing and spitting of old Nestor (I, iii, 172–8).[15] Ulysses, as to him, is totally preoccupied with his own image and he regards the theatre as an instrument of political manipulation rather than a means of criticism or of satire of authority. Such subversion of the hierarchical order disquiets and even panics him and, in his *saeva indignatio*, he betrays the symptoms of what the painter Dali, after Lacan has called 'critical paranoia'. The image which the world sends back to him is 'tortive' (I, iii, 9), distorted, dangerous.

Indeed, nobody in *Troilus and Cressida* seems really sure of his or her identity. Everyone must be identified and this is constantly checked and confirmed as if they were confronted with police forces: 'Who comes here?', 'Is this the lady Cressid?', 'What's Thersites?', 'It is Cassandra?', etc. On the whole, identity does seem problematic, sometimes in the eyes of the protagonists themselves as we have seen with Cressida. In a number of cases, characters are reduced to mere role-playing. In a world undermined by doubt, there is no adequation between being and appearance. Sometimes the characters do not recognize each other, as when Aeneas, sent by Hector as a messenger, refuses to understand that he is indeed addressing Agamemnon (I, iii, 247) or when the Greek generals walk past Achilles and utterly ignore him to suggest that he no longer exists in their eyes.

If the Greeks are so swollen with pride that a little pin-prick is needed to blow them down to their true dimensions, the Trojans tend to see their present reality obliterated at the expense of the intemporal archetypes into which they are projected. This, for example, may be seen in the lovers' oaths which Pandarus will subsequently make his:

> If ever you prove false to one another [...] let all pitiful goers-between be called to the world's end after my name: call them Pandars: let all constant men be Troiluses, all false women Cressids, and all brokers between Pandars
> (III, ii, 197–202)

This way of placing one's own image *sub specie aeternitatis* ('to the world's end') by attaching one's own name to a proverbial saying for the times to come, does amount to putting all characters in a strange ahistorical weightlessness, somewhere between myth and reality.

But this is only an extreme, atypical case and what prevails in *Troilus and Cressida* is the conflict of perspectives. For example, how can we reconcile the words of a very martial Prologue ('in armour') evoking 'the ministers and instruments of cruel war' (lines 4–5) and 'those broils' (27) with what Aeneas, a little later, says when he mentions 'this dull and long-continued truce' (I, iii, 262)? It is true that, all along the play, we are confronted with a 'phoney war', with plots, manipulations, speeches, in short with all sorts of make-believes rather than with the action initially promised. So it comes as no surprise to us that the ancient heroes and medieval knights should have been exchanged against the roles of politicians. Thus, one sees that Ulysses' great speech on degree, interrupted by Aeneas's untimely arrival, has only one practical effect, that of inventing some mean trick to rig the lottery that will designate Hector's adversary, so that Ajax may be favoured at the expense of Achilles. The political wisdom which is constantly invoked is of a purely rhetorical order as expediency or crafty behaviour regularly predominate in the course of the action. But these contradictions point to the existence of some more important games of perspective, those linked to spatial and temporal representations.

In *The Rape of Lucrece*, Shakespeare gave a painstaking description of the details of the setting of the Trojan war on the painting hanging on the walls of Lucrece's palace:

> At last she calls to mind where hangs a piece
> Of skilful painting made for Priam's Troy,
> Before the which is drawn the power of Greece,
> For Helen's rape the city to destroy,
> Threatening cloud-kissing Ilion with annoy;
>   Which the conceited painter drew so proud
>   As heaven, it seemed, to kiss the turrets bowed
>   (lines 1366–72)

In *Troilus and Cressida*, one finds the ramparts of the city on the one hand and the Greeks' tents on the other. Shakespeare is not happy with a simple *trompe l'oeil* setting and he uses all the resources provided by an overhead perspective on the ramparts that plunges on to the battlefield. This is why, according to Alexander, Hecuba and Helen may enjoy a vantage-point on the battlefield:

>   Up to the eastern tower,
> Whose height commands as subject all the vale,
> To see the battle
>   (I, ii, 2–4)

We find the same device in the passage where Pandarus and Cressida take their stance in an elevated position in order to watch the warriors returning from the war ('Here, here, here's an excellent place, here we may see them most bravely', I, ii, 183–4).

Shakespeare also alternates between scenes inside and outside the walls as he changes the points of view according to which camp the characters are in. Perspective also varies with the light which is that of dawn in the beginning ('Before the sun rose he was harness'd light' as Hector's mother and wife say when they observe him from the top of the walls in I, iii, 8), then darkens progressively until it becomes a mere chiaroscuro in the scene

of Cressida's betrayal to end in a Caravaggio-like nocturnal under ink-black
stormy skies at the time of Hector's death.

Perspective further depends on the observer's position. First, there is
Achilles' quasi-surgical vision surveying all the details of his adversary's body
before the battle:

> Now Hector, I have fed mine eyes on thee;
> I have with exact view perus'd thee, Hector.
> [...] I will the second time,
> As I would buy thee, view thee limb by limb
> (IV, v, 230–7)

Hector replies to this: 'O, like a book of sport thou'lt read me o'er / [...]
Why dost thou so oppress me with thine eye?' (IV, v, 238–40). It is also
Pandarus's case who, in a facetious conceit, plays at counting for Cressida
the number of hairs on Troilus's chin to make them a miniature representation
of Priam's family: among his 52 hairs, the white one represents the old
patriarch (I, ii, 162–4). This vision is taken through a magnifying glass.
Short-sighted vision may be blurred when taken too closely, as it is the case
for Thersites who constantly puts his nose in it. So everything he says is
warped, distorted by the lack of distance, like the battle which he transforms
into a scene of bull-baiting in Act V (V, vii, 9–12). The animalization of
things human comes from the fact that he fails to see the scene in its right
perspective and that details are exaggerated and the lines distorted. The
obsession with monstrosity is partly the result of long-sighted vision. Another
type of error of perspective is linked to the reverse effect, i.e. to excessive
distance so that short-sightedness is then responsible for the artistic fuzziness
that bars contact with reality.[16] When he describes Cressida, Troilus views
her with the eyes of the idealist inventing an imaginary topography which
highlights her beauty (I, ii, 100–4). In this play, the description of things
is a question of perspective as much as of humour and this is the message
which Agamemnon wants to convey to Achilles when he declares:

> A stirring dwarf we do allowance give
> Before a sleeping giant. Tell him so
> (II, iii, 139–40)

For Achilles has lost all sense of proportion: 'Things small as nothing [...]
/ He makes important' (II, iii, 170–1). It is in the same light that the
dialogue between Troilus and Cressida about 'the monstrosity of love' should
be understood, as it poses the problem of the contradiction between the
infinite nature of desire and the limits of performance (III, ii, 79–82).
Everything boils down to a question of accommodation and, as Troilus
himself says, one cannot see clearly what is looked at too closely: 'I do fear
besides / That I shall lose distinction in my joys' (III, ii, 24–5).

This principle of perspective also underlies the structure of the play,[17]
built on a mirror-like pattern with parallelisms and antitheses between the
Greeks and the Trojans, between the love affairs and the politics of war.

Just as certain characters like Pandarus and Thersites or Hector and Ulysses reflect the desire to establish a form of symmetry between the two camps, others like Helen and Cressida, or Achilles and Ajax, are built according to the technique of reflection or analogy. The symmetry is found again in the echoes from scene to scene, since the one in which the Trojans deliberate to decide whether Helen should be kept or not finds its counterpart in the previous one in which the Greek chiefs lament over the quarrels and the bad discipline that weakens their army. Certain compositions are more complex, like Act IV scene v, where two events take place simultaneously and echo each other by a series of ironical correspondences. This is when Ajax and Ulysses are trumpeting the event of the single combat against Hector; but it is Cressida who arrives in his place and she is going to be greeted by a series of kisses before Ulysses treats her like a common whore; the trumpet is heard again and the transition with Hector's arrival is made thanks to a pun, to a double image that encapsulates the two realities of love and war – 'the Trojan [s] trumpet'.[18] Such contamination of meaning is evidently not fortuitous and it is a kind of anamorphosis played with the ear that blends two perspectives in one and the same ambiguous sound.

Another structural effect of perspective consists in building the whole play around an empty, almost absent figure, namely the character of Helen whose appearance in Act III scene i, in the geometrical centre of the play, is as brief as it is disappointing. She is the cause of seven years' war, as the prologue says in lines 9–10, and everything about her seems fraught with a mysterious, ambivalent fascination. Now the few words that she exchanges with Paris and Pandarus make her appear a somewhat insignificant creature. If she is a living legend she is also an illusion which is made real only by distance or rumour. Looked at closely and in her privacy, she is a non-entity.[19] Instead of the magical icon we expect to see, we find only a make-believe, a deceptive image that leads to mistaken judgements. Thersites had coined a neat and sexually evocative phrase to render this feeling of evasiveness, of receding reality when he referred to 'the eye of Helen's needle, for whom he [Ajax] comes to fight' (II, i, 82–3). Helen's misleading eye is like a needle's eye. It is both everything and nothing. But, paradoxically, it is also the eye of the cyclone as she moves around in a world of boredom, languor and decadent voluptuousness while the tempest of war and destruction rages about her. So physical beauty or *venustas* is only a fantasy, a collective hallucination as, at the core of the dramatic and strategic design, we find only emptiness. As on Velazquez's painting of *Las Meniñas* in Madrid's Prado museum, the play is organized around an absence upon which the onlookers' attention is nevertheless bound to converge.[20] Beauty, like ugliness or the masks that disguise or make up reality, is also a matter of perspective. In *Troilus and Cressida*, it all boils down to looks that are too distant or too close and to errors of accommodation.

This is why Shakespeare is careful to insist on the importance of time in a play where everything is seen according to a series of retrospective or prospective glances that try to situate the present in connection with history and myth. One of the characteristics of *Troilus and Cressida* is that the future is known in advance, so that it has the effect of making the present unreal. The speech which Ulysses delivers to Achilles on the ephemeral nature of reputation, may indeed be read as an emblematic parable putting in perspective the figure of Time itself:

> Time hath, my lord, a wallet at his back
> Wherein he puts alms for oblivion,
> A great-siz'd monster of ingratitudes.
> [...] to have done is to hang
> Quite out of fashion, like a rusty mail
> In a monumental mockery
> (III, iii, 145–53)

The destructive and iconoclastic time of the play, traditionally designated as *tempus edax rerum*, is nothing but a mockery, a make-believe allegory, a forgetful figure that remembers nothing and nobody. This is of course another of these deceptive speeches of Ulysses, aiming at making Achilles come out of his reserve as well as of his tent, but it is also used as a means of ironical focus indirectly intended at those who refuse to listen to prophets or to the warnings of fate and to those who give vain promises – two attitudes that nevertheless foreshadow the impending disasters (III, ii, 182–7). Such an anticipation, which brings the perspective of annihilation into the heart of the present moment, turns love into a *memento mori*, a proleptic warning which reveals how closely the fate of the city is linked to that of its most famous woman. Cressida's betrayal, which repeats Helen's earlier adultery, looks ahead to Sinon's betrayal of Troy and to the city's final destruction by fire.

In this play, the existence of a dual perspective in space and time, that is of a reading of the past and of the future which is not only bifocal or binocular but truly bi-textual, takes us back to a hidden mystery which is only disclosed in the end. This contributes to making *Troilus and Cressida* the equivalent of those secret paintings or *Vexierbilde*, the fashion for which had already been introduced into England by painters such as Holbein.

Indeed, in Elizabethan England as in Shakespeare's text, the word perspective had the technical meaning of an optical game with strange or curious effects or of a painting built in such as way as to produce a fantastic or distorted image, whose meaning can only appear under a specific angle of vision. These optical tricks created chimaeras by multiplying or by superimposing images and they stood for symbolic conflicts in vision or perspective.[21] The symbol of a double world where an appearance may be replaced by another, the anamorphosis allows for dual perspective where the frontal vision only affords a series of puzzling or disquieting images while a side-glance allows the truth to be revealed. Shakespeare resorted to that device in his comedies as well as in tragic situations, in *Richard II* for instance, when Bushy says to the queen:

For sorrow's eye, glazèd with blinding tears,
Divides one thing entire to many objects –
Like perspectives, which, rightly gazed upon,
Show nothing but confusion; eyed awry,
Distinguish form

(II, ii, 16–20)

This passage was probably inspired by Holbein's famous painting of *The Ambassadors* (1553) which Shakespeare may have seen hanging in Whitehall on the occasion of a performance there. The oblong streak at the bottom of the painting representing the two French ambassadors with the instruments of trivium and quadrivium in the background cannot be deciphered when looked at face on ('rightly gaz'd upon'), while the image emerges as what it is really, i.e. as a skull distorted by perspective, when it is 'ey'd awry', i.e. seen from the right-hand side of the picture. This dual point of view is clarified by the succession of two images that transform the painting into a small-scale theatre with its stage and setting changes.[22]

In *Troilus and Cressida* it is Agamemnon who calls attention to the idea of the curious perspective when he resorts to the image of the knot in the wood that 'infects the sound pine and diverts its grain / Tortive and errant from his course of growth' (I, iii, 7–9) or, further down, in the circumlocutions through which he shows to Hector his good intentions towards him and speaks of 'this extant moment [...] / Strain'd purely from all hollow bias drawing'   (IV, v, 167–8). It would seem that these metaphors have no other purpose than to make us familiar with the existence of biased perspectives which single-minded characters like Troilus will simply not imagine, let alone accept.

This seems to be what the central scene of Act V is driving at. This is a scene in which Troilus watches Cressida's behaviour with Diomedes. Act V scene ii is powerfully put in perspective inasmuch as Cressida's dialogue with Diomedes is being overheard and interpreted at four different levels: by Troilus who is eavesdropping upon them, by Ulysses who is a witness of the scene and by Thersites who has an overall view and watches them watching. Finally, there are the spectators whose looks envelop those of the different actor–spectators of the scene. It is not exactly a case of a play within the play as in *A Midsummer Night's Dream* or *Hamlet*, but it is certainly a *mise en abyme* whose effect is to distance Troilus's reactions and to prevent the drama from veering into pathos or tragedy.

What Troilus overhears is the visual error of which Cressida accuses herself before she yields to Diomedes' advances:

Troilus farewell! One eye yet looks on thee,
But with my heart the other eye doth see.
Ah, poor our sex! this fault in us I find:
The error of our eye directs our mind.
What error leads must err; O, then conclude,
Minds sway'd by eyes are full of turpitude

(V, ii, 106–11)

The squint that seems to afflict cross-eyed Cressida serves to understate and to unmetaphor the inconstancy of the human heart. For Troilus it is something as incomprehensible as unacceptable:

> This is not she. O madness of discourse,
> That cause sets up with and against itself!
> Bifold authority
>   (V, ii, 141–3)

Being thus made a witness of the duplicity of his beloved results in blowing to pieces Troilus's world picture as well as the laws of ordinary logic. He experiences a form of mental disjunction, an ontological breakdown that is the equivalent of schizophrenic hallucination. To convey his present double-bind and the inner contradiction that afflicts him, he juxtaposes two antithetical phrases, 'This is, and is not, Cressid' (line 145), that reflect his incredulity.[23] He finds himself in a situation analogous to Duke Orsino's in *Twelfth Night* when put in presence of Viola's twin:

> One face, one voice, one habit, and two persons!
> A natural perspective, that is, and is not
>   (V, i, 217–18)

In the darker world of the problem plays, the double is no longer externalized as the twin in the comic game of errors but it is perceived as an instance of moral duplicity, of the 'bifold authority' that leads Troilus to the door of madness. Indeed, he is placed in a position where he cannot believe his own eyes:

> Within my soul there doth conduce a fight
> Of this strange nature, that a thing inseparate
> Divides more wider than the sky and earth;
> And yet the spacious breadth of this division
> Admits no orifex for a point as subtle
> As Ariachne's broken woof to enter
>   (V, ii, 146–51)

Troilus's unfocused vision leads him to create an apocryphal mythology that rolls into one the names of Ariadne and Arachne ('Ariachne') and which offers a whole range of fresh intertextual perspectives for the reader. His slip, the sign of his state of mental confusion, amounts to a form of verbal anamorphosis that opens up two contradictory directions of analysis. On the one hand, one finds the myth of the labyrinth with the image of Ariadne abandoned by Theseus, which is Troilus's situation in reverse and, on the other, that of Arachne's woof with its miniature representation of the sexual deviations and metamorphoses of the gods; its destruction by Pallas led Arachne to despair so that she hanged herself. It has often been argued that the image of the 'broken woof' is to be read as the sign of Troilus's inner wound or as a subliminal image of defloration. But it is also an image of self-mutilation in which this unbearable extra eye is put out. Troilus, the witness of a self-division and of a double perspective, experiences here a painful trauma.[24] Normally, the contradictory sides of a given reality appear only after time has revealed its successive facets. In fact, the play's scene adumbrates another underlying scene which becomes visible later in a retrospective apprehension of meaning. This second level of meaning serves to expose the deceptiveness of beauty and of the quest of honour. Like Troilus's love, they are a form of blindness due to an effect of perspective. Helen's beauty then appears as one of the faces of death lurking beneath her skin. *Venustas* was only a mask for *vanitas* and the sight of woman's voluptuous body conceals the skeleton in the cupboard. The seduction of appearances embodied by Helen and Cressida, just like Thersites' ugliness incidentally, was only a mask, a form of cunning, a game of perspective used to delay the ultimate revelation of the dance of death.

All this becomes fully apparent at the end of Act V, when passions are let loose after the long period of inactivity. The ravages of the Sagittary, the implacable archer who brings desolation and death in the Greek camp, remind us of the medieval allegory of the Triumph of Death. Hector is attacked when unarmed and just after getting hold of the wonderful suit of armour he desired. It is significant that the latter should contain a rotten carcass, the emblem in a stage *Vanité* and a *memento mori* with an immediate and devastating irony as far as Hector is concerned. He has just met with the image of his own destiny.

*   *   *

In *Troilus and Cressida*, Shakespeare debunks and undermines Homer's legendary story. Neither a chronicle, nor comedy, nor tragedy, the play is moreover situated in the middle of nowhere in the Folio, where it is printed as a sort of afterthought or last minute addition as it appears between *Henry VIII* and *Coriolanus* without being previously announced in the initial 'catalogue'. This is a first effect of perspective found again in the many *trompe l'oeil* arrangements of a play whose entire structure is governed by a quasi-absence, that of Helen, whom the Prologue however presents as the *primum mobile* of the current wars.

Such decentring, where essential elements seem to be rejected on to a sort of outer circle, with Pandarus and Thersites acting as the satirical and gloating voyeurs of the paltry or squalid actions inside the inner circle of the plot that have nothing to do with the noble ideals of the characters of ancient myth, is another striking characteristic of the play. It is pointing to the invention of a new geometry with perspective, optical illusion and *mise en abyme* as its main component parts.

The multiple perspectives represented by the various characters and by the plot, namely the phoney war and the games of seduction, desire and pleasure, become interwoven in a series of complex arabesques but they only open on to blind windows and lead to nowhere. Through this highly stylized play that extensively resorts to dramatic alienation, Shakespeare brings home to us the idea that life is nothing but theatrical settings and role-playing. Behind the shimmering veil of appearances and the fantasies of feminine seduction, we are led to acknowledge the pathetic emptiness of its characters and the universality of the experience of betrayal. Cressida's inconstancy is no simple accident, it reveals a division of the human being, a loss of the feeling of identity linked to the prevalent triumph of relativism and individualism.

   Troilus and Cressida is a play based on the principle of uncertainty which, by borrowing from the techniques of perspective and anamorphosis, takes up, in a more sophisticated form, the main elements of fifteenth-century Moralities. The myths of Love, Honour and Beauty all break up under our eyes and they lead the protagonists to an experience of nothingness where the dust that accumulates on the ruined walls of the city offers the first and last images of the play. *Troilus and Cressida* finally appears as an un-substantial world of shadows where everything is put in perspective or only exists through perspective. As Pandarus reveals in his concluding soliloquy ('Good traders in the flesh, set this in your painted cloths', V, x, 45–6), the play seems entirely made up of a succession of cardboard elements, painted panels, *trompe l'oeil* figures. So that the only reality that is left to exist in the end is that of the theatre – a machinery generating dreams and illusions.

NOTES

1. All references to the play are to the Arden Shakespeare, ed. Kenneth Palmer (London and New York: Methuen, 1982).
2. See Philippe Comar, *La perspective en jeu. Les dessous de l'image* (Paris: Gallimard (Collection Découvertes), 1992), pp. 20–4.
3. See Alexander Schmidt, *Shakespeare Lexicon and Quotation Dictionary* (Berlin, 1902, reprint New York: Dover Publications, 1971), 2 vols. See also Ernest B. Gilman, *The Curious Perspective. Literary and Pictorial Wit in the Seventeenth Century* (New Haven and London: Yale University Press, 1978), pp. 40–1ff.
4. The expression, introduced by André Gide à propos paintings by Memling, Quentin Metsys or Velasquez, to designate a scene reflected in miniature in a mirror inside the main scene of the picture, is borrowed from the heraldic language where it designates a coat of arms whose design is duplicated in small compass in a second one, *Journal 1889–1939*, Gallimard, Éditions de la Pléiade (Paris, 1960), p. 41 (year 1893). The technical equivalent for this would be dramatic embedding, alienation effect or even effect of infinite recession (game of mirrors). On this see *The Show Within: Dramatic and Other Insets. English Renaissance Drama (1550–1642)*, ed. François Laroque, Collection Astraea, (Montpellier, 1992), 2 vols.
5. In this connection see Raymond Gardette, 'Images d'espace dans *Troilus and Cressida*' in *Shakespeare. Troilus and Cressida*, (Actes du colloque des 9–10 novembre 1990), Lyon, 1991, p. 56. The concept of parody as '*enchâssement du vieux dans du neuf*' is borrowed from Linda Hutcheon's article, 'Ironie et parodie. Stratégie et structure', *Poétique*, 36 (November 1978), p. 469.
6. Ann Thompson, *Shakespeare's Chaucer* (Liverpool, 1978), p. 160.
7. This, according to Erwin Panofsky, was a special vantage point from which

men of the Renaissance could see the ancient world:

> [There is an] inward correspondence between perspective and what may be called the general mental attitude of the Renaissance: the process of projecting an object on a plane in such a way that the resulting image is determined by the distance and location of a 'point of view' symbolized, as it were, the *Weltanschauung* of a period which had inserted a historical distance – quite comparable to the perspective one – between itself and the classical past.

Life and Art of Albrecht Dürer, p. 261 [quoted in Ernest Gilman, *The Curious Perspective*, p. 28].

8. See Ann Thompson, 'The Characters of Oblivion: Shakespeare De-constructs Troy', in *Shakespeare. Troilus and Cressida*, p. 101.
9. In this connection see Antoine Compagnon, *La seconde main ou le travail de la citation* (Paris: Seuil, 1979), p. 279.
10. See Brian Gibbons, *Shakespeare and Multiplicity* (Cambridge: Cambridge University Press, 1993), p. 9.
11. See the entry 'Perspective' in *L'atelier du peintre et l'art de la peinture*, Dictionnaire des termes techniques (Paris: Larousse, 1990).
12. See R.J. Kaufmann, 'Ceremonies for Chaos' in *Troilus and Cressida*, Casebook Series, ed., Priscilla Martin (London: Macmillan, 1976), pp. 164–5.
13. Éliane Cuvelier, '*Troilus and Cressida*. Stratégies de manipulation', in *Shakespeare. Troilus and Cressida*, p. 121; see also R.J. Kaufmann, 'Ceremonies for Chaos' in *Troilus and Cressida*, Casebook Series, pp. 164–5.
14. R.J. Kaufmann, op. cit., pp. 162–4.
15. In this connection see Éliane Cuvelier's article, '*Troilus and Cressida*. Stratégies de manipulation', in *Shakespeare. Troilus and Cressida*, pp. 112–14.
16. In this connection, see Ann Lecercle's interesting analysis in her article entitled 'Words, Wards, Watches: Going-Between in *Troilus and Cressida*' in *Shakespeare. Troilus and Cressida*, p. 129;

> Error is of the eye in *Troilus and Cressida*. It is through a knot in the wood that medieval sorceresses like Mélusine were seen in their true light. What is essential in Chaucer, the Medieval tales and Shakespeare at this period is the constant framing of vision 'in between'.

17. See W.T. Jewkes, "To Tell my Story': The Function of Framed Narrative and Drama in *Hamlet*', Stratford-Upon-Avon Studies No. 20, *Shakespearian Tragedy* (London: Edward Arnold, 1984), pp. 31–2 and 44.
18. See A.P. Rossiter, *Angel with Horns, Fifteen Lectures on Shakespeare* (London: Longman, 1961), reprint 1989, p. 133; see also Pierre Iselin, 'Hark What Discord Follows': Musique, médiatisation et disconvenance dans *Troilus and Cressida*', in *Shakespeare. Troilus and Cressida*, pp. 157–8.
19. See Arnold Stein, 'The Disjunctive Imagination', in *Shakespeare. Troilus and Cressida*, p. 189.
20. See Michel Foucault's analysis of the painting in *Les mots et les choses*, Paris, Gallimard (Bibliothèque des Idées) (Paris, 1966), pp. 20–31.
21. See Ernest B. Gilman, *The Curious Perspective. Literary and Pictorial Wit in the Seventeenth Century*, chapter 2, 'The Curious Perspective in England', pp. 50–66; Gary Schmidgall, *Shakespeare and the Courtly Aesthetic* (Berkeley and San Francisco: University of California Press, 1981), pp. 125–34 ('Illusion and the New Perspective').
22. Jurgis Baltrusaitis, *Anamorphoses. Les perspectives dépravées* (Paris: Flammarion, 1984), p. 101; Raphaëlle Costa de Beauregard, 'Remarques à propos de l'utilisation de l'art de la miniature dans *Troilus and Cressida*', in

Shakespeare. Troilus and Cressida, p. 56.
23.   See Elizabeth Freund, '"Ariachne's Broken Woof": the Rhetoric of Citation in *Troilus and Cressida*', in *Shakespeare and the Question of Theory*, ed. P. Parker and G. Hartman (London, 1985), p. 23; Ann Lecercle, 'Words, Wards, Watches', pp. 126–7.
24.   On this, see John Kerrigan's analysis in his introduction to *Motives of Woe. Shakespeare and 'Female Complaint'. A Critical Anthology* (Oxford: Clarendon Press, 1991).

CHAPTER TWENTY

Mannerism and Anti-Mannerism in *Love's Labour's Lost*: 'The Words of Mercury are Harsh After the Songs of Apollo'

Sidney Thomas

Love's Labour's Lost inevitably invites discussion by paradox. It is Shakespeare's most light-hearted and sportive comedy, yet the merriment is interrupted and the scene begins to cloud with an announcement of death. It is a love comedy, yet at its close Jack hath not Jill. It is deliberately artificial in conception, structure, and language, yet it concludes with an attack on the artificial life. It reveals Shakespeare's debt to his predecessors and contemporaries more clearly than any other of his plays, yet it is one of his boldest and most original experiments in form. Finally, it is totally unlike any other play he was ever to write, yet it contains, in microcosm, much of the matter and style of his later work.

Most, if not all, of these paradoxes can be subsumed under a more general paradox: *Love's Labour's Lost* is Shakespare's most mannerist play, yet it is also his farewell to mannerism. It is, uniquely among his plays, a self-conscious aesthetic manifesto, a statement of what he accepts and rejects in the artistic practice of his own time. To understand, not simply *Love's Labour's Lost*, but the direction in which the young Shakespeare was moving, the view of life and art which he was arriving at, we need to understand mannerism as one of the dominant art styles of the later sixteenth century.

But to do this, we must first disabuse ourselves of the currently fashionable notion that mannerism is 'the manifestation of a rebellious, expressionistic "constant of the European spirit"'.[1] We have had, in recent years, a number of attempts by cultural historians to use mannerism as *the* key to the understanding of virtually all the major creative figures of the later sixteenth and early seventeenth centuries. Mannerism has become an umbrella term covering not only a multitude of visual artists, from Pontormo to Velazquez,[2] but also such composers as Gesualdo and Monteverdi, and such writers as Donne and, not least, Shakespeare.

Nowhere has the case for mannerism as a style expressive of profound social and personal alienation been more forcefully and unequivocally stated than in an influential work by Arnold Hauser.[3] For him, mannerism is 'an expression of unrest, anxiety, and bewilderment generated by the process of alienation of the individual from society and the reification of the whole cultural process'.[4] With this as his major assumption, Hauser can then proceed to the dogmatic certainty of his categorization of Shakespeare: 'That the author of *Romeo and Juliet*, as well as of *Hamlet*, *Measure for Measure*, and *Troilus and Cressida*, and even *Othello*, was a mannerist will be readily admitted, but when he wrote *Antony and Cleopatra* he was a mannerist still.'[5]

Acknowledging his discipleship to Hauser, Cyrus Hoy has lately gone one step further in transforming Shakespeare into a complete mannerist: 'Shakespeare's final artistic style ... may indeed be viewed as the ultimate expression of mannerist principles in Shakespeare's art.'[6] Indeed, for Hoy 'mannerist principles' underlie not only Shakespeare's art, but all of Jacobean tragedy as well, so that Jonson's *Sejanus* is no less mannerist than *Antony and Cleopatra*.[7]

It is easy to understand the strong (one is tempted to say the fatal) attraction of such a critical approach for present-day scholars. To interpret mannerism as an art of shock, tension and *angst*, and then to classify Shakespeare as a mannerist, is to make him our contemporary, a sharer in our world-view, alienated as we see ourselves alienated. It is to give his work a comforting and familiar relevance, to bring him as close to us as a Kafka or a Beckett, to dignify the art of our own time with the cachet of Shakespeare's genius.

We may well be sceptical, to begin with, of any attempt to group together, as exemplars of the same aesthetic 'principles', works created over a rapidly changing period of a century or more, in countries of differing social, political, and religious systems, and art forms at varied stages of development. If a Bronzino court portrait and *Hamlet* are both expressions of mannerism, then there is clearly something wrong with our definition of mannerism. The more it explains, the less it explains.

Further, the Hauser conception of mannerism is not, as a literary scholar might innocently assume, that which is universally held by art historians. Rather, it is a view vigorously opposed by most students of mannerism, who hold to an interpretation most eloquently stated by John Shearman, who contends that mannerism is marked, not by 'qualities inimical to it, such as strain, brutality, violence, and overt passion', but rather by 'poise, refinement and sophistication'. And he goes on to assert that mannerism is an artistic language of 'articulate, if unnatural beauty, not one of incoherence, menace and despair: it is, in a phrase, the stylish style'.[8]

Like Hauser, Shearman finds mannerist qualities not only in the visual arts, but also in the writing of the period. In line with his much more limited and specific idea of mannerism as an art of sophistication and refinement, however, he discovers its literary analogues not in Shakespearian tragedy, but in such examples of the handbook of manners as Stefano Guazzo's *La civil conversazione* of 1574.[9] This book, translated into English by George Pettie and Bartholomew Young as *The Civile Conversation* in 1586, attracted the attention of Francis Douce in 1839 as a possible source of both Jacques's 'All the world's a stage' speech and of Timon's epitaph.[10]

More recently, Sir Edward Sullivan[11] has attempted to make a case for Shakespeare's extensive borrowing from Guazzo. Many of the verbal parallels he points out between the Pettie–Young translation and Shakespeare's plays are such commonplaces as to mean very little, but others, such as those for *Hamlet*, are quite striking, especially in their cumulative effect. He suggests, with a certain plausibility, that the idea of the academe in *Love's Labour's Lost* may have come from Guazzo's discussion of Italian academies. John W. Draper,[12] more convincingly, has argued that the social convention of the *conversazione* was widely known throughout Europe, and would certainly have attracted Shakespeare's attention. However, he treats the *conversazione* simply as a genre of formal courtly debate, and therefore sees the influence of such works as Guazzo's on *Love's Labour's Lost* as limited to such debates, of which he identifies two in the play.

The Guazzo–Pettie–Young work has, however, a deeper significance for Shakespeare's early comedies, and particularly for *Love's Labour's Lost*. *The Civile Conversation* is precisely the kind of model of upper-class social behaviour, of elegant raillery and witty game playing, that the young actor from Stratford would have turned to for guidance when he attempted an urbane comedy of aristocratic life. Though in the direct tradition of Castiglione's *The Courtier*, the Guazzo book lacks the gravity, the philosophic idealism, the sense of social purpose which inform the earlier work. The passionate lyricism of Bembo's great discourse on love and beauty in the fourth book of *The Courtier* finds no echo in Guazzo. As if in deliberate contrast, the corresponding section of *The Civile Conversation* reaches a climax of polish and refinement of conduct and language.

It is this fourth book of Guazzo's manual of etiquette that provides perhaps the clearest link between continental mannerism and Shakespeare's early style. It describes a banquet 'betweene six Lords and foure Ladies' at which a ruler is selected by lot, through a procedure involving a random reference to a Petrarch sonnet. The Queen then chosen declares it 'my will and pleasure ... that some pretie sporte of solitarinesse may be deuised amongst you ... That euerie one of us shall chuse to himselfe a conuenyent place for a solitarie life, with declaring the occasion mouing him thereunto, & confirming it with some prouerbe.'[13]

After recording a series of witty answers given by members of the company to questions propounded by the Queen, Guazzo concludes: 'By this banquet men may learne to take their meate temperatelie, to exercise their stile modestlie, to sport and iest discreetlie, to use concord without roisting, learning without vaineglorie, curtesie without blemish or fault.'[14]

We do not, of course, need to assume that Shakespeare knew and used the Guazzo book in order to argue that there is a strong element of mannerism in *Love's Labour's Lost*. Here, if anywhere in Shakespeare, we can find a parallel to the 'stylish style' in the visual arts. None of Shakespeare's plays is more glittering with artifice, more openly addressed to a sophisticated coterie.

Nonetheless, much of *Love's Labour's Lost* inescapably reminds us of *The Civile Conversation*, particularly of its fourth book. The play opens, almost as if in direct reference to Guazzo, with Navarre and his friends devising 'some pretie sporte of solitarinesse', and the whole action of the play, until the final scene, is only the elaboration of a game, a succession of choreographic approaches and withdrawals, a progression by set speeches and witty retorts.

It is, above all, in the language of the play that Shakspeare's debt, not simply to Guazzo, but to the whole tradition represented by Guazzo, is most apparent. In a very real sense, as many recent commentators have noted, *Love's Labour's Lost* is a play about language, a play on words and through words.[15] For most of its length, it is an anthology of false and affected modes of discourse. The most conspicuous and fantastical of the word-mongers, the one who most needs to learn to exercise his style modestly, is, of course, Armado, 'a man in all the world's new fashion planted'. In his delight in fire-new-words, his intemperate hyperboles, his offences against decorum in language and behaviour, he constantly violates the mannerist ideal of true poise and refinement.

Nathaniel and Holofernes, the curate and the schoolmaster, are more familiar and traditional figures, whose literary origins go back to antiquity. But in the context of the play, their excesses of pedantry form still another element in the mannerist attack on crudity and exaggeration in speech. Their learning is condemned by its vainglory, and comes to nothing. 'They have been at a great feast of languages and stol'n the scrapes,' says Moth. And when Holofernes condescendingly rebukes Dull, 'Thou hast spoken no word all this while,' his reply is just and final, 'Nor understood none either, sir' (V, i, 131–3).

In contrast to the pretentious falsity, in its various modes, of the speech of Armado, Nathaniel and Holofernes, the language of the lords and ladies seems to offer examples of true wit and elegance. The King and his friends, the Princess and her attendants, appear, at first glance, very patterns of how to sport and jest discreetly, and how to use courtesy without blemish or fault. Each of them is a virtuoso of repartee, a master-mistress of felicitous and perfectly tuned discourse. The obvious delight which Shakespeare takes in their quickness, precision and grace of discourse is matched by the delight with which we respond to it. This is Shakespeare the whole-hearted mannerist, exuberant in his command of words and in his ability to mirror and please an aristocratic audience. It is almost as if he is responding to the injunction of the King to the poet Lodowick in the anonymous *Edward III*:

Better than bewtifull thou must begin,
Deuise for faire a fairer word than faire,
And euery ornament that thou wouldest praise,
Fly it a pitch aboue the soare of praise.[16]

But in the end mannerism is not enough for Shakespeare. To say, as John W. Draper does, that 'the theme of *Love's Labour's Lost* is the predominance of love over study in youthful minds'[17] is to miss the point of the play. The lovemaking of the lords is as mannered and unreal as the construction of their little academe. They are no more truly serious in the one than they were in the other. The sonnets in which they phrase their formal passion, the masque of Russians with which they woo the ladies of France, continue on another plane the game-playing with which the comedy has begun. Berowne's great speech on love at the end of Act IV is, for all its eloquence, an intricate set piece embellished with all the tricks of rhetoric, and produced as a response to the King's plea, 'Then leave this chat: and, good Berowne, now prove / Our loving lawful and our faith not torn.' Language can make all things right (IV, iii, 280–1).

That nothing has really changed with the lords' surrender to love is fully evident in the second scene of Act V, where the game of wit achieves its ultimate complexity as paradox is piled on paradox. 'They do it but in mocking merriment,' says the Princess, 'And mock for mock is only my intent.' And then she continues:

There's no such sport as sport by sport o'erthrown –
To make theirs ours, and ours none but our own.
So shall we stay, mocking intended game,
And they, well mock'd, depart away with shame.
                        (V, ii, 153–6)

Artifice met with artifice, thrust with counter-thrust – all goes almost to the very end as the Princess has planned it. But then, in one of the most dramatic reversals in Shakespeare's plays, none the less so for being so quietly managed, Marcade enters with the news of the French king's death. He makes his announcement and then, having spoken no more than two dozen words, 'My tale is told,' he says and vanishes. At this point, the whole conventional world of the play crumbles: artifice is overwhelmed by reality.[18]

But this is no accidental effect, no sudden improvisation on the part of Shakespeare to bring his play to a conclusion. It has been prepared for from the beginning; every flourish of style has been designed to lead up to the moment when style itself is defeated. In the customary world of Shakespearian comedy, journeys end with lovers meeting. Here, the journey is yet to take place, and it is therefore clear why the comedy cannot end like any old play.

As language has been the vehicle through which the make-believe world of the play has been created, so it is the vehicle by which that world is to be destroyed. Even before the appearance of Marcade, Berowne has proclaimed his renunciation of the mannerist style:

Taffeta phrases, silken terms precise,
Three-pil'd hyperboles, spruce affection,
Figures pedantical — these summer flies
Have blown me full of maggot ostentation.
I do forswear them; and I here protest
By this white glove (how white the hand, God knows!)
Henceforth my wooing mind shall be express'd
In russet yea's and honest kersey no's.
And to begin: wench, so God help me, law!
My love to thee is sound, sans crack or flaw
                                (V, ii, 407–16)

The forswearing of spruce affection, however, is announced in an elaborately patterned speech of alternately rhyming lines rounded off with a couplet, making a mockery of Berowne's promise, a few lines earlier, never to woo in rhyme. And when Rosaline replies 'Sans "sans", I pray you', he confesses that he still has 'a trick of the old rage'.

The reformation of Berowne, as of the other lords, is still to come. It is projected to a time and a world outside of the play, when love's labour shall have become truly a labour of love: only then can love's labour's lost be changed into love's labour's won. 'And therewithal to win me if you please, / Without the which I am not to be won,' says Rosaline to Berowne,

You shall this twelvemonth term from day to day
Visit the speechless sick and still converse
With groaning wretches; and your task shall be,
With all the fierce endeavour of your wit
To enforce the pained impotent to smile.
                                (V, ii, 834–46)

And Berowne replies:

To move wild laughter in the throat of death?
It cannot be; it is impossible.
Mirth cannot move a soul in agony.
                                (V, ii, 841–3)

Shakespeare is never again, in any of his comedies, as serious about his vocation as an artist as he is at this moment. *Love's Labour's Lost*, we may remember, was probably written during, or immediately after, the terrible plague years 1592–4. At no other time during his career can the limitations of wit, of language and art itself, have been so apparent to Shakespeare. The speech in which Rosaline responds to Berowne's outburst is the clearest statement in the play of this awareness: ... If sickly ears,

Deaf'd with the clamors of their own dear groans,
Will hear your idle scorns, continue them,
And I will have you, and that fault withal;
But if they will not, throw away that spirit,
And I shall find you empty of that fault,
Right joyful of your reformation.
                                (V, ii, 849–55)

'That fault' which Rosaline reprehends in Berowne and whose reformation she awaits is not simply the exercise of a gibing spirit, the wormwood of his wit. It is rather the elevation of artifice to a way of life, the insulation from reality, the rules of the game elaborated and refined to an ultimate degree. It is, in short, the mannerist style and the mannerist mode of being which are here being decisively rejected. Or so it would seem.

Shakespeare, however, even so early in his career, is already Shakespeare and avoids the too easy and obvious solution. The antithesis between art and nature, the shattering of the play world against the hard surface of reality – this is what the comedy is about, but it is not all that it is about. The supreme power and grace of language, the exercise of wit, art itself, are still to be tested. It may be that they will fail: to move wild laughter in the throat of death may be impossible, but it is still to be attempted.

As with all major creative artists, it is the totality of Shakespeare's career that finally establishes the meaning of any one of the works that make up that career. That word-play and wit do not insult reality but can be deeply serious and penetrating, that truth can be expressed through artifice – these are concepts that are central to the plays of Shakespeare's maturity, whether expressed in the antic disposition of Hamlet or the riddles of the fool in *Lear*. They receive perhaps their ultimate statement in the colloquy between Polixenes and Perdita in Act IV scene iv of *The Winter's Tale*:

Pol.   Wherefore, gentle maiden
Do you neglect them? [i.e. gillyflowers]
Per.   For I have heard it said
There is an art which in their piedness shares
With great creating nature.
Pol.   Say there be.
Yet nature is made better by no mean
But nature makes that mean. So, over that art
Which you say adds to nature, is an art
That nature makes ...
                              This is an art
Which does mend nature – change it rather; but
The art itself is nature.
                                      (IV, iv, 85–97)

And we answer with Perdita: 'So it is'. The words of Mercury do not cancel out the songs of Apollo. The paradoxes of *Love's Labour's Lost* do not so much contradict as reinforce each other. Harsh reality intrudes upon the mannered world of the King of Navarre's park, but it opens it up to the world outside rather than destroys it. Mannerism, in the end, is absorbed into anti-mannerism. It is rejected as an ideal, but retained as a stratagem, both of language and behaviour. Only in this sense can it be true to speak of the Shakespeare of the great tragedies and of the last plays as a mannerist.

NOTES

All quotations from Shakespeare are from the Kittredge–Ribner edition (Waltham, MA: Ginn), 1971.

1. Craig Hugh Smyth, 'Mannerism and *Maniera*', *The Renaissance and Mannerism: Studies in Western Art* (*Acts of the Twentieth International Congress of the History of Art*, vol. II, Princeton, 1963), p. 197.

2. See, for example, Wylie Sypher's reference to 'Velazquez' Maids of Honor (1656), a belated mannerist composition', *Four Stages of Renaissance Style* (Garden City, NY: Doubleday, 1955), p. 171.

3. *Mannerism* (New York: Knopf, 1965), 2 vols.

4. Ibid., Vol. 1, p. 111.

5. Ibid., Vol. 1, p. 342.

6. 'Jacobean Tragedy and the Mannerist Style', *Shakespeare Survey* 26 (1973), 64. For Hoy, Hauser's book is a 'definitive account of mannerism' (49).

7. 'Jonson might be termed the Bronzino of Jacobean mannerism' (ibid., 56).

8. *Mannerism* (Baltimore, MD: Penguin Books, 1967), p. 19. See also the same author's 'Maniera as an Aesthetic Ideal', *The Renaissance and Mannerism: Studies in Western Art*, pp. 200–21. For a similar view of mannerism, see Alastair Smart, *The Renaissance and Mannerism in Italy* (New York: Praeger, 1971), p. 167; and S.J. Freedberg, *Painting in Italy 1500 to 1600* (Baltimore, MD: Penguin Books, 1971), p. 144. ('... The passion of Parmigianino's *Vision of St. Jerome* is not an emotion about the subject matter of the picture so much as it is an emotion about art. Its excitement derives from the intensity and quick, mannered fineness with which aesthetic sensation is experienced ... the ultimate meaning of the altarpiece is its power of aesthetic artifice.')

9. Shearman, *Mannerism*, p. 41.

10. *Illustrations of Shakespeare* (London, 1839), pp. 185, 358.

11. Introduction to *Pettie's Guazzo* (The Tudor Translations, Second Series VII. London: Constable, 1925), Vol. I, pp. xxxviii–xcii.

12. 'Shakespeare and the *Conversazione*', *Italica*, 23 (1946), 7–17.

13. *The Civile Conversation* (London, 1586), Aaiii[r].

14. Ibid., Ccviii[v].

15. See, for example, William Matthews, 'Language in *Love's Labour's Lost*', *Essays and Studies*, 17 N.S. (1964), 1–11; James L. Calderwood, '*Shakespeare Metadrama* (University of Minnesota Press, 1971), pp. 52–84; William C. Carroll, *The Great Feast of Language in 'Love's Labour's Lost.'* (Princeton University Press, 1976); and Malcolm Evans, 'Mercury Versus Apollo: A Reading of *Love's Labour's Lost*', *Shakespeare Quarterly* 26 (1975), pp. 113–27.

16. *Edward III* (London, 1596, Cl[r]. These lines occur in a scene often ascribed to Shakespeare.

17. Draper, 16 (see note 12).

18. This development is brilliantly treated by Bobbyann Roesen in her essay '*Love's Labour's Lost*', *Shakespeare Quarterly*, 4 (1948), 411–26. See also her later discussion of the play, Anne Righter, *Shakespeare and the Idea of the Play* (London: Chatto & Windus, 1962), pp. 110–12.

PART SIX

Shakespeare and Criticism

CHAPTER TWENTY-ONE

The Rehabilitation of *King Lear* and *Troilus and Cressida*

Kenneth Muir

The two plays to which William Elton devoted many years of his life, with such learning and intelligence, that we are all his debtors, have been appreciated by the theatre-going public only within living memory. *King Lear* was played during the eighteenth century only in Nahum Tate's adaptation,[1] with its restoration of the King and Cordelia's marriage to Edgar. This adaptation was preferred by Samuel Johnson, who found the original too painful; and it was only by the romantic critics, Coleridge, Lamb and Hazlitt, that the Tate version was generally condemned. Lamb, indeed, declared that none of Shakespeare's tragedies could be acted,[2] because performance inevitably fell short of the reader's idea of them. Gradually Tate's alterations were abandoned, but even at the end of the nineteenth century, Bradley believed that *King Lear*, although a poetic masterpiece, was not a good stage play.[3] He had the excuse that no audience between 1660 and 1910 had had the opportunity of seeing the play performed in a way that allowed Shakespeare's stagecraft to be judged fairly.

Johnson's preference for Tate was due to the admitted painfulness of the original. He admits that

> a play in which the wicked prosper and the virtuous miscarry may doubtless be good, because it is a just representation of the common events of human life; but since all reasonable beings naturally love justice, I cannot easily be persuaded that the observation of justice makes the play worse.

Johnson complains that 'Shakespeare has suffered the virtue of Cordelia to perish in a just cause, contrary to the natural ideas of justice ... and to the faith of the chronicles'.[4] But if Shakespeare had followed the story in the Chronicles, familiarized by the condensed version in *The Faerie Queene*, he would have known that Queen Cordelia was deposed by her nephews and imprisoned by them, so that, despairing of ever regaining her liberty, she killed herself. Johnson would have been even more outraged by such an ending. Nor is his description of the play as one 'in which the wicked prosper and the virtuous miscarry' an accurate one. All the wicked characters die: Cornwall killed by his servant, Oswald killed by Edgar, Regan poisoned by Goneril, Goneril committing suicide when her plots miscarry, Edmund slain by Edgar, who ascends the throne on the death of Lear. The prosperity of the wicked is short-lived.

All the same, it may well be that the tragic nature of the tragedy delayed its rehabilitation. I am reminded of a stranger who sat next to me at a performance of *Twelfth Night* years ago, who told me how much he enjoyed Shakespeare's comedies, but that '*Hamlet* and *King Lear* erred on the tragic side'.

Troilus and Cressida suffered an even longer eclipse. The only recorded performances after the Restoration until the beginning of the present century were in Dryden's absurd travesty in which all the best poetry was mangled and Cressida remained faithful to Troilus. There was a performance in Munich in 1898, based apparently on Shakespeare's original, and perhaps suggested by the tribute paid by Goethe in his conversations with Eckermann[5]: 'If you would like to know Shakespeare's unfettered spirit, read *Troilus and Cressida*.' But accounts we have of the Munich performance and of others in various European cities do not encourage the belief that the directors understood the play.

It was still unperformed in England and most literary critics branded it as one of Shakespeare's unpleasant plays, written when he was going through a bad patch in his private life. It was 'the work of a man whose soul is poisoned with filth'. 'An ugly, inconsistent and unpleasant performance'.[6] Moreover the play was thought to be badly constructed; nothing happens in the first two acts except two long-winded debates in the Greek camp and in Troy.

Several things combined to bring about the rehabilitation of these two plays. The first was the gradual realization, based on scholarly research and critical acumen, that Shakespeare's stagecraft was dependent on the kind of stage for which the plays were written; and therefore that productions designed to attract the general public, philistines, barbarians and all, were uniformly disastrous. The time wasted in scene-changing, the interference with the order of the scenes, and the decimation of the text made the judicious grieve. Bernard Shaw had emphasized this throughout his dramatic criticism, and he had always stressed the central importance of the poetry.[7]

> The Bard has already become a mere stalking-horse for the scene painter, the costumier and the spectacular artists generally. His plays were presented in mutilated fragments divided into acts with long waits between, in which form they were so horribly boresome, being mostly unintelligible, that only the most powerful personal fascination would induce playgoers to endure him.

That is why Shaw applauded the productions of William Poel, even though the casting was frequently odd, the acting inadequate, the cuts disgraceful: they were less boring than the West End perversions.

Harley Granville Barker had played the part of Richard II in Poel's 1899 production, before he became actor and director at the Court Theatre, where many of Shaw's best plays were performed. Later, when he directed three of Shakespeare's plays at the Savoy theatre (1912–14), he improved on Poel's methods in several significant ways. He made hardly any cuts; he had excellent professional casts, including his wife, Lillah McCarthy; he had beautiful sets and costumes; and he jettisoned traditional stage business. Some critics complained of his innovations, and the speed of the delivery of the lines was such that Arnold Bennett, for one, found it difficult to follow.[8] But these productions transformed the way in which Shakespeare was performed, not merely at the Old Vic, where shortage of money limited their artistic possibilities, and at Stratford-upon-Avon, but in the productions of Gielgud and others, where longer rehearsal periods, brilliant designers and appropriate music added to the effectiveness of the whole.

Yet Barker and Shaw were well aware that the Elizabethan type of stage, with its platform half-surrounded by the audience, had an intimacy which could never be achieved in a theatre with a proscenium arch, footlights and a front curtain.

Troilus and Cressida had at last been revived in England by Charles Fry in 1907, but the critics still thought that the play was dull and unactable. Five years later Poel produced the play with himself as Pandarus. He had actresses playing Aeneas and Paris and, still more bizarrely, Thersites. Some of the best poetry was cut. Yet the production became historically famous because Edith Evans, a young amateur, played Cressida. When the production transferred to Stratford-upon-Avon, a splended young actor, Ion Swinley, played Troilus. The play aroused some critical interest and an appraisal by an excellent critic, John Palmer.[9]

Ten years were to elapse before the next production of the play by the Marlowe Society at Cambridge, with an all-male cast. The production proved to be a landmark in the play's history. For the first time since Shakespeare's day – perhaps for the first time ever – there was a fully appreciative audience. Many of its members were veterans who had spent the best years of their lives on the Western front. Whether or not they had read the war poems of Sassoon and Rosenberg, they shared their disenchantment with the war. Colonel Bonamy Dobrée, Professor of English Literature at Leeds, when he came to see my production at York in 1936 told me of his reactions to the 1922 production. He, like many others in the audience, considered the debunking of illusions regarding war and sex as salutary and relevant to the immediate post-war period, and relevant also to the years between the Treaty of Versailles and the signing of the Munich agreement.

It is not surprising that *Troilus and Cressida* found a ready welcome in 1922, for the literature being written appealed to the same audience. Ezra Pound's *persona* declared that a myriad had died in the war[10]

> For an old bitch gone in the teeth
> For a botched civilisation.

This botched civilization had been depicted by T.S. Eliot in his first three volumes, *The Waste Land* not then being regarded as a step in the poet's pilgrimage to the Church of England. James Joyce used the Homeric tale of Ulysses to depict the sordid realities of life in Dublin, as Shakespeare had used the tale of Troy to attack the idealization of war and sex.[11] Bernard Shaw in *Heartbreak House* had anatomized the deficiencies of the ruling class. Noel Coward, before he realized his talent for comedy, had depicted in *The Vortex* a Hamlet of our days, a drug addict with a tortuous relationship with his corrupt mother. In several novels of the period young men on leave or demobilized are devastated by the infidelity of their Cressidas.[12] Adultery seemed to be an appropriate derivation of adult.

Since the Marlowe Society production, *Troilus and Cressida* has remained in the repertory. There have been numerous productions in London and elsewhere, some in modern dress. There have been frequent revivals at Stratford-upon-Avon. It is not likely that it will ever be banished from the theatre. History had enabled us to catch up with Shakespeare.

No one would now publicly admit that Charles Lamb was right when he declared that Shakespeare's *King Lear* could not be acted, except in the banal sense that no production is perfect. Granville Barker's great preface to the play showed how the storm-scenes could be performed and his anonymous production in which he groomed Gielgud for the part demonstrated that his advice was eminently practical.[13] During the last 60 years any regular play-goer within reach of London or Stratford, could have seen a number of admirable Lears, including Redgrave and Olivier and (some would add) Wolfit; and there were television and film versions, especially Kozintsev's, to remind us of its wider ramifications. But, as with *Troilus and Cressida*, the play needed more than great acting, a new understanding of Elizabethan stage conventions and the acceptance of poetry as the one real essential, for audiences to undergo the disagreeables evaporated by the intensity of which Keats spoke.[14] It required too a new willingness on the part of audiences, not merely to prefer *Hamlet* to *The Mousetrap*, but to accept a tragic view of life. We have now a largely agnostic population, well able to respond to the subtext of the play, that William Elton regarded as a coded message to the freethinkers of Shakespeare's audience. Even Christians, as in Shakespeare's day, can accept that life on earth is inescapably tragic. Those who have lived through two world wars, through blitzes and famines, through the Holocaust and Gulag, through Hiroshima and the threat of Aids, through the notable lack of wisdom in the best-intentioned governments, are unlikely to feel that *King Lear* is too awful to be endured. Here, too, History has made us catch up with Shakespeare. Yet the treatment of the play by some directors, regarding it as a forerunner of the Theatre of Cruelty, a prime example of the Theatre of the Absurd, may suggest that today we need another coded message, addressed this time to the surviving Christians in the audience, who may not believe in a future life or in the fictional accretions to the gospel story, but who do take the Sermon on the Mount seriously, and believe that it is better to be Cordelia than her sisters, Edgar than Edmund, Kent than Oswald, Albany than Cornwall. Shakespeare gave the devil his due, but he would not have approved of directional whitewashing of the criminals.

NOTES

1. See Kenneth Muir, 'Three Shakespeare Adaptations', in *Leeds Phil. and Lit Soc. Proceedings* (1959), 233–8. Tate's father, Faithful Tate was a Puritan poet of some charm.
2. *Works of Charles Lamb*, vol. 3, ed. William Macdonald, n.d. (Phoenix Book Company), pp. 17–39.
3. Bradley, *Shakespearean Tragedy* (Macmillan, 1904), pp. 198–9.
4. *Dr. Johnson on Shakespeare*, ed. W.R. Wimsatt (Penguin Shakespeare Library, 1969), p. 126.
5. Everyman's Library edn (1931), p. 123.
6. Agnes Mure Mackenzie (Heinemann, 1924); John Bailey (English Heritage Series, 1929).
7. *Shaw on Theatre*, ed. E.J. West (Hill and Wang, 1959), p. 126.
8. Arnold Bennett, *The Journals*, 3 October 1912. He reported a week later that George Moore preferred *Charley's Aunt* to Barker's *Winter's Tale*. It may be mentioned that Bernard Shaw, despite his admiration for Barker, admitted that he was not at his best with Shakespeare because of his dislike of the grand manner, which he regarded as 'ham'.
9. Palmer afterwards wrote a book on Ben Jonson, a biography of Molière and a study of modern French dramatists.
10. Ezra Pound, *Shorter Poems* (Faber, 1928), p. 176.
11. *Ulysses* (1922).
12. Richard Aldington, *Death of a Hero* (1929), written a few years later, is a typical example.
13. Two recent tapes by Ronald Watkins (*Shakespeare's Globe: The Actor's Task* and *Lear's Storm*) demonstrate the brilliance of Shakespeare's stagecraft and Watkins's resilience. He was acting 60 years ago. I acted with Watkins 65 years ago in a performance of Blake's *The Ghost of Abel*: Watkins was Jehovah, I was Satan.
14. Letter of 22 December 1817.

CHAPTER TWENTY-TWO

Wilson Knight and Shakespeare's Last Plays[1]

Philip Edwards

Wilson Knight was a pioneer in recognizing the importance of Shakespeare's last plays, or 'romances'. *Myth and Miracle: An Essay on the Mystic Symbolism of Shakespeare*, was published in 1929. In his biography of his brother, Knight tells us that *Myth and Miracle* was actually 'a booklet version' of a fuller study written in 1928 but never published, called *Thaisa*.[2] The typescript of *Thaisa* is in the Shakespeare Library of the City of Birmingham Public Libraries, bound up with letters of rejection from several publishers, including one signed by Richard de la Mare from Faber and Gwyer, the firm which T.S. Eliot had just joined.[3] *Myth and Miracle* had been preceded by Colin Still's essay on *The Tempest* (*Shakespeare's Mystery Play*, 1921), but all the same it was a voice in the wilderness, largely unheeded. It was a spirited and vigorous work, a manifesto, challenging what Knight considered to be the inessential preoccupations of Shakespeare scholarship ('the side-issues of Elizabethan and Jacobean manners, politics, patronage, audiences, revolutions and explorations'), and demanding that we should 'fix attention solely on the poetic quality and human interest of the plays concerned'.

During the two following decades the climate of critical opinion changed dramatically. D.G. James's outstanding essay, 'The Failure of the Ballad-Makers', appeared in 1937 (in *Scepticism and Poetry*); James quoted *Myth and Miracle*, and acknowledged a debt to Knight's work. In 1938, E.M.W. Tillyard's book, *Shakespeare's Last Plays*, arguing that Shakespeare's work had moved on from realism to symbolism, showed a somewhat ungracious awareness of what Knight had been doing. In 1947, Knight published *The Crown of Life: Essays in Interpretation of Shakespeare's Final Plays*; he reproduced *Myth and Miracle* as the book's opening essay. By this time, the sharp sense of discovery had been dulled. *The Crown of Life* is a more stolid work, concerned with detail rather than heuristics, and not helping its cause with its culminating eulogy of patriotism and protestantism in the chapter on *Henry VIII*.

Wilson Knight's work was always controversial, but it was very influential. There are some interesting and significant changes in his outlook on the last plays between *Thaisa* and *The Crown of Life*. These have not been

258

recorded. At this distance in time from Knight's innovative work, when so many revolutions in Shakespeare criticism have taken place, it is worth trying to describe and assess just what it was that Knight had to say about the romances.

In the very first sentence of *Myth and Miracle*, Knight explained that his concern was to authenticate and justify what he called 'curiosities of the supernatural descending on the purely human interest'. Shakespeare, he went on to argue, had reached the limit of what could be done in the 'direct representation' of 'a normal play' (pp. 13, 19).[4] 'Shakespeare has passed beyond interest in imitation' (p. 23). He was now employing myth to express the miraculous. People and events in the final plays are to be understood metaphorically not literally.

For Shakespeare was looking beyond the living scene, beyond the collisions and disasters of mortal life. (Knight was more expansive on immortality in *Thaisa* than in the published work.) Death is a delusion. All mortal life is only an interruption of our true immortal, spiritual life; it is a descent into the unreal. The finest spirits are conscious of this wider mode of existence, which dwarfs our mortal life. Shakespeare's belief in immortality, Knight wrote, enabled him to discern 'the true nature and purpose of the sufferings of humanity' (p. 22); the fact and the mystery of those sufferings had previously been the terminus of his dramatic explorations. Immortality was now to be expressed symbolically by victorious love; by the reunion of lovers such as Pericles and Thaisa in *Pericles* or Leontes and Hermione in *The Winter's Tale* who had been separated by what appeared to be death. The divine control which places suffering in a context of immortality was expressed metaphorically by characters such as Cerimon in *Pericles*, who brings the 'dead' Thaisa back to life; or by the sudden descent of Jupiter on the back of an eagle in *Cymbeline* to explain the workings of Providence.

It is the theophanies – metaphorical or vicarious divine appearances – on which I wish to concentrate. Knight's justification of these supernatural moments (the resurrection of Hermione in *The Winter's Tale*, for example, or the masque in *Cymbeline* and Katharine's vision in *Henry VIII*) is perhaps the best-known aspect of his work on the last plays, and also the aspect which most exposed him to adverse criticism. These theophanies were central to him, being the most positive indications that Shakespeare's gaze was now mystical and transcendent. It was greatly daring to go straight to Cerimon's revival of Thaisa, who had been buried at sea as having died in childbirth, as 'one of the pinnacles of Shakespeare's art' – in spite of the admitted coarseness of the poetic fabric of this mangled text. Superlatives were common: the entry of Jupiter in *Cymbeline* is 'a priceless possession to the interpreter of Shakespeare' (p. 19).

Knight was not outwardly disturbed that so many of these visions are somewhat questionable in their aesthetic quality. The language of *Pericles* may be a special case, but there are linguistic problems also in *Cymbeline* and *Henry VIII*. In the former, the language of the vision is so stiff and

stilted that its authenticity had been frequently questioned; the scene
of the vision in *Henry VIII* was often attributed to Fletcher. Knight went
on to the offensive. 'These scenes have had a poor deal', he wrote in
The Crown of Life (p. 195). He mentioned other scenes of supernatural
visiting which had been challenged by scholars, such as the Hecate scenes
in *Macbeth*.

> Is it possible that twentieth-century scholarship is merely attributing to Shakespeare
> its own dislike of the visionary and the supernatural? And that its stylistic
> judgements merely reflect that dislike? (p. 196).

But in spite of Knight's splendid and successful rescue of the authenticity of
the vision in *Cymbeline*, it seems clear that below the surface he was uneasy
about the aesthetic and theatrical quality of the theophanies. As I shall explain,
he later suppressed some of the misgivings which he voiced in *Thaisa*, but
even in *The Crown of Life* he can say (quite unexpectedly) of the vision in
Cymbeline: 'It is, of course, no part of my present purpose to argue that the
vision in question is a good vision or the theophany effective on the stage
... It is ... possible that Shakespeare was not himself wholly satisfied' (p. 196)
He then remarked that in *Henry VIII* 'the emphasis is, except for the soft
music, wholly on silent ... dumb-show and ritual'. This remark looks forward
to what he writes in the chapter on *Henry VIII*: 'This silent ritual is probably
Shakespeare's most satisfying projection of that visionary intuition already
found emphatic in [his] recent works' (p. 327).

There has been a good deal of mockery of this view that the ultimate
expression of the vision of England's greatest poet should be wordless, yet
it is at the heart of Knight's thinking about the last plays, and it is a perfectly
respectable position to hold, that, given the inadequacy of language, visionary
intuitions and apprehensions best express themselves in silence. Unfortunately, Knight undermined the strength of his own position because, needing
to emphasize the authenticity and importance of the spoken theophanies,
he overdid his praise of them. His eagerness to display the evidence of
the later Shakespeare's religious insight ran away with him, and repressed
his awareness of their shortcomings. As a result, there are considerable
inconsistencies in what he wrote.

In *Myth and Miracle*, discussing the two major scenes in *Pericles* of the
raising of Thaisa and the reunion of Pericles and Marina, Knight showed
great perception in picking on the resonance of words he found shimmering
in the mud.

> Did you not name a tempest,
> A birth and death?
>   (V, iii, 33–4)

But no such incandescence could be pointed to in the masque in *Cymbeline*.
Posthumus is languishing in prison, believing that Imogen has been killed
on his orders. With a stage-direction for 'solemn music' there appear 'as in
an apparition' his dead parents and brothers. The appeal to Jupiter for mercy

on the suffering Posthumus, speaking in a curiously antiquated chant. Then Jupiter appears.

> *JUPITER descends in thunder and lightning, sitting upon an eagle. He throws a thunderbolt. The Ghosts fall on their knees.*
> *Jupiter.* No more, you petty spirits of region low,
> Offend our hearing. Hush! How dare you ghosts
> Accuse the Thunderer, whose bolt, you know,
> Sky-planted, batters all rebelling coasts?
> Poor shadows of Elysium, hence, and rest
> Upon your never-withering banks of flowers.
> Be not with mortal accidents oppressed.
> No care of yours it is; you know 'tis ours.
> Whom best I love I cross; to make my gift,
> The more delayed, delighted. Be content,
> Your low-laid son our godhead will uplift;
> His comforts thrive, his trials well are spent.
> Our Jovial star reigned at his birth, and in
> Our temple was he married. Rise and fade.
> He shall be lord of Lady Imogen,
> And happier much by his affliction made.
> This tablet lay upon his breast, wherein
> Our pleasure his full fortune doth confine.
> And so away; no farther with your din
> Express impatience, lest you stir up mine.
> Mount, eagle, to my palace crystalline.   *Ascends.*
>   (V, iv, 93–113)

Of this scene, 'a vivid revelation of a kindly Providence behind mortality's drama', Knight wrote: 'It is our one precise anthropomorphic expression of that beyond-tragedy recognition felt through the miracles and resurrections of sister-plays and reaching Christian formulation in *Henry VIII*' (p. 202). He also wrote:

> We may practically equate Shakespeare's Jove with Jehovah, whilst also observing that, since representation of the supreme deity cannot be completely successful (as Milton also found), Shakespeare probably gains rather than loses in *Cymbeline* by reliance on a semi-fictional figure allowing a maximum of dignity with a minimum of risk. (p. 202)

This is a puzzling sentence. I suppose the meaning is that if you wish to represent the Christian God in literature or on the stage you are well advised to use the iconography of a different religion, making it clear to the audience that you know you are speaking in metaphors. Of course, the decision to present Jove here is not a prudential matter. The play is set in Roman Britain, so we have a Roman deity. This was the way (Shakespeare was saying) the Romans imagined their god. But Knight's phrase, 'a maximum of dignity with a minimum of risk', is a poser. This god does indeed descend from a machine. To maintain dignity while mounted on a property eagle must have been quite a task for the actor at the Globe (where Simon Forman saw the play in 1611). I would have thought that Shakespeare was allowing himself a *maximum* of risk. The formal language, the machinery, the classical legend, are all firmly in the convention of the court masque. It seems to me that Shakespeare was not creating illusion but showing illusion being created; not trying to convey a sense of the divine but exhibiting with considerable detachment a theatrical image of the divine. It is notable that in *Thaisa* Knight's praise of the divine image in *Cymbeline* was much more cautious.

Knight's extended commentary in *The Crown of Life* on the statue-scene in *The Winter's Tale* is one of his most impressive pieces of writing. It is a powerful recreation, in prose narrative and quotation, of the effect of the scene on an audience. But this narrative excludes from consideration the maximum of risk which Shakespeare took in bringing Hermione back to life on stage. For of course Hermione is not 'brought back to life'. She never died. There is a major difference here from the Cerimon/Thaisa situation in *Pericles*. In that play the chest containing Thaisa's body is washed ashore. Cerimon, who has acquired by intense study what seem like preternatural powers of healing, believes it would still be possible to 'kindle again' 'the fire of life' within her, and by his great efforts she is revived – brought back to life.

The revival of Hermione is quite different. For 16 years everyone has assumed that she died after collapsing at her trial. Leontes and Perdita visit the chapel where Paulina has been arranging the making of a statue of Hermione. But in the final scene the 'statue' turns out to be Hermione herself, who is thus reunited with her amazed and delighted husband and daughter. Though we were told in the previous scene that Paulina had visited a certain 'removed house' 'twice or thrice a day ever since the death of Hermione', no explanation of Hermione's long concealment is given; she herself simply says she 'preserved' herself in the hope of seeing again her banished daughter.

Paulina persuades Hermione to pretend to be a statue. Then, with words of magical resonance, she acts as though she is bringing a statue to life. However marvellous to the standers-by, however moving to the audience, the scene is a deception, quite unlike the resuscitation of the virtually dead Thaisa.

In this scene, Knight wrote, Paulina, who 'has functioned throughout as the Oracle's implement, becomes now its priestess' (p. 123). He spoke of 'her voice quivering with the Sibylline power she wields' as though she actually were bringing stone into life. Indeed, the nature or condition of Hermione before she steps down to greet Leontes is left uncertain in Knight's commentary. For all one can see, Knight thought that Hermione had really died, and that Shakespeare had left a real mystery about her survival or coming back to life. 'The poet,' he wrote, 'carefully refuses to elucidate the mystery on the plane of plot-realism' (p. 125). 'We are not, in fact, to search for answers on this plane at all: *the poet himself does not know them*' (pp. 125–6; my emphasis). And a footnote says that Shakespeare 'purposely drives the miraculous to a limit not touched in *Pericles*'. It is clear that Knight does not accept that the restoration of Hermione is essentially Paulina's *coup de théâtre*, with herself choosing the rôle of priestess in a drama which she herself has written in order first to punish Leontes and then when he is penitent to reward him – miming, indeed, the workings of Providence as they are expounded by Jupiter in *Cymbeline*. Knight chose to see the restoration of Hermione as a miracle.

It is here that the unpublished *Thaisa* is helpful, for it is much less vague about the plot of *The Winter's Tale*. Knight expressed his impatience with 'commentators who waste time defending or attacking Shakespeare for the absurdity of Hermione's sixteen years deception' (pp. 24–5). The story of the play counted for little or nothing. Shakespeare wanted scenes of resurrection, of the repudiation of death, of the assurance of divine watchfulness. It didn't really matter to him what the context of the miracle might be; everything was concentrated on the magic of the moment. 'The restoration of Hermione asserts at once the unreality of death and the truth of love' (p. 62). In his father's eyes, though not in the audience's eyes, Ferdinand (in *The Tempest*) is brought back from the dead. This also is a 'myth of death's unreality'. Providing such scenes in the theatre involved Shakespeare in all sorts of narrative improbabilities. But he didn't care. The probability of art was jettisoned in the process of overturning the probabilities of life itself. So, in reading the restoration of Hermione as a miracle, Knight was not misreading the events which led up to it; he was disregarding them.

It is therefore curious (to return to *The Crown of Life*), that Knight did not choose to identify the theophany in *The Tempest* as a miracle. The masque in which divine beings bless the contract of marriage between Ferdinand and Miranda he brushed aside with the words: 'the goddesses are mere etceteras, called up and puffed away at Prospero's will' (p. 196). Prospero is for Knight a metaphor both for the power of art and for the workings of God. It is very surprising that he should dismiss this demonstration of divine blessing as a contrivance. The word he uses is not contrivance but 'fabrication'. It is because he already has a metaphor for God in the play, in Prospero, that he cannot accept a lower layer of metaphor for divine protection; he finds it too patently theatrical. But its theatricality is no greater, surely, than the theatricality of the theophany in *Cymbeline* or the miracle in *The Winter's Tale* or the theatricality of Prospero himself. The theatricality of a play within a play does not stand in contradiction to the theatricality of the outer play: it corresponds with, mirrors and intensifies its theatricality. It may well be said that the ostentatious theatricality of the entry of the divine figures in a masque organized by Prospero, and terminated at his bidding, mirrors and intensifies the theatricality of all the divine shows contrived by the art of Shakespeare in his final plays.

Knight noted how the witness of the masque, Ferdinand, is entranced. 'To Ferdinand the visionary masque "makes this place Paradise" (IV, i, 124)' (p. 246). Actually, Ferdinand says that it is the maker of the masque who makes this place Paradise.

So rare a wondered father and a wise
Makes this place Paradise.

Knight then wrote a remarkable sentence about Prospero cancelling the masque as he remembers the threat of Caliban's conspiracy. 'Prospero's abrupt dismissal of the Masque makes a neat comment on the limitations of paradisal speculation in a brutal world.' The limitations of paradisal speculation! Shakespeare is seen to be rebuking Ferdinand for his gullibility. Now Knight many times uses the word 'paradisal' without the least hint of scorn. *Myth and Miracle* speaks of the 'paradisal radiance' of *Pericles*, for example. It is naturally a question why that particular 'paradisal radiance' should be free from the 'limitations of paradisal speculation' obvious to Knight in the theophany of *The Tempest*.

Knight went on to remind us of the renowned speech which follows Prospero's cancellation of the masque. 'The dismissal is ... followed ... by a repudiation not only of fantasy, but of human fabrication at its grandest (towers, palaces, temples), ... and even of "the great globe itself" and all its children, themselves but fantasies.' But Prospero, Knight continued, was not a figure of 'negation'. In his very existence 'some supreme positive is mysteriously defined'. By his 'summary dismissal of creation's marvels, some great otherness, some Nirvana of which all these are but transient symbols, is conjured into momentary possession'. This platonism suggests the language which Shelley gave to Demogorgon in *Prometheus Unbound*.

> If the abysm
> Could vomit forth its secrets ... But a voice
> Is wanting, the deep truth is imageless.

There is a recession of images, layer after layer, from Juno and Ceres who are the fantasies and fabrications of Prospero to all other fabrications and appearances on earth. But Knight makes a special case of Prospero, who is the fantasy and fabrication of Shakespeare, as an index to an unknowable reality, the great otherness which cannot be imaged.

Consistency seems to be wanting here, in diminishing the status of Prospero's masque, and in elevating the status of Prospero, while at the same time seeming to accept Shakespeare's recognition that all the fabrications of human art are equally evanescent, transient symbols only of imperceptible truth.

At this point it is necessary to note the very important contribution which Knight made to the study of the last plays in locating and analysing the ubiquitous references to art. We can concentrate on what he said about Marina in *Pericles*. He picked up the importance of what most of us had taken to be routine commendations of Marina in the quaintly archaic Gower choruses – how she was good at knitting, sewing, embroidery, music, singing, even writing.

> She sings like one immortal, and she dances
>   As goddess-like to her admired lays.
> Deep clerks she dumbs, and with her nee'le composes
>   Nature's own shape, of bud, branch, or berry,
> That even her art sisters the natural roses ...
>   (V, Chorus)

Knight linked her artistic ability – sistering nature itself – which enabled her to bring back the vitality of the aged and despairing man who proves to be her father, with the representation of Marina in the play as herself a work of art: statue, monument, palace. The two essential references which Knight gave are from Pericles' awestruck recognition of this healing saint.

> Thou seem'st a palace
> For the crowned truth to dwell in.
> (V, i, 121–2)

> Thou dost look
> Like Patience gazing on kings' graves and smiling
> Extremity out of act.
> (V, i, 137–9)

'The whole world of great tragedy,' wrote Knight, '... is subdued to an over-watching figure, like Cordelia's love by the bedside of Lear's sleep. ... Patience is here an all-enduring calm seeing *through* tragedy to the end' (p. 65). (The end being eternity.) Knight said that Marina is 'as it were, art incarnate', and again, 'all but art personified. She is that to which all art aspires, which it seeks to express' (pp. 62, 64). Perhaps this last sentence does not fully convey the power of the figure of Marina, who is both the energy of artistic creation and its product. Just as nature can be *natura naturans* and *natura naturata*, so the word art can be used both for a potency and for the effect of that potency. When Coleridge said that 'nature itself ... is the art of God' he was using each of the terms, nature and art, as both power and product.

Knight associated the repeated references to 'monumental art' with Yeats's poem 'Sailing to Byzantium', in which the old man retreats from the living scene towards 'monuments of unageing intellect'. Yeats is indeed the poet for testifying to the power of the poet to create images which direct the dreams of humanity towards their proper fulfilment. In 'The Statues', Grecian boys and girls 'pressed at midnight in some public place / Live lips upon a plummet-measured face.' Marina is the product of Shakespeare's art, and she is one of his creations who also simulates his own creativity. She functions as a Miranda and a Prospero. It is as a skilled artist that she can restore Pericles to full life, and, as his recovered daughter she is the fulfilment of his dreams.

Shakespeare's preoccupation in his last plays with the fabrications of art and with the healing power of these fabrications relates directly to the nature and meaning of the theophanies which Knight so extensively explored. In my view every one of them is offered in the terms Knight used for the masque in *The Tempest*, as a manifest fabrication denoting 'the limitations of paradisal speculation', recognizing at the same time humanity's need for metaphysical reassurance, the power of art to provide such assurance, and also the extreme improbability that the images of art can actually penetrate the darkness that surrounds us. 'Mirror on mirror mirrored is all the show.'

The most masterful of images may turn out to be a circus-animal – like the bear in *The Winter's Tale*.

It is difficult to believe that the theophanies of the last plays represent Shakespeare's personal enlightenment about ultimate meaning. They creak too much, and seem to wish to be heard creaking. I pointed out earlier that it is possible in *The Crown of Life* to discern that for all his advocacy Wilson Knight had his misgivings about the way the miracles were presented. His dissatisfaction with their aesthetic quality is much more pronounced in the early *Thaisa*. 'What symbols would not be crude?' he asked (p. 31). 'I do not think that he [Shakespeare] was satisfied with the final plays' (p. 32). 'I think [corrected to 'perhaps'] the freshness of his Perdita joyed him more than the mystic truth of Hermione's resurrection. But he did not relax the quest.' In *Cymbeline* the theophany may have 'added clarity to religious meaning', but 'it lacks artistic life' (p. 33). 'Religion is killing his art' (p. 34). Although *The Tempest* was a triumph, it was only a pause on a necessary progression towards silence. Knight argued that music was a more powerful vehicle of mystical vision than words and images. The importance of music in connection with theophany in the last plays shows Shakespeare's awareness of this. He was moving 'beyond expression'. After *The Tempest*, Knight argued, Shakespeare had no need of the theatre. The deep truth is imageless.

It will be clear that as time went on the need to insist on the importance of the theophanies led Knight to a certain amount of soft-pedalling on their awkwardness. Indeed, in discussing *The Winter's Tale* in *The Crown of Life* he wrests the theophany from its context and treats it as unalloyed miracle, an intimation of immortality. But at the same time, at the risk of some self-contradiction, he was pursuing the basic argument, made plain in *Thaisa*, that there is hostility between theatre and truth. 'Religion is killing his art' – and theatrical art is misrepresenting his religious discoveries. The inadequacy of his attempts to represent transcendent vision in the language of the theatre enforces a progression towards silence.

Knight's later tendency to overpraise the aesthetic quality of the theophanies was unfortunate. It lowers the quality of Shakespeare's artistic values and of his religious thinking. His own earlier uncertainties map out an extended effort by Shakespeare, ending in failure, to provide theatrical symbols for mystical vision. (This is similar to the theme of D.G. James's essay mentioned earlier.) The sense of failure moved Shakespeare first towards music and then into silence. This view is much more coherent than the rather confused picture presented in *The Crown of Life*, and it makes more sense to those of us who find the initimations of immortality in the last plays unconvincing. To me, the uneasiness of the theophanies suggests an insistence by Shakespeare that all metaphysical reassurance is a human construct. But to disagree with Wilson Knight is not to derogate his work; one can learn a great deal from him without accepting his conclusions or even at times the validity of his arguments.

NOTES

1. An earlier version of this essay was given as a paper at a conference at Leeds University in memory of Wilson Knight in April 1986.
2. *Jackson Knight: A Biography* (Oxford: Alden Press, 1975), pp. 119–20.
3. There is also a signed copy of the poem *Marina*, which Eliot sent to Knight two years later!
4. Page references are to the reprinted *Myth and Miracle* in *The Crown of Life*.

CHAPTER TWENTY-THREE

Contemporary Versions of *King Lear*

Claus Uhlig

Such indeed is Shakespeare's canonical authority that any theory of literature or culture which cannot illuminate at least aspects of his works is doomed to failure from the start. Hence all those recent attempts to invade or even appropriate Shakespearean texts that the community of Renaissance scholars and critics has witnessed over roughly the past two decades. Thus the poet's works have become a strongly contested site, no longer habitable for critics who still ground their thought in idealist and liberal humanist assumptions or operate with notions such as an art-work's 'organic unity' or an interpretation's 'objective correctness'. He or she who wants to enter the Shakespearean universe today must radically break with traditional notions of author, text-context dialectic and audience, trying instead to conceive of their mutual relations or their respective interactions with culture and society at large in new ways, while further taking into account the altered, that is, diminished role of language in the process of creating meaning.

Yet does it really help to complain (Vickers, 1993)? In other words, has the literary or even political and ideological appropriation of Shakespeare not always been a cultural phenomenon throughout history (Marsden, 1991)? Consequently, the study of the past, be it a literary period with its ideas and conventions, an individual writer within the context of the genres he used, or only – as for the moment, and that for obvious reasons in a *Festschrift* devoted to the author of *'King Lear' and the Gods* (1966) – a single play and its contemporary reception, should be seen as liable to the shifting sands of scholarly and critical fashions. This one must try to come to terms with. From a broad historicist angle of vision (and who would not like to transcend his or her ideological position to reach such a vantage point?), the invasion of recent theory (in the widest sense) into the territory of Shakespeare studies, then, is to be accepted as a datum of history itself. Whether ephemeral or full of potential for the future (Grady, 1991), all post-isms of today combine to accelerate the already fast process of change, to sharpen our own awareness of history, and to provide us with a multiple, if ever-shifting, hermeneutics. The meanings a community of interpreters generate thus inevitably emerge as both culturally and historically conditioned, sometimes to the detriment of the past, sometimes highlighting features overlooked heretofore.

To a smaller or larger extent, all scholars and critics working in the Renaissance have become conscious of the fact that the task of interpretation itself is intertextually and interculturally constituted, to be understood as an act whereby the creative discourses of the past and the scholarly discourses of the present tend to interact, even to become fused. If the questions we ask of texts are different from what they were a generation ago, then the answers we get are different, too. Quite predictably, we now often find disorder and uncertainty where about half a century ago scholars found order; and we look for debate, subversion, and ideological contradiction (Sinfield, 1992) instead of harmony and agreement. More precisely, recent critical currents, while refusing to differentiate between formerly autonomous texts and their respective social and cultural 'backgrounds', seek to oust unifying and collective notions of so-called dominant Renaissance beliefs and practices by insisting on the fragmentary, heterogeneous, and marginal in their impatience with monolithical concepts of history that belie the plurality of historical discourses and the conditioning of texts by contexts. And fully imbued with its own political experience in regard to official ideologies and established institutions, contemporary scholarship cannot but view the literary text as one mode of expression among others in the whole sphere of social action and representation both past and present.

Bearing all this in mind, I propose to review four major recent trends in Shakespeare criticism, i.e. deconstruction, psychoanalysis, new historicism together with cultural materialism, and feminism – in an attempt to assess their respective contribution to our understanding of just one play, namely, *King Lear*.

＊   ＊   ＊

Let us start with perhaps the most prominent project in today's efforts to undermine traditional critical securities, deconstruction. Mainly inspired by Derrida, deconstruction, the post-structuralist approach to philosophy and literature, in its radical linguistic scepticism has come to question all the hidden assumptions, which even up to structuralism assured the permanence and coherence of western culture, by denying the one-to-one relation between signifier and signified that was still inherent also in semiotics, for example. For deconstruction the difference of signifier and signified is abolished, with each signifier relating to several signifieds which in turn become signifiers themselves pointing to, and being defined by, yet other signifieds as signifiers. Owing to this obvious circularity, deconstruction spreads out instability and negates the very possibility of definite meaning that is assumed to be never fully present but always absent, dispersed in a chain of signifiers. From a temporal perspective, all utterances become meaningful only, if at all, by referring to signs preceding them, which is tantamount to saying that, at a given time and in a specific context, every sign always implies traces of other signs. Taking the world of human experience to be structured like a language, deconstruction thereby likewise insinuates that neither autonomous individuals nor self-evident truths – the transcendental signifier that guarantees meaning – actually exist (Eagleton, 1983; Felperin, 1985; Atkins and Bergeron, 1988).

To be sure, deconstruction itself stresses its subversive qualities, seeing that its critical procedures can be used to destroy notions such as textual autonomy, the mimetic nature of texts, authorial self and intention, or for that matter, textual coherence. Even belief in something like history seems impossible now, not to mention the categorical dissolution of generic boundaries and the very concept of literature itself (Norris, 1985, p. 47). But since it would be pointless to continue with this privative description of the critical movement in question, it should be noted that of late deconstructionist criticism has tended to reintroduce notions of referentiality and stability into the process of the production of meaning. Relying on passages in Derrida's work that admit a certain determinative influence of author and historical context on the meaning of signs, the critical mode under discussion has up to a point rehabilitated authorial intention and contextualism in literary studies once again. As a consequence, deconstructionists have even come round to argue in favour of linking deconstructionist and new historicist methods (Waller, 1988). Parallel to this, Christopher Norris has shown the difference between 'pure' deconstruction and its tempered version as resulting from different interpretations of Derrida's statement that there is 'no outside to the text' (Derrida, 1976, p. 158). This can either be understood as denying the existence of any reality beyond the text – in consequence leading to extreme formalism and textual solipsism – or as asserting the mere linguistic nature of our experience of the world, a view amounting to a reintroduction of relativistic notions of referentiality.

Often too theoretically self-conscious for its own good (Atkins and Bergeron, 1988; Cohen, 1987), deconstructionist criticism not surprisingly comes up with analytical results that are predetermined by its very assumptions – yet one more instance of hermeneutic circularity. Still, if a critic of that persuasion succeeds in proving the existence of deconstructionist ideas in Renaissance literary theory itself, he might well feel legitimized to employ the said method in the analysis of Renaissance texts at large, further encouraged by the built-in deconstructive nature of theatre and the very act of performance achieving, as it seems, meaning through dispersal (Waller, 1988). In a similar vein, readings of Shakespeare's plays are inclined to parallel his puns and paradoxes with Derridean wordplay in general, attempting to demonstrate Shakespeare's fundamentally deconstructionist views on the issues of language and meaning (Parker and Hartman, 1985).

A case in point with special reference to *King Lear* would be Jackson I. Cope's contribution to *Shakespeare and Deconstruction*, edited by G. Douglas Atkins and David M. Bergeron (1988), an essay undertaking to interpret the play in the light of Derrida's conception of language. Cope especially emphasizes the importance of marginality and non-reality for the construction of meaning in *King Lear*. The play's architecture for him is further undermined by its flouting of Christian and tragical expectations that are nevertheless implied in its text(s). The play centres on hopes for redemption that turn out to be 'nothing', probably the blank, in the Lacanian sense, of the transcendental signifier. Derrida's notion of the necessary absence of the self in expression is exemplified by the exile that results from Cordelia's attempt to speak plainly or to say 'nothing' (I, i, 86–9). Similarly, Lear, the outcast on the heath, is reduced to essential nothingness. Thus the play is enacted on the margins: all central characters – Lear, Gloucester, Kent, Cordelia and Edgar – are exiles. The centrality of marginality in *King Lear* is brought into relief particularly through the figure of the fool, who in his madness and irrationality points to the unnaturalness of man's nature and society. Man is always blinded in his inability to see his real self because he is entrapped in language, i.e. at the same time, in society. Having, along the lines indicated, suggested a more or less speculative rapprochement between Derrida's metaphoric talk about language and the more furious poetry against the paradox of language in *Lear* (p.275), Cope then goes on to parallel Foucault's and Derrida's metaphors about light and dark, day and night, sight and blindness with passages in *King Lear* – to the effect that he finally sees all characters, in the wake of the fool, as giving up light for darkness and sight for the insight that there is no escape from 'nothing' and 'never'. Thus, and to his own satisfaction, he has 'argued some language of Derrida, of Foucault, of modernism into restive coexistence with the language of *Lear*' (p. 279).

Through an analogously eclectic manner, Jonathan Goldberg, in his essay 'Perspectives: Dover Cliff and the Conditions of Representation' (1984, 1988), couples Derrida with another influential French thinker, this time Lacan, adding references to the history of seeing and the representation of reality in the arts as well as in the theatre. He starts with identifying 'Dover' as the place of Lacanian desire, a place that promises relief and deliverance, where Lear will meet Cordelia again, where Gloucester will find peace, where everything will become good in the end – only to reveal Dover cliff as an illusion. It stands for the impossibility of the signifier ever to reach the signified, thus simultaneously also pointing up the limits of representation, with Edgar's realistic description paradoxically underlining the inability of stage and language to actualize what is represented in his speech (IV, vi, 11–24). Whether one can follow Goldberg in regarding Dover cliff as standing for hope and desire as well as for the problem of theatrical representation in general might be a moot point; his historical linking, however, of the cliff's description with principles of Renaissance painting as delineated, for example, in Alberti's *Della pittura* is most interesting, resulting as it does in the affirmation: 'Vision depends upon both blindness and invisibility; it rests upon a vanishing point' (*Shakespeare and Deconstruction*, p. 252). According to Goldberg, in Edgar's description two modes of seeing, two perspectives exist. The first is the optical illusion of anamorphosis that does not centre on a vanishing point but requires the viewer to take different points of view; it is related to the theatrical illusion as multiplicity. The second is the perspective of illusionistic painting, theatrical reality and representation. In Shakespeare's time the latter version was evolving and beginning to supersede the first, enabling Goldberg to spell out the consequences of this process for *King Lear* and its audience, and that again in an illuminating way, whereas I find his dragging in of Lacan and Derrida with regard to the problem of representation itself too far-fetched to be convincing, especially since neither the *Lear* text(s) nor the other Shakespearean plays invoked for support bear out his concluding and more playful points.

To give a third and final example of deconstructionist readings of *King Lear*, Michael McCanles on his part also relies on the authority of two French master-minds, i.e. Foucault and Lacan. In 'Shakespeare, Intertextuality, and the Decentered Self' (1988), he adopts their view that there exists no such thing as a centred self that would not depend on the simultaneous existence of a decentred self. Accordingly, he reminds us that in Shakespeare characters often define themselves by adopting the speech of other characters from outside the play, a speech that is recognizably not their own; and this technique stresses the fact that there is no centred self without decentring identification with outside discourses. Applied especially to *Lear*, this assertion permits him to understand the play first and foremost as the old king's search for an authentic identity that is assumed to have been lost but actually never existed (I, iv, 238). Finally, despite all efforts, what is staged is the dissolution of the king's identity, so that McCanles feels entitled to see Lear's shattered and fragmented personal identity, from the opening scene onwards, not so much as a consequence of his madness as rather a result of his inability to combine his contradictory longings for love and justice in one coherent discourse. Thus it cannot be decided whether the play has an 'optimistic' or a 'pessimistic' ending – a problem that once confronted Professor Elton, as will be remembered even today – since we do not know 'which Lear we see die over Cordelia's dead body' (*Shakespeare and Deconstruction*, p. 207). Needless to say that this very undecidability, be it related to Lear himself or to the play as a whole, prepares the way for the essay's inconclusive conclusion, a result by nature so dear to true deconstructionists.

* * *

Not unlike deconstruction, psychoanalytical criticism, especially as practised by Lacan and his followers, has by now developed its own self-vindicating strategies. In rewriting Freudian psychoanalysis, Lacan's theories are clearly indebted to the post-structuralist theorem of the principal impossibility of ever realizing complete presence, coherence, or autonomy of meaning. This basically linguistic assumption structures his account of the nature of human identity and psyche. Accordingly, for Lacan a human being's sense of self, and that from early childhood on, is formed not autonomously but by a process of identification with other objects in the world. One main consequence of this is that the human self can never be quite itself for want of complete unity with its objects of identification. Therefore a centring of the self is possible only by decentring it. Our sense of a unitary self is just a fiction, although a necessary one, without which we would not be able to survive. Through the father's entry into its life and the parallel discovery of sexuality, every child has to learn that identity depends on difference and absence. At the same time language is discovered, which is likewise grounded in the principles of difference and absence. But contrary to pure deconstructionist thought, language for Lacan has a symbolic function: it stands in for the object that is not present. In this symbolic state, a child begins to accept that its desire for complete unity with its mother can never be fulfilled in reality. All that is available is merely symbolic substitution in a world of language where meaning can never be fixed and is always dispersed. To a greater extent than in Freudian psychoanalysis, the autonomy and coherence of the self are thus undermined in Lacan's radically linguistic understanding of the human psyche. In the end, human identity for him is formed through a social process and can be defined only with and against an 'other' (Eagleton, 1983; McCanles, 1988).

These and similar ideas have now begun to take hold of American psychoanalytical criticism, as it is – especially in the present context – represented for us in the collective volume *Representing Shakespeare*, edited by Murry M. Schwartz and Coppélia Kahn (1980). Here, we again witness a rejection of older humanist notions of autonomous, self-sufficient human individuals, capable of coherent self-expression in rational discourse, and that predictably in favour of a foregrounding of the socialized nature of even the innermost recesses of an individual's soul. Convinced that in representing the 'other' we also represent ourselves, the editors of the said volume, in contrast to traditional psychoanalytical criticism, argue that any reading of a Shakespearean play must be seen not as a discovery of meaning but rather as its construction on the part of the critic, who cannot abstract his or her interpretation from the present moment of writing. What is more, for the editors and contributors to *Representing Shakespeare*, the poet's texts and language reenact central aspects of the process of individualization, seeing that the latter could be defined in terms of representation and its dramatic quality (pp. xii–xiv).

Thus C.L. Barber for one, writing on 'The Family in Shakespeare's Development' (pp. 188–202), views the poet as very much concerned with, if not obsessed by, questions of opposites, identity, family, authority and destruction, although, compared to the younger contributors to the volume, his style is sober and his psychological stance rather traditional. According to him, Shakespeare's great tragedies essentially dramatize the loss of the 'sacred-in-the-human' (p. 188), and this conviction subsequently informs his reading of *King Lear*, seeing that the universe of the play confronts us with a world where religious feeling and need are directed towards the human family and its extensions in society. That way human relationships, with Lear and Cordelia in the end assuming an almost iconic character, stand in, so to speak, for Professor Elton's *deus absconditus* (pp. 199–201). Yet, needless to add, since Lear and Cordelia remain finite persons in a finite world, they cannot but exemplify the tragic failure of any attempt to gain sacred status for human beings.

Apart from taking Shakespeare's tragedies to present versions of the Oedipus complex tragically unresolved (p. 196), the essay discussed is not so much psychoanalytical as sociological and historical in orientation. This, however, is soon to change in Richard P. Wheeler's more provocative article, likewise to be found in *Representing Shakespeare*. Wheeler locates *King Lear* in the Shakespearean canon of tragedies by relating the play to two central ways of gaining self-fulfilment and self-identity in moments of extreme crisis. On the one hand, there is fulfilment in trust; on the other, fulfilment in autonomy. Grounding his argument in Mahler's theory of the establishment of identity and trust during the early process of mother–child separation, he goes on to group *Lear*, together with *Hamlet*, *Othello* and *Antony and Cleopatra*, among the trust-type tragedies, because in all these plays the longing for mutuality is stronger than the wish for autonomy and power. Now, owing to this systematic alignment of *Lear* with tragedies of similar thematics in Wheeler's sense, his interpretation unfolds more or less automatically, pointing up the fear of losing autonomy through merging with the other that inhabits the plays of the trust/merger type – plays that as a rule end tragically in mutual destruction.

More than just a case study in applied psychoanalysis with reference to Shakespearean texts, David Willbern, also writing in *Representing Shakespeare*, but this time fashionably dependent on Derrida and Lacan, most daringly speculates on 'Shakespeare's Nothing' (pp. 244–63), yet again his results are all too predictable for those readers who are themselves conversant with contemporary Paris thought. It therefore comes as no surprise to learn that there is both a positive and a negative side to 'nothing' in *King Lear*, the one comprising denial, absence, lack and negation, the other referring to the ground of being and those moments of silence without which speech would be impossible. And thanks to this ultimately deconstructionist dialectic, Willbern, after a series of semantic disquisitions, is able to drive home the argument that in *King Lear* the audience, the poet, and the theatrical production combine to give meaning to 'nothing'.

*   *   *

To those scholars and critics impatient with deconstructionist wordplay or psychoanalytical ingenuity, American new historicism or, alternatively, British cultural materialism might, at least at first sight, have seemed a more rewarding approach to Renaissance literature in general and to Shakespeare's texts in particular. Trying still to maintain a more or less stable relationship between referent and sign, signifier and signified, new historicists and cultural materialists, in their uncompromising contextualization of literary texts, strongly rely on a marxist notion of ideology, albeit extended and redefined. Accordingly, ideology is understood not as a form of political propaganda but as the dominant discourse in a society that consists of a set of practices, ideas, ways of conduct and interpreting the world, pervading everyday life and being perpetuated by institutions such as education, family, religion, culture and law (Dollimore and Sinfield, 1985; Howard and O'Connor, 1987). The main functions of ideology, in this view, are to legitimate the existing order and to give out particular interests, for instance those of the ruling class, as universal ones. Ideology thus creates the illusion of a society as unity, static and unchangeable, but of necessity comprising contradictions and conflicts. Moreover, to reach its aims the ideological apparatus must suppress all kinds of subordinate and marginal discourses that often are oppositional, threatening to undermine the asserted unity and stability of society. While applying several techniques in this process, one of the most sophisticated moves designed, on the part of ideology, to neutralize the danger coming from adversary positions lies in the method of containment that tries to integrate oppositional discourses into the dominant one and thus forces them to support the existing order.

Now, with regard to literature, neither new historicists nor cultural materialists are willing to grant it autonomous status. Instead, they see it deeply implicated in the process described and are eagerly bent on analysing the interplay of dominant ideology and marginal discourses in literary texts or cultural institutions such as the theatre – often in terms of subject, gender, and class (Cohen, 1987; Wayne, 1987). Consequently, literature is seen as a site of ideological struggle, which holds especially true with regard to its most prominent institution, the theatre – for most scholars and critics narrowed down, of course, to the theatre of Shakespeare and his time (Greenblatt, 1988; Weimann, 1988). In method, however, the two critical currents under review appear to be richer, seeing that, in addition to marxism, they as a rule tend to buttress their expositions with post-structural thought. This is above all conspicuous in the rejection of individual autonomy, authorial intention, and the possibility of universal meaning (if ever there was such a thing). What is more, both trends also like to emphasize the role of the marginal or the 'other' in their readings of literary works, because for them cultural meaning is primarily constructed through the interaction between dominant and suppressed discourses in a given society. Seeing literature, as they do, entwined with social processes of a larger order, both cultural materialism and new historicism ultimately do not even shirk from dissolving the boundaries of the literary text itself, depriving it of its former privileged status by merging it with its historical contexts.

Notwithstanding protests from an older school of marxism still holding on to the referential and symbolic nature of theatrical language in general and its particular ability to appropriate the real in society and history

(Weimann, 1988), British cultural materialists and American new historicists meanwhile have refined their approach to the Renaissance and Shakespeare, although they differ from each other in important respects, and that especially with regard to the problem of containment. British materialists favour a type of criticism that is politically engaged and outspoken about its support of leftist politics, preferably with a revolutionary intent. Therefore they aim at destroying the dominant conservative view of Shakespeare in Britain by stressing the subversive potential of his plays and demonstrating the ideological nature of the received picture of the poet (Dollimore and Sinfield, 1985). Contrary to this position, American new historicists tend to be politically evasive, if not conservative at heart. With respect to Shakespeare's plays, this is tantamount to an emphasis on the neutralizing power of strategies of containment, owing to which the poet's plays can be read as supporting the dominant ideology. Thus Greenblatt, for example, while taking into account the possibility of subversion in the theatre despite containment, is on the whole more inclined to underline the apolitical, aesthetic nature of the theatre as a cultural institution during the age of Elizabeth I. According to him, only theatre's essentially 'nonuseful' and 'unpractical' character offered the possibility of almost unlimited representation on the stage (*Negotiations*, pp. 18f.) – a point of view almost amounting to a re-aestheticization of literature, although from a historical perspective.

Still, while one may therefore well ask what is so 'new' about new historicism (Veeser, 1989; Thomas, 1991), its difference from cultural materialism as discussed just now is not so significant as not to warrant the stressing of important affinities between the two critical currents. They seem to centre first and foremost around the concept of history itself, now no longer conceived as unifying or monolithic but rather as contradictory or precarious, blatantly comprising the most divergent forms of discourse at any given time and especially not excluding marginal or dissident voices. In other words, not any longer, as in the good old days of Tillyard for instance, regarded as the sphere of ideas, history has of late become the battleground of ideologies in conflict and struggles for power. Moreover, the act of criticism itself is these days, and rightly so, presented as always ideologically committed, serving to further present interests in the construction of past meanings. Hence both critical trends under review, interested as they are in Shakespeare as a contemporary cultural institution of conservatism and very emblem of the literary, are much concerned with both the historical and ideological nature of the hermeneutic activity of producing meaning – an activity closely to be watched through studying not only the history of theatrical production but also the ways of assimilating literature in such institutions as film, TV and education. What thus emerges to the dismay of cultural materialists in particular, is the perpetuation of a conservative picture of Shakespeare as both genius of all mankind and great national poet of Britain, a picture that is concurrently gratifying the institution involved in the promoting and the author Shakespeare, whose status thereby becomes even more sacrosanct (Dollimore and Sinfield, 1985; Cohen, 1987; Wayne, 1987).

Being time now for some exemplification, pride of place should to all intents and purposes be given to Stephen Greenblatt for his having been associated with new historicism for quite a while now. Notably his much-quoted contribution to the study of *King Lear*, 'Shakespeare and the Exorcists' (1984), reprinted in his *Shakespearean Negotiations* (1988), shows that school's methods of interpretation at work to perfection. Taking for granted the social nature of aesthetic energy, Greenblatt, via *King Lear*, explores the paths and bypaths on which social energy, seen as circulating dialectically between margin and centre, context and text, and amenable to study through a society's ceremonies, metaphors, everyday practices, clothing, stories and so on, is transformed into aesthetic energy in a process of exchange, appropriation and acquisition, implicating the theatre as well as other culturally defined zones and institutions. He pursues his argument by once again linking *King Lear* with Harsnett's *A Declaration of Egregious Popish Impostures*, but contrary to previous source studies, he now sheds new light on an established mutual relationship by stressing the cultural fact that the two texts in question are part of the sixteenth- and seventeenth-century's struggle for a redefinition of religious and social values, especially the attempt to reorient the concept of the 'sacred'. When all is said and done, however, one's previous impression of the play as a whole is not radically altered by Greenblatt's interpretation, although the institutional exchange he posits as taking place between *A Declaration* and *King Lear* must be granted. That way the church can be seen as allowing the theatre to use powerful religious practices, while the theatre in turn appears as underwriting the church's condemnation of these practices as fakes. Yet in the end, *King Lear*, owing to the scepticism pervading the text in more than one place, tends to undermine the official position. For in Harsnett, neohistorically manipulated into being devoid of transcendence, its supposed lack means a liberation from lies, whereas Shakespeare depicts a world lacking the supernatural as totally without hope and full of despair instead, not even managing to suppress the demonic principle for good.

Seeing that even with Greenblatt we are thus more or less back at C.L. Barber's 'post-Christian' play or, for that matter, W.R. Elton's 'pessimistic' version, one comes to realize that the so-called 'new' is more often than not the thinly disguised 'old'. In the case of the interpretation of *Lear* by David Aers and Gunther Kress, contributed to their collective volume *Literature, Language and Society in England 1580–1680* (1981), the novelty of approach along the lines under discussion consists in relying on a rather traditional model of marxist criticism, although seemingly set through with the Althusserian notion of ideology's effect on the unconscious. They further amplify their exposition with Marcuse's statement that great lierature always works toward undermining the existing order, drawing its strength from an internal conflict between affirmation and negation of that order – a

conflict, moreover, that is acted out on the linguistic level, since ideology
is reified in language and thereby submerged below the level of consciousness.
Small wonder, then, that the *Lear* emerging from premises like these is one
full of indecisiveness, a quality inherent from the beginning and lasting to
the end of the play, ultimately resulting, as it appears to Aers and Kress,
from Shakespeare's inability to imagine a working alternative for either the
destructive new bourgeois ideology or the corrupt old system (pp. 98f.).

From the point of view of ideology so fascinating for the school of criticism
to occupy us with just one more illustration, James H. Kavanagh, writing
for *Alternative Shakespeares*, edited by John Drakakis (1985), also tackles
King Lear. Following in his turn Macherey's and Balibar's concept of
interaction between language, literature, and ideology in an Althusserian
sense, he reads the tragedy as an attempt to reconcile the competing ideologies
to be found in the poet's times by means of a work of art. More precisely,
in *Lear* we are told to witness the crisis of a patriarchal and individualist
order, as opposed by hierarchical and feudal loyalties. Both ideologies are
then presented as confronting each other, constituting two views of the world,
two different conceptions of 'nature' that are mutually exclusive (p. 157).
That way they at the same time work to the detriment of any effect of
reconciliation the play might otherwise be taken to have produced for its
original audience. Much of this, it should be remembered, was heard more
than 30 years ago (Danby, 1948), but in contrast to the urbane language of
criticism prevalent then, these 'new' insights are now phrased with a
presentistic sense of urgency, giving modern audiences the feeling of being
intimately involved in the process of creating meaning, and that, of course,
from their own ideological climate of opinion.

Still, all this is relatively mild if compared to Jonathan Dollimore's *Radical
Tragedy* (1984) which pushes cultural materialism to its extreme when, in
his version of *King Lear*, he strips the text of all kinds of humanist, Christian,
even existentialist concepts. According to this reductionistic reading, *Lear*
is, 'above all, a play about power, property, and inheritance' (p. 197).
Particularly the family relationships in the play are seen as exclusively
determined by material concerns. Furthermore, Lear's conversion to humanism is questioned as no justice results from this, and the king's despair on
the heath, far from leading to self-examination, only betokens his separation
from all sources of self-justification, whether stoical, Christian, or humanist
in kind. Finally – and predictably – the play's ending is regarded as completely pessimistic since it refuses to view man as a tragic figure that finds
fulfilment in death.

* * *

The sort of reductionism instanced from Dollimore's indeed 'radical'
contribution to Shakespeare studies and all too familiar from innumerable
other marxist interpretations of literature can now also be shown at work

in feminist criticism, the last of the four recent critical currents under scrutiny in the present article. For, while methodically drawing from sources that in their spectrum reach from liberal humanist positions to deconstructionist practices, its thematic focus always is the issue of gender. Examining most of the time the ways women are presented in literary texts and female identities are constructed through literature, feminist critics are as attentive to ideologies as their historicist or materialist counterparts; and not least owing to this awareness, the overall impact of feminist criticism on literary studies has been to undermine the male-centred viewpoints of traditional criticism, thereby subverting the ideology of male superiority and dominance (Thompson, 1988; Callaghan, 1989). In addition to that, it should be clear that feminist criticism, far from just being one more theory among others, is rooted in a definite political movement that started back in the 1960s and 1970s, and began to invade Shakespeare studies during the early 1980s (Cohen, 1987; Grady, 1991).

To characterize it further with regard to the dramatist, feminist criticism, despite its one-dimensional orientation, has by now generated quite a variety of, sometimes mutually antagonistic, approaches to Shakespeare's work. On the face of it, two groups of feminist critics could be distinguished. There are, on the one hand, those who stress the misogyny of the poet's work either as the product of a misogynist author or as the result of Elizabethan misogyny at large, and, on the other hand, feminist critics of a more apologist temperament who are inclined to regard Shakespeare as a kind of proto-feminist, far ahead of his times in his presentation of women. And to this latter group the poet's apparent misogyny had been mainly constructed by male misogynist criticism and production of his plays. Methodically speaking, further differentiations seem indicated within feminist Shakespeare criticism, i.e. three main categories can be singled out: a liberal humanist view, a psychoanalytic approach (at home mainly in the United States), and a materialist version (especially strong in Britain) (Cohen, 1987). As appears appropriate, they are all three of them governed by their respective pre-dilections, a circumstance holding little surprise for those scholars familiar with both postmodern theory and the Shakespeare canon. Other studies, more adventurous in intent, discuss the subversive potential of female discourse or, again, the questioning of gender identity in the theatre, as occasioned especially through cross-dressing (Dollimore, 1990). Yet, whatever the thrust of their argument, it should in all fairness be admitted that none of the feminist contributions I have read naïvely assumed a simple mimetic relationship between literary text and socio-cultural context. Instead, and in keeping with today's advanced hermeneutical awareness, each reading offered was conscious of the fact that any meaning we wish to give to a text of the past is always a reconstruction of meaning and as such inevitably informed by present ideological needs and constraints.

In this respect, Kathleen McLuskie's *Lear* essay 'The Patriarchal Bard' (1985) in particular is very much to the point. She begins with remarks on the play's connection of female insubordination and general chaos, threatening the male order of human nature. In contrast to its sources, she goes on, *King Lear* presents female evil, as exemplified above all in Goneril and Regan, purely in terms of gender, sexuality and family relations. Only resort to the patriarchal principle could control female anarchy and lust and thus restore the universal order of family and state. But obviously the results of such a feminist analysis of ideological structures and gender relations in *Lear* are at loggerheads with the emotional responses the play elicits from the audience which is manipulated into identification with Lear and the patriarchal ideology he stands for. Now, since all this is a nuisance to a feminist critic, it has to be changed. Yet as the only possibility to subvert the misogynist impact of *King Lear*, McLuskie proposes a different staging of the play. Its emotional effect could be undermined, she believes, by emphasizing its historical otherness, conspicuous as it is, for example, in its gerontocratic orientation and its representation of family relations as dominated by material interests. By historicizing her argument in this manner she hopes to undercut the play's ideology, finally allotting to feminist criticism the task of giving perspectives beyond the mere abolition of patriarchy. And in view of the fact that one can conceive of other forms of social organization and affective relationships that do not necessarily lead to chaos, it might yet pay to try to resist or subvert the 'patriarchal bard'.

Patriarchy, again, is also the butt of Coppélia Kahn's psychoanalytically informed criticism of the play when writing on 'The Absent Mother in *King Lear*' (1986). Searching for the maternal subtext of the tragedy and the hidden mother in the king's psyche, she takes, for a start, exception to a patriarchal model of the family in which children come to be seen solely as products of the father. Lear's conception of patriarchy, although in accordance with the situation obtaining in the English Renaissance, nevertheless tragically fails when he wants to put it into practice. In the resulting crisis, he falls into a state of 'hysteria', in which Kahn sees a resurgence of Lear's suppressed identification with his mother. Extending her argument further, she characterizes *King Lear* as not only a family drama but also a tragedy of the male predicament in general. Here, Chodorow's account of early human development is resorted to for support, especially in regard to its bearing on the formation of personal identity. During this process a daughter's female identity comes naturally to her by identifying with her mother as woman, whereas a son has painfully to break away from the infantile union with his mother, gaining his male identity through a final rejection of femininity. This psychoanalytical model of explanation is then superimposed on the play, i.e. related to Lear's traumatic experience of separation from a maternal presence in the guise of his three daughters. And the fact that these gender conflicts in *King Lear* are connected with, and intensified by, generational conflicts adds to the poignancy of a play at the end of which the old king has come to realize that daughters are not mothers.

Admittedly, then, this psychoanalytical reading of *King Lear* focusing as it does on the 'absent mother' – one cannot help being reminded of Lady Macbeth's missing children as commented upon more than half a century ago by L.C. Knights (1933) – carries conviction up to a point, but not further, for ultimately it seems too much immersed in contemporary concerns, if not obsessions, to answer to the ideal of disciplined, non-speculative scholarship. Confronted with Kahn's as well as with McLuskie's essays and pondering their implications for *King Lear*, one almost is tempted to say that we might well need another play.

❊   ❊   ❊

This last, not quite serious remark of mine is tantamount to admitting that the recent trends in Shakespeare criticism surveyed, if ever so briefly and selectively, in the present article have definitely made a difference to our whole conception of the poet and his times. In other words, many Shakespearians brought up with the ideal of scholarship alluded to must, to their nostalgic regret, feel jolted out of comfort and complacent agreement with previously accepted but now rejected 'Elizabethan world pictures' or 'Elizabethan compromises'. In a world which is becoming ever more competitive, even more radical readings of Shakespeare's texts are bound to appear on the scene, forcing the minority hitherto in institutional command or academic authority to listen to the voices of the marginalized and repressed majority that has been excluded from 'culture' for so long. While thus a further politicization of Shakespeare studies is to be anticipated, there is certainly nothing to fear with regard to the poet's international status: the icon will stay in the canon. Only the ways we worship Shakespeare will change. The 'new' critical currents reviewed in the preceding pages have already borne witness to this. Unfortunately, most of the time they had to be characterized in privative terms ('undermine', 'destroy', 'negate', 'abolish', and so on), pointing to losses we can now only recoup through great intellectual effort if we wish to repossess 'our own' Shakespeare again. For exacting they are indeed, these more often than not free-wheeling 'scholastic' inquiries, written in the spirit of interdisciplinarity and 'mutual illumination' not of the arts alone but of everything with everything. To those who still feel securely in possession of their Shakespeare and, on top of that, have a grasp of postmodern theorizing, the critical scene as it presents itself today worldwide is most stimulating and rewarding. Yet, while due allowance must be made for the pastness of the past, its resuscitation in the present cannot but yield a present-day picture which then in turn alters the past itself. A historicist of the purest water will not condone this inevitable interaction. But rather than letting the past be buried in oblivion for ever, it seems better to revive it, albeit at the cost mentioned, namely, of being rooted in the present.

Shakespeare – who else survives like him? – is now the prime agent in this critical and hermeneutical process of interaction between present and past, past and present. What is more, when adding to the Elizabethan and

Jacobean dimensions of his works the history of their reception – or appropriation – through time, we may expect to get an even more complex perception of the poet than we enjoy already, and that in no small measure due to the recent critical trends discussed in the foregoing. That they had, as I pointed out, mostly their own axe to grind, using Shakespearean texts as mere pretexts, should not disturb us unduly, for that is the way critics imbued with a sense of 'novelty', if not even a conviction of 'urgency', are used to write. All in all, it is a pleasure to watch them in performance; it would, of course, be more pleasurable for any scholar now alive to participate in the work of renewal under way or, better still, to assist in heralding the next shift in critical paradigm.

BIBLIOGRAPHY

Aers, David, Bob Hodge and Gunther Kress (eds), *Literature, Language and Society in England 1580–1680* (Dublin: Gill and Macmillan; Totowa, NJ: Barnes and Noble, 1981).

Aers, David and Gunther Kress, 'The Language of Social Order: Individual, Society and Historical Process in *King Lear*', in Aers *et al.* (eds), *Literature, Language and Society*, pp. 75–99.

Atkins, G. Douglas and David M. Bergeron (eds), *Shakespeare and Deconstruction* (New York: Lang, 1988).

Barber, C.L., 'The Family in Shakespeare's Development: Tragedy and Sacredness', in Schwartz and Kahn (eds), *Representing Shakespeare*, pp. 188–202.

Callaghan, Dympna, *Woman and Gender in Renaissance Tragedy: A Study of 'King Lear', 'Othello', 'The Duchess of Malfi' and 'The White Devil'* (New York: Harvester Wheatsheaf, 1989).

Cohen, Walter, 'Political Criticism of Shakespeare', in Howard and O'Connor (eds), *Shakespeare Reproduced*, pp. 18–46.

Cope, Jackson I., 'Shakespeare, Derrida, and the End of Language in *Lear*', in Atkins and Bergeron (eds), *Shakespeare and Deconstruction*, pp. 267–83.

Danby, John F., *Shakespeare's Doctrine of Nature: A Study of 'King Lear'*, (London: Faber and Faber, 1948; repr. 1972).

Derrida, Jacques, *Of Grammatology*, trans. Gayatri Chakravorty Spivak (Baltimore: The Johns Hopkins University Press, 1976).

Dollimore, Jonathan, *Radical Tragedy: Religion, Ideology and Power in the Drama of Shakespeare and His Contemporaries* (Brighton: Harvester, 1984).

Dollimore, Jonathan, 'Critical Developments: Cultural Materialism, Feminism and Gender Critique, and New Historicism', in Stanley Wells (ed.), *Shakespeare: A Bibliographical Guide* (Oxford: Clarendon Press, 1990), pp. 405–28.

Dollimore, Jonathan and Alan Sinfield (eds), *Political Shakespeare: New Essays in Cultural Materialism* (Manchester: Manchester University Press, 1985).

Drakakis, John (ed.), *Alternative Shakespeares* (London: Methuen, 1985).

Eagleton, Terry, *Literary Theory: An Introduction* (Oxford: Blackwell, 1983; repr. 1985).

Elton, William R., *'King Lear' and the Gods* (San Marino, Calif.: The Huntington Library, 1966).

Felperin, Howard, *Beyond Deconstruction: The Uses and Abuses of Literary Theory* (Oxford: Clarendon Press, 1985).

Goldberg, Jonathan, 'Perspectives: Dover Cliff and the Conditions of Representation', in Atkins and Bergeron (eds), *Shakespeare and Deconstruction*, pp. 245–65.

Grady, Hugh, *The Modernist Shakespeare: Critical Texts in a Material World* (Oxford: Clarendon Press, 1991).

Greenblatt, Stephen, *Shakespearean Negotiations: The Circulation of Social Energy in Renaissance England* (Berkeley: University of California Press, 1988; repr. Oxford: Clarendon Press, 1990).

Howard, Jean E. and Marion F. O'Connor (eds), *Shakespeare Reproduced : The Text in History and Ideology* (London: Methuen, 1987; repr. New York: Routledge, 1990).

Kahn, Coppélia, 'The Absent Mother in *King Lear*', in Margaret W. Ferguson, Maureen Quilligan and Nancy J. Vickers (eds), *Rewriting the Renaissance: The Discourses of Sexual Difference in Early Modern Europe* (Chicago: University of Chicago Press, 1986), pp. 33–49.

Kavanagh, James H., 'Shakespeare in Ideology', in Drakakis (ed.), *Alternative Shakespeares*, pp. 144–65.

Knights, L.C., *Explorations: Essays in Criticism Mainly on the Literature of the Seventeenth Century* (London: Chatto and Windus, 1946; repr. Harmondsworth: Penguin, 1964).

McCanles, Michael, 'Shakespeare, Intertextuality, and the Decentered Self', in Atkins and Bergeron (eds), *Shakespeare and Deconstruction*, pp. 193–211.

McLuskie, Kathleen, 'The Patriarchal Bard: Feminist Criticism and Shakespeare: *King Lear* and *Measure for Measure*', in Dollimore and Sinfield (eds), *Political Shakespeare*, pp. 88–108.

Marsden, Jean I. (ed.), *The Appropriation of Shakespeare: Post-Renaissance Reconstructions of the Works and the Myth* (New York: Harvester Wheatsheaf, 1991).

Norris, Christopher, 'Post-structuralist Shakespeare: Text and Ideology', in Drakakis (ed.), *Alternative Shakespeares*, pp. 47–66.

Parker, Patricia and Geoffrey Hartman (eds), *Shakespeare and the Question of Theory* (New York: Methuen, 1985).

Schwartz, Murray M. and Coppélia Kahn (eds), *Representing Shakespeare: New Psychoanalytic Essays* (Baltimore: The Johns Hopkins University Press, 1980).

Shakespeare, William, *King Lear*, ed. Kenneth Muir, The Arden Edition (London: Methuen, 1952; repr. 1961).

Sinfield, Alan, *Faultlines: Cultural Materialism and the Politics of Dissident Reading* (Oxford: Clarendon Press, 1992).

Thomas, Brook, *The New Historicism and Other Old-Fashioned Topics* (Princeton, NJ: Princeton University Press, 1991).

Thompson, Ann, '"The Warrant of Womanhood": Shakespeare and Feminist Criticism', in Graham Holderness (ed.), *The Shakespeare Myth* (Manchester: Manchester University Press, 1988), pp. 74–88.

Veeser, H. Aram (ed.), *The New Historicism* (New York: Routledge, 1989).

Vickers, Brian, *Appropriating Shakespeare: Contemporary Critical Quarrels* (New Haven: Yale University Press, 1993).

Waller, Gary, 'Decentering the Bard: The Dissemination of the Shakespearean Text', in Atkins and Bergeron (eds), *Shakespeare and Deconstruction*, pp. 21–45.

Wayne, Don E., 'Power, Politics, and the Shakespearean Text: Recent Criticism in England and the United States', in Howard and O'Connor (eds), *Shakespeare Reproduced*, pp. 47–67.

Weimann, Robert, *Shakespeare und die Macht der Mimesis: Autorität und Repräsentation im elisabethanischen Theater* (Berlin-Weimar: Aufbau-Verlag, 1988).

Wheeler, Richard P., '"Since first we were dissevered": Trust and Autonomy in Shakespearean Tragedy and Romance', in Schwartz and Kahn (eds), *Representing Shakespeare*, pp. 150–69.

Willbern, David, 'Shakespeare's Nothing', in Schwartz and Kahn (eds), *Representing Shakespeare*, pp. 244–63.

Index